The Memory Process

The Memory Process

Neuroscientific and Humanistic Perspectives

edited by Suzanne Nalbantian, Paul M. Matthews, and James L. McClelland

The MIT Press
Cambridge, Massachusetts
London, England

MIT Press books may be purchased at special quantity discounts for business or sales promotional use. For information, please email special_sales@mitpress.mit.edu or write to Special Sales Department, The MIT Press, 55 Hayward Street, Cambridge, MA 02142.

This book was set in Stone Sans and Stone Serif by Toppan Best-set Premedia Limited. Printed and bound in the United States of America.

Library of Congress Cataloging-in-Publication Data

The memory process : neuroscientific and humanistic perspectives / edited by Suzanne Nalbantian, Paul M. Matthews, and James L. McClelland.
    p. ; cm.
Includes bibliographical references and index.
ISBN 978-0-262-01457-1 (hardcover : alk. paper) 1. Memory. I. Nalbantian, Suzanne. II. Matthews, Paul M. III. McClelland, James L.
[DNLM: 1. Memory. BF 371 M5337 2011]
BF371.M463 2011
153.1′2—dc22
                                                                    2010005429

10 9 8 7 6 5 4 3 2 1

Contents

Acknowledgments

The instigation for this book came from the Interdisciplinary Memory Symposium in Neuroscience and the Humanities held at Cold Spring Harbor Laboratory in 2007 and organized by Suzanne Nalbantian. That productive interchange was made possible by the generous financial support of Joanna Rose, Mary Phipps, the MMC Corporation, and the gracious hosting of Dr. Jan Witkowski at the Banbury Center. We also wish to thank our MIT Press editor Robert Prior, who accepted this book for publication with the vision of venturing across disciplinary boundaries.

Introduction

Suzanne Nalbantian

The Memory Process offers an interdisciplinary approach to the understanding of human memory with contributions from both neuroscience and the humanities. It is based on the conviction that the future for breakthroughs in memory research lies in a convergence of these two perspectives. The aim of the book is to forge key connections between the latest findings in scientific memory research and insights from various sectors in the humanities (literature, philosophy, theater, art, and music) on this timely subject.

This kind of consilience, to borrow the term biologist Edmund O. Wilson used to describe such unified knowledge, brings to fruition the goal of two prescient, worldly French thinkers, Paul Ricoeur and Michel Serres. Ricoeur, a philosopher of hermeneutics and literary theory, predicted that the overriding orientation of neuroscience in the future would be to juxtapose objective experimentally recorded activities with the "incredible richness" of a "lived biology."[1] Serres, a philosopher of science, metaphorically invoked the Greek god Hermes to suggest that there had to be messenger work between the cultures of humanists and scientists.[2] Through the interchange of intradisciplinary (within neuroscience) and cross-disciplinary (between neuroscience and the humanities) approaches, this book offers a means toward tangible advances in the field of memory studies by opening up new avenues for empirical study and testing.

With fresh evidence from both sides of the divide, *The Memory Process* seeks to identify commonalities not only within the field of neuroscience but between it and the humanities across disciplinary lines. Its leading premise is that memory is multifaceted and has multiple phases prompted by inputs from different levels of functioning. The range of memory studies is vast, from a primitive understanding of memory in the study of reflexes and conditioning in animals to the complex, malleable personal memory experiences of human beings. The extension of memory studies from laboratory animals to humans is here furthered through the recourse to the humanities.

The nineteen chapters of this book offer varying approaches to the encoding, consolidation, and retrieval of memory. On the scientific side, chapters 1–8 and chapter 19 convey both fundamental concepts and ongoing debates from the perspectives of genetics and epigenetics, functional neuroimaging, connectionist modeling, dream analysis, and neurocognitive studies, with findings drawn from both animal research and human neuropsychology. On the humanities side, chapters 12–19 together present repositories of memory data from comparative literature, art, music, film, and theater. Their selective analyses offer pertinent information to scientists about the human memory experience beyond laboratories and experimental control. In the middle of the book, chapters 9–11 serve as a bridge between neuroscience and the humanities from the vantage point of philosophy and ethics, offering exterior measures of truth and forecasting, veridicality of knowledge and prolepsis, by which to judge the scientific findings with humanistic criteria.

The humanities can also reap rewards from this interchange. Neuroscience offers interpretive information, which the memory process gives to both the fundamental levels and the highest strata of artistic style and creativity. By drawing on modern neuroscientific memory studies, the study of artworks can be detached from stale theories and subjective interpretations of hermeneutic relativity. For our time, a new scientific vigor can nurture analysis of the arts, anchoring their connection to the material world. Since memory is a detectible, even measurable ingredient in this perspective, as opposed to more elusive functions such as creativity or consciousness, it provides a reliable basis for linking literature and the allied arts to the basic human condition. Through this kind of interdisciplinarity, the volume's humanistic chapters demonstrate how the basic core of artistic works can be reexamined in light of a changing, intellectual zeitgeist brought about by memory studies.

In the scientific arena, the explosively expanding field of memory research, with its different points of emphasis, needs to be sifted to yield shared perceptions. The modern neuroscience of memory has explored behavioral properties, faculties, and physiology, as revealed by studies of brain lesions and impairments, evolution, and biochemistry. Researchers have treated the gamut of memory studies, ranging from the molecular and cellular levels to the circuit and network levels, and onto the system level, which reaches the psychology of mind and behavior. Insights have been drawn from both animal and human models.

Since the 1990s, dubbed the Decade of the Brain, scientific memory researchers have engaged in lively debates over familiar issues such as stability, veridicality, and localization. The old storehouse versus connectionist debates of a decade ago have turned into the cellular, local, serial (bottom-up) versus systems (top-down) debates discussed in the chapters that follow. Considerations of localization versus integration and functional specificity versus interaction are also in play. *Construction, reconstruction, stabilization, lability* are words used to help us understand the gestation and metamorphosis of memory. There is increasing appreciation of the role of affective components and unconscious perceptions in memory encoding and in biasing recollection. The contributors to this volume expose commonalities in understanding memory within the large spectrum of study while maintaining healthy candor about unsolved mysteries.

As with most disciplines, neuroscience has taken on different orientations in its evolution, and the study of memory is naturally involved in this progression. Rejecting the metaphysical dimensions of mind as spiritual in the legacy of transcendental philosophers such as Plato, Descartes, Bergson, and Kant, modern neuroscientists first emerged as atheistic materialists. Material man could be reduced to neurons, synapses, and general bodily states, as explained in Jean-Pierre Changeux's *Neuronal Man* (1985), Joseph LeDoux's *Synaptic Self* (2002), and Antonio Damasio's *Descartes' Error* (1994), respectively. Correspondingly, memory studies were brought into biological contexts—cellular, molecular, and anatomical ones.

Concurrently, the Anglo-American terrain of logical empiricism gave philosophical legitimacy to the exploratory wave of neurophilosophy, providing a new terrain for a more global, interdisciplinary exploration of memory in the larger scope of unified brain/mind theories. This hybrid field was established by Patricia Churchland in her 1986 book *Neurophilosophy: Toward a Unified Science of the Mind-Brain*. The search for an empirically based theory of mind, raising the key issue of "how macro phenomena are produced by neuronal phenomena,"[3] led researchers into the twilight zone of consciousness studies alongside the steady neurobiological progress of the discipline. In the early 1990s, the search for neurobiological correlates of subjective experience, of a narrative progression of mental events (Daniel Dennett), of consciousness proper (John Searle), of vision or "qualia" (Francis Crick), established a wider framework for the study of the organization of the memory process.[4] Most productively in this context, neural architecture began to be applied to memory studies. In 1988, Bernard Baars was an initiator of global workspace theory, demonstrating that the superstructure of the cortex was the communication center or "theater" for conscious long-term memory. A decade later, Stanislas Dehaene, Michel Kerszberg, and Jean-Pierre Changeux devised a neuronal workspace model that sought to conjoin neurobiological processing with a concept of organized and adaptive consciousness activity that involved selective memory within a global framework of the brain. In more general terms, Gerald Edelman and Giulio Tononi in 2001 proposed a synoptic view of memory as "a system property" of a unified field of consciousness with a theory of reentry circuits that help build memory structures. The neurologist Marsel Mesulam pursued the search for pathways from sensation to cognition, contending that subjective biases give a "transcendental" function to the brain in its interpretive organization of sensory inputs and its impact on memory.[5]

With such precedents, we have entered a syncretic age in which the mind is beginning to be dissected as a biological superstructure. Two of our era's best-known neuroscientists, Antonio Damasio and Eric Kandel, have renewed the call for a focus beyond the functional brain alone to the larger issue of the science of the mind.[6] This agenda has great implications for the study of memory. Insights into the multiple cognitive aspects of memory are emerging from attempts to connect cellular and molecular analysis to systems theories. But if this larger enterprise is to be directed toward understanding the mental dimensions of memory, interdisciplinary scrutiny can take us to a whole new level of analysis.

In this endeavor, philosophers are well positioned to serve as mediators between science and the arts. They can ask the important questions of how existence (ontology), knowledge claims (epistemology), and selfhood (metaphysics) can be considered in the descriptive phenomenological studies of memory. The three philosophers in this volume, Bickle, Hirstein, and Glannon, do just that. John Bickle (chapter 9) isolates the foundational neuroscientific bases of memory's ontology and thereby lobbies for an uncompromising reductive approach to the study of memory to help concretely bridge mind to its foundational molecules. William Hirstein (chapter 10) takes on the epistemological criterion, speculating on the extent to which the truth or "reality" can be a measure in subjects' memory experiences, whether pathological or normal. Walter Glannon (chapter 11) tackles the issue of human identity, which he sees at the heart of the memory process but at the mercy of interventions of neuroscientific advances.

The continuous neurocognitive modeling of memory has already incorporated new elements, widening the epigenetic breadth of memory studies. Most of us would agree that memory is an important part of human identity. Indeed, we might readily change the Cartesian dictum "I think, therefore I am" to "I remember, therefore I am." This orientation has entered folk psychology with, for example, the curiosity about Capgras syndrome, popularized by Richard Powers's novel *The Echo Maker*, linking memory loss from severe brain injury to disturbing identity problems. Some scientists have also become cognizant of the subjective factor of selfhood or "autonoetic awareness." This expression points to the fact that the consciousness of time (e.g., psychological time) and the awareness of self are special aspects of subjective experience that must be brought into the studies of human memory. The humanists in this volume naturally go much further in this endeavor, showing how memory is crucially related to human identity, selfhood, and self-knowledge. Sophisticated literature is especially revealing in this regard, as demonstrated in chapters 12–15 (part IV) by literary scholars Nalbantian, Richardson, Foster, and Favorini.

Others corroborate the linkage of identity and memory in varied contexts. Most dramatically, from a clinical standpoint, Matthews' discussion of Alzheimer's disease (chapter 5), as a severe pathology with its impact on all types of conscious recollection of facts and autobiographical episodes (declarative memory), highlights the close relationship between memory and our view of what constitutes the self. Hirstein (chapter 10) shows that when confabulation, or memory distortion, occurs in normal populations, it can be construed as a natural inclination of "completion phenomena" for memories that are not strong enough to present an integrated virtual self in society. Glannon (chapter 11) who also recognizes the role of memory in shaping personhood, considers the threat to that identity caused by brain injuries, on the one hand, and the intervention of pharmacological agents, on the other. And Fernando Vidal (chapter 19) showcases the connection between memory and "cerebral" selfhood in his study of celebrated movies. Memory deficits caused by accident, illness, or even science-fiction-film manipulation portraying retrograde amnesia are shown to alter the selves of the characters, their personalities and identities, in movies that proceed from matters of brain to those of the mind. For Vidal, movies display experiential, cultural aspects of memory that go beyond neuroscientific explanations of synaptic plasticity in neurobiological animal models to render alternative human memory models through the medium of filmic expression. This cultural formation of memory has its own validity, superseding scientific data in a larger context of human actualization and experience.

Neuroscientists can be limited by the demands for precision and extreme specialization to ensure accurate and complete tests of hypotheses. Humanists can challenge with large questions and bring their different perspective to help move findings to larger integrative synoptic viewpoints. With the new connections proposed and the new questions asked by humanists, more avenues for empirical research can be found. This humanistic optic, communicated through highly descriptive phenomenological studies, enhances and adds experiential context to the scientific findings. Humanistic interpretations of literature, art, music, and theater can provide a data bank (from human subjects) that offers insights into the sequence and interactions of memory processing unattainable with the time-limited results of fMRIs or controlled experiments on studies of sea slugs (*Aplysia*), mice, rats, fruit flies, and monkeys. Chapters 12–17, by Nalbantian, Richardson, Foster, Favorini, Freedberg, and Hertz, provide examples of how the arts bring to life and elaborate upon neuroscientific theories. Case studies of memory events are analyzed as evidentiary material and interpreted with scientific cross-references.

For Suzanne Nalbantian (chapter 12), striking episodes or images from a novel can reveal distinct categories of memory processing that current neuroscientists such as Changeux, Stickgold, McClelland, and Rolls have been discussing. While offering a taxonomy of memory processing gleaned from a group of twentieth-century autobiographical authors, she also examines creative features of episodic memory that underlie the varieties of normal memory processing. For Alan Richardson (chapter 13), the memory-based imagination of Romantic works of poetry and prose is compatible with a sophisticated understanding of what is being called "prospective memory" processing, the ability of memory systems to affect anticipatory behavior, as described by Daniel Schacter, Thomas Suddendorf, and Michael Corballis. For John Foster (chapter 14), "specimen passages" from selected literary memoirs reveal the vicissitudes of long-term episodic memory. External factors such as mood at the time of writing, language in which the remembered event was first documented, and interfering testimony of an event demonstrate the socialization of memory, as described by Katherine Nelson and Robyn Fivush. For Atillio Favorini (chapter 15), theater, especially modernist drama, can reflect the process of memory's organization, with dramatic scenes organizing action-in-time. This coincides with Gerald Edelman's concept of theatrical metaphor as providing conceptual and perceptual linkages in a systems-level approach that enacts the reconstruction of relationships with reentered data.

Turning to art and music, we are also reminded of the active participation of the listener/viewer in the construction of meaning that automatically involves memory. In reformulating the role of memory in art, David Freedberg (chapter 16) shows how a visual gesture in an image in a painting can reveal memory's embodiment, as it provokes the viewer's empathy for the subject of the painting. This is in line with Antonio Damasio's view of the baseline of somatic responses that govern aspects of consciousness. Freedberg shows how procedural memory and emotional memory in unmediated, automatic responses to art can be more significant than cognitive, prefrontally modulated aspects of long-term cultural memory. For David Hertz (chapter 17), music is the ultimate memory art; it is totally dependent on memory for its significance because it calls upon the listener's recall of a remembered past of patterns in a musical piece. In accord with David Huron's and Oliver Sacks's observations, Hertz describes various kinds of memory in music. He shows how stylistic variations in different musical compositions, involving sequence, echo, tonality, or cumulative form, demonstrate the creative manipulations of musical memory by composers.

The established classifications of memory systems figure in all the chapters of this volume, particularly because the distinct kinds of memory relate to different circuitry in the memory process. But as more insights into interactions between different types of memory are found, such definitions can be contextualized in light of new theories and new experimental findings. For example, music has been shown to conjoin several forms of memory according to the function of time, as sensory memory moves to short-term, long-term, and emotional memory. With visual art, sensory, working, and emotional memory can take precedent over explicit, cognitive memory processing. In some of the literary material, it can be seen how long-term autobiographical memory displaces short-term memory. The accepted classifications, drawn from experimental studies of both healthy and impaired subjects, can therefore be revisited according to the interdisciplinary perspectives that *The Memory Process* offers.

Understanding the physiological and neurological bases of memory and its classifications requires at least a limited knowledge of the architecture of the brain. Neurons (figure I.1) are the fundamental elements for information processing in the brain. Each neuron has a complex network of input processes known as "dendrites" (figure I.2) that capture information and a single output process known as the "axon." Cognitive processes rely on large networks of neurons organized into interacting functional

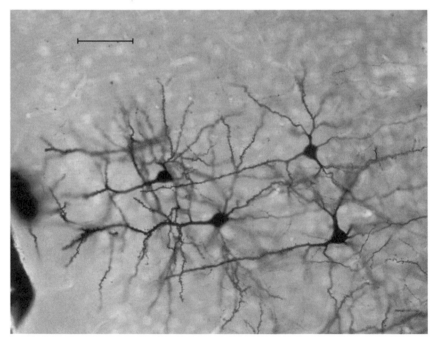

Figure I.1
Neurons in the cortex of a rodent brain. The image illustrates large central neuronal cell bodies with neurites extending from them. An extensive network of dendrites captures input to the neuron via synapses at the specialized granular regions known as "synaptic boutons." Scale bar: 50 μm.
Image courtesy of Dr. Zoltan Molnar, University of Oxford.

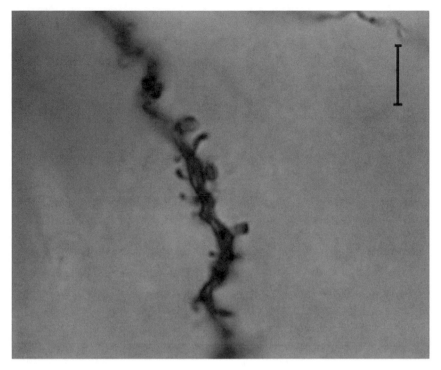

Figure I.2
Individual dendrite of the type shown in figure I.1 at higher magnification. The bulging specializations (synaptic boutons) that accommodate synapses are readily apparent. These dynamic structures are stabilized by appropriate repetitive input such as that responsible for long-term potentiation (LTP). Scale bar: 5 μm.
Image courtesy of Dr. Zoltan Molnar, University of Oxford.

modules. The modularity inherent in this functional architecture gives rise to regional functional specializations. The outer surface of the brain is formed by neurons organized in layers of the neocortex, which is specialized for executive functions, perception, and higher-level control of action. The middle part of the brain has a simpler pattern of organization of neurons known as "paleocortex" that includes the hippocampus (figure I.3), a region critical for declarative memory. Deeper within the substance of the brain are large ovoid clusters of neurons that form part of the subcortical gray matter (thalamus, basal ganglia). At an even higher level of organization, the brain can be divided into major structures or lobes (frontal, parietal, temporal, and occipital; figure I.4). The hippocampus is

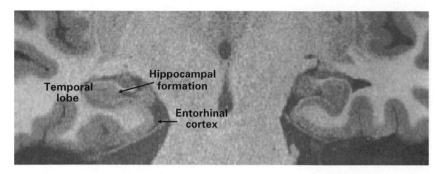

Figure I.3
Coronal human MRI image acquired in vivo, showing the temporal lobe, hippocampal formation, and entorhinal cortex. The medial temporal regions of both brain
hemispheres are clearly visible. The darker rim is the gray matter of the brain, where
the cortical neurons are found. The lighter regions are white matter, through which
myelinated axons connect neuronal regions.
Image courtesy of Dr. Bruce Fischl, Harvard University.

in the medial temporal lobe, near or adjacent to the amygdala and rhinal
cortex, respectively. The rhinal cortex has subregions known as the "perirhinal, entorhinal, and parahippocampal cortices," which receive especially extensive input from wide areas of the brain, a key to its integrative
functions for declarative memory. The amygdala plays a major role in the
limbic system, which mediates emotional responses.

To return to classifications, *episodic memory* (figure I.5) has been brought
to the forefront by humanistic studies that are concerned with long-term
autobiographical memory. In the 1970s and 1980s, the psychologist Endel
Tulving, a major figure in development of the modern taxonomy of
memory, championed the term *episodic memory* to describe source memory,
as distinguished from the generic semantic memory of facts and information.[7] Defined as the personal memory of events that are consciously and
declaratively recollected, this particular form of memory, which we all
experience as humans, involves the specificity of time and place and is
rich in vivid detail. But it also can be the most vulnerable type of memory.
Robert Stickgold (chapter 4) shows that, although episodic memories are
strengthened in slow wave sleep (SWS), they are eliminated as accurate
records of events in REM sleep. Paul Matthews (chapter 5) reviews how
neuropathology (on a neurobiological level) and neuroimaging (at a neural
systems level) have strengthened foundations for distinctions between

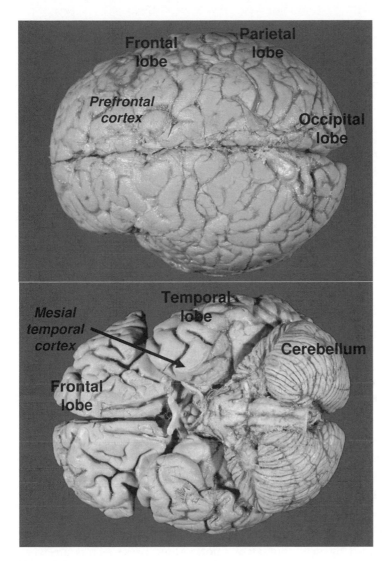

Figure I.4

Major features of brain surface anatomy. In the dorsal view (upper image), the brain hemispheres have similar surface anatomy defined by the bulging folds of gyri. Specific hollows formed between adjacent gyri (known as "sulci") define the large, functionally specialized regions of the brain (lobes), whose approximate locations are shown. The *occipital lobe* includes cortex functionally specialized for visual processing; the *parietal lobe* includes highly associative cortex that allows large-scale integration of information (as well as cortical mediation of somatic sensation); and the *frontal lobe* includes both cortex specialized for the control of motor functions and associative cortex involved in working memory and executive control, found in the *prefrontal cortex*. In the ventral view (lower image), the *temporal lobe* forms part of the base of the brain. The medial temporal region includes the *hippocampal formation* and related neocortex. The *cerebellum* is a specialized "hindbrain," structurally and functionally distinct from the *cerebrum*.

Images courtesy of Dr. Zoltan Molnar, University of Oxford.

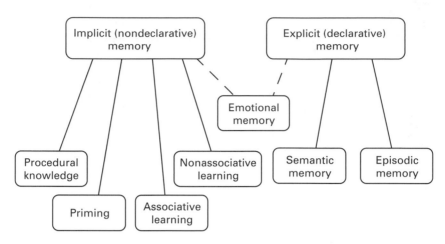

Figure I.5
A taxonomy of memory. Major divisions of implicit and explicit memory have been defined empirically. Evidence for the classification has come from studies of memory deficits in patients with focal brain lesions and from experimental studies of healthy subjects. As discussed in several chapters of this volume, emotional memory has emerged as a useful construct integrating aspects of both implicit and explicit memory systems.

episodic and other forms of memory. He focuses in depth on the fundamental, critical role of the hippocampus in declarative memory. As seen in clinical case studies, including that of HM, as described by Matthews, McClelland, Bickle, Hirstein, and Glannon, episodic memory can be subject to anterograde and retrograde amnesia. But even without neurological damage, episodic memory is fragile, degrades with time, and can even be altered by new context or information. These factors are what the humanists Nalbantian, Richardson, and Foster address in their analysis of autobiographical memory.

This precious kind of human memory has a compelling history. More than a century ago, in 1896, the French philosopher Henri Bergson distinguished between spontaneous "pure memory" of the first reading of a book and the learned recollection of its content in *Matter and Memory*. He considered spontaneous memory to be a higher form of memory precisely because it retained its place and date. His contemporary the American philosopher William James had written in *Principles of Psychology* (1890) about the "warmth" and "intimacy" of retrieving "memory proper," an autobiographical memory with the familiar context of its close associations. Both philosophers were distinguishing episodic memory from semantic or working memory long before such terms existed. Although this rudimentary distinction has prevailed over the years, fresh insights into episodic memory are presented by various chapters in this volume.

In scientific terms, William Hirstein (chapter 10) shows how autobiographical memories are naturally distorted without the normal executive management and supervision of memory retrieval by the prefrontal lobes. Nalbantian (chapter 12) analyzes the way specific source memories are actually retrieved through the art of autobiographical modern fiction. Richardson (chapter 13) discusses the expansion of the episodic memory system and the exploitation of its fragility by episodic future thinking among writers of the Romantic era. Foster (chapter 14) points to the vicissitudes as well as continuities of episodic memory as exemplified by modern memoir writers. Barbara Tillmann, Isabelle Peretz, and Séverine Samson (chapter 18) reveal that music can create robust emotional memory markers for long-term episodic memory and its lived context.

Semantic memory (figure I.5) is the other form of explicit (declarative) memory, connected to learning. It is the basis of our knowledge of facts and general information without a spatiotemporal context. Nonetheless, some say that semantic memory is derived from episodic memory, seeing the two kinds of memory as points along a continuum from general to specific. Theorists differ in how they view the mechanistic basis of semantic and episodic memory. Some propose relatively distinct memory systems for the two types (with different storage mechanisms for them), although semantic information can be contained within an episodic memory. Stickgold (chapter 4) gives new perspectives to semantic memory by showing its predominant expression in the dream state, which naturally extracts semantic memory from episodic memory as part of the process of memory consolidation. In James McClelland's connectionist model (chapter 6), a parallel distributed complementary memory system including different brain regions contributes to the storage and retrieval of both general knowledge and episodic memories. In his theory, every act of retrieval involves joint contributions of these systems: the medial temporal lobe plays an especially important role in the fast storage of item- or event-specific information and the neocortex of the brain serves as the eventual, long-term storage site of oft-repeated general information. McClelland's theory is consistent with Hirstein's observation (chapter 10) that in unusual conditions of confabulation, semantic memory can interact with episodic memory, linking fictional autobiography with surrounding fictional history in erroneous ways.

Working memory is a form of short-term memory that holds memory temporarily for goal-directed purposes. The term (with roots in William James's notion of "primary memory") was first introduced in modern times by a tripartite model of Alan Baddeley and Graham Hitch in 1974. More recently, in 2000, Baddeley added a fourth component called an "episodic buffer," which along with the central executive component brings out links across domains between working memory, conscious awareness, and long-term memory. According to the model, the decision-making mechanism of working memory involves "prospective memory" processing, whose short-term information store guides planning for the future.[8] Paul Matthews, in his extended discussion of working memory (chapter 5), points out that functional brain imaging reveals how this type of memory is in fact involved in the interaction between associative neocortical regions and other areas of the brain. It is interesting that the Baddeley-Hitch model may have a serious impact on the study of the interaction of working memory and emotion, which can be observed especially in the realm of music. Tellingly, Tillmann, Peretz, and Samson (chapter 18) show how music involves general working memory circuitry such as the frontoparietal networks.

Implicit memory (figure I.5) allows unconscious recollection to guide perception or action and behaviors. One can say it is part of what we *do not know we know.* It is distinguished from explicit memory, which involves conscious recall. As the term is used by Peter Graf and Daniel Schacter (1985), it is manifested in language (either with visual or auditory presentation) or in object priming subserved and thought to be independent of the medial temporal lobes.[9] It is reflected in unconscious priming, whereby familiar words or structural forms are made more accessible and therefore likely to be used with no conscious recollection of the prior experience that gave rise to them. Associations and complex ideas can also be primed, and it is likely that such priming introduces content into the imagery of dreams, involving nonassociative connections that lead to qualitative changes in memory. Nondeclarative implicit memory also includes functional procedural, automatic, and noncognitive memory relating to motor skills and habits that often require repetition and are subserved by the corticostriatal system. It is knowledge of how to perform a task. Unlike declarative conscious memories, procedural memory has been found to be unimpaired in cases of amnesia resulting from damage to the hippocampus. Notably, as Stickgold (chapter 4) shows us, sleep leads to the enhancement of procedural memory. Implicit memory is also manifested in reflex responses governed by the cerebellum. Freedberg (chapter 16) shows how implicit procedural memory in bodily responses to a work of art supersedes long-term declarative memory in aesthetic responses.

Emotional memory (figure I.5) crosses the border between implicit and explicit memory processing. It is mediated by different areas of the brain, involves different brain states and a complex interaction between emotion and cognition. Years ago, of course, Freud had turned memory pathologically into a symptom of neurosis, which in his view was the result of unconscious suppression of traumatic memory. Likening memory to the German children's toy *Wunderblock,* he had set long-term unconscious memory on an underlying wax tablet and short-term conscious memory on the transparent celluloid paper.[10] While Freud was maintaining that indelible "repressed" memory never reached the celluloid surface as straightforward conscious awareness, his wax metaphor was also suggesting that such highly emotional memories were lasting, hidden memory imprints. Perhaps Freud's most lasting legacy is his revelation of the multidimensional nature of memory and the influence of cognitive and emotional context on recollection. His theory of repressed memory, however, has come under widespread scrutiny with "memory wars" fueled by recent neuropsychological evidence. For example, dream researchers like J. Allan Hobson have argued that "dream content is emotionally salient on its face" and is not disguised.[11] For his part, Stickgold (chapter 4), in his account of the physiological basis of dreams, shows how the emotional core of memories is enhanced and revealed during sleep, leading to the construction of meaning in memories.

As *The Memory Process* demonstrates, the study of emotional memory has a wide range, from rodent behavior experiments in the laboratory (LeDoux and Doyère), to neurospsychological systems analysis (Rolls), to real-life clinical cases of traumatized people (Glannon), to human relationships as represented in modernist literature (Nalbantian and Foster) or imagined in futuristic films (Vidal), to memory segments spared by music

(Tillmann, Peretz, and Samson). Using a neurobiologically based bottom-up strategy, neuroscientists such as LeDoux and Doyère (chapter 7) have brought to the forefront the intricacy of both the biological retention and erasure of the emotional memory of fear. This variability is attributed to the inherently labile characteristics of fear traces when retrieved in the amygdala networks along with the way they were encoded and embedded. Their work on fear memory in animals falls in the category of implicit emotional memory. As a leading authority on memory and emotion, Edmund Rolls (chapter 8) has offered a neuropsychological systems approach, analyzing emotional memory in its wide variety of human manifestations in a contextual construction, which works toward its preservation. He argues that it principally involves two distinct systems, one mediated implicitly by the amygdala and the other explicitly by the hippocampus. Interestingly (and even disturbingly where major effects are seen with simple pharmacological interventions, as with the beta-blocker propranolol), Glannon (chapter 11) describes how the emotional component of a complex memory trace can be extracted or deleted, while the declarative, episodic subject matter of the memory is left intact.

The scope of emotional memory also presents distinctions between encoding specificity and mood-dependent retrieval. This viewpoint is taken up by the humanists. Nalbantian (chapter 12) shows how the encoding of personal experiences with emotion and registered in poetic language seals autobiographical memories and ensures their retrieval. Foster (chapter 14) shows how mood at the time of retrieval may affect the representation of a past event or experience. Tillmann, Peretz, and Samson (chapter 18) show how music, invested as it is with emotion, interacts with long-term memory processes. Whereas Glannon (chapter 11) treats the ethical considerations of the new pharmacological means of arresting or erasing emotional memory, Vidal (chapter 19) presents the popular cultural view, as witnessed through movies, that emotionally charged memories are among the most permanent ones that ultimately cannot be erased. Hence the study of emotional memory and its complexity leads us to address the question of the permanence of memory in general.

It is notable that in this volume the old concept of the engram, originally designating a physical, material trace, is treated in a new way as it evolves into more of a generic term. Matthews (chapter 5) describes the tools of neuroimaging and illustrates how they have been applied to a modern redefinition of the memory engram in terms of electrophysiological activity and connectivities in the brain. Historically speaking, Karl Lashley, who popularized the engram in the title of his celebrated 1950 paper "In Search of the Engram," was seeking, but not finding, where it was stored. Ironically, however, his work spurred future scientists to search for the ways in which memory traces could be located. In 1949, Lashley's student Donald Hebb established a legacy in searching for engrams not in any single unities but in neuronal assemblies. He discovered synapses as the sites in the hippocampus that could be modified biochemically and structurally by incoming experience in the construction of memory.[12] Hippocampal synaptic connectivity was suggested as the basis for such cell assemblies with the introduction of the concept of long-term potentiation (LTP) by Tim Bliss and Terje Lømo in 1973.[13] LTP displays key features of the kind of brain plasticity that Hebb postulated must be at the basis of memory: the active synapses on a neuron are selectively strengthened, enhancing their functional association and creation of an element of the memory trace. Gary Lynch and colleagues (1990) associated long-term potentiation with morphological changes in the neuron, specifically in the shape of dendritic spines.[14] Other researchers have identified a cascade of molecular changes affecting synapses (after learning) that lead to this dendritic remodeling for long-term maintenance of the enhanced connectivities from which memory emerges.

Consolidation theory was set forth in 1994 by Larry Squire and Pablo Alvarez. Their neurobiological network model connected memory sequentially to the medial temporal lobe networks for temporary memory storage, and predominantly to the neocortex for long-term memory storage. The structures implicated in the medial temporal lobe were the hippocampal formation consisting of the hippocampus and the anatomically related entorhinal, perirhinal, and parahippocampal cortices. The study of human episodic memory impairment with retrograde amnesia led these researchers to the concept of memory consolidation.[15] Along with this standard model, based largely on the preservation of human episodic memory, the systems-oriented research of James McClelland and colleagues was introducing (in the 1980s and 90s) a parallel distributed processing framework, which shifted the focus to the permanence of neocortical memory. This theory (described by McClelland in chapter 6) provoked the search for memory that is gradually "fixed" over time in a permanent form, as traces are transferred but also multiplied in different regions of the brain. Lynn Nadel and Morris Moscovitch subsequently proposed the multiple trace theory of memory, with Moscovitch continuing to ask the important question in the new millennium "Are different types of memories consolidated in different structures?"[16] Studies proliferated in an effort to understand consolidation behaviorally and biologically in different stages across different regions of the brain in systems studies.

Meanwhile, bolstering consolidation theory and the standard model, James McGaugh asserted in 2000 that new factors had to be introduced into the analysis of consolidation, notably the critical involvement of the amygdala and its modulatory influences of neuroplasticity in other brain regions.[17] McGaugh concentrated on the hormone adrenaline (epinephrine), as a "stress-responsive neuromodulator" that could be analyzed for enhancement of certain types of memory. The subject of chemical enhancement of memories is of continuous interest. Serotonin, dopamine and norepinephrine were among monaminergic neurotransmitters studied as possible agents for stabilizing memories. Enhancing activity of the cholinergic agonist acetylcholine, which is released by neurons widely projecting to brain regions mediating memory, was demonstrated to modulate memory in clinically useful ways.

From neuropathological investigations in the 1950s through the renaissance of the cognitive neurosciences with neuroimaging methods in the 1990s and early years of the twenty-first century, neuroscientists have provided progressively more refined localizations for critical processes of memory, as Paul Matthews (chapter 5) shows us. Initially, this came from studies relating natural lesions to memory impairments in humans, in conjunction with tests of the effects of selective brain lesioning in animals. By the end of the 1990s, however, functional magnetic resonance imaging (fMRI) was directly mapping brain activity responsible for memory in human volunteers. Studies using fMRI emphasized how highly distributed brain systems for memory are. An increasing range of molecular imaging studies with positron-emission tomography (PET) are allowing direct studies of the underlying neurochemistry both in living animals and in humans.

Even as the systems-level description of memory processes was refined, molecular consolidation theory became prominent. The advent of advances in cell and molecular biology was also turning the focus of memory consolidation to the ongoing process at postsynaptic sites in dendrites with the activation of NMDA receptors and kinases. The essential notion of the CREB protein "switch," was shown to be necessary for memory formation and consolidation.[18] This functioning was demonstrated in the sensitization of motor reflexes in animal studies initiated by the study of the sea slug *Aplysia* by Eric Kandel and extended in studies of the fruit fly *Drosophila* by Tim Tully and Jerry Yin, and on to rats and mice by Alcino Silva and others. This work allowed classical neuropharmacological and neurobiological approaches to be integrated, establishing, for example, relations between signaling by the neurotransmitter serotonin and CREB-dependent transcription of genes for the long-term effects of the memory process. The implications of this work have been wide and varied. For example, Alcino Silva (chapter 2) has argued that molecular genetic approaches actually paved the way for reconsolidation theory.

The first decade of the twenty-first century has brought serious challenges to consolidation theory (as a one-time process) with the growing prominence of various versions of memory reconsolidation. Long-term memory has been shown to become unstable upon retrieval or reactivation. Active molecular mechanisms at retrieval are necessary for long-term memory stabilization, revealing that all or only some stored elements of the original memory are subject to modification. This approach was especially pertinent to the study of the cellular mechanisms in the amygdala that underlie Pavlovian fear conditioning, as conducted by Joseph LeDoux. In 2000, along with LeDoux, Karim Nader and others brought reconsolidation theory to the forefront by demonstrating that in rat studies fear memories when reactivated upon retrieval are rendered labile, are destabilized, and require new protein synthesis to persist over time.[19] In 2009, Nader and Oliver Hardt understandably called for "a new model of memory which successfully integrates both consolidation and reconsolidation."[20]

Indeed, after a decade of investigation into the changeability of memory, studies of reactivation of consolidated memory are yielding new theories, which go beyond reconsolidation. In particular, chapters 1, 3, and 7 (Dudai, Changeux, LeDoux and Doyère) in this book do offer a new conceptual framework for conceiving the continuing process of stabilization that reconciles both memory's persistence through some form of engram traces and its continuously "active," highly plastic state that is susceptible to changes. It is notable, however, that such constant reshaping of memory proves to be a normal phenomenon in much of the humanistic material.

In the context of this lively evolution in memory theory, *The Memory Process* presents a range of neuroscientific discussions, treating the persistence of memory (Dudai), the lability of memory (LeDoux and Doyère), the stabilization of memory (Changeux), the construction of memory (McClelland and Rolls), the functioning of memory (Matthews), the transience of memory (Silva), the modality of memory (Stickgold), and the permanence of memory (Tillmann, Peretz, and Samson). Certain qualifications and refinements of these scientific views are offered by the humanistic chapters. Notably, however, there emerges a growing consensus that notions of redundancy, selection, reconstruction, and transformation have replaced views of memory based on representation and replication.

A constructive view of memory is presented in chapters 3, 6, and 8, by Changeux, McClelland, and Rolls, which link memory to learning and the acquisition of knowledge in a human neurocognitive framework. Jean-Pierre Changeux (chapter 3) presents a chain of repeating events that are governed by the prefrontal cortex, as demonstrated by a global neuronal workspace model. The physical "knowledge" or "emotion" traces, presumed to exist latently, are induced, broadcast dynamically by executive function, and evolve into patterns of synaptic connectivity that Changeux calls "stored epigenetic memory." Stabilizing a memory trace involves testing and selection of hypotheses about information that has been partially retained. McClelland (chapter 6), in the context of his network system theory of memory, has championed a view of the memory trace as a pattern of adjustments or changes to the strengths of the synaptic connections among neurons. In this view—one widely though not universally shared among neuroscientists—memories have a physical substrate, but the physical substrates of different memories are overlaid in overlapping sets of connections, much as two or more holograms can be overlaid on the same photographic plate. Offering another version of constructive memory processing, Edmund Rolls (chapter 8) explains how the memory trace is stored with its context, grasping the larger picture from the cue, the clue, the scrap, the remnants of memory, replicated in various parts of the brain. A consequence is that one can recover a whole memory cued by only a part of it that. We might say that the weaving together of those scraps is like the work of a creator. In yet another interpretation, Matthews, from his neuroimaging perspective (chapter 5), shows that memory traces may be viewed as a functional property.

The notion of the transience of memory is presented by Dudai, Silva, and LeDoux and Doyère, drawn especially from molecular neurobiological animal studies. Despite his earlier view of the "fragility of the engram," Yadin Dudai (chapter 1) maintains it as a useful concept (of some kind of biological change) with which to measure modification and transformation. Currently, he holds that in humans reconsolidation actually might help to strengthen at least part of the memory trace in the conglomerate of what he calls a "society of engrams." Assessing the growing trend of memory lability theories, Alcino Silva (chapter 2) accepts the natural and necessary inaccuracy of memory. With his history of CREB studies, he seeks to present a revolutionary standpoint by viewing consolidation theory (and its avatar of reconsolidation) as a questionable template in memory research. He poses the following question as he moves from transgenic mice to humans. If memory is so labile, is it ever really fixed? Instead, he contends that memory mechanisms "are designed for constant editing, engineered for fine-tuning information with experience" not for accuracy or permanency. In their study, Joseph LeDoux and Valérie Doyère (chapter 7) analyze the complexity of consolidation theory by pointing to tagging, erasure, and updating, which can occur at certain stages of reconsolidation of fear memory. They also demonstrate how emotional and declarative aspects of memory can be separated in the course of reconsolidation during the selective time windows of opportunity that can either strengthen or weaken such memories.

In contrast, sleep studies and research on musical memory have concentrated on the classical model of long-term memory as largely fixed, although able to be reinforced. From their vantage point, Tillmann, Peretz, and Samson (chapter 18) show how music demonstrates the retention of long-term memory through a musical lexicon of musical tunes that is stored through a lifetime in the right temporal lobe. Musical memory improves over time, bolstered by cultural exposure and hierarchical structures of a musical system. The view that sleep participates in the consolidation of memory has its own venue. As Nalbantian points out in chapter 12, Robert Stickgold and J. Allan Hobson had over the years focused on cholinergic activation in altered states of consciousness, including phases of sleep, which serve as the basis for modulated memory production. In this volume, Stickgold (chapter 4) stresses that REM sleep enhances systems-level processes of triage producing qualitative changes in memory that convey their meaning both in terms of their gist and their emotional core. He distinguishes between the stabilization and strengthening of episodic memories in slow wave sleep (SWS) and their elimination as accurate records of events in REM sleep. Understanding the detail of distinctions between how memories are consolidated in waking and sleep states is a major future area for research.

The study of dreams brings another dimension to the analysis of the human memory process, that of the imagination, which appears to apply to the waking state as well. This component has been identified across the border between the scientists and humanists as they witness the modulation of memory. Strikingly scientists such as Dudai, Silva, Changeux, Stickgold, and Rolls have come to recognize certain signs of the imagination in the memory process. Dudai (chapter 1) finds that in the case of episodic memory imagination is a useful factor that changes, updates and extends the previous knowledge and demonstrates the advantageous plasticity of memory. Silva (chapter 2) implies that imagination is a property of memory that helps to bend memories to their "self-serving fictions." Changeux (chapter 3) proposes that imagination is part of the novelty of the spontaneous activity of "prerepresentations," latent forms of memory that can be stabilized within the global neuronal workspace. Stickgold (chapter 4) says that the literary imagination functions in a way that is similar to that of the dreaming brain and its natural, nonassociative handling of memories. Rolls (chapter 8) raises the developing case for nondeterministic components ("noise") in driving creativity by allowing alternative possible futures to be built on the experiences of the past. With his scientific perspective, Hirstein (chapter 10) shows how confabulation can be seen as a normal event in the first stage of memory processing; memory has to be edited in a top-down manner by the executive function of the frontal lobe for it monitoring and correction.

Juxtaposed with these kinds of scientific observations, many of the humanists have identified the imaginative component they find to be inherent in memory. In analyzing various forms of the imagination, humanists tap literary material for its productive blend of fact and fiction. This kind of discussion also leads naturally to the consideration of the epistemic truth claim or veridicality of human memory. This takes us back to Nalbantian, Richardson, Foster, and Favorini. Nalbantian (chapter 12) says that autobiographical fiction serves to "heighten," not belie, the truth of the raw memory material. She demonstrates that the veracity of this creative composition of memory can then be measured against the veridical baseline of autobiography. In the context of Romantic literary texts, Richardson (chapter 13) shows how the very fragility of episodic memory proves not to be a flaw but an adaptive advantage in imaginative reconstruction for future thinking. Foster (chapter 14) witnesses in autobiographical texts the fusion of memory with the imagination with writers such as Nabokov who create composite memories that are full of facts, but not entirely factual. Favorini (chapter 15) uses a theater-based metaphor to describe the memory process as a "scripting of recollection" that is manifest in the dramatic imagination that does not "picture" the past, but reconstructs and recategorizes it. The dramatic instantiation of memory reflects the natural temporal ordering and succession of an altered memory system that incarnates memory in the present.

Many of the contributors to this volume adventurously reconsider basic assumptions about the memory process, viewing it as transformative, selective, and adaptive. The Argentinian poet-writer Jorge Luis Borges intuitively rejected the metaphor that memory was stored in, for example, a granary or warehouse. He offered instead the metaphor of the mirror, by which memory becomes a fluid montage of myriad reflections. Like the literary writers with their memory tropes, current neuroscientists are arriving at their own metaphors for the memory process. Dudai, for example, replaces the traditional "storehouse" with a "phoenix" metaphor, suggesting memory's perennial transfiguration. The dynamism that is described helps to put life into the connectionist models, metastability into the substantialist ones and probability into the cellular ones. Old models are challenged by a nonlinear definition of causality in the investigation of the memory process, suggested by Silva, Changeux, LeDoux and Doyère, and Bickle. This leads to the questioning of methodology in memory research, particularly by Silva and Bickle. How far can we construe the etiology of memory modeling if memory storage is not a stepwise constructive process but an indeterminate one of constant transformation that depends on a convergence of correlated, emergent occurrences (Silva, Bickle), the alternating active/inactive states of memory plasticity after retrieval (Dudai, LeDoux and Doyère) or the productive creation of redundancies (Changeux, McClelland)? Moreover, the genetic and epigenetic sides of the workings of memory are being viewed interactively in an interrelated, symbiotic relationship. As Changeux shows, genetic coding is modulated according to the input of experience; but conversely, as Silva reports from transgenic studies, mutations in genomes can disrupt behaviorial plasticity. And as words such as *pattern*, *fluidity*, and *rhythm* emerge in the study of memory, there is growing recognition that memory is not only composed of some identifiable traces, but also is a process and activity. This perspective on memory can be aligned with the analysis of humanistic works that show how memory is relational (Favorini, Hertz), provisional (Foster, Freedberg) and artistically constructive (Nalbantian, Richardson, Vidal). The science and art of memory are herewith conjoined.

This book's efforts to engage the two different approaches to memory provided by neuroscience and the humanities have yielded points of convergence and issues for further debate. In our era of continued strain on the humanities, *The Memory Process* shows how valuable they are in offering pertinent information and insight to scientists about human memory—its origins, accessions and rendering—outside of laboratories and experimental controls as an untapped source of case studies in human experience. In our era of the humanization of science, this volume shows how scientific criteria may lend new rigor and new perspectives for understanding the rich material of humanistic studies. It is hoped that this book will stand as a touchstone in the ongoing exploration of the memory process and as a model for effective interdisciplinary exchange.

Acknowledgment

I am grateful to Paul M. Matthews for his commentary on this introduction.

Notes

1. Jean-Pierre Changeux and Paul Ricoeur, *What Makes Us Think?* trans. M. B. DeBevoise (1998; reprint, Princeton, NJ: Princeton University Press, 2000), 73–74.

2. Michel Serres, *Hermes: Literature, Science, Philosophy*, ed. Josué Harari and David F. Bell (Baltimore: Johns Hopkins University Press, 1982).

3. Patricia Churchland, *Neurophilosophy: Toward a Unified Science of the Mind-Brain* (Cambridge, MA: MIT Press, 1986), 478.

4. See Daniel Clement Dennett, *Consciousness Explained* (Boston: Little, Brown: 1991); John R. Searle, *The Rediscovery of the Mind* (Cambridge, MA: MIT Press: 1992; and Francis Crick, *The Astonishing Hypothesis: The Scientific Search for the Soul* (New York: Scribner; Maxwell Macmillan International, 1994).

5. See Bernard Baars *A Cognitive Theory of Consciousness* (New York: Cambridge University Press, 1988); Stanislas Dehaene, Michel Kerszberg, and Jean-Pierre Changeux, "A Neuronal Model of a Global Workspace in Effortful Cognitive Tasks," *Proceedings of the National Academy of Sciences USA* 95 (1998): 14529–1453; Gerald Edelman and Giulio Tononi, *A Universe of Consciousness: How Matter Becomes Imagination* (New York: Penguin, 2001); Marsel Mesulam, "Representation, Inference, and Transcendent Encoding in Neurocognitive Networks of the Human Brain," *Annals of Neurology* 64 (2008): 367–378.

6. See Antonio Damasio, "How the Brain Creates the Mind" and Eric Kandel, "The New Science of Mind," in *The Best of the Brain from Scientific American*, ed. Floyd E. Bloom (New York: Dana Press, 2007): 58–75.

7. See Endel Tulving, "Episodic and Semantic Memory," in *Organization of Memory*, ed. E. Tulving and W. Donaldson (New York: Academic Press, 1972), 381–403. E. Tulving, *Elements of Episodic Memory* (Oxford: Clarendon Press, 1983).

8. See Alan D. Baddeley and Graham Hitch, "Working Memory," in the *Psychology of Learning and Motivation: Advances in Research and Theory*, ed. Gordon H. Bower (New York: Academic Press, 1974), 8:47–89; and Alan D. Baddeley, "The Episodic Buffer: A New Component of Working Memory?" *Trends in Cognitive Science* 4 (2000): 417–423.

9. See Peter Graf and Daniel L. Schacter, "Implicit and Explicit Memory for New Associations in Normal and Amnesic Subjects," *Journal of Experimental Psychology: Learning, Memory, and Cognition* 11 (1985): 501–518.

10. Sigmund Freud, "Notiz über den 'Wunderblock,'" *Internationale Zeitschrift für Psychoanalyse* 11 (1): 1. GW, XIV.

11. See Mark Solms, "Freud Returns," *Scientific American* 290 (May 2004): 82–88; J. Allan Hobson, "Freud Returns? Like a Bad Dream," *Scientific American* 290 (May 2004): 89.

12. K. S. Lashley, "In Search of the Engram," in *The Neuropsychology of Lashley: Selected Papers of K. S . Lashley,* ed. Frank A. Beach et al. (New York: McGraw Hill, 1960), 500–501; Donald O. Hebb, *The Organization of Behavior: A Neuropsychological Theory* (New York: Wiley, 1949).

13. T. V. P. Bliss and T. Lømo, "Long-Lasting Potentiation of Synaptic Transmission in the Dentate Area of the Anaesthetized Rabbit Following Stimulation of the Perforant Path," *Journal of Physiology* (London) 232 (1973): 331–356. See also Guilherme Neves, Sam F. Cooke, and Tim V. Bliss, "Synaptic Plasticity, Memory

and the Hippocampus: A Neural Network Approach to Causality," *Nature Reviews Neuroscience* 9 (2008): 65–75.

14. Gary Lynch and Dominique Muller, "Steps Between the Induction and Expression of Long-Term Potentiation," *Neurotoxicity of Excitatory Amino Acids,*" ed. Alessandro Guidotti (New York: Raven Press, 1990).

15. Pablo Alvarez and Larry Squire, "Memory Consolidation and the Medial Temporal Lobe: A Simple Network Model," *Proceedings of the National Academy of Sciences USA* 91 (1994): 7041–7045. See also Larry Squire and Pablo Alvarez, "Retrograde Amnesia and Memory Consolidation: A Neurobiological Perspective," *Current Opinion in Neurobiology* 9 (1995): 169–177.

16. Morris Moscovitch, "Consolidation: A Systems Approach to Remote Memory and the Interaction between the Hippocampal Complex and Neocortex," in *Constructive Memory,* ed. Boicho Kokinov and William Hirst (Sofia: New Bulgarian University, 2003), 50.

17. James McGaugh. "Memory—A Century of Consolidation," *Science* 287 (2000): 248–251.

18. Pramod K. Dash and Binyamin Hochner, "Injection of the cAMP-Responsive Element into the Nucleus of *Aplysia* Sensory Neurons Blocks Long-Term Facilitation," *Nature* 345 (1990): 718–721. See also Alcino J. Silva et al., "CREB and Memory," *Annual Review of Neuroscience* 21 (1998): 127–148.

19. Karim Nader, Glenn E. Schafe, and Joseph LeDoux, "Fear Memories Require Protein Synthesis in the Amygdala for Reconsolidation after Retrieval," *Nature* 406 (2000): 722–726.

20. Karim Nader and Oliver Hardt, "A Single Standard for Memory: The Case for Reconsolidation," *Nature Reviews Neuroscience* 10 (March 2009): 232.

I   Scientific Foundations

1   The Engram Revisited: On the Elusive Permanence of Memory

Yadin Dudai

That memory involves enduring physical changes in the organism has been proposed, using era-dependent metaphors, since antiquity.[1] More than a century ago, Richard Semon introduced the term *engram* to refer to such a change.[2] It gained popularity, however, only when a group of researchers, most notable among them Karl Lashley, embarked on a systematic hunt for engrams, using lesions to determine which parts of the brain impair the ability of animals to form and maintain memories. That search proved futile: "This series of experiments," wrote Lashley in 1950 toward the end of his career, "has yielded a good bit of information about what and where the memory trace is not ... I sometimes feel, in reviewing the evidence on the localization of the memory trace, that the necessary conclusion is that learning just is not possible ... Nevertheless, in spite of such evidence against it, learning does sometimes occur."[3]

Lashley's disillusion was quickly forgotten, however, or probably suppressed in the collective memory of memory scientists, and the search for the engram was soon revitalized. Reasons were proposed why Lashley failed in his attempts to localize the physical trace of memory, and advanced methodologies were recruited to the game. These included localized brain stimulation, recording of nerve cell activity in the behaving animals, and, ultimately, functional brain imaging in humans. This renewed search yielded an abundance of fascinating data on memory systems in the brain, on the neural circuits that subserve them, and on cellular and molecular mechanisms that might make memory possible.

With this massive accumulation of new data on brain mechanisms of memory in the background, it seems like a proper time to revisit the engram. How enduring is the hypothetical physical change, if at all? What is its relevance to the expression of memory? The *Zeitgeist* in the neurobiology of memory was until recently that the engram is indeed a lasting change induced by the learning experience, not much unlike the inscriptions on wax tablets proposed by Plato in the dialogue *Theaetetus*. This view is now changing, however, which comes as no surprise to students of human psychology and cognition, who for years have claimed the most intriguing attribute of long-term memory to be its frailty rather than its stability.[4] Yet it is of interest to the science of memory as a whole to appreciate why the aforementioned conceptual change is taking place in brain research.

In analyzing the current transition in the interpretation of the engram, it is useful to spell out at the outset the two major, long-standing hypotheses in the neurobiology of memory. One is the "dual trace hypothesis," the other the "consolidation hypothesis." Derived mostly from the works of William James and Donald Hebb, the dual trace hypothesis posits that memory traces exist in two forms.[5] One is ephemeral (short-term memory, STM), the other long-term and stable (long-term memory, LTM). The consolidation hypothesis posits that for memory to become long-term, it must undergo a maturation process, which renders the trace resistant to some agents and treatments that can impair or erase short-term memory.[6] The consolidation hypothesis further assumed that consolidation occurs just once per item.

The dual trace and consolidation hypotheses are closely related. For the trace to be dual, transition from one form to another has to take place, which is consolidation; and for consolidation to take place, a change in the nature of the memory trace has to be assumed. Both hypotheses embrace a universal unifying concept in biology: Living entities develop and grow. Both consider learning to be an experience-dependent process in which the "teaching stimulus" triggers a local, restricted developmental shift in the relevant areas of the brain, involving local growth processes in interconnected sets of nerve cells. Memory is hence the outcome of growth processes in the neuronal circuits that encode the newly acquired information. Seen this way, brains never reach full maturity (admittedly, not a particularly surprising conclusion, scientific evidence notwithstanding). Edwin Holt epitomized this viewpoint in 1931: "Growth and learning are one continuous process, to the earlier phases of which we give the one name, and to the later ... the other."[7] Or, an earlier similar view: "For every act of memory," said Alexander Bain, "...

there is a specific grouping or coordination of sensations and movements, by virtue of specific growth in the cell junctions."[8] Elaborate experience-dependent growth theories paved the way to the discovery that de novo macromolecular synthesis, characteristic of development and growth in all tissues, is indeed required for long-term memory. The concept of trace transition via consolidation hence fits the idea that like organs and organisms, memories mature over time.

It is noteworthy that the term *consolidation* is used in memory research to denote hypothetical memory stabilization processes at different levels of brain organization. Molecular neurobiologists refer to postencoding stabilization of synaptic or cell-wide information storage, which is completed within hours or days after encoding, as "cellular" or "synaptic consolidation." Cellular consolidation is universal and has been identified in all species capable of acquiring long-term memory. But there is also an additional process, called "systems consolidation," which refers to the postencoding reorganization of information in distributed corticohippocampal circuits. This process requires weeks, months, possibly even years to complete.[9] In this chapter, unless otherwise indicated, *consolidation* refers to both synaptic and systems types of memory maturation.

The consolidation hypothesis thus implies two interrelated attributes of long-term memory: *unidirectionality* along the time arrow and *stability* over time. In particular, it was assumed that once consolidation is over, the memory item becomes resistant to a variety of amnesic agents, such as inhibitors of protein synthesis.

Retrieval Renders Old Memories Malleable Again

Ample evidence from human cognitive psychology indicates that recollection involves reconstruction of information rather than mere replication. In parallel, animal studies have provided intriguing evidence that reactivation of items in long-term memory opens a window of susceptibility to amnesic agents, long after the completion of the postulated post-encoding consolidation. This phenomenon, termed "reconsolidation," was nevertheless practically neglected for decades. There were two reasons for this neglect. First, the interpretation of the data on the apparent susceptibility of reactivated memories to interference in terms of a process of recurrent consolidation was challenged. Second, the dominance of the consolidation hypothesis tended to interfere with proper discussion of the idea of reconsolidation. Ultimately, the accumulating data made their impact, and in recent years the study of reconsolidation has become a major focus of interest in both human and animal research.[10]

In terms of the cellular and circuit mechanisms, reconsolidation is not a faithful replay of consolidation. Both processes do, however, share dependence on de novo macromolecular synthesis in nerve cells. To date, several boundary conditions have been identified that constrain reconsolidation. These include the degree of "dominance" of the reactivated trace compared to other associations of the same cue (i.e., the ability of that specific trace to control behavior after retrieval); competition with concomitant memory extinction; and, most pertinent to our discussion here, conditions that promote new encoding in or immediately after retrieval.[11]

Close examination of the data and discussions in the field unveils three potential versions of the reconsolidation hypothesis. The "strong version" posits that the regained plasticity applies to all the elements of the original memory and may indeed end up in the erasure of that memory. The "intermediate version" posits that there is a core memory that is stable and unaffected by the reconsolidation, although some stored elements of the original trace can still be modified and even erased. The "weak version" posits that the original memory trace is unaffected, and the transient augmentation of plasticity refers only to new information added to the older memory during or immediately after retrieval. The weak version does not deviate from the classical consolidation hypothesis, as it simply claims that new information consolidates; thus not really "reconsolidation." It is so far unclear which of the other versions fits reality better, the "strong" or the "intermediate." Yet even if upon memory reactivation the core representation becomes susceptible to amnesic agents (i.e., as the "strong version" predicts), related memory associations seem to be spared.[12]

Whereas in laboratory settings reconsolidation is usually unveiled by detecting susceptibility to memory impairment after retrieval, in real life the process might provide an opportunity for the strengthening of the trace. This observation, along with the finding that reconsolidation is promoted by the induction of an encoding state in the retrieval situation, raises the possibility that the role of reconsolidation may be to update memory. That is to say, the process promotes adaptation of the retrieved trace to the retrieval context. However, whereas the consolidation hypothesis postulates that the original memory is securely consolidated, updating notwithstanding, the reconsolidation hypothesis, even in its "intermediate version" (see above), assumes that at least part of the original trace regains susceptibility to change. Some data support a role for reconsolidation in the updating of long-term memories. The current discrepancy on the role of reconsolidation in updating in different systems and paradigms might be related to boundary conditions on reconsolidation, which are not yet completely understood.

Malleability in the Absence of Retrieval

Recent data demonstrate that long-term memory (at least up to a few months after encoding) is susceptible to certain amnesic agents, even in the absence of explicit memory reactivation, that is, in the absence of retrieval. These agents are inhibitors of an enzyme, the atypical isozyme of protein kinase C (PKC) called PKMζ. PKCs are molecules composed of a catalytic subunit, which catalyzes the modification of the substrate proteins in vivo, and a regulatory subunit, which inhibits the catalytic subunit by binding to it via a specific part, termed the *pseudosubstrate domain*. In the absence of the regulatory subunit, the enzyme becomes constitutively active, or "autonomous." PKMζ is the autonomous form of PKCζ. In laboratory experiments, PKMζ can be selectively inhibited by a number of inhibitors, notable among them a cell-permeable form of the pseudosubstrate protein sequence, called the zeta inhibitory peptide (ZIP). PKMζ has been reported to be critical to the maintenance of long-term potentiation (LTP), a popular cellular model of learning in the hippocampus.[13] The persistently active PKMζ acts on specific synaptic substrates, leading to modification of the microstructure of the synapse and, ultimately, to a substantial increase in the number of functional postsynaptic receptors for the major transmitter glutamate (particularly receptors of the subtype called "AMPA"). All this culminates in persistent enhancement of synaptic transmission, presumed to encode the experience-dependent alteration in the activity of the specific neuronal circuit, that is, the cellular manifestation of the memory formed by the specific experience.

Long-term spatial information in the hippocampus, subserved by LTP, was shown to critically depend on persistent activity of PKMζ.[14] This was demonstrated by the microinfusion of the selective inhibitor ZIP into the hippocampus of the behaving rat. Additional forms of hippocampus-dependent memories and some forms of amygdala-dependent memories were also shown to be impaired by the PKMζ inhibitor. Although the hippocampus is indeed well known to play a critical role in some types of memory, it is the neocortex that is considered to serve as the ultimate repository of many types of long-term memory in the mammalian brain. Microinfusion of ZIP into the neocortex was shown to rapidly erase remote memories in the behaving rat. The affected brain area was, however, still able to reacquire a new memory association, implying that information was depleted from the storage apparatus but the apparatus itself was not damaged.[15] These data thus suggest that PKMζ permanently maintains the cellular machinery that embodies long-term memory. When the enzymatic activity is blocked briefly, the experience-dependent synaptic modifications collapse, and so does the specific memory. One possibility is that the target of PKMζ is a synaptic "tag" that is formed when new information is encoded, but is then degraded rapidly by dephosphorylation. In the absence of this tag, although the enzymatic activity recovers from the inhibition, the enzyme can no longer locate the proper phosphorylation site and therefore the tag is not regenerated and memory is lost.

Two main conclusions emerge from the findings concerning the role of PKMζ in long-term memory persistence. First, that some specific inhibitors (e.g., ZIP) can cause rapid, irreversible amnesia even in the absence of explicit memory reactivation. Thus postretrieval "reconsolidation" is not the only window of opportunity in which an item in long-term memory can be modified. And second, neuronal changes that subserve long-term memory are not indelible modifications in synaptic structure, but remain dependent on ongoing enzymatic activity and thus are capable of rapid and dynamic alterations by experimental manipulations.

What might be the role of a mechanism that permits rapid erasure of long-term memory? Several possibilities come to mind. First, in situ, the cellular mechanism that requires persistent phosphorylation by PKMζ might be regulated in selected synapses, possibly in a graded manner, resulting in fast, restricted modulation of local synaptic properties. Such rapid, local modulation of long-term synaptic plasticity might, for example, be useful in the course of fast incorporation of new experience into existing associative knowledge schemas in the neocortex, without necessarily activating other related associations that are accessed at the time of change.[16]

Second, rapid inhibition of PKMζ in specific synapses might result in a rapid shift of synapses to a reduced level of activity or even to a silent state. This might be useful when previous accumulating modifications culminate in catastrophic "freezing" (e.g., a stable local minimum trap) of the computational abilities of the neuronal circuit, a situation that might be remedied by "rebooting." (We can note again the abundance of era-dependent metaphors in discussions of brain function). And third, as some computational models suggest, circuits might saturate, a situation that might benefit from erasure because it releases computational space for processing and storing new information.

Selective inhibitors of PKMζ are, at this time, the only agents found capable of rapidly erasing certain types of long-term and remote memory associations in the mammalian brain in the absence of explicit memory reactivation. Since phosphorylation of synaptic proteins is implicated in many cellular models of memory encoding, and since the phosphorylation of a target protein can be reversed by another type of enzyme, protein phosphatase, further research on protein phosphatase inhibitors may lead to identification of additional types of memory erasers.

Memories Active and Inactive

The recent findings concerning modifiability of long-term memory have revitalized an alternative conceptual framework to the aforementioned dual-trace and consolidation hypotheses. This alternative conceptual framework portrays memory items in two alternating states: active and inactive.[17] "Active" is the state of the memory trace immediately after encoding and retrieval. Occasionally the memory trace might also become activated independent of encoding and retrieval. Otherwise, the trace is "inactive." Over time, so goes the hypothesis, the trace alternates between the active and inactive states. The data on consolidation and reconsolidation indicate that whenever active, the trace enters a special state ("post-activation state"), in which it is highly plastic and susceptible to interference by amnesic agents. This runs counter to the dual trace hypothesis, which predicts no augmented plasticity after retrieval once consolidation is over.

It is noteworthy that the active/inactive types of models neither nullify the existence of a unique initial consolidation process nor preclude an early maturation phase for each item in memory immediately following

its encoding. As noted above, studies comparing consolidation to reconsolidation show that reconsolidation is not a faithful recapitulation of
consolidation. In addition, studies on the role of PKMζ in neural plasticity
and memory show that memories are not sensitive to PKMζ inhibitors in
the first hours after training. All this implies that the properties of a fresh
memory are different from those of an old one. But once long-term memory
is established, the active/inactive models assume that the memory is still
malleable and not stored as an indelibly consolidated item. Resorting to
metaphors, the combination of the dual trace model with the consolidation hypothesis connotes a "storehouse" class of metaphors, [18] whereas the
more recent data on the high plasticity of the long-term trace and the
"cyclic" models that stem from these data favor a "phoenix" type of metaphor: Occasionally, items in memory get the opportunity to be reborn
again and again.

The Advantage of Instability

The findings that items in long-term memory are prone to change either
upon their reactivation in retrieval (i.e., reconsolidation) or even in the
absence of such explicit reactivation (e.g., by interfering with persistent
activity of the cellular information-keeping machinery), may at first seem
counterintuitive. It does seem advantageous to abort the formation of
long-term memory in the consolidation window to eliminate new information that is judged by the brain to be superfluous or only of temporary
value. But, once information is judged to be valuable for long-term use and
hence consolidated, why should it be modified over time? Similar to the
answer to any other teleology-driven question in science, the answer to
this question as well is supposed to be *a priori* speculative. Still, the intellectual exercise is worth playing. First and foremost, the possibility should
not be excluded that this potential frailty of declarative long-term memory
reflects an inherent mechanistic shortcoming of the biological system,
rather than adaptivity. That said, it is still worthwhile to consider adaptive
possibilities. The first that comes to mind is that memories too robust are
a potential disadvantage, as they may not fit anymore to guide the proper
action and reaction in a changing environment. The updating process, as
noted above, is highly valuable. Updating in retrieval can benefit from
the existence of the reconsolidation window. Updating outside the time

window of reconsolidation may further facilitate fast incorporation of new experience into existing associative knowledge schemas in the absence of superfluous activation of indirect associations.[19]

The price paid by the organism for this plasticity may be the reduced veracity of stored information. It is noteworthy that for at least one type of memory system, episodic memory, this has been proposed as an advantage rather than an imperfection.[20] It has been postulated that the function of the cognitive system that we dub "episodic memory" is primarily to permit generation of mental time travel and particularly the imagination of scenarios of future events rather than storing the memory of past events. If indeed "episodic memory" is primarily a mental future-time-travel organ, the fact that items in long-term memory change over time is not a disadvantage, but rather an advantage. The reason is that imagination permutates and extends our previous experience, not unlike the recursiveness proposed to underlie the faculty of language; and hence too rigid a memory may lead to poor imagination, one that plays scenarios of the future that are only similar to the past.[21] Thus the elementary neuronal mechanisms that permit recurrent updating of items in long-term memory may have also permitted us to evolve a more effective imagination, clearly a faculty of great phylogenetic value.

Engrams as Palimpsests

Is the engram permanent then? Given that synapses, cells, and circuits seem to be in constant flux, that experience-dependent modifications in neural systems have ample opportunities to become redone and possibly undone, and that the engram refers to the physical trace formed in encoding, the first answer that comes to mind is no. But this answer is rather simplistic. To arrive at a more realistic one, we need to consider two fundamental issues. The first is the level of details that are valuable for the organism to remember. The second is the distinctiveness or "individuality" of engrams, that is, the distinct set of informational attributes that reflect the unique event that had led to the formation of the engram and are supposed to be "stored" in that specific engram.

Memory systems seem to differ from one another in the resolution of the information that makes the memory item valuable to the organism. For example, some skills are critically dependent on fine details. Yet to remember superfluous details of events could be counterproductive, as illustrated in the biographies of the real-life mnemonist Solomon Shereshevsky and his fictional counterpart, Funes, from Jorge Luis Borges's fascinating story.[22] That fine details concerning the content and timing of events become unreliable as time goes by is thus not necessarily a design flaw in our memory systems. On this issue, the cognitive evolutionary perspective is different from that of the individual struggling to remember a pertinent detail. We indeed feel uncomfortable and embarrassed when attempting in vain to recall exactly what happened during last year's vacation. But from a phylogenetic point of view, this information is rarely critical. The gist of the experience, or the processed and distilled mental narrative, is usually more important than the accuracy of the details. Narratives can assimilate and parsimoniously represent the valuable impact of experience. Giving up on superfluous details could allow the brain to promote generalization and facilitate appropriate response to both expected and unexpected cues. It is also probably easier on the capacity of the memory system.

In the process of forming mental narratives, engrams merge, losing much of their original individuality. They join the distributed, large and dynamic "society of engrams" that comes to constitute our memory. To consider an engram as a discrete, well-defined long-term physical trace is hence a bit naive. In real life, engrams are palimpsests, reflecting physical traces of many layers of past events.[23] Molecular, synaptic, and cellwide mechanisms, of the types described earlier in this chapter, allow the engrams to do just that.

The permanence of memory traces is hence evasive. Discrete, fine-grained mnemonic traces, assumed to be formed in encoding, are likely to be ephemeral. What persists is their increasingly diluted contribution to memory palimpsests that keep metamorphosing so long as the brain endures. But stripping engrams of their individuality doesn't render the concept of the engram useless. Keeping this concept alive, over a century after Semon had proposed it, reminds us that items in memory are indeed embedded in some type or another of physical change in the biological material and drives us to search for the algorithms used by biological learning machines and for their implementation in identified biological nuts-and-bolts. And as the recent exciting developments in neuroscience demonstrate, the search for the engram can indeed unveil surprising new and useful properties of memory systems at all levels, from the molecular to the behavioral.

Notes

1. Yadin Dudai, *Memory from A to Z: Keywords, Concepts, and Beyond* (Oxford: Oxford University Press, 2002).

2. Richard Semon, *The Mneme* (1904; reprint, London: George, Allen and Unwine, 1921). Throughout this chapter, the term *engram* will be used interchangeably with *memory trace*, hence implying that the *trace* is a physical change in the nervous system.

3. Karl S. Lashley, "In Search of the Engram," *Symposia of the Society for Experimental Biology* 4 (1950): 454–482.

4. Daniel L. Schacter, ed., *Memory Distortion* (Cambridge, MA: Harvard University Press, 1995).

5. William James, *The Principles of Psychology* (1890; reprint, New York: Dover, 1950); Donald O. Hebb, *The Organization of Behavior: A Neuropsychological Theory* (New York: Wiley, 1949).

6. Yadin Dudai, "The Neurobiology of Consolidations, or, How Stable Is the Engram?" *Annual Review of Psychology* 55 (2004): 51–86.

7. Edwin B. Holt, *Animal Drive and the Learning Process* (New York: Holt, 1931).

8. Alexander Bain, *Mind and Body: The Theories of Their Relation* (London: Henry King, 1872).

9. James L. McClelland and Nigel H. Goddard, "Considerations Arising from Complementary Learning Systems Perspective on Hippocampus and Neocortex," *Hippocampus* 6 (1996): 654–665.

10. Karim Nader and Oliver Hardt, "A Single Standard for Memory: The Case for Reconsolidation," *Nature Reviews Neuroscience* 10 (2009): 224–234.

11. Richard G. M. Morris et al., "Memory Reconsolidation: Sensitivity of Spatial Memory to Inhibition of Protein Synthesis in Dorsal Hippocampus during Encoding and Retrieval," *Neuron* 50 (2006): 479–489.

12. Jacek Debiec et al., "Directly Reactivated, but Not Indirectly Reactivated, Memories Undergo Reconsolidation in the Amygdala," *Proceedings of the National Academy of Sciences USA* 103 (2006): 3428–3433.

13. Douglas S. Ling, Larry S. Benardo, and Todd C. Sacktor, "Protein Kinase Mzeta Enhances Excitatory Synaptic Transmission by Increasing the Number of Active Postsynaptic AMPA Receptors," *Hippocampus* 16 (2006): 443–452.

14. Eva Pastalkova et al., "Storage of Spatial Information by the Maintenance Mechanism of LTP," *Science* 313 (2006): 1141–1144.

15. Reut Shema, Todd C. Sacktor, and Yadin Dudai, "Rapid Erasure of Long-Term Memory Associations in Cortex by an Inhibitor of PKMz," *Science* 317 (2007): 951–953.

16. Dorothy Tse et al., "Schemas and Memory Consolidation," *Science* 316 (2007): 76–82.

17. Donald J. Lewis, "Psychobiology of Active and Inactive Memory," *Psychological Bulletin* 86 (1979): 1054–1083.

18. Henry L. Roediger III, "Memory Metaphors in Cognitive Psychology," *Memory & Cognition* 8 (1980): 231–246.

19. D. Tse et al., "Schemas and Memory Consolidation"; J. Debiec et al., "Directly Reactivated, but Not Indirectly Reactivated, Memories Undergo Reconsolidation in the Amygdala."

20. Yadin Dudai and Mary Carruthers, "The Janus Face of Mnemosyne," *Nature* 434 (2005): 567.

21. Marc D. Hauser, Noam Chomsky, and William T. Fitch, "The Faculty of Language: What Is It, Who Has It, and How Did It Evolve?" *Science* 298 (2002): 1569–1579.

22. Alexander. R. Luria, *The Mind of a Mnemonist* (London: Jonathan Cape, 1969); Jorge Luis Borges, "Funes, His Memory," in *Collected Fictions* (1944; reprint, New York: Viking: 1998).

23. Yadin Dudai, *Memory from A to Z.*

2 Molecular Genetic Approaches to Memory Consolidation

Alcino J. Silva

Science continually reinvents the world around us, the tools we use, the way we communicate, our economy, even our belief systems. Neuroscience also changes the world within, shaping how we imagine ourselves, refocusing our consciousness with more and more accurate representations of the mysterious biology that determines who we are. Human memory is often thought of as a computer drive full of events, faces, emotions, with files of our catalogued pasts, some fragile and nearly unreadable, but most intact, waiting for the right moment to be recalled. This surprisingly common view of memory can be traced to one of the longest-lasting and most influential theories in neuroscience research: the consolidation theory.[1] According to this theory, our senses—sight, smell, hearing, touch, and taste—bring the world to the brain, which uses a stepwise process to file away the parts that are useful, interesting, distressing, and important. Such ostensible consolidation assures the stability and the reliability of these memories.

This chapter describes how recent neuroscientific findings, including those from molecular genetics, are leading researchers to question the strong version of this theory and to formulate a more dynamic and adaptive view of memory. Recent molecular and cellular cognition studies in many laboratories, including my own, have led me to dramatically reconsider basic assumptions about memory processes. This reevaluation reflects exciting new molecular genetic findings that are changing the way memory is imagined and studied.

One of the key legacies of the consolidation theory is that memory cements information in the brain in sequential, stepwise fashion, with an initial labile phase lasting a few hours, where memories can more easily be disrupted, and later phases where memory is far more resilient to interference. This multiple-phase description has served as a useful account of many important results in memory research and continues to play an important role in the taxonomy of memory phenomena. Embedded within the theory, however, are assumptions about the fidelity and reliability of processes designed to faithfully represent information in the brain that are neither useful nor data-driven.

Even though many of our memories are vivid and some may even be accurate, most of what we remember of our daily lives is neither exact nor rich in detail.[2] There is overwhelming neuropsychological evidence that evolution did not design our memories to be video cameras faithfully and precisely recording our daily experiences.[3] For example, a key memory system in the brain is specifically structured to extract from experience unconscious rules and abstractions that allow organisms to deal with the ever-changing world that surrounds them in an expedient and self-serving manner. There is also evidence that we may change our memories, if only a little, each time we recall them.[4] The fluidity of memory may reflect the challenges inherent in engineering brains able to make life-and-death decisions at a moment's notice in noisy, uncertain, and ever-changing environments. Memory is about survival, not accuracy.

According to the consolidation theory, the troublesome lapses or errors of memory that we all experience are no more than the necessary failings of an imperfect system forced to work with the difficult compromises of evolution. One of the implicit assumptions of the strong version of the theory is that unreliable memories are the result of our genetic heritage, our environment, and our behavior, or the failure of one or more. The consolidation theory states that memory involves multiple steps or phases of memory mediated by an ensemble of molecules, cells, and neuronal circuits. Failure of any one of these components could easily account for memory's imperfections.

It is important to note that the influential consolidation theory, introduced more than a century ago, still manages to capture much of what we know about memory. Despite its obvious shortcomings, it continues to have a strong grip both on how we conceive and imagine memory mechanisms and on how we plan and execute memory experiments.[5] Moreover, it explicitly or implicitly accounts for most of the findings in molecular and cellular cognition, a new neuroscience field, in which molecular genetics plays a key role. To explain how recent molecular genetic results seem to contradict the strong version of the consolidation theory, I now turn to that field.

The distinguishing feature of molecular and cellular cognition is a dogged determination to account for psychological phenomena with fully integrated molecular, cellular, and system explanations. Crucial to the development of the field was the transgenic revolution that swept through biology in the late 1980s and early 1990s.[6] Transgenic mice (expressing a modified gene) and knockout mice (having specific gene deletions or modifications) are powerful molecular genetic tools that changed the face of biology and that continue to have a key role in most areas of biology.[7] At the time, however, neuroscience had not yet fully joined the molecular genetics revolution; it was splintered into various disciplines, with molecular biologists busy cloning new genes, physiologists discovering new mechanisms of neuronal communication, and psychologists exploring the neuroanatomy of memory. Each discipline operated in its own separate world, hardly ever crossing the experimental boundaries of neighboring disciplines and rarely exploring the potential of multidisciplinary studies. The reason for this was simple. There were few experimental tools to bring together the work in these separate disciplines. Molecular biologists had very few ways to test the function of the genes they were cloning in neurons, much less in living animals. Physiologists had great difficulty exploring the mechanisms of "memory" phenomena such as long-term potentiation (LTP) in behaving animals, and psychologists had little incentive and few strategies to try to to incorporate emerging neuroscientific concepts and findings in their working hypotheses and experimental approaches.

Nevertheless, at the time many neuroscience luminaries called for the integration of these separate disciplines in developing explanations of brain function.[8] In the late 1980s, the transgenic revolution sweeping through biology suggested a way to accomplish just that. Mutant mice could be used to integrate molecular and cellular approaches with behavioral studies.[9] Thus mutant mouse lines were engineered with mutations in putative "memory" genes, and these mice were then used to conduct electrophysiological and behavioral studies of the function of the disrupted genes. By integrating the molecular, electrophysiological, and behavioral analysis of the mutant mice, there was the opportunity to connect the function of the disrupted molecule with the specific physiological mechanisms disrupted in the mutants and with the behavioral profile of the mutant mice.[10]

The prospect of genetically engineering mammals and then using the mutants to glimpse the innermost workings of the brain was exciting. Consequently, in a relatively short time a large number of different laboratories took the lead from early studies and joined the genetics revolution. The gene that brought this revolution to neuroscience was alpha-calcium-calmodulin kinase II (αCaMKII), which encodes a synaptic kinase thought to modulate neuronal communication in brain regions, like the hippocampus, involved in memory.[11] The choice of genes was at first limited since few mammalian genes were thought to be involved in learning and memory. Once mice were genetically engineered with a mutation that disrupted αCaMKII, they were studied by a team of neuroscientists including physiologists and psychologists.[12] These early studies found that the αCaMKII-mutant mice had severe learning problems, especially in hippocampal tests such as the Morris water maze, a test for spatial learning. Thus initial physiological analysis of the mutants was focused on a hippocampal region (Ca1) required for spatial learning. These studies found that mutant neurons had profound deficits in a specific synaptic phenomenon: long-term potentiation (LTP), a significant development since Donald Hebb had proposed an LTP-like mechanism as the basis for learning and memory in 1949.[13] According to Hebb, synapses change their biochemistry and even their structure during learning; these changes are used later to retrieve the stored information, just as the physical changes (burns) in compact disks are used by computers to later retrieve the information stored there.

Moreover, in the mid-1980s, Richard Morris and colleagues had demonstrated that a drug that blocked a key synaptic calcium channel required for long-term potentiation (the N-methyl D-aspartate receptor, or NMDAR) impaired both hippocampal LTP measured in vivo and hippocampal-dependent spatial learning and memory in the water maze behavioral test Morris had developed a few years earlier.[14] Strikingly, activation of the NMDA receptor, which supposedly happens in the hippocampus during spatial learning, results in increases in calcium in postsynaptic sites and consequently in the activation of αCaMKII.[15] These two studies suggested that NMDA receptors are activated during learning; with calcium entering postsynaptic sites in dendrites, activating αCaMKII, and thus triggering long-lasting changes in synaptic function required for spatial learning and memory. The striking *convergence* of these two distinctly different studies (one relying on a pharmacological manipulation in rats and the other on a genetic manipulation in mice) was the foundation stone for a large series of related studies that have now demonstrated a causal link between synaptic mechanisms, hippocampal (Ca1) long-term potentiation, and spatial learning and memory.[16] Not surprisingly, the many transgenic studies that followed the initial αCaMKII experiments implicated a large number of other molecules in the regulation of LTP and memory.

For example, two years after the publication of the αCaMKII papers, similar genetic studies implicated the transcription factor cAMP-responsive element-binding protein (CREB) in the stability of long-term potentiation and in the "consolidating" of memory.[17] Unlike previous genetic manipulations, the CREB mutation did not affect either the early stages of long-term potentiation or short-term memory. Instead, the mice showed deficits in the stability of long-term potentiation and in long-term memory. Pioneering physiological studies in *Aplysia* by Eric Kandel's group and subsequent behavioral analysis in *Drosophila* by Jerry Yin and Tim Tully, as well as many other published studies, echoed these findings.[18] Interestingly, CREB is activated by intracellular signaling pathways turned on by the activation of NMDA receptors, again providing a surprising degree of integration and coherence to these molecular genetic findings of memory research.

The consolidation theory had an all-encompassing influence on how these processes were imagined and the results interpreted. As mentioned above, the biochemistry and physiology of memory were thought of as stepwise processes that take sensory perception and develop fully consolidated memories, just as a stepwise chemical process develops a photographic negative into a fully processed print. In both cases, the initial information is faithfully preserved, and the function of the ensuing processes is to simply develop the memory into its mature and permanent state. The CREB findings had a considerable impact because this transcription factor was an important link in the long-term potentiation and memory hypothesis. The proteins made by this transcription factor were supposed to stabilize (i.e., consolidate) the neuronal changes initiated by NMDA receptors, αCaMKII, and a myriad of other synaptic-signaling molecules.

Indeed, so strong was the influence of the consolidation theory that very little attention was paid to the obvious *transformative* properties of these dynamic molecular and cellular processes. The activation of αCaMKII, CREB, and all of the other numerous molecules implicated in memory, the induction and stability of the synaptic mechanisms they regulate, and the circuit processes that support the representations of information in the brain (e.g., hippocampal place fields) are all highly dynamic and probabilistic in nature: they do not manifest the determinism, inflexibility, finality, and "solidity" implicit in the consolidation theory. The flow of calcium into synaptic sites during learning and the activation of kinases, phosphatases, and other synaptic molecules are far from being Newtonian wheels in a complex biological machine designed with deterministic principles in mind. The evidence suggests an altogether different picture. The molecules and physiological processes implicated in memory by the genetic research touched on above, function in a sea of probabilistic events. Their unreliable nature may actually be a virtue. The complexity of their functions and the probabilistic nature of their activities may generate a plurality of brain functional states that can be selected and fine-tuned with experience, so that appropriate responses are developed to the endless problems that face behaving brains in the Darwinian arena of evolution.

Probabilities, rather than certainties, dominate the molecular events of memory and the physiologies they control. For example, action potentials, which reflect neuronal activity, are physiological events generated by channels in the cell membrane. When triggered in one cell, they can activate neurotransmitter release, so that the information they convey can be passed on through the neuronal chains of communication in the brain that turn action into reaction and behavior. But action potentials are often ignored by synaptic terminals involved in memory.[19] Neurotransmitter release is a highly probabilistic event since not every action potential results in the release of neurotransmitter. In the Ca1 region of the hippocampus, for example, synaptic terminals ignore incoming action potentials a significant percentage of the time. When a neurotransmitter is actually released and reaches the opposing dendritic receptor sites, another set of probabilistic events takes over the activation of channels and the ionic currents that send the incoming message into the intracellular molecular networks deciding whether to ignore or act upon the signals received.[20] Probabilistic events also dominate the signaling machinery that transmits and transforms those signals and the output processes that pass along the transformed signals to the appropriate centers in the brain. The patterns of activation in these centers are also probabilistic and infused with a character of controlled chaos that permeates all levels of biological complexity. Such emergent complexity seems inconsistent with the deterministic and stepwise reliability implied in the classical consolidation theory of memory. In contrast, the probabilistic nature of the biochemistry and physiology of memory is more easily reconcilable with the statistical nature of semantic structures underlying memory.[21]

Nevertheless, despite all evidence of such indeterminism, molecular and cellular mechanisms of memory continue to be framed within a two-stage consolidation model, in which an initial labile stage (dependent on NMDA receptors and kinases such as αCaMKII) is followed by a memory consolidation stage (dependent on CREB and other molecules that regulate transcription and then translation) when acquired information is permanently etched into the brain's neuronal circuits. Thus, it has been proposed that products of CREB-dependent transcription mediate neuronal structural growth that "locks" memories in neuronal networks.

For many years, the overwhelming influence of the consolidation theory stymied recognition of the probabilistic nature of molecular and cellular events. Indeed, molecular and cellular neuroscientists disregarded psychological data that demonstrated the dynamic, capricious, and self-serving nature of memory and that clearly contradicted the idea of memory as stable, reliable, and objective.[22] This psychological information, in fact, was consistent with an emerging body of biological data on molecular, cellular, and system mechanisms that were just as dynamic and capricious as memories themselves.

Particularly noteworthy in this regard are "the seven sins of memory" in Daniel Schacter's book of that title: transience, absentmindedness, blocking, misattribution, suggestibility, bias, and persistence.[23] Each of these attributes defines qualities that characterize the vast majority of our memories. Indeed, most if not all of our memories may suffer from at least one of these sins. If that is so, they are not sins, but simply reflections of fundamental properties of memory. Indeed, the power of our memory systems may lie in their susceptibility to many internal and external factors that constantly update, change, edit, and even bend fact to self-serving fictions.

In my view, the beginning of the end of the strong version of the consolidation theory can be traced back to the publication in 2000 of two highly influential papers on reconsolidation: a lucid review by Susan Sara and a research paper by Karim Nader and colleagues.[24] Essentially, these and other papers, some even dating as far back as the 1960s, argued that memories actually undergo "consolidation-like processes" nearly every time they are recalled (hence, the unfortunate term *reconsolidation*, likely to confuse unaware readers for years to come), and that interfering with consolidation mechanisms during recall weakens or even erases these memories.[25] Discovering these nearly forgotten studies was a real shock to many neuroscientists in the grip of the consolidation theory: How could it possibly be true that every time we recall something, we need to store it all over again? Wouldn't this cycle of recall and restorage risk the adulteration or even loss of memory? How could a brief recall episode paired with blockers of consolidation mechanisms (e.g., protein synthesis inhibitors) disrupt a previously "consolidated" memory? If each recall episode could potentially change every one of our memories, what did *consolidation* really mean? Certainly, this fluid view of memory was problematic for a theory that speaks of memory as a cement-like process. So surprising were the reconsolidation findings and so glaring was their contradiction of the predominant consolidation paradigm that they were greeted with considerable skepticism, including my own. Fortunately, Sheena Josselyn and Satoshi Kida, two postdoctoral fellows in my laboratory, overlooked my misgivings, and decided to use a new state-of-the-art transgenic inducible system to test the possible role of CREB in memory "reconsolidation."[26] A key property of this transgenic system is that it can be quickly turned on and off. A protein's function is studied by expressing a small fragment that disrupts the protein's normal functioning. The disrupting protein fragment is then sequestered away inside the cell in a molecular cage of "heat-shock" proteins that prevent it from interacting with other proteins. Adding tamoxifen, the activator of this transgenic system, changes the conformation of the protein fragment and destabilizes the sequestering cage.

Kida's and Josselyn's hard work paid off. Using this transgenic approach, they were able to show that CREB was needed both shortly after learning for memory formation and after recall for memory reconsolidation. Disrupting CREB at either time resulted in amnesia. Their results demonstrated that the process of recall itself placed emotional memories into a labile state that required CREB for stability: interfering with CREB function specifically during recall disrupted memory. Our laboratory had previously demonstrated that CREB is required for initial memory storage; these new experiments showed that the same transcription factor it is also involved during additional rounds of consolidation following recall. Dramatically, the disconcerting aspect of these findings was that they confirmed the idea that recall destabilized the memory that had been originally consolidated. If cherished memories may be liable to change each time they are recalled, what aspects of our biographical pasts can we really trust? If memory was truly this fluid, how could we go on believing in the strong version of the consolidation dogma? Indeed, emerging results are suggesting that memory mechanisms are designed, not for accuracy and permanency, but instead, for constant editing and fine-tuning of information with experience.

It is important to note that the CREB results described above turned out not to be an exception to the rule. Many subsequent findings by Yadin Dudai, Karim Nader, and Oliver Hardt demonstrated that much of the molecular machinery that we thought stored memories into a "permanent" state is also required for stabilizing memories each time they are recalled.[27] Coming as they have from a large number of experiments performed in many laboratories with many forms of memory and in several species, these and other reconsolidation findings have attracted a great deal of attention, not only because of their obvious implications to mainstream concepts of memory, but also because of their potential application in neuropsychiatric therapies. Memory mechanisms may explain why traumatic experiences lead to posttraumatic stress disorder (PTSD) and why hedonic experiences with substances of abuse lead to drug addiction.[28] Reconsolidation-based strategies may provide a much-needed window of opportunity to weaken initially strong memories that result in maladaptive behavioral responses and thus to treat a large number of people afflicted by related mental health problems.

Results from studies of remote memory have also questioned some of the most basic assumptions of the classical version of the consolidation.[29] Until recently, the molecular and cellular analysis of memory had been focused almost exclusively on the acquisition and processing of information. Amazingly, nothing was known about the molecular and cellular mechanisms that stabilize memory over weeks, months, and years, although the neocortex, by virtue of its potentially large storage capacity, was widely thought to be involved in the "permanent" storage of complex memories, such as spatial and contextual memories in mice. Studies from a few laboratories, including my own, uncovered direct evidence for the involvement of cortical networks in remote contextual and spatial memory.[30] My colleagues and I came across hints that remote memory is not simply a cortical version of the earlier hippocampus-dependent memory. We noted in our mouse studies, for example, that remote (cortical) memories seemed more general, as if they were semantic versions of their earlier, more specific (episodic-like) counterparts.[31] In their elegant 1995 study, James McClelland and colleagues had proposed that the brain uses two different, but complementary memory processing systems to store declarative (hippocampus-dependent) memories: a hippocampus-based system ideally suited for fast acquisition and high content; and a neocortical system optimized for gradually interleaving new information into previously formed semantic structures.[32]

Interestingly, my laboratory has shown that immediately after being trained to recognize a chamber with its own wall configuration and odor, mice can easily distinguish it from another, similar chamber.[33] Over time, however, as the memory for the chamber ages and becomes hippocampus independent, the mice can no longer distinguish between the two chambers. This erosion of memory happens normally without any further exposure to chambers of any kind. Since the memory is just as strong a month after training as it is the day after, the animal does not forget its training chamber. But what changes is the accuracy of the memory. The idea that memory changes over time, that it is even dependent on different brain structures is not easily reconciled with the rigid views of memory embodied in the classical version of the consolidation theory. Just as with the reconsolidation work, remote memory studies suggest a more dynamic and plastic view of memory, one that is in stark contrast with the solid one-dimensional imagery of the classical consolidation theory.

In retrospect, the notion of memory consolidation has made important contributions to research, including the concept that memory has multiple distinct phases with unique molecular, cellular, and behavioral properties. The reconsolidation theory has simplified and unified experimentation, focusing considerable effort on mechanisms that capture information in the brain. A number of powerful experimental paradigms have emerged, such as fear conditioning, that highlight the photographic-like aspects of memory.[34] These paradigms usually involve simple tasks and very strong training. Not surprisingly, under these unusual circumstances, trained animals express stronger and more stable memories than usual. Further ethologic learning tasks, such as social recognition (the ability of one animal to recognize and remember another after a brief encounter), have revealed the more fragile and unstable aspects of memory. However useful it may have been, the consolidation dogma and the experimental framework it generated distorted both popular and scientific ideas of memory; it distracted neuroscience research from a variety of pertinent and fascinating questions concerning the dynamic, constructive, metamorphic, and transformative properties of memory.

The compelling nature of the consolidation theory and its continuing grip on our imagination stems not from science alone, but from a deeply engrained need to trust our remembrances of things past. Life is often made more bearable by cherished memories, moments we hold on to and wholeheartedly believe happened the way we remember them. But science is a merciless arbiter, and emerging genetic evidence is bearing down ever more heavily on this moribund workhorse of memory research.

Notes

1. James L. McGaugh, "Memory—A Century of Consolidation," *Science* 287 (2000): 248–251.

2. Daniel L. Schacter and Donna R. Addis, "The Cognitive Neuroscience of Constructive Memory: Remembering the Past and Imagining the Future," *Philosophical Transactions of the Royal Society of London* B 362 (2007): 773–786; Daniel L. Schacter, Kenneth A. Norman, and Wilma Koutstaal, "The Cognitive Neuroscience of Constructive Memory," *Annual Review of Psychology* 49 (1998): 289–318.

3. Daniel Offer et al., "The Altering of Reported Experiences," *Journal of the American Academy of Child and Adolescent Psychiatry* 39 (2000): 735–742.

4. Karim Nader and Oliver Hardt, "A Single Standard for Memory: The Case for Reconsolidation," *Nature Reviews Neuroscience* 10 (2009): 224–234.

5. J. L. McGaugh, "Memory—A Century of Consolidation."

6. Mario R. Capecchi, "The New Mouse Genetics: Altering the Genome by Gene Targeting," *Trends in Genetics* 5 (1989): 70–76.

7. On the use of transgenic tools and the great effort placed in developing mutant mice for studies in immunology, development, and cancer, see M. R. Capecchi, "Targeted Gene Replacement," *Scientific American* 270 (March 1994): 52–59.

8. Patricia Churchland and Terry Sejnowski, *The Computational Brain* (Cambridge, MA: MIT Press, 1992).

9. A. J. Silva et al., "Deficient Hippocampal Long-Term Potentiation in Alpha-Calcium-Calmodulin Kinase II Mutant Mice," *Science* 257 (1992): 201–206; A. J. Silva et al., "Impaired Spatial Learning in Alpha-Calcium-Calmodulin Kinase II Mutant Mice," *Science* 257 (1992): 206–211.

10. Anna Matynia et al., "Genetic Approaches to Molecular and Cellular Cognition: A Focus on LTP and Learning and Memory," *Annual Review of Genetics* 36 (2002): 687–720.

11. A. J. Silva et al., "Deficient Hippocampal Long-Term Potentiation in Alpha-Calcium-Calmodulin Kinase II Mutant Mice"; A. J. Silva et al., "Impaired Spatial Learning in Alpha-Calcium-Calmodulin Kinase II Mutant Mice"; R. M. Hanley et al., "Functional Analysis of a Complementary DNA for the 50-Kilodalton Subunit of Calmodulin Kinase II," *Science*, 237 (1987): 293–297; John Lisman, Howard Schulman, and Hollis Cline, "The Molecular Basis of CaMKII Function in Synaptic and Behavioural Memory," *Nature Reviews Neuroscience* 3 (2002): 175–190.

12. A. J. Silva et al., "Deficient Hippocampal Long-Term Potentiation in Alpha-Calcium- Calmodulin Kinase II Mutant Mice"; A. J. Silva et al., "Impaired Spatial Learning in Alpha-Calcium-Calmodulin Kinase II Mutant Mice."

13. Donald O. Hebb, *Organization of Behavior: A Neuropsychological Theory* (New York: Wiley, 1949).

14. R. G. M. Morris et al., "Selective Impairment of Learning and Blockade of Long-Term Potentiation by an N-Methyl-D-Aspartate Receptor Antagonist, *AP5*," *Nature* 319 (1986): 774–776.

15. J. Lisman et al., "The Molecular Basis of CaMKII Function in Synaptic and Behavioural Memory."

16. Yong-Seok Lee and Alcino J. Silva, "The Molecular and Cellular Biology of Enhanced Cognition," *Nature Reviews Neuroscience*, 10 (2009): 126–140; but see Guilherme Neves, Sam F. Cooke, and Tim V. P. Bliss, "Synaptic Plasticity, Memory and the Hippocampus: A Neural Network Approach to Causality," *Nature Reviews Neuroscience* 9 (2008): 65–75.

17. Roussoudan Bourtchuladze et al., "Deficient Long-Term Memory in Mice with a Targeted Mutation of the cAMP-Responsive Element-Binding Protein," *Cell* 79 (1994): 59–68; Satoshi Kida et al., "CREB Required for the Stability of New and Reactivated Fear Memories," *Nature Reviews Neuroscience* 5 (2002): 348–355.

18. Pramod K. Dash, Binyamin Hochner, and Eric R. Kandel, "Injection of the cAMP-Responsive Element into the Nucleus of *Aplysia* Sensory Neurons Blocks Long-Term Facilitation," *Nature* 345 (1990): 718–721; see also the *Drosophila* behavioral

and other studies reviewed in Alcino J. Silva et al., "CREB and Memory," *Annual Review of Neuroscience* 21 (1998): 127–148.

19. Christina Allen and Charles F. Stevens, "An Evaluation of Causes for Unreliability of Synaptic Transmission," *Proceedings of the National Academy of Sciences USA* 91 (1994): 10380–10383.

20. Seiji Ozawa, Haruyuki Kamiya, and Keisuke Tsuzuki, "Glutamate Receptors in the Mammalian Central Nervous System," *Progress in Neurobiology* 54 (1998): 581–618.

21. James L. McClelland, Bruce L. McNaughton, and Randall C. O'Reilly, "Why There Are Complementary Learning Systems in the Hippocampus and Neocortex: Insights from the Successes and Failures of Connectionist Models of Learning and Memory," *Psychological Review* 102 (1995): 419–457.

22. Daniel L. Schacter and Kenneth A. Norman, "The Cognitive Neuroscience of Constructive Memory," *Annual Review of Psychology* 49 (1998): 289–318.

23. Daniel L. Schacter, *The Seven Sins of Memory: How the Mind Forgets and Remembers* (Boston: Houghton Mifflin, 2001).

24. Susan J. Sara, "Strengthening the Shaky Trace through Retrieval," *Nature Reviews Neuroscience* 1 (2000): 212–213; Karim Nader, Glenn E. Schafe, and Joseph E. LeDoux, "Fear Memories Require Protein Synthesis in the Amygdala for Reconsolidation after Retrieval," *Nature* 406 (2000): 722–726.

25. Yadin Dudai, "The Neurobiology of Consolidations, or, How Stable Is the Engram?" *Annual Review of Psychology* 55 (2004): 51–86.

26. S. Kida et al., "CREB Required for the Stability of New and Reactivated Fear Memories."

27. Y. Dudai, "The Neurobiology of Consolidations, or, How Stable is the Engram?"; K. Nader and O. Hardt, "A Single Standard for Memory: The Case for Reconsolidation."

28. Jonathan L. C. Lee et al., "Disrupting Reconsolidation of Drug Memories Reduces Cocaine-Seeking Behavior," *Neuron* 47 (2005): 795–801; Courtney A. Miller and John F. Marshall, "Molecular Substrates for Retrieval and Reconsolidation of Cocaine-Associated Contextual Memory," *Neuron* 47 (2005): 873–884.

29. Paul W. Frankland et al., "Alpha-CaMKII-Dependent Plasticity in the Cortex is Required for Permanent Memory," *Nature* 11 (2001): 309–313; Paul W. Frankland et al., "The Involvement of the Anterior Cingulate Cortex in Remote Contextual Fear Memory," *Science* 304 (2004): 881–883.

30. Brian J. Wiltgen et al., "New Circuits for Old Memories: The Role of the Neocortex in Consolidation," *Neuron* 44 (2004): 101–108.

31. Brian J. Wiltgen and Alcino J. Silva, "Memory for Context Becomes Less Specific with Time," *Learning & Memory* 14 (2007): 313–317.

32. J. L. McClelland, B. L. McNaughton, and R. C. O'Reilly, "Why There Are Complementary Learning Systems in the Hippocampus and Neocortex."

33. B. J. Wiltgen and A. J. Silva, "Memory for Context Becomes Less Specific with Time."

34. Markus Fendt and Michael S. Fanselow, "The Neuroanatomical and Neuro-chemical Basis of Conditioned Fear," *Neuroscience & Biobehavorial Reviews* 23 (1999): 743–760.

3   The Epigenetic Variability of Memory: Brain Plasticity and Artistic Creation

Jean-Pierre Changeux

The voluntary and conscious retrieval of long-term memories is a global brain process that mobilizes several levels of organization nested within the human brain. It first proceeds from the level of the gene and the species-specific functional organization that characterizes the human brain to the level of neuronal organization and networks, the development and maturation of which are exceptionally long in the human species. Throughout this period of synaptic growth and selective stabilization, *epigenetic* patterns of connections are laid down with changing environmental conditions, ultimately operating within the alert "conscious subject" in a "global neuronal workspace."[1] Over decades of research, I have used the term *epigenetic* to denote the productive interaction between genetic information and environmental changes—a phenomenon at the core of the brain's plasticity and memory.[2] Memories, which are evoked with the scrutiny of the personal and historical evolutions of artistic and scientific representations, do not follow as obscure and random a path as it may seem. They engage strong selection mechanisms following what I have referred to as "epigenetic rules"—mental tools that mathematicians and artistic creators have imposed on themselves from the beginning of time, and that have evolved throughout the course of history.[3]

Brain Complexity and Epigenetic Variability

Memory can fruitfully be examined in this epigenetic context. The adjective *epigenetic* is derived from *epigenesis*, a noun composed of two Greek roots: *epi*, meaning "on" or "upon," and *genesis*, meaning "birth." In the present context, *epigenetic* combines two notions: superimposition upon the action of the genes, chiefly as a result of learning and experience; and coordinated, organized development.

The human brain is made up of approximately 86 billion neurons, each neuron having an average of 10,000 discontinuous contacts (or synapses) with multiple connections. Thus there are some 10^{15} synapses in the human encephalon, or approximately 600 million synapses per cubic millimeter. The number of possible combinations between neurons is truly astronomical—on the same order of magnitude as the number of positively charged particles in the universe. In addition, the efficiency of these synaptic contacts varies as a function of experience to the extent that no limit can legitimately be placed on the functional combinations of the brain's neuronal networks.

It is important to remember that the neuronal systems of the brain are not assembled after the fashion of a computer, with prefabricated parts fitted together in accordance with a blueprint that exactly specifies the nature and purpose of each circuit and switch. If this were the case, an error in even the smallest detail of the implementation of a program could have catastrophic consequences. In contrast, and as provided for in the epigenetic model, the brain's neuronal systems are established in stages, with considerable margins of variability, and are subject to processes of selection that proceed by means of trial and error. At certain critical stages of development, the connectivity of the network is refined. The state of activity of the developing network, whether spontaneous or evoked, works to regulate this process.

One should remember, too, that the total amount of DNA present in the haploid human genome comprises some 3.1 billion base pairs, but no more than 20,000–25,000 gene sequences.[4] The exons coding for the complexity of brain organization thus represent only 1.2% of our genome. Moreover, this number of structural genes does not vary greatly from mouse to monkey to human, despite a massive increase in the number of cells (from about 70 million in the mouse to 86 billion in humans).[5] Mammalian brain anatomy has evolved dramatically from a poorly corticalized lissencephalic brain with about 10–20 identified cortical areas to a brain with an extremely high relative cortical surface, multiple gyri and sulci, and possibly as many as 100 identified cortical areas.[6] Thus there exists a remarkable nonlinearity between the evolution of brain anatomy and that of the total number of genes.[7] The extended regulation by the state of activity of the neuronal network during development may contribute to this increase in complexity.

Another aspect of brain organization, often underestimated, is its variability. For example, careful anatomical and functional studies of Brodmann's areas (regions of the cortex with distinct patterns of neuronal organization) show that their topology varies from one individual to another.[8] This individual variability is often attributed to heredity. But both anatomical and behavioral studies of genetically identical *monozygotic* twins (originating from the same fertilized egg or zygote) clearly demonstrate that their brains are not in fact identical. On the neuronal and synaptic scale, significant variations in connectivity have been detected among neurons in genetically identical (*isogenic*) animals. For example, in isogenic members of the small invertebrate species *Daphnia magna*, the numbers of sensory cells in the eye and neurons in the optical ganglion are preserved, along with the principal categories of synaptic contacts; yet the exact number of synapses and the precise form of the axonal branches vary.[9] Similar observations have been reported with respect to the dendrites of Müller motor neurons in a parthenogenetic fish. A variable element is introduced in neuronal connectivity during development of the adult network. This is a plausible consequence of the way in which the neurons of the network are assembled; it represents the stored trace—as singular patterns of connection—of the outcome of the trials and errors undergone by constituent axons and dendrites during their growth phases.[10]

In humans, about half of all adult connections that contribute to the epigenetic memories are formed after birth, and their numbers continue to change—rising and then falling off—until death. Although the length of the gestation period is roughly comparable in chimpanzees and humans (224 days and 270 days, respectively), the postnatal development of the brain lasts considerably longer in man (70% of adult cranial capacity is reached at 3 years of age in humans compared to only 1 year in chimpanzees). The global evolution of synaptic density in the cerebral cortex of both monkeys and humans includes a rapid phase in which 90% of all synapses are formed (at a rate of about 40,000 per second).[11] Every minute of a baby's development is accompanied by the laying down of more than 2 million synapses in the brain. Birth occurs exactly in the middle of this rapid phase of synaptic development. There follows a longer phase, lasting until puberty, in which this rate of growth levels off, subsequently declining until the approximate number of synapses that will be preserved during adulthood is reached. In humans, the duration of the rapid phase is shorter in a sensory area such as the visual cortex, where it lasts for about two or three years after birth, than in an association area such as the prefrontal cortex, where it lasts for up to ten years.

The process of synapse formation has great importance from a functional point of view since the prefrontal cortex, which is rich in neurons found in layers II and III, plays such a central role in memory and other higher cognitive functions.[12] The human infant displays a great number of synaptic combinations that are progressively shaped by epigenetic interactions with the physical, social, and cultural aspects of the outside world. These, in turn, give rise to a series of overlapping critical periods of development through which the newborn then young brain passes before reaching the adult stage. Various growth factors contribute to the epigenetic regulation of synaptic development. Within the Darwinian context of evolution, the brain is open to the environment through variation-selection-amplification. The addition and subtraction of synaptic connections persist beyond childhood and adolescence, producing a stable balance during adulthood. The equilibrium becomes more fragile as the organism ages, however, and shifts in favor of regression in the final phase of senescence leading up to death.

The epigenetic hypothesis suggests an original approach to the problems of genetic parsimony and nonlinear evolution. It gives fresh insight into the acquisition, testing, and transmission of new knowledge, and to the appearance of culture—which developed in an exceedingly brief period of evolutionary time.

The Selective Stabilization of Synapses and the Storage of Cultural Memory

Only in recent years has the epigenetic evolution of neuronal connectivity been described in a mathematically rigorous way. The simple model that Philippe Courrège, Antoine Danchin, and I originally proposed in 1973 describes the basic ingredients of synaptic evolution at the stage of maximum diversity for a given neuronal network.[13] This model distinguishes a minimum of three synaptic states: labile, stable, and regressed.

Its central premise is that the evolution of the connective state of a given synapse is controlled within a precise time frame by the totality of the message constituted by the signals arising from spontaneous and evoked activity in the postsynaptic cell. Such activity regulates the stability, regression, and, in some cases, regeneration of the nerve ending in the developing cell by means of "trophic signals," propagated in a direction opposite to that of the nerve impulse, in a retrograde manner. The characteristic connectivity and functional potential of a given nerve cell with its *stored epigenetic memory*—what I have called its "singularity"—is thus the result of selective stabilization by the activity of the particular distribution of synaptic contacts that have survived from all those present when diversity was greatest.

The model also has microscopic learning rules formulated in mathematical and biochemical terms to describe more precisely these elementary changes in synaptic efficiency as a function of experience. In particular, it includes the best-known such rule, introduced in 1949 by the Canadian psychologist Donald Hebb, namely, that the "strength" of a given connection increases when there is a temporal coincidence between pre- and postsynaptic activities.[14]

Any realistic model of the epigenesis of neuronal networks in the brain will need to take into account not only the interaction of inhibitory and excitatory neurons but also the possible contribution of reinforcement or reward mechanisms that facilitate rapid changes in synaptic efficiency. In formal terms, this circumstance is already contemplated by the Changeux, Courrège, and Danchin 1973 model, which provides for the possibility that the whole of the signal message received by the postsynaptic cell (including reward signals) controls retrograde synaptic selection. It is obvious that the specific role of reward—and, conversely, error or "punishment"—signals in the evolution of cerebral connectivity during development must be more adequately correlated with learning behaviors.[15]

The 1973 model demonstrated a *variability theorem* that, more than thirty-five years later, still seems to be of great interest. The theorem holds that, for any given neuronal network, a single afferent message can stabilize different patterns of connections while preserving the same output despite the deterministic character of the model. The concept of functional reproducibility in the face of anatomical variation has subsequently been developed by several research teams and remains the subject of lively discussions. In fact, the variability theorem casts new light on the paradoxical constancy of brain function that is observed despite the striking variability of neuroanatomical organization. Indeed, the recording of temporal patterns of neuronal activity in the form of a connectional geometry that varies from one individual to another while nonetheless producing effectively the same functions or behaviors may in fact provide the basis for one of the most important "bridging laws" between psychology and the neuroscience.

This conclusion is of importance when one considers cultural memories and, in particular, oral and written languages. That different individuals within the same language community are able to understand each other despite the different connectivities of their brains provides support for the variability theorem. Moreover, reading and writing were "invented" by human societies long after the genetic endowment of humans, as *Homo sapiens*, was established. Acquisition of literacy exploits the *epigenetic* capacities of the developing brain to develop stable memories for new skills. For example, the inability to read alters the patterns of selective stabilization of phonological pathways for processing new words. Learning to read and write leaves profound epigenetic memory traces in the child's brain that persist until adulthood. Training in reading and writing not only selects preexisting pathways—that is, appropriates undifferentiated pathways that, in other conditions, might be used for other purposes (such as tactile reading in the case of Braille)—but it also stimulates the outgrowth of additional axon terminals. Even though none of these results individually constitutes a definitive test of the model of selective stabilization of developing synapses, taken together, the results are consistent with the notion that such stabilization plays a crucial role in the storage of *cultural memory* as a whole.

The Neuronal Habitus

The conception of gene expression and epigenetic evolution as interrelated, nonlinear, and highly contextualized phenomena exposes the fallacy underlying two highly influential views of human memory and intelligence. The first (inspired by Plato's conception of the overall innate dispositions of the human mind) postulates a specialized gene for intelligence, language, and even grammar, neglecting epigenesis. The second postulates the exclusive influence of environmental factors in mental development, neglecting genetics. As we have seen, the opening up of the genetic envelope to epigenetic variability and to evolution by selection is made possible by the incorporation of a random component in synaptic development within cascading and nested sequences of synaptic outgrowth, sequences that correlate with the acquisition or loss of particular skills or abilities. The period of pre- and postnatal development is marked by a series of crucial events, all of them included in a universal genetic envelope: the infant's first applications of practical knowledge; the emergence of reflective consciousness, and subsequently of a theory of mind; and the learning of language, epigenetic rules, and social conventions. This makes possible both the diversification, transmission, and evolution of culture and the individual developmental differences that make each human unique.

The individual character of each person is thus constructed as a function of what the sociologist Pierre Bourdieu has called the "habitus":[16] a unique synthesis of an individual's genetic endowment, circumstances of birth and upbringing, and sociocultural environment, as experienced by the individual. Both innate knowledge and the innate disposition to acquire further knowledge and consciously test its truth develop through the *genetic* evolution of species. The exceptionally long period of *epigenetic* evolution undergone by the human brain enables it to incorporate information about the external world that is not obtainable by genetic mechanisms. This process also makes possible the production of a cultural memory not directly subject to the intrinsic limitations of the brain, thus capable of being epigenetically transmitted at the level of the social group. Thus a few essentially quantitative changes in the genotype and cerebral connectional phenotype suffice to bring about qualitatively new changes in human brain function that not only allow culture to emerge but also provide access to consciousness.[17]

Neuronal Architecture for Access to Consciousness: The Global Neuronal Workspace

In this epigenetic context, the neuronal workspace model (figure 3.1), which I devised in 1998 together with Stanislas Dehaene and Michel Kerszberg, serves as a useful framework for the scrutiny of the memory process. Although an emotionally reactive, sentient being, the newborn

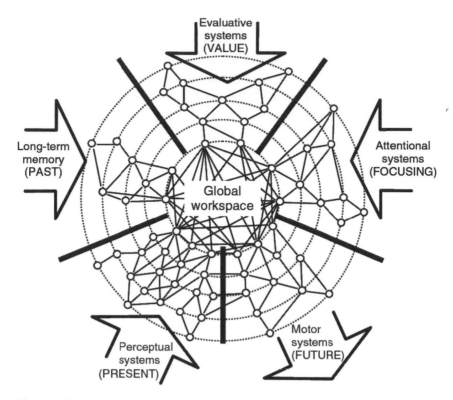

Figure 3.1
Neuronal workspace model.
Reproduced from Stanislas Dehaene, Michel Kerszberg, and Jean-Pierre Changeux, "A Neuronal Model of a Global Workspace in Effortful Cognitive Tasks," *Proceedings of the National Academy of Sciences USA* 95 (1998).

must still develop rationality and self-consciousness.[18] These psychological functions develop progressively over time, together with the memories of the semantic lexicon. The prefrontal cortex becomes accessible to delayed-response tasks by the age of 12 months. A working memory and global neuronal workspace start to contribute to cognitive tasks, which are no longer automatic and demand a conscious mental effort.

The neural bases of consciousness have been, in recent years, the subject of intense debates.[19] The formal neuronal network that Stanislas Dehaene and I initially proposed in 1991 for the Wisconsin Card Sorting and other cognitive tasks served as starting point for the development of a more general model in 1998 that included the "global workspace" suggested in

1989 by Bernard Baars on psychological grounds.[20] The Dehaene, Kerszberg, and Changeux 1998 model accounts for the unitary character of
consciousness and the access of a broad diversity of representations to
consciousness, as well as for the available brain imaging data.

The 1998 model's neuronal network distinguishes, in simplified, formal
terms, two main computational spaces within the brain (figure 3.1) with
two activities that have bearing on memory production.[21] The first is a
processing network composed of parallel, distributed, and functionally
encapsulated processors, each processing a particular type of information
in competition with each other. They operate on sensory and motor
systems, with stored long-term memories (including autobiographical
memory and self), attentional and evaluative systems, and, more extensively, emotions. The processor neurons establish bottom-up and top-
down projections with the neurons of the global neuronal workspace,
which is the second computational space. It differs from Baars's global
workspace in that cortical neurons with long-range excitatory axons recip-
rocally connecting distinct cortical areas play an essential role in the
genesis of the conscious workspace.[22] These neurons selectively mobilize
or arrest through descending connections in a top-down mode the ascending inputs of the specialized processor neurons. In an appropriate state of
awareness or attention, they broadcast signals to the multiple cortical areas
that are associated with subjective experience and the ability to report it.
Out of the multiple active cortical representations that could become conscious, only one representation receives the top-down amplification that
mobilizes it into consciousness. Such "dynamic mobilization," which produces a single global representation at a time, distinguishes this process
from unconscious performance.

Workspace neurons in the prefrontal cortex test internal hypotheses
or prerepresentations that furnish a context for the reactivation by the
hippocampus of long-term memories stored in the cerebral cortex that
are linked to sensory perception and action. "Long-term memory circuits
provide the workspace with an access to past percepts and events."[23] When
memories are selected by internal evaluation, they are then integrated as
part of the representations of the workspace through the hippocampus.
They may spontaneously recombine with each other, with representations
evoked by the interaction with the outside world, or with both.[24] Imagination thereby introduces some "novelty" in these prerepresentations.

Accordingly, the memories that are evoked are not direct recall of past events, but reconstructions from physical traces stored in the brain in latent form. How these traces—cognitive, emotional, or both—are registered depends on the topology of synaptic connections as well as on their efficiency in transmitting nerve signals.[25] Darwinian competition strengthens some of the transient networks as memory objects become stable neuronal traces.

It has been widely accepted since Hebb's 1949 study that the representations, images, ideas, or mental states that form in our brain *spontaneously* or as a consequence of *interactions* with the outside world can be identified as created by the correlated (or coherent) transient, dynamic electrical and chemical activity of a defined, distributed population of neurons. The graph of the neurons mobilized together with the frequency and coherence of the impulses flowing in the graph is anticipated to carry the "meaning"— or, following linguist Ferdinand de Saussure, the "signified" (*signifié*)—that would result from the selective stabilization of fleeting prerepresentations spontaneously produced by the brain.[26] The conjecture is that the brain would generate in the global neuronal workspace "crude," transient, and labile prerepresentations or hypotheses that vary from one instant to the next. The infant brain would thus operate in a projective way constantly testing hypotheses on the outside world, and later on its own inner world. A simple mechanism may lead to the selection of the relevant prerepresentation and to its storage not only as a stable synaptic or neuronal but also as a semantic trace in the brain. The mechanism is based on the positive or negative reinforcement (reward or punishment) received from the outside world as it is mediated by the release of specific brain neurotransmitters, such as dopamine, acetylcholine, or serotonin.[27] Accordingly, the efficacies of the synapses concerned would change if, for instance, a reward neurotransmitter reached the surface of the neurons at or near the moment the neurons were actively mobilized by the relevant prerepresentation. Determinations of temporal coincidence could be accomplished, for instance, by "multihead" molecules, called "allosteric proteins," which include neurotransmitter receptors.[28] Those like the acetylcholine nicotinic receptor are known to undergo slow regulatory transitions of potentiation, desensitization, or both, which can be regulated by a variety of effectors.[29]

Among the many neuronal systems engaged in memory storage and retrieval, the system in which acetylcholine is the neurotransmitter (termed *cholinergic*) has a particular significance. The "cholinergic hypothesis" suggests an important, though not exclusive, role of cholinergic input in learning and memory.[30] Moreover, acetylcholine binds to two principal categories of receptors: nicotinic receptors that are ligand-gated ion channels and muscarinic receptors that are G-protein-linked receptors. Involvement of neuronal nicotinic receptors in learning and memory processes has been recognized for decades. In rats, nicotine and nicotinic agonists specifically improve learning in different test procedures, including the radial-arm maze and object recognition task. In humans, nicotine decreases working memory errors in both smokers and nonsmokers by decreasing distractability and improving attention functions. Among the diverse subtypes of nicotinic receptors, the $\alpha 4\beta 2$ receptors have been shown to be critically involved in cognitive functions in genetically modified mice.

Muscarinic receptors have also long been known to play key roles in cognitive function and learning processes. The muscarinic antagonist scopalamine is a classic amnesic drug. Mice lacking the M2 receptor subtype show significant deficits in behavioral flexibility and working memory using the Barnes circular maze and the T-maze delayed alternation tests, respectively. The cholinergic system thus represents an important contribution to memory storage and retrieval.[31]

Characterized by progressive memory loss and cognitive decline, Alzheimer's disease is accompanied by a loss of neurons and synapses, especially cholinergic synapses in the basal forebrain, cerebral cortex, and hippocampus—and by a substantial reduction in both muscarinic and nicotinic acetylcholine receptors (AChRs). Early studies indicated that acute nicotine administration improved performance of patients with Alzheimer's disease in cognitive tasks, whereas acute administration of the noncompetitive (channel blocker) antagonist mecamylamine resulted in the dose-dependent impairment of performance. Several pharmacological options have recently emerged for the development of novel $\alpha 4\beta 2$ nAChR, and $\alpha 7$ nAChR ligands as candidate drugs to treat Alzheimer's disease.[32]

Along with the cholinergic system's contribution to regulation of access to consciousness, a crucial issue that my colleagues and I have scrutinized is the access of stored memories into the global neuronal workspace and consciousness. It is not a simple matter of retrieval, of direct recall, but rather the result of a *reconstruction* process of internal testing and selection from among alternative accounts. Recall can be viewed as a reconstruction during which reactivated memories may be unconsciously biased by preexisting knowledge or by the emotional resonance of actual memories of past experience. The content of memories may even be deliberately modified and revised through the incorporation of new information meant to strengthen its plausibility. So-called inaccuracies or distortions can take place in this context. Memory consists of understanding a past event: it is a reconstruction of the past event through information that has only partially been retained. This recall of stored knowledge is therefore never complete, and is often biased by the process of recollection itself, which also requires decision-making at the point of recollection.[33]

Artistic Creation and Memory Storage

The epigenetic internalization of the personal history of an individual, together with that of the individual's sociocultural environment, raises tremendous problems of analysis and formalization. Each human brain melds, in a singular manner, multiple nested evolutions by variation selection: the genetic evolution of the species, along with the many epigenetic evolutions from experience and memory traces stored both inside the brain and outside the brain, as a society's cultural heritage, for example.

Memory retrieval experiments and other cognitive tasks that unfold sequentially over time produce temporal sequences, a "mental flow," analogous to that of music. Each "note" is mobilized serially as the outcome of distinct processes described above, and then is held online in working memory until a moment of resolution is reached to create a well-formed, time-ordered sequence or "melody" of consciousness.

During the "mental experience" of creative work, these multiple evolutions overlie and connect with each other. Beginning with the first "confused shapes" (Leonardo da Vinci), randomly born bits on which, according to the French poet and essayist Yves Bonnefoy, "the imaginary rests," one can distinguish the "first idea," a still crude outline that is nevertheless importantly connected to the subject's own definition. Then this mental object, sifted through the filter of reason, becomes reality on paper by multiple "external drawings" of the graphic sketch, or *disegno*. Representations from the "internal circuit" give way to precise movements of the hand and fingers (often acquired after a long period of practicing one's art) that finally direct the pen or the paintbrush. A cascade of activity in premotor, then motor areas extends the internal, implicit evolution of mental creation.

Despite the progressive rebuilding and restructuring that takes place in climbing up the hierarchical ladder of cortical regions, we are still far removed from that "singing state" evoked by another French poet, Paul Valéry, that "musical place of words," where images, words, and rhymes meet at the point of poetic creation. But it seems that we are getting closer with an important brain imaging study by Bernard Mazoyer and his colleagues.[34] These researchers compared the cerebral activity of monolingual French-speaking subjects to whom three types of stimuli were presented aurally: a story in Tamil, which they could not understand; a list of French words that they could understand; and finally, a well-structured story in French. Investigators found that the more comprehensible the stimuli became, the more activation was found in the left hemisphere, with the number and intensity of the activations increasing. Multiple cerebral domains find themselves "stuck together" (cum prehendere) when a subject comprehends. With complete understanding of the story, the prefrontal cortical region comes into play: an essential component of the global neuronal workspace, the lesioning of which affects attention, reasoning, and mental planning. The prefrontal cortex contributes to mental synthesis, to organizing thoughts into intentions. It helps to build mental representations that relate to social interaction. It plays a central role in attributing mental states to others (theory of mind), in recognizing the so-called moral emotions such as sympathy and violence inhibition and, of course, the ability to integrate past memories and present information into a decision-making process leading to action in a social world.[35]

If artistic creation is part of the personal history of the artist within the artist's unique sociocultural environment, it stems from an anterior historical evolution. A painting or artwork thus can be viewed as a complex synthesis of memes that are transmitted by one painter to another through the artwork. Although the material artwork is more reliable than the unstable human brain, ensuring the permanence of those memes, their transmission through art can be viewed as the result of selection processes over centuries. Art historians can trace evolutions only because painters borrow patterns, figures, and forms from others. These elements become units of replication or memes that are perpetuated through time. It is well known that memes of form and meaning from the ancient world, for example, were adapted to the cultural contexts of the Renaissance. Paintings therefore communicate a longitudinal evolution of memes of form and a vertical intersection of numerous memes of meaning—all of which the artists incorporate in their own individual expression.[36] For instance, at the origins of Picasso's *Demoiselles d'Avignon*, Hélène Seckel would place *Saint John's Vision* by El Greco, followed by the *Bathers* by Cézanne, the *Turkish Bath* by Ingres, and, among Picasso's own works, the *Harem* of 1906 and *Two Nudes* from the same year, with an obvious influence of African art, and finally several sketches for the painting itself.[37] Such historical evolution of art engages a rather severe selection mechanism following specific *epigenetic rules* that creators have imposed on themselves from the beginning of time, and have helped develop throughout the course of history.

In conclusion, the access to consciousness, in which evoked memories occupy a central place, is a neurological process that is beginning to be understood but still requires a better knowledge of its neural bases and of its genesis through the relationships of the individual with his or her physical, social, and cultural environment and unique personal history.[38] It is fundamentally an "endogenous process." Spontaneous activity of the nervous system has long been postulated as a critical mechanism of the *epigenesis of neuronal networks* and of the top-down processes taking place in the *global neuronal workspace*.[39] The brain is *not* a simple input-output processing device but an open, motivated, and self-organizing system operating in a *projective* manner.[40] Molecular mechanisms are at work in the brain both bottom-up and top-down in its genetic and epigenetic construction. The brain can indeed be viewed as an *intentional organ*, originating from the synthesis of multiple *nested* evolutionary processes taking place at *several interacting levels* of selection and variability (genes, neurons, networks of neurons, shared social and cultural organizations). These interlocking processes operate with different time scales and with considerable neural plasticity that integrate the phylogenetic, ontogenetic, social, and cultural history of the human species in its "memories."

Notes

1. Jean-Pierre Changeux, Philippe Courrège, and Antoine Danchin, "A Theory of the Epigenesis of Neural Networks by Selective Stabilization of Synapses," *Proceedings*

of the National Academy of Sciences USA 70 (1973): 2974–2978; Stanislas Dehaene, Michel Kerszberg, and Jean-Pierre Changeux, "A Neuronal Model of a Global Workspace in Effortful Cognitive Tasks," *Proceedings of the National Academy of Sciences USA* 95 (1998): 14529–14534. See also Jean-Pierre Changeux and Stanislas Dehaene, "The Neuronal Workspace Model: Conscious Processing and Learning," in *Learning Theory and Behavior*, ed. R. Menzel, vol. 1 of *Learning and Memory: A Comprehensive Reference* (Amsterdam: Elsevier, 2008), 729–758. Still in formalization development, the neuronal workspace model has some shortcomings. A specific challenge for the future is to integrate in the model connections to the workspace self-representations that might allow the simulated organism to reflect on its own internal processes.

2. Jean-Pierre Changeux, *The Physiology of Truth: Neuroscience and Human Knowledge*, trans. M. B. DeBevoise (2002; reprint, Cambridge, MA: Harvard University Press, 2004).

3. Jean-Pierre Changeux, *Raison et plaisir* (Paris: Odile Jacob, 1994); S. Dehaene, M. Kerszberg, and J.-P. Changeux, "A Neuronal Model of a Global Workspace in Effortful Cognitive Tasks."

4. J. Craig Venter et al., "The Sequence of the Human Genome," *Science* 291 (2001): 1304–1351; Eric S. Lander, "Initial Sequencing and Analysis of the Human Genome," *Nature* 409 (2001): 860–921.

5. Frederico A. C. Azevedo et al., "Equal Numbers of Neuronal and Nonneuronal Cells Make the Human Brain an Isometrically Scaled-Up Primate Brain," *Journal of Comparative Neurology* 513 (2009): 532–541.

6. Vernon Mountcastle, *Perceptual Neuroscience: The Cerebral Cortex* (Cambridge, MA: Harvard University Press, 1998).

7. Jean-Pierre Changeux, *Neuronal Man: The Biology of Mind*, trans. Laurence Garey (1983; reprint, New York: Pantheon, 1985); J.-P. Changeux, *The Physiology of Truth: Neuroscience and Human Knowledge;* Gerald Edelman, *Neural Darwinism: The Theory of Neuronal Group Selection* (New York: Basic Books 1987); George L. Gabor Miklos and Gerald M. Rubin, "The Role of the Genome Project in Determining Gene Function: Insights from Model Organisms," *Cell* 86 (1996): 521–529.

8. Helmuth Steinmetz et al., "Brain (A)symmetry in Monozygotic Twins," *Cerebral Cortex* 5 (1995): 296–300.

9. Françoise Levinthal, Eduardo Macagno, and Cyrus Levinthal, "Anatomy and Development of Identified Cells in Isogenic Organisms," *Cold Spring Harbor Symposia on Quantitative Biology* 40 (1976): 321–331.

10. J.-P. Changeux, *Neuronal Man: The Biology of Mind.*

11. Jean-Pierre Bourgeois, "Synaptogenèses dans le néocortex des primates," *Neuropsy* 12 (1997): 506–510; Jean-Pierre Bourgeois, "Synaptogenesis, Heterochrony, and

Epigenesis in the Mammalian Cortex," Nobel Symposium on "Genetic versus Environmental Determination of Human Behaviour and Health," *Acta Paediatrica Suppl.* 422 (1997): 27–33; Jean-Pierre Bourgeois, "Synaptogenèses et épigenèses cérébrales," *Épigénétique* 21 (April 2005): 428–433.

12. J.-P. Changeux and S. Dehaene, "The Neuronal Workspace Model: Conscious Processing and Learning."

13. J.-P. Changeux, P. Courrège, and A. Danchin, "A Theory of the Epigenesis of Neural Networks by Selective Stabilization of Synapses"; J.-P. Changeux and A. Danchin, "Selective Stabilization of Developing Synapses as a Mechanism for the Specification of Neuronal Networks," *Nature* 264 (1976): 705–712; Gerald Edelman and G. Tononi, "Selection and Development: The Brain as a Complex System," in *The Lifespan Development of Individuals: Behavioral, Neurobiological and Psychosocial Perspectives*, ed. David Magnusson (Cambridge: Cambridge University Press, 1996), 179–204.

14. J.-P. Changeux, P. Courrège, and A. Danchin, "A Theory of the Epigenesis of Neural Networks by Selective Stabilization of Synapses."

15. Thomas Gisiger, Michel Kerszberg, and Jean-Paul Changeux, "Acquisition and Performance of Delayed-Response Tasks: A Neural Network Model." *Cerebral Cortex* 15 (2005): 489–506; Thomas Gisiger and Michel Kerszberg, "A Model for Integrating Elementary Neural Functions into Delayed-Response Behavior," *PLoS Computational Biology* 2 (2006): e25; Jeffrey P. Gavornik et al., "Learning Reward Timing in Cortex through Reward Dependent Expression of Synaptic Plasticity," *Proceedings of the National Academy of Sciences USA* 106 (2009): 6826–6831.

16. For a discussion of Pierre Bourdieu's concept of "habitus," see Roy Nash, "Bourdieu on Education and Social and Cultural Reproduction," *British Journal of Sociology of Education* 11 (1990): 431–447; and Jean-Pierre Changeux, in *Croyance, raison, déraison*, ed. Gérard Fussmann (Paris: Odile Jacob, 2006).

17. Stanislas Dehaene and Jean-Pierre Changeux, "Neural Mechanisms for Access to Consciousness," in *The Cognitive Neurosciences III*, ed. Michael Gazzaniga (Cambridge, MA: MIT Press, 2004), 1145–1157.

18. Hugo Lagercrantz and Jean-Pierre Changeux, "The Emergence of Human Consciousness: From Fetal to Neonatal Life," *Pediatric Research* 65 (2009): 255–260.

19. F. Crick and C. Koch, "Some Reflections on Visual Awareness," *Cold Spring Harbor Symposium on Quantitative Biology* 55 (1990): 953–962; Gerald M. Edelman, *The Remembered Present: A Biological Theory of Consciousness* (New York: Basic Books, 1989); Rodolfo Llinás and Denis Paré, "Of Dreaming and Wakefulness," *Neuroscience* 44 (1991): 521–535; John Searle, "Consciousness," *Annual Review of Neuroscience*, 23 (2000): 558–559; S. Dehaene and J.-P. Changeux, "The Neuronal Workspace Model: Conscious Processing and Learning."

20. Stanislas Dehaene and Jean-Pierre Changeux, "The Wisconsin Card Sorting Test: Theoretical Analysis and Simulation of a Reasoning Task in a Model Neuronal Network," *Cerebral Cortex* 1 (1991): 62–79; Bernard J. Baars, *A Cognitive Theory of Consciousness* (New York: Cambridge University Press, 1988).

21. The seminal Dehaene, Kerszberg, and Changeux 1998 model was updated in 2003, 2005, and 2008. See Stanislas Dehaene, Claire Sergent, and Jean-Pierre Changeux, "A Neuronal Network Model Linking Subjective Reports and Objective Physiological Data during Conscious Perception," *Proceedings of the National Academy of Sciences USA* 100 (2003): 8520–8525; Stanislas Dehaene and Jean-Pierre Changeux, "Ongoing Spontaneous Activity Controls Access to Consciousness: A Neuronal Model for Inattentional Blindness," *PLoS Biology* 5 (2005); J.-P. Changeux, P. Courrège, and A. Danchin, "A Theory of the Epigenesis of Neural Networks by Selective Stabilization of Synapses"; J.-P. Changeux and S. Dehaene, "The Neuronal Workspace Model: Conscious Processing and Learning."

22. S. Dehaene, M. Kerszberg, and J.-P. Changeux, "A Neuronal Model of a Global Workspace in Effortful Cognitive Tasks."

23. S. Dehaene, M. Kerszberg, and J.-P. Changeux, "A Neuronal Model of a Global Workspace in Effortful Cognitive Tasks," 14530.

24. J.-P. Changeux, *The Physiology of Truth: Neuroscience and Human Knowledge.*

25. See Jean-Pierre Changeux and Paul Ricoeur, *What Makes Us Think: A Neuroscientist and a Philosopher Argue about Ethics, Human Nature, and the Brain*, trans. M. B. DeBevoise (1998; reprint, Princeton, NJ: Princeton University Press, 2000).

26. Ferdinand de Saussure, *Course in General Linguistics*, trans. Wade Baskin (1916; reprint, Glasgow: Fontana/Collins, 1977).

27. G. Edelman and G. Tononi, "Selection and Development: The Brain as a Complex System"; Stanislas Dehaene and Jean-Pierre Changeux, "A Simple Model of Prefrontal Cortex Function in Delayed-Response Tasks," *Journal of Cognitive Neuroscience* 1 (1989): 244–261; P. Read Montague, Peter Dayan, and Terrence J. Sejnowski, "A Framework for Mesencephalic Dopamine Systems Based on Predictive Hebbian Learning," *Journal of Neuroscience* 16 (1996): 1936–1947; Christopher D. Fiorillo, Philippe N. Tobler, and Wolfram Schultz, "Discrete Coding of Reward Probability and Uncertainty by Dopamine Neurons," *Science* 299 (2003): 1898–1902; Stanislas Dehaene and Jean-Pierre Changeux, "Reward-Dependent Learning in Neuronal Networks for Planning and Decision Making," *Progress in Brain Research* 126 (2000): 217–229.

28. S. Dehaene and J.-P. Changeux, "A Simple Model of Prefrontal Cortex Function in Delayed-Response Tasks"; S. Dehaene and J.-P. Changeux, "The Wisconsin Card Sorting Test: Theoretical Analysis and Simulation of a Reasoning Task in a Model Neuronal Network"; Jean-Pierre Changeux and Stuart J. Edelstein, "Allosteric Mechanisms of Signal Transduction," *Science* 308 (2005): 1424–1428.

29. Jean-Pierre Changeux and Stuart J. Edelstein, *Nicotinic Acetylcholine Receptors: From Molecular Biology to Cognition* (Paris: Odile Jacob, 2005).

30. Raymond T. Bartus et al., "The Cholinergic Hypothesis of Geriatric Memory Dysfunction," *Science* 217 (1982): 408–414.

31. J.-P. Changeux and S. J. Edelstein, *Nicotinic Acetylcholine Receptors: From Molecular Biology to Cognition*.

32. See Antoine Taly et al., "Nicotinic Receptors: Allosteric Transitions and Therapeutic Targets in the Nervous System," *Nature Reviews Drug Discovery* 8 (2009): 733–750.

33. Daniel Schacter, *Searching for Memory: The Brain, the Mind and the Past* (New York: Basic Books. 1996); Elizabeth Loftus, "Creating False Memories," *Scientific American* 277 (September 1997): 71–75.

34. See B. M. Mazoyer et al., "The Cortical Representation of Speech," *Journal of Cognitive Neuroscience* 5 (1993): 467–479.

35. See J.-P. Changeux and P. Ricoeur, *What Makes Us Think*.

36. See Jean-Pierre Changeux, "Art and Neuroscience," *Leonardo* 27 (1994): 189–201.

37. Hélène Seckel, *Les Demoiselles d'Avignon*, Catalog of the exhibition by Picasso Museum, Exhibition at the Musée Picasso, Paris, January 26–April 18, 1988,

38. See J.-P. Changeux and S. Dehaene, "The Neuronal Workspace Model: Conscious Processing and Learning."

39. J.-P. Changeux, P. Courrège, and A. Danchin, "A Theory of the Epigenesis of Neural Networks by Selective Stabilization of Synapses." S. Dehaene and J.P. Changeux, "Ongoing Spontaneous Activity Controls Access to Consciousness."

40. J.-P. Changeux, *The Physiology of Truth: Neuroscience and Human Knowledge*.

4 Memory in Sleep and Dreams: The Construction of Meaning

Robert Stickgold

Perhaps the most complex accomplishment of the human brain is the construction of meaning—a process that requires the analysis of large bodies of data and the identification of associations, relationships, regularities, and rules in the world around us. Each and every one of us does this constantly, from the moment we are born to the moment we die, discovering or creating our own *personal meaning* of the world. Science, the arts, and literature, for their part, attempt to discover or create, not a personal, but rather a *universal meaning* of the world. Although almost all of the time consciously spent in pursuit of this meaning occurs during waking, this chapter presents evidence that the states of sleep and dreaming contribute as much to our discovery and creation of meaning—both personal and universal—as does the state of conscious wakefulness, and quite possibly more.

Memory Systems

In discussing the construction of meaning, we start with memory. Although the human mind does not begin as a tabula rasa, the construction of meaning nonetheless depends critically on the knowledge gained through experience and introspection. Such knowledge is stored within the brain as memories. Cognitive neuroscience divides memories into several distinct categories and subcategories, based on their nature. Understanding these divisions is important because the interaction between sleep and memory appears to be dependent on the category of memory being considered.

In what is perhaps the most common taxonomy, human memories are categorized, at the top level, as declarative or nondeclarative.[1] Declarative memories (figure 4.1A), which are either episodic or semantic, are memories that can be directly reported by an individual. Episodic memories are

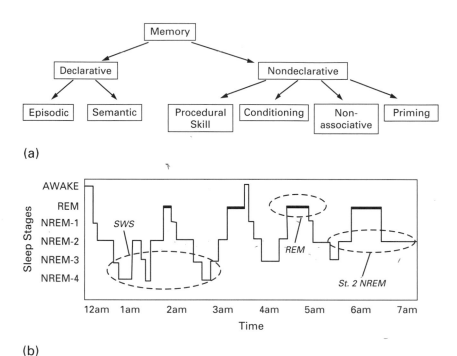

(a)

(b)

Figure 4.1

Memory systems and the sleep cycle. (A) Memory systems—human memory is most commonly divided into declarative forms, with further subdivisions into episodic and semantic; and nondeclarative forms, subdivided into an array of different types including procedural skill memory. (B) The human sleep cycle—across the night, NREM and REM sleep cycle every 90 minutes in an ultradian manner, whereas the ratio of NREM to REM sleep shifts. During the first half of the night, stages 3 and 4 NREM (SWS) dominate, whereas stage 2 NREM and REM sleep prevail in the latter half of the night. EEG patterns also differ significantly between sleep stages, with electrical oscillations such as K-complexes and sleep spindles occurring during stage 2 NREM, slow (0.5–4 Hz) delta waves developing in slow wave sleep, and theta waves seen during REM sleep.

Reprinted from M.P. Walker and R. Stickgold, "Sleep-Dependent Learning and Memory Consolidation," *Neuron* 44 (2004): 121–133. Courtesy of Elsevier, Ltd.

memories of life events that can be brought back into conscious awareness and at least partially reexperienced. Thus remembering walking into the room you are currently in, what you had for dinner last night, a recent conversation with a friend, your college graduation, and where you were when you heard about the 9/11 attacks in New York City are examples of episodic memories. In contrast, semantic memories are memories of general information. Your age and birthday, the capital of France, the sum of five plus five, and the meaning of the word *memory* are all examples of semantic memories. Episodic and semantic memories are declarative memories because they are directly accessible to conscious recall. As discussed below, the sleep-dependent stabilization of declarative memories is most often associated with a particular stage of sleep, referred to as "slow wave sleep."[2]

In contrast to declarative memories, nondeclarative memories (figure 4.1A) cannot be brought into conscious awareness. Perhaps the most commonly recognized subcategory of nondeclarative memory is procedural memory. Just as declarative memories are memories of "what," procedural memories are memories of "how." How to tie your shoe, ride a bicycle, play the piano, and repair an aortic aneurysm represent motor procedural memories of increasing complexity. Procedural learning normally begins with declarative memories (e.g., "Place the right lace over the left lace and tuck it under") but, with increasing practice, as the skills are mastered, they become automatic, and often end with the loss of the original declarative memories (e.g., the keyboard key pressed when the right ring finger moves up one row from the "home" keys). Less commonly recognized is the wide range of perceptual procedural skills. How to distinguish different coins either by sight or touch, calculating whether to stop as a traffic light turns yellow, and selecting a ripe, but not overripe banana are all examples of such perceptual procedural memories and skills.

Beyond perceptual and motor procedural skills, there is a wide range of complex cognitive procedural skills that can be learned. These require the development of new cognitive strategies, which are constructed outside of conscious awareness.[3] Playing chess, deciding where to park, what to order at a restaurant, and whom to marry are examples of behaviors that depend on complex cognitive procedural skills. In such situations, although we usually have a sense of why we decided the way we did, we are unable to explain these reasons with enough clarity that an observer could reliably replicate our behavior in the future. Sleep can lead to the absolute enhancement of all forms of procedural memories, leading to improved performance on procedural tasks after sleep. This enhancement also shows specific sleep stage dependencies, different from those seen for declarative memories.

Although these memory systems have been defined according to their behavioral and phenomenological characteristics, they are also differentiated by the brain systems they bring into play. The formation of declarative memories is dependent on the hippocampus, a midline brain structure tucked beneath the temporal lobes of the cerebral cortex. Bilateral destruction of the hippocampus produces classic amnesia and prevents the formation of new declarative memories. The recall of such memories when initially formed is also dependent on the hippocampus. But over time, these memories evolve, their recall ceases to depend on hippocampal activity, much of the episodic detail is lost, and they become more and more semantic in nature. In contrast, hippocampal damage does not prevent the formation of new procedural (nondeclarative) memories.

Associations, Relationships, Regularities, and Rules

The construction of meaning involves the interpretation of information that is learned. This chapter presents the results of scientific experiments that indicate how sleep facilitates such construction through the identification and retention of associations, relationships, regularities, and rules in the world around us. It describes sleep's ability to perform tasks that separately test each process. The establishment of associations within the brain requires the formation or strengthening of bidirectional connectivity between two or more memories, such that the activation of each memory increases the probability the other will be activated. Associations generally form when the objects of two memories share properties, such as memories for two dogs, or for a car and a bus, or for cars and buses in general. Such associations form the basis of similes. Relationships also involve formation of connections between memories, although these can be in just one direction. They can be more specifically linked to a type of relationship (larger than, the mother of, a kind of, etc.) and are usually learned, rather than automatically formed. Thus the association between one car and another can be made automatically based on physical similarities, whereas the relationship between a particular car and its owner is based on separately learned connections. Interestingly, object transformations in dreams, in which one object suddenly (and impossibly) transforms into another are based on associations of similarity, and not on learned relationships.[4]

Although associations and relationships form between preexisting memories within the brain, the extraction of regularities and the discovery of rules require the formation of metaconstructs within the memory systems. These can act as the implicit definitions of categories such as dogs, books, verbs, and teachers. In their simplest form, they are arguably the physical instantiation of Platonic forms,[5] existing only in the patterns of neural connectivity that represent the extracted regularities of a group of objects. The discovery of rules similarly requires the extraction of metaconstructs from a given group of individual memories. Rules are to relationships what regularities are to associations. Thus they describe how one set of objects follows from a second set, how thunder follows from lightning, how ice follows from the cooling of water, or how anger follows from betrayal.

Associations, relationships, regularities, and rules are the products of complex and sophisticated mechanisms of memory processing. Although they are most notably formed as a consequence of conscious reflection, the vast majority of this effort goes on without intent and outside of awareness. Surprisingly, much of it occurs preferentially, or even exclusively, during sleep.

Meaning

As off-line memory processing proceeds within the brain, creating associations, relationships, regularities, and rules, meaning begins to arise. From an evolutionary perspective, the construction of "meaning" refers to the integration of new memories into preexisting memory networks to provide an enhanced context from within which preexisting information can better inform future action. From a phenomenological perspective, this same integration provides a context that facilitates recognition of associations and relationships between new memories and elements in these networks, and that promotes identification of regularities of which the new memory is a part, and of rules that apply to it. Phenomenological awareness of these connections places new memories within the context of an individual's life to date, but also within the imaginal space of the individual's future, helping to create both an understanding of the world and a sense of the self in time. Although the details of how meaning is extracted or constructed remain unclear, much of this happens, not while we are awake, but rather while we sleep.

The Physiology and Chemistry of Sleep

The invocation of the muses who inspire the creation of literature and the arts is an ancient tradition. Perhaps a more modern version would be the invocation of "whiskey for the first draft and coffee for the rewrite." What these share is the concept that writing occurs preferentially in an altered state of consciousness, whether brought about by the muses or the modern pharmacopoeia. Yet the most common route to altered states is simply to sleep.

A night of sleep normally consists of a series of about five cycles of alternating rapid eye movement (REM) sleep and non-REM (NREM) sleep (figure 4.1B). NREM sleep is further divided into four stages of increasingly deep sleep, with the two deepest stages, stages 3 and 4, collectively referred to as "slow wave sleep" (SWS) because of their characteristic EEG profiles. A typical REM cycle starts with light stage 2 NREM sleep, followed by deep slow wave sleep, back to lighter stage 2 NREM sleep, and ending with a period of REM sleep. Although each sleep cycle lasts approximately 90 minutes, slow wave sleep dominates the earlier cycles and REM sleep dominates the later ones. Within each cycle, the brain and mind pass through a series of distinct states (table 4.1).

Stage 1 NREM Sleep

The initial state of sleep attained at sleep onset is stage 1 NREM, a transitional state normally lasting only a few minutes and characterized by short, vivid dreams that are usually simple images or brief narratives, less complex than REM sleep dreams. These dreams are often related to presleep thoughts, and sleep onset can involve an almost imperceptible shift from logical thoughts to bizarre thoughts and hypnagogic images.

Stage 2 NREM Sleep

Stage 2 represents the onset of true sleep, and is usually attained within a few minutes of sleep onset. It is seen throughout the night, without any clear bias toward earlier or later hours, and is intermediate in character between REM and slow wave sleep. Stage 2 dreaming shifts across the night. Early in the night, stage 2 dreams are short, thoughtlike, and of minimal vividness. As the night progresses, they become more dreamlike, longer, and more vivid. Stage 2 is defined largely by its signature EEG pattern, with relatively fast, low-amplitude waves often lost in the noise, but highlighted by occasional isolated large amplitude waves and bursts of highly structured wave patterns.

Table 4.1
Characteristics of Sleep stages

	Stage 1 NREM	Stage 2 NREM	SWS	REM
Timing	Sleep onset	All night	Early night	Late night
EEG patterns	Fast, desynchronized	Moderately synchronized	Slow, highly synchronized	Fast, desynchronized
Neurochemistry	ACh ↑ NE ↑ 5-HT ↑	ACh — NE — 5-HT —	ACh ↓ NE ↑ 5-HT ↑	ACh ↑↑ NE ↓↓ 5-HT ↓↓
HC → cortex	?	?	↑↑	↓↓
Cortex → HC	?	?	↓↓	↑↑
Limbic: DLPFC	?	?	↓↓	↑↑
Dreaming	Short vivid, single scenes	Less vivid, more thoughtlike	Minimal, thoughtlike	Long, vivid, complex, bizarre

Note: Sleep stages differ both in their physiological features and in the formal properties of their dreams. Arrows and dashes reflect relative levels of activity; "↑" indicates high; "—" indicates moderate; "↓" indicates low; "?" indicates an absence of experimental data for that cell. ACh, acetylcholine; DLPFC, dorsolateral prefrontal cortex; 5-HT, serotonin; HC, hippocampus; NE, norepinephrine.

Slow Wave Sleep

Stages 3 and 4 of NREM sleep together constitute slow wave sleep (SWS), characterized by an EEG pattern of large, slow waves, resembling a child's drawing of waves on the ocean, which indicates highly synchronized firing of neurons in the cortex. Most of a night's slow wave sleep occurs during the first two REM cycles, in the first half of the night (figure 4.1B). Later in the night, periods of NREM sleep are often exclusively lighter, stage 2 NREM sleep. Reports of dreaming are relatively rare, and tend to be minimal in vividness, length, and content. Although there is some dispute over whether this reflects impoverished dreaming or a problem with recall after awakenings from slow wave sleep, the consensus is that dreaming is diminished in this state.

Slow wave sleep differs from other stages of sleep in other dramatic ways. One of these is the activity of neuromodulatory systems. Several neurotransmitters modulate brain activity, sculpting it to produce more or less reliable and accurate communication within neural networks. Although greater reliability and accuracy might seem obviously preferential, within complex neural networks this is not always true: reduced reliability can lead to activation of associations that would not otherwise be selected. Thus the activation of neural nets representing the synthesis of new associations, relationships, and schemas requires reduced accuracy within these networks. Based on behavioral studies, increases in neuromodulation by norepinephrine (NE) and serotonin (5-hydroxytryptamine, or 5-HT) lead to more reliable activity.[6] In contrast, the neuromodulator acetylcholine (ACh) would appear to have the opposite effect. It is thus striking that slow wave sleep is characterized by relatively high levels of norepinephrine and serotonin, but reduced levels of acetycholine in the brain (table 4.1), a condition that should maximize the reliability of neural network activity.[7]

Slow wave sleep also shows changes in the patterns of regional brain activation and communication.[8] In addition to a general decrease in brain activity in almost all regions, there is a shift in the pattern of communication between major memory regions. Information appears to flow out of the hippocampus into the cerebral cortex, where individual elements of episodic memories are stored (table 4.1). Such activity corresponds to that required for the reactivation of episodic memories. In contrast, flow into the hippocampus, critical for the formation of new memories, appears to be blocked.

Taken as a whole, the physiology of slow wave sleep suggests a system evolved to reliably reactivate episodic memories and possibly stabilize and strengthen them, although poorly constructed for the discovery of new associations and insights.

REM Sleep

In almost every way, REM sleep is the antithesis of slow wave sleep (table 4.1). The majority of a night's REM sleep comes in the last third of the night. The EEG pattern is fast and desynchronized. The levels of norepinephrine and serotonin drop to near zero, whereas levels of acetylcholine are high.[9] In some regions, such as the hippocampus, acetylcholine levels are higher than in waking.[10] This pattern of neuromodulation leads to less reliable transmission within neural nets, a poor state for predictable outputs from such networks, but an optimal one for the activation of new patterns of activity associated with the discovery of new relationships within and among neural networks. Such patterns, in turn, can lead to new relationships among the neurons in a network and, at another level, to the modification of conceptual schema and the development of insight.[11] This can be seen behaviorally by waking subjects from REM sleep or light, stage 2 NREM sleep, and having them quickly (in one or two minutes) complete cognitive tests, before the brain's neurochemistry has had a chance to adjust to the waking state. When this is done, subjects awakened from REM sleep are more effective at activating weak associations (e.g., thief-wrong) than normally strong ones (e.g., right-wrong), and can even solve anagrams more quickly, than when awakened from stage 2 NREM sleep.[12]

At the level of regional brain activation, REM sleep shows a pattern markedly different from that seen in slow wave sleep.[13] As the brain shifts from slow wave to REM sleep, regions in the front of the brain, most notably the dorsolateral prefrontal cortex (DLPFC), become even less active than their already suppressed levels during slow wave sleep. In contrast, other regions, along the midline of the brain, in the limbic region of the cortex become even more active, sometimes more active than in the waking state. This particular constellation of changes seems functional. The dorsolateral prefrontal cortex is considered the center of executive control and logical reasoning in the brain. In contrast, the limbic system mediates emotional responses, both behavioral and memorial, being activated not only during emotional responses but during the processing of emotional memories as well. Thus, during REM sleep, the brain appears to shut down logical reasoning and crank up emotionality. At the same time, communication between the hippocampus and cerebral cortex reverses direction, with information now flowing into the hippocampus, but not out, a condition that would make it potentially impossible for episodic memories to be reactivated. Finally, dreaming is at its peak. REM sleep dreams are more frequent, more vivid, longer, more bizarre, and more emotional than those in NREM sleep, and as the night progresses, all of these features become even more intense.

As a whole, REM sleep seems to prime the brain for a bottom-up process of creative discovery and constructing meaning. Logical reasoning is turned down, emotional thinking is ramped up; strong associations are down; weak associations are up; recall of episodic memories is down. In such a state, the brain is forced to rely on semantic and conceptual information stored across widely distributed regions of the cortex, and on the weaker, less obvious associations among them. The net result is the fine-tuning and frank reconstruction of the individual's understanding of the self and the world, and of the relationship between them. Arguably, there is no better description of the function of literature, or of the nature of dreams.

Sleep and the Evolution of Memories

The last ten years has produced a stunning amount of evidence for an important and, in some cases, critical role for sleep in the evolution of memories. Sleep leads to the enhancement of memories for procedural skills, so that, following a night of sleep, performance is enhanced for recently learned visual, auditory, and motor skills.[14] Sleep stabilizes and prevents interference with verbal memory, and may even enhance emotional memories.[15] But beyond these relatively straightforward processes, which can be performed by simply strengthening newly formed memories within the brain, sleep also facilitates systems-level processes that lead to qualitative changes in memories. For example, sleep contributes to the slow evolution of memories, from clear and accurate records of recent events into generalized memories of the gist of events, placed within the context of memories from disparate times, and used to develop new conceptual memories describing the rules and meanings of events in our lives.

Emotional Memories

Over time, what we seem to remember most from our past are emotional events. And even for those events, our memories are remarkably sparse, with memories of the emotional core of the event often maintained "as if it were yesterday," although much of the surrounding detail is lost. But this is not just a sign of the ravages of time. It is, in all likelihood, a robustly evolved mechanism for maintaining only those memories considered most important. Moreover, evidence now suggests there is an active process, occurring during sleep, that leads to this selective retention of the emotional core of our memories. In a 2007 emotional memory experiment, subjects viewed about 75 pictures, each of which had a central object (e.g., a crashed car) embedded in a scene (e.g., a city street).[16] As in real life, subjects were not asked to memorize the scenes, but merely to judge whether each was one they would be more or less likely to approach or avoid. Later, the pictures were deconstructed, and on a surprise test, subjects were asked to separately identify the objects (e.g., the crashed car) and the background scenes (e.g., the city street) they had seen before.

In constructing the pictures, all of the background scenes were designed to be emotionally neutral. But though half of the foreground objects were similarly neutral, the other half were aversive (e.g., a crashed car or dead cat). To look at the specific effect of sleep on these memories, half the subjects were trained in the morning and tested 12 hours later that evening, without intervening sleep (the wake group), whereas the other half were trained in the evening and tested 12 hours later, the next morning, after a night of sleep (the sleep group; figure 4.2).

When the performance of subjects in the wake group was analyzed, there was no evidence of any differences based on sleep or stimulus type. Subjects tended to do about 10% worse at recognizing both the neutral and aversive objects and their backgrounds, than other subjects tested just 20 minutes after originally viewing the pictures. Subjects in the sleep group also did about 10% worse for both the neutral objects and the backgrounds. But, in contrast, subjects in the sleep group were actually slightly *better* at recognizing the emotional objects in the morning than they were the night before. This single condition—just the emotional object and not its background, and just after a night of sleep—stood out from all the rest as being selectively maintained over the 12-hour interval. Thus, whereas neutral scenes decay across the day and night, and emotional scenes likewise decay

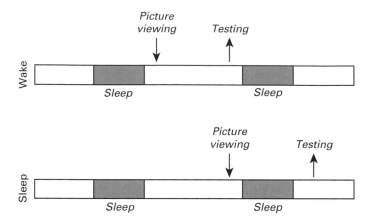

Figure 4.2
Wake-sleep paradigm. To distinguish sleep-dependent changes in memory from changes resulting from the simple passage of time, separate tests are performed over 12-hour periods that consist of either daytime wakefulness (napping is prohibited) or a night including a normal period of sleep. Additional studies control for the possibility of circadian confounds.

across the day, memories for the emotional core of our daily events are selectively and actively maintained, and possibly even strengthened, while we sleep.

Gist Memories

In addition to remembering the emotionally salient events of our lives, we also remember the gist of events. Rather than remembering all the details initially recorded in an episodic memory, the brain can relatively quickly cut to the chase, winnowing out details of no relevance. Over time, the gist is all that's left of most of those memories. As has been noted by others, it is altogether fitting and proper that we should do this. We want to remember what the capital of France is, but not where we learned that fact, or who else was there, or what the weather was like on that day.

As with emotional memories, sleep appears to selectively retain memories for the gist of studied material.[17] When subjects heard a list of words related to a central, "gist" word not included in the list, they often falsely believed that this gist word was actually included. Thus, after hearing the list *nurse, sick, lawyer, medicine, health, hospital, dentist, physician, ill, patient, office, stethoscope*, as many as two-thirds of subjects falsely believed that the word *doctor* was also on the list. The brain appears to identify the gist of the list so strongly that it becomes indistinguishable from the words actually heard.[18]

When subjects heard eight of these lists read to them in the morning and were asked 12 hours later that evening to recall as many of the words as possible, their correct recall of words actually heard and their incorrect recall of the gist words associated with each list were 30% to 40% lower than shortly after hearing the lists. If, instead, they were trained in the evening, and tested 12 hours later the following morning, after a night's sleep, their recall of the studied words was still about 20% worse than shortly after hearing the lists, but their "recall" of the gist words was actually 5% better than the evening before. Sleep appears to selectively maintain the "memory" of the gist words, while allowing memory of the words actually heard to decay, resulting in a memory the next morning that is less accurate, but more useful, than the night before. Thus it appears that the extraction and retention of the gist of events in our lives may also be largely a sleep-dependent process.

This extraction of gist is notably different from what has been described above as the selective maintenance of emotional memories. The emotional memory effect represented the stabilization and even enhancement of memories of pictures seen during waking. But the gist memory study was intentionally designed so that the gist words of the studied list were never actually seen. In fact, the gist memories, insofar as the subjects believed that they had seen the gist words, were false memories. Thus the study's findings suggest that sleep may help construct, rather than extract, the gist of the word lists. Sleep appears to be a state in which the brain specifically acts to construct the meaning of events in our lives. Indeed, since *gist* can be defined as the substance or essence of a speech or text, like a Platonic form, it is never actually seen, but rather is constructed within the mind and falsely perceived as being of the outer world.

Sleep and the Extraction of Rules

Constructing meaning often involves looking across a large number of similar events and finding the rules that govern the general category of events. Thus we learn that clouds suggest possible rain, black thunderheads probable rain, and thunder and lightning highly probable, immediate rain. Only by taking numerous examples into account at one time can the brain extract these individual rules, and only by more complex comparisons can it come to an understanding of the relationship among these simpler rules. What's important is that, even though we can learn these facts didactically, more often we come to understanding them without intentionally analyzing the data behind them. Rather, our understanding arises from analyses performed without intent and outside of conscious awareness. In at least some instances, the analyses also appear to occur preferentially, if not exclusively, during sleep.

When subjects were shown initially meaningless cues (playing cards with varying numbers of squares, triangles, circles, or diamonds) and asked to predict the outcome (rain or sun), they performed only at chance. But as they began to sense that some cards were more frequently associated with one outcome than the other, they began also to infer rules governing the relationship between cue and outcome. If trained in the morning and tested 12 hours later that evening, subjects showed no improvement in performance. But when trained in the evening and tested 12 hours later the next morning, after a night of sleep, their performance improved by 10% to 15%.[19] Sleep appears to provide an environment within which the brain can more effectively extract the rules governing earlier experiences, allowing the individual to more successfully identify optimal responses to similar circumstances the next day.

Inference and Insight

Such findings of sleep-dependent memory processing extend to more complex systems. In a 2006 study of transitive inference, subjects were taught relationships between pairs of objects and asked to infer relationships between other pairs. It was found that sleep enhanced their ability to perform such inferences.[20] And in two very different tests of insight, subjects showed dramatically more insight into previously studied material after "sleeping on it," with increases ranging from 40% to 150%.[21]

Sleep and the Construction of Meaning

The wide range of memory processes that now appear to occur exclusively or preferentially during sleep represents a veritable guide to the processes involved in the construction of meaning. Identifying what's important, extracting or constructing its gist, inferring larger conceptual structures, discovering insights—all of these are part and parcel of constructing meaning, and contribute to our ability to understand the world within which we live. How sleep performs this synthesis remains unknown in its details.

Associative Processing in REM and NREM Sleep

The construction of meaning involves identifying the relationships among disparate facts and memories. We understand the meaning of an event when we have placed it in the context of previous experiences and can use its relationship to those experiences to better predict how to respond to similar circumstances in the future. Two studies that measured cognitive performance during brief awakenings from different sleep stages provide insight into how the brain processes memory associations during sleep.

In one study, subjects were shown two letter strings in rapid succession, a word followed by either another word or a nonword, and were asked to indicate, as quickly and accurately as possible, whether the second letter string was a word. For each pair of words, the two were either strongly related semantically (e.g., hot-cold), weakly related (e.g., thief-wrong), or semantically unrelated (e.g., fish-tape). In classic studies using this semantic priming protocol, responses to strongly related target words (e.g., cold) are faster than for weakly related targets (e.g., wrong), and these in turn are faster than for unrelated targets (e.g., tape). But when subjects were tested moments after awakening from REM sleep, they showed significantly faster responses to weakly than to strongly related targets, and no difference between strongly related and unrelated targets (figure 4.3).[22]

A second study, using the same REM and NREM awakening protocol, looked at the ability of subjects to solve anagrams. As with the weak priming in the first study, subjects were able to solve more anagrams when awakened from REM sleep than from light, stage 2 NREM sleep.[23] Taken together, these two studies suggest that the brain, during REM sleep, is in a state that facilitates the activation of normally weak associations, perhaps even at levels greater than those seen for normally strong associations. This represents a brain state in which novel and unexpected associations are more readily identified, enhancing creativity, the discovery of insight, and the construction of meaning. But it is also a state optimal for generating the classically bizarre and hyperassociative content of dreams.

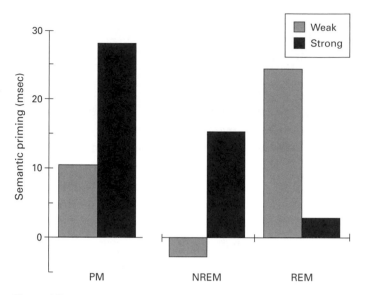

Figure 4.3

Sleep-related changes in semantic priming. Subjects were either tested during the afternoon (PM) or immediately following awakenings from stage 2 NREM or REM sleep. For each test session, median reaction times were calculated for correct responses to strongly related, weakly related, and unrelated word pairs. Strong priming—the difference in median response time for strongly related and unrelated word pairs; weak priming—the difference in median response time for weakly related and unrelated word pairs. Differences between weak and strong priming were statistically significant for the PM and REM conditions ($p \leq .01$), but not in the NREM condition ($p = .17$).

Modified from R. Stickgold et al., "Sleep Induced Changes in Associative Memory," *Journal of Cognitive Neuroscience* 11 (1999): 182.

Dream Construction

Before there was literature, before there were oral traditions and storytelling, there were dreams. Indeed, across the millennia and across cultures, dreams arguably represent the ur-literature of our species. As such, they provide the basic structure of literature, containing narrative, emotionality, bizarreness, sudden shifts in time and place, metaphor, and meaning.

To take just one example, dreams and literature are both complex admixtures of fiction and truth. In both cases, it is usually impossible to clearly distinguish between the story and the author's or dreamer's actual life. One dream study collected 364 instances of incorporating waking events into dream elements from the 300 dream reports of 29 subjects, and analyzed the similarities and differences between each waking event and the dream element it inspired.[24] The waking events, identified by dreamers as the sources of dream elements, were recalled as "episodic" memories and contained relatively accurate and complete recapitulations of the actual events as they unfolded over time. In contrast, the process of dream construction invariably selected only discrete elements from these events, placing them in different physical locations and contexts, with different actors and actions, retaining only the overall gist and emotional tone of the original event, and shedding almost all of the detail found in the episodic memory of the original event. Thus dreaming seems to reflect the same preferential activation of weak associations over strong associations seen in more direct cognitive testing of sleep-dependent memory processing, while showing the same restrained relationship to reality that is seen in literature.

But a fundamental difference still remains between dreams and literature. Unlike literary works, dreams are constructed without intent. Although Freud argued against this position, referring to "an intention which is realized through the dream,"[25] J. Allan Hobson and Robert McCarley have found that the dream process has "its origin in sensorimotor systems, with little or no primary ideational, volitional, or emotional content."[26] This concept of a bottom-up rather than top-down process of dream construction distinguishes dreaming from literature. Even when a literary work is perceived by the author to "write itself," there is no question but that the author continually directs the writing process. In contrast, there is no evidence for any similar guidance in dream construction. Rather, the construction process appears more like a "drunken sailor's walk" from one weak association to the next.

Dream construction, then, can be seen as similar to the off-line processing of memories characterized, in part, by the sleep studies described above. It differs from them, however, in two important ways. First it is unclear why such memory processing would need to occur within conscious awareness, that is, during dreaming. In fact, consciousness constrains information processing to a single stream of thought, while the nonconscious aspects of the brain can process parallel streams of information simultaneously. An explanation is needed for why some forms of memory processing should require this single-stream mode. Second, none of these sleep-dependent memory processes would appear to require the construction of a narrative, that is, of a series of events occurring across space and time. The processes of strengthening specific memories, identifying associated memories, extracting patterns, and constructing rules have no obvious need for narrative construction. This would also seem to require further explanation.

Dream Narrative

The questions of how and why dreams are constructed as narratives remain largely unexplored at the brain level function. Recently, two relevant theoretical constructs have been proposed. Although both are designed to explain waking rather than dreaming brain activity, they both bear importantly on the questions at hand. The first of these is the concept of a resting or "default" brain state.[27] Studies of regional brain activity have identified a coherent network of brain regions that are coactive when an individual is doing no particular task, typically while lying in a brain scanner awaiting instructions to perform some task. These brain regions are believed to control what has been called the "default brain mode." In this context, it is striking that patterns of brain activation seen during REM sleep[28] largely overlap with this default network. When a meta-analysis of brain imaging studies asked which categories of cognitive tasks led to similar activation patterns in waking, it was found that envisioning the future (prospection), remembering the past (recall of autobiographical memories), conceiving the viewpoint of others (theory of mind), and spatial navigation utilize this same core brain network.[29] All of these, whether recalling the past or imagining the future, arguably involve the process of "scene construction," moving through space and time.[30] Insofar as this reflects the "default" activity of the brain, they suggest a striking conclusion—that narrative construction *is* the default mode of the brain.

The second relevant new theoretical construct is the "prospective brain,"[31] for which the function of memory is not to relive the past, but to project the future. According to this concept, memory systems evolved not to allow us the pleasures and pains of reminiscence, but to provide us with tools that would help us perform more successfully in the future.

Put together, these two new concepts suggest that a major function of the brain is not that different from the function of literature.[32] When not actively engaged otherwise, the brain appears to be involved with the "remembrance of things past,"[33] with divining the thoughts and intents of others, and imagining future worlds and scenarios. For literature, as for the resting brain, its greater purpose is both to create a personal understanding of the world in which we live and to expand its boundaries. Thus both these default brain processes and literature help us navigate through our personal world more effectively and creatively. All of these functions arguably are more evident in the dreaming brain than anywhere else.

Dream Consciousness

Although the forms of sleep-dependent memory processing described above do not appear to require narrative construction, neither do they appear to require conscious awareness, both of which occur during dreaming. Conscious awareness of the activation and synthesis of thoughts, feeling, and images is what distinguishes dreaming from the myriad other brain processes occurring while we sleep.

The brain mechanism generating this consciousness and the specific function of the conscious aspect of dreaming remain unknown. Even discussing them seems of questionable value because neither has been successfully addressed with regard to normal waking consciousness. But in trying to link sleep, memory, dreams, meaning, and literature, such a discussion also seems unavoidable. At one level, the explanation of why we dream is relatively straightforward. When we sleep, the brain shifts into a series of specific brain states, which, among other functions, permit the offline processing of memories. For some forms of memory processing, specific brain processes are utilized, and these in turn require the coordinated participation of a specific set of brain structures. It is a property of these brain structures that, when so coactivated, they produce the phenomenon of conscious awareness, and specifically an awareness of the sensations associated with their specific activation. During waking, activation of these regions produces conscious awareness of current sensory input along with recalled and reconstructed sensations of past experiences stored in memory. During sleep, with the concomitant blockade of sensory input, dreaming is the resultant phenomenological experience. Unanswered, for both waking and dream consciousness, are the harder questions of exactly which brain regions are required, how conscious experience arises from their activation, and how the specific sensations associated with one particular activation of the system become the content of conscious experience.

But we can say something more now. Perhaps conscious experience is generated specifically by activation of the default network observed during both waking and sleep, a network involved in the production of narratives within the brain. If this is true, then the construction of narratives— dreams, stories, autobiographical memories, future projection—requires consciousness. However, "requires" is used here in the sense that the production of narratives necessarily involves the production of conscious experience, not in the sense that conscious experience contributes a necessary element to the process of narrative construction. This is important because it remains unclear whether dreaming, or consciousness in general, serves a function or instead merely represents an epiphenomenon of brain processing. Still, I would suggest that the brain processes proposed for the default network and for memory processing during sleep are inextricably intertwined with consciousness itself, and that narrative construction, a hallmark of dreaming, cannot occur during sleep without its appearance in conscious experience, that is, in dreaming.

Acknowledgments

This chapter is based on a talk given at the Memory in Neuroscience and the Humanities Conference, Cold Spring Harbor Laboratory, New York, October 31–November 2, 2007. I wish to thank Jessica Payne, Matthew Tucker, and Erin Wamsley for discussions and editing advice. The chapter's work was supported by grants from the National Institutes of Health of the United States, MH48,832 and MH65,292.

Notes

1. Larry R. Squire and Stuart Zola-Morgan, "Structure and Function of Declarative and Non-declarative Memory Systems," *Proceedings of the National Academy of Sciences USA* 93 (1996): 13515–13522; Endel Tulving, "How Many Memory Systems Are There?" *American Psychologist* 40 (1985): 385–398.

2. Werner Plihal and Jan Born, "Effects of Early and Late Nocturnal Sleep on Declarative and Procedural Memory," *Journal of Cognitive Neuroscience* 9 (1997): 534–547.

3. Carlyle Smith and Danielle Smith, "Ingestion of Ethanol Just Prior to Sleep Onset Impairs Memory for Procedural but Not Declarative Tasks," *Sleep* 26 (2003): 185–191.

4. Cynthia D. Rittenhouse, Robert Stickgold, and J. Allan Hobson, "Constraint on the Transformation of Characters and Objects in Dream Reports," *Consciousness and Cognition* 3 (1994): 100–113.

5. Plato, *The Republic* (Oxford: Oxford University Press, 1993), Book VII, 514a–520a.

6. David Q. Beversdorf et al., "Noradrenergic Modulation of Cognitive Flexibility in Problem-Solving," *NeuroReport* 10 (1999): 2763–2767; David Q. Beversdorf et al., "Effect of Propranolol on Verbal Problem-Solving in Autism Spectrum Disorder," *Neurocase* 14 (2008): 378–383. C. Richard Clark, Gina M. Geffen, and Laurie B. Geffen, "Catecholamines and Attention: 2. Pharmacological Studies in Normal Humans," *Neuroscience and Biobehavioral Review* 11 (1987): 353–364.

7. Jeffrey P. Sutton, Adam N. Mamelak, and J. A. Hobson, "Network Model of State-Dependent Sequencing," in *Advances in Neural Information Processing Systems*, ed. J. E. Moody, S. J. Hanson, and R. P. Lippmann (San Mateo, CA: Morgan Kaufmann, 1992), 283–290.

8. Allen R. Braun et al., "Regional Cerebral Blood Flow throughout the Sleep-Wake Cycle," *Brain* 120 (1997): 1173–1119; Pierre Maquet et al., "Functional Neuroanatomy of Human Slow Wave Sleep," *Journal of Neuroscience* 17 (1997): 2807–2812; J. Allan Hobson, Robert Stickgold, and Edward F. Pace-Schott, "The Neuropsychology of REM Sleep Dreaming," *NeuroReport* 9 (1998): R1–R14. György Buzsáki, "The Hippocampo-neocortical Dialogue," *Cerebral Cortex* 6 (1996): 81–92.

9. J. Allan Hobson, Robert W. McCarley, and Peter W. Wyzinski, "Sleep Cycle Oscillation: Reciprocal Discharge by Two Brainstem Neuronal Groups," *Science* 189 (1975): 55–58.

10. Hideki Kametani and Hiroshi Kawamura, "Alterations in Acetylcholine Release in the Rat Hippocampus during Sleep-Wakefulness Detected by Intracerebral Dialysis," *Life Sciences* 47 (1990): 421–426.

11. Ullrich Wagner et al., "Sleep Inspires Insight," *Nature,* 427 (2004): 352–355; Denise J. Cai et al., "REM, not Incubation, Improves Creativity by Priming Associative Networks," *Proceedings of the National Academy of Science USA,* (2009).

12. Robert Stickgold et al., "Sleep-Induced Changes in Associative Memory," *Journal of Cognitive Neuroscience,* 11 (1999): 182–193.

13. Pierre Maquet et al., "Functional Neuroanatomy of Human Rapid-Eye-Movement Sleep and Dreaming," *Nature,* 383 (1996): 163; J. Allan Hobson, Robert Stickgold and Edward F. Pace-Schott, "The Neuropsychology of REM Sleep Dreaming," *Neuroreport,* 9 (1998): R1–14.

14. Sara Mednick, Ken Nakayama and Robert Stickgold, "Sleep-Dependent Learning: A Nap is as good as a Night," *Nature Neuroscience,* 6 (2003): 697–698; Robert Stickgold et al., "Visual Discrimination Task Improvement: A Multi-step Process Occurring

During Sleep," *Journal of Cognitive Neuroscience,* 12 (2000): 246–254; Nadine Gaab et al., "The Influence of Sleep on Auditory Learning: A Behavioral Study," *Neuroreport,* 15 (2004): 731–734; Matthew P. Walker et al., "Practice with Sleep Makes Perfect: Sleep-Dependent Motor Skill Learning," *Neuron,* 35 (2002): 205–211; Reto Huber et al., "Local Sleep and Learning," *Nature,* 430 (2004): 78–81.

15. W. Plihal and J. Born, "Effects of Early and Late Nocturnal Sleep on Declarative and Procedural Memory"; Jeffrey M. Ellenbogen et al., "Interfering with Theories of Sleep and Memory: Sleep, Declarative Memory, and Associative Interference," *Current Biology* 16 (2006): 1290–1294; Jessica D. Payne et al., "Sleep Preferentially Enhances Memory for Emotional Components of Scenes," *Psychological Science* 19 (2008): 781–788.

16. J. D. Payne et al., "Sleep Preferentially Enhances Memory for Emotional Components of Scenes."

17. Jessica D. Payne et al., "The Role of Sleep in False Memory Formation," *Neurobiology of Learning and Memory* 92 (2009): 327–334.

18. James Deese, "On the Prediction of Occurrence of Particular Verbal Intrusions in Immediate Recall," *Journal of Experimental Psychology* 58 (1959): 17–22; Henry L. Roediger and Kathleen B. McDermott, "Creating False Memories: Remembering Words Not Presented in Lists," *Journal of Experimental Psychology: Learning, Memory & Cognition* 21 (1995): 803–814.

19. Ina Djonlagic et al., "Sleep Enhances Category Learning," *Learning & Memory* 16 (2009): 751–755.

20. Jeffrey M. Ellenbogen et al., "Human Relational Memory Requires Time and Sleep," *Proceedings of the National Academy of Science USA* 104 (2007): 7723–7728.

21. Ullrich Wagner et al., "Sleep Inspires Insight"; Denise J. Cai et al., "REM, Not Incubation, Improves Creativity by Priming Associative Networks".

22. Robert Stickgold et al., "Sleep-Induced Changes in Associative Memory".

23. Matthew P. Walker et al., "Cognitive Flexibility across the Sleep-Wake Cycle: REM-Sleep Enhancement of Anagram Problem Solving," *Cognitive Brain Research* 14 (2002): 317–324.

24. Magdalena J. Fosse et al., "Dreaming and Episodic Memory: A Functional Dissociation?" *Journal of Cognitive Neuroscience* 15 (2003): 1–9.

25. Sigmund Freud, *The Interpretation of Dreams* (1900), at http://psychclassics .yorku.ca/Freud/Dreams/dreams.pdf/, 42.

26. J. A. Hobson and R. W. McCarley, "The Brain as a Dream-State Generator: An Activation-Synthesis Hypothesis of the Dream Process," *American Journal of Psychiatry* 134 (1977): 1347.

27. Marcus E. Raichle and Abraham Z. Snyder, "A Default Mode of Brain Function: A Brief History of an Evolving Idea," *NeuroImage* 37 (2007): 1083–1090, 1097–1089.

28. J. A. Hobson, R. Stickgold, and E. F. Pace-Schott, "The Neuropsychology of REM Sleep Dreaming."

29. Randy L. Buckner and Daniel C. Carroll, "Self-Projection and the Brain," *Trends in Cognitive Sciences* 11 (2007): 49–57; R. Nathan Spreng, Raymond A. Mar, and Alice S. Kim, "The Common Neural Basis of Autobiographical Memory, Prospection, Navigation, Theory of Mind, and the Default Mode: A Quantitative Meta-analysis," *Journal of Cognitive Neuroscience* 21 (2009): 489–510.

30. Demis Hassabis and Eleanor A. Maguire, "Deconstructing Episodic Memory with Construction," *Trends in Cognitive Science* 11 (2007): 299–306.

31. Daniel L. Schacter, Donna R. Addis, and Randy L. Buckner, "Remembering the Past to Imagine the Future: the Prospective Brain," *Nature Reviews Neuroscience* 8 (2007): 657–661.

32. Suzanne Nalbantian, *Memory in Literature: From Rousseau to Neuroscience* (Basingstoke, UK: Palgrave Macmillan, 2003).

33. Marcel Proust, *Remembrance of Things Past*, trans. C. K. Scott Moncrieff and Terence Kilmartin, 3 vols. (1913–27; reprint, New York: Random House, 1981).

II Scientific Phenomena and Functioning

5 The Mnemonic Brain: Neuroimaging, Neuropharmacology, and Disorders of Memory

Paul M. Matthews

Neuropathology and neuroimaging provided the foundations for the twentieth-century renaissance of cognitive neuroscience in memory studies. Research applying these tools led efforts to relate a psychological view of memory to an understanding of the brain and the way it works. This chapter briefly reviews these approaches and considers how imaging of memory-related phenomena at a systems level can be related to underlying cellular and molecular mechanisms. Integration across these levels provides the basis for current efforts to develop treatments that may limit or even reverse disorders of memory. The complexity of the challenge and even the definition of what we consider a disorder of memory are illustrated by the concluding clinical vignettes. These highlight the need for consilience in memory studies if we are to powerfully and humanely translate our understanding of memory into strategies for improving health and well-being.

Neuroimaging of Memory

The Tools of Neuroimaging

The structure of the brain can be imaged noninvasively using X-ray computerized axial tomography (CT) or magnetic resonance imaging (MRI). Because MRI images reflect the distribution and properties of water, they are ideal for defining the structure of a soft tissue such as the brain. Moreover, MRI does not rely on the use of radiation, as does CT. For more than two decades, MRI therefore has been the primary tool for imaging the brain. Sensitivity of the MRI image to certain physicochemical properties of water in a tissue leads to changes in the signal from different kinds of cells or with different patterns of organization of cells in a tissue. This enables direct correlations to be made between brain pathology and memory performance with living subjects after surgical resections for the treatment of epilepsy, for example, or after damage to a specific brain region by a stroke or trauma.

A related technique called "functional MRI" (fMRI) builds on the same basic methodology. Neuronal signaling triggers increased metabolism and locally increased blood flow. fMRI detects the small increases in oxygenated blood that accompany this increased metabolism through its effects on the water signal.[1] Because the technique relies on testing for *differences* in brain activity *between* cognitive states, however, it defines only brain regions that show changes in activity between two states.

Absolute measurements of brain metabolism can be made directly with positron-emission tomography (PET), although experiments that use this neuroimaging tool are technically much more demanding. PET relies on incorporating a positron-emitting radioisotope into a tracer molecule of interest, for example, glucose (the primary fuel for the brain) for studies of brain activity. When the labeled molecule is injected, its distribution into the brain can be followed over time by placing an array of detectors around the head that are able to sense the photons produced by the decay of the isotope. PET can also be used to map the distribution of specific neurotransmitter receptors in the brain. PET studies can be correlated with fMRI studies or with structural anatomical studies to more precisely define the neurochemical mechanisms by which neurons interact, providing a powerful way to link molecular events to descriptions of memory at a systems level.

Structural Imaging: Relating Specific Deficits of Memory to Focally Injured Brain

The first contributions of neuroimaging to understanding how the brain is organized for memory came with imaging brain lesions in patients and relating lesional anatomy to their specific memory deficits. The simple concept motivating these studies was that behavioral deficits after lesions define the functions normally performed by the lesioned regions.

As discussed in several chapters of this volume, the fundamental importance of the medial temporal lobe to processes for declarative memory was established by clinical studies of the patient HM, who suffered from a severe form of epilepsy that responded poorly to medical treatment.[2] Using a radical new neurosurgical procedure, the American neurosurgeon William Beecher Scoville removed the seizure-generating medial temporal regions of HM's brain bilaterally. The surgery successfully reduced the frequency of HM's seizures, but left him with profound declarative memory deficits.

HM lost the ability to encode new information either about his own experiences (episodic memory) or about the world (semantic memory). Moreover, his memory of his own life prior to the surgery was severely limited, although semantic knowledge of events earlier than several years before the time of the surgery appeared to be relatively spared. Although his language comprehension was unaffected, he could not use words that had come into the lexicon since the date of his surgery. But even though his longer-term declarative memory was profoundly impaired, his working memory relatively unaffected. Thus he could repeat an examiner's name over seconds to minutes during a testing session, for example, but as soon as he was distracted or given sufficient competing information to attend, the name was forgotten.

HM also retained good implicit (skill) memory. Although his motor performance overall was somewhat impaired relative to that expected from a healthy person (likely reflecting nonspecific consequences of his chronic epilepsy), he could learn new skills. If briefly shown a "priming" list of words and then asked to complete a series of word stems (e.g., *epi-*), HM could preferentially complete the stems according to the previously shown priming word (e.g., *epilepsy*) with a facility approaching that of a normal person. These and related observations thus clearly dissociated declarative and implicit memory as distinct psychological processes.

Recent MRI studies of HM's brain have provided a more detailed description of its anatomy than had been available from the original neurosurgical report (figure 5.1, plate1).[3] The lesion was highly selective: the portion of the anterior medial temporal lobe that was removed bilaterally included the entorhinal cortex and about half of the the hippocampus and immediately adjacent structures. These brain regions therefore must mediate processes necessary for declarative memory.

A related study of three other patients with brain lesions of different sizes, but all confined to the hippocampus and adjacent entorhinal cortex, suggested that the severity of memory impairment can be related directly to the extent of (bilateral) damage to the hippocampal formation.[4] Moreover, this work showed that *larger* bilateral lesions, even

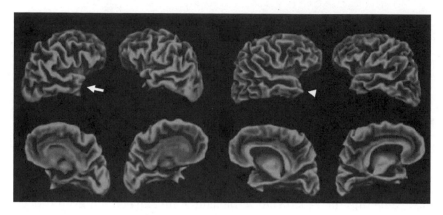

Figure 5.1 (plate 1)
Magnetic resonance images of HM's brain, scannèd in late life. Images on left show a reconstruction of its surface anatomy, with the folds of gyri digitally enhanced as green colors. Images on right show a healthy control brain for comparison (small arrowhead), clearly highlighting bilateral surgical loss of the anterior temporal lobes in images on left (arrow).
Modified with permission from David H. Salat et al., "Neuroimaging H.M.: A 10-Year Follow-Up Examination." *Hippocampus* 16 (2006): figure 3.

when still confined to the hippocampus, can produce retrograde amnesia for fifteen years or longer. These studies together directly identified the hippocampus as a central locus for declarative memory processing. They also demonstrated that the hippocampus not only subserves new memory formation, but also that it plays a critical role in accessing long-term memory in a temporally graded fashion.

Functional Imaging: Understanding How the Hippocampus Works with the Rest of the Brain to Create Memories
Functional brain imaging studies that allow direct associations between memory behavior and brain activity in healthy subjects have contributed to an increasingly precise functional-anatomical dissection of declarative memory. Peter Wais of the University of California at San Diego, summarizing the results of the fMRI studies published up to the time of his review (July 2008), has provided a simplified empirical description of how the different medial temporal structures may work together to allow both recognition that something is known and the associated full recollection.[5] Activity of the perirhinal cortex during encoding of a memory is needed both for the experience of "knowing" something and to recollect the

context in which it became known. By contrast, activity limited to the hippocampus and parahippocampal cortex is associated with recollecting the memory context alone. Wais's summary reemphasizes the role of the hippocampus for episodic memory, but extends results from lesion studies with a segmentation of local functions in rhinal cortex. This and much related work shows that the hippocampus does not function in isolation: the medial temporal cortex supports cognition for memory by functioning as an integrated unit.[6]

Mapping changes in brain activity with fMRI during recollection of semantic memories for events of the previous thirty years, Larry Squire's laboratory has further refined our understanding of how functions of the medial temporal lobe are integrated with more distant regions of the brain for semantic memory.[7] Activity in the medial temporal lobe (specifically, in the left hippocampus, amygdala, and at the right tip of the temporal lobe) showed reduced activity for more remote memories (figures 5.2, 5.3, plate 2). By contrast, regions in the frontal and parietal neocortex showed

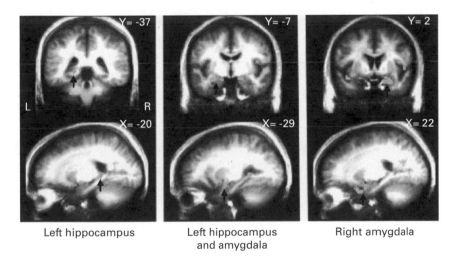

Left hippocampus   Left hippocampus   Right amygdala
                          and amygdala

Figure 5.2 (plate 2)
Functional magnetic resonance images illustrating how activity in the hippocampal formation is greater during recollection of more recent memories. The images (in different views) highlight regions of brain that show greater activity (more yellow along an orange-yellow color spectrum) for more recent memories. Regions with time-dependent recall activity include particularly the left hippocampus.
Reproduced with permission from Christine N. Smith and Larry R. Squire, "Medial Temporal Lobe Activity during Retrieval of Semantic Memory Is Related to the Age of the Memory," *Journal of Neuroscience* 29 (2009): figure 4.

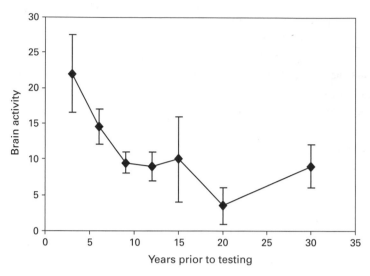

Figure 5.3

Quantitative measurements of brain activity in the left hippocampus and amygdala as a function of the age of the memory (as highlighted in the middle images of figure 5.2). Activity in these medial temporal structures decreased as subjects recalled more distant memories. Data from the same experiment also demonstrate increased activity in a widely distributed set of neocortical regions (prefrontal and lateral temporal cortices and the precuneus and cuneus).

Adapted from Christine N. Smith and Larry R. Squire, "Medial Temporal Lobe Activity during Retrieval of Semantic Memory Is Related to the Age of the Memory," *Journal of Neuroscience* 29 (2009): figure 4.

large increases in activity with recollection of the more remote memories. Thus, although the medial temporal lobe has a uniquely critical role in declarative memory formation and recall, activity subserving recollection of declarative memories becomes more highly distributed in the brain over time.

What Is So Special about the Hippocampus?

As discussed in chapter 6 of this volume, James McClelland and colleagues put forward a compelling theoretical model about twenty-five years ago to describe the way that the hippocampus might work with other parts of the brain to mediate memory.[8] They hypothesized that memories first are stored in a system (which they initially localized in the hippocampus) that is highly flexible but unable to maintain them intact for the longer term. This system acts over time to encode long-term memories in a second system with more slowly formed, but more permanent connections (which McClelland and colleagues localized to regions of the neocortex). As illustrated by Squire's work (figures 5.2, 5.3, plate 2),[9] functional imaging studies of healthy subjects have provided empirical support and further refined these concepts. Another illustration is provided by recollection of faces. Activity in the hippocampus is sustained during presentations of novel faces, but is only transient for recollection of familiar faces.[10]

More direct evidence that the role of the hippocampus in memory retrieval is time limited comes from a recent study of memory for the *positions* of faces on a projection screen, a task that probes spatial memory. Differences in the patterns of brain activation after short and longer delays before recall were contrasted.[11] The longer-term delays allowed an overnight period for consolidation of the memories. Increased neocortical activation in the frontal and parietal cortices and in the thalamus, as well as in an occipital brain region specialized for face recognition (the fusiform gyrus), were found after memory consolidation. Activity in the hippocampus itself decreased with time. Together, these studies suggest that the hippocampus has a particular role in supporting flexible, short-term memory storage.

A second emerging concept is that the structure and activity of the hippocampus are unique not only for the functional flexibility they confer, but also because they allow *relational* information integration. Studies of spatial memory well illustrate the concept. Rodents can be trained to find a path to food along an experimental maze. Individual neurons (place cells) in the hippocampi of rodents trained in navigation tasks were shown to be tuned to specific regions of space.[12] Their organization and experience-dependent functions create a world-centered (allocentric) map of their environment in the hippocampus.

Working with Eleanor Maguire and others in University College, London, John O'Keefe has provided compelling neuroimaging evidence that a similar hippocampal system must be used for spatial memory in humans. In one experiment, O'Keefe, Maguire, and colleagues introduced healthy subjects to a virtual reality town, which they were allowed to explore during a period of familiarization.[13] The investigators then asked their subjects to navigate "virtually" between specific places in the town while activity in their brains was mapped using PET. As expected, after a period of exploration, the subjects all performed as if they had a mental map of the virtual town. When subjects navigated to specific places, fMRI showed selective activation of the right hippocampus (figure 5.4, plate 3), further confirming a role for the hippocampus in spatial memory.

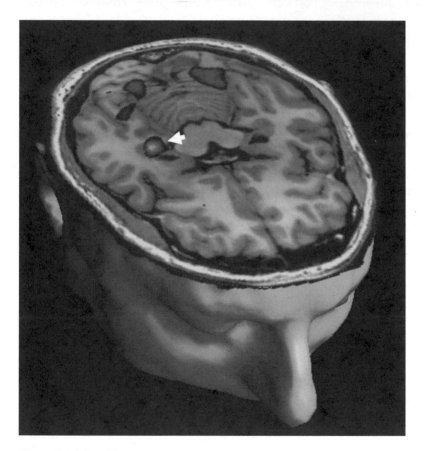

Figure 5.4 (plate 3)
Three-dimensional reconstruction of the brain at the level of the right hippo-campus, representing statistically significant increases in brain activity in subjects performing a virtual reality spatial navigation task. Note the prominent activation (blob in the right hippocampus; arrow), which mediates important processing functions of spatial memory, crucial to navigation. Activations at the back of the brain are related to visual cortex activity with the task.
Images courtesy of Prof. Eleanor A. Maguire, University College, London.

The experiment also added to evidence suggesting that hippocampal functions are lateralized, with specialization of the right hippocampus for spatial memory.

Creation of a spatial map in the hippocampus demands new specializations of place cells and the creation of new connections between them. This implies that the structure of the hippocampus must be able to change as demands for spatial learning change. In follow-up studies, O'Keefe, Maguire, and colleagues showed that the posterior right hippocampus was larger in more experienced London taxi drivers, who must develop and regularly use a comprehensive mental map of the entire metropolis of greater London ("The Knowledge"; figure 5.5, plate 4). The relative increase in size of the hippocampus correlated with years in the job.[14]

A 2009 rodent study has better explained some aspects of what might account for this.[15] The hippocampus is one of the rare regions in the brain where new neurons are continually born throughout life (most of the cells in the brain found in old age are also present at birth). The new work has shown that if animals are treated so that neurogenesis in the hippocampus is blocked, then, although the treated animals are still able to navigate, their ability to do so according to fine map relations is impaired relative to untreated control animals. This suggests that the hippocampus adds new cells to its structure as demands for greater spatial detail in memory increase- that it literally grows as the cognitive map becomes more information rich.

How spatial memory is encoded in the hippocampus provides a paradigm for the way that this brain structure supports memory formation more generally. Spatial memory involves creating a framework for relations between map points, but relational learning has a much broader role in the way we remember.[16] Narrative recall, for example, can be viewed as recollection of relationships between time and concepts within the narratives. John O'Keefe has extended his concept of hippocampal processing for spatial memory. His general "cognitive map" theory posits that the functional role for the hippocampus in episodic memory is derived from the need to relationally integrate a linear sense of time with language-based reference points.[17] Others have suggested a related, but less specific, role for the hippocampus in episodic memory: flexibly establishing relational associations between information widely distributed across neocortical regions.

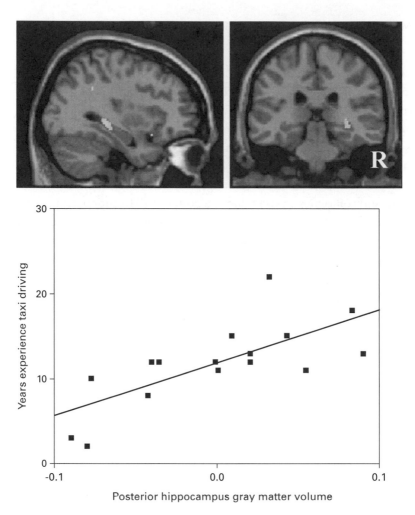

Figure 5.5 (plate 4)
Functional brain images derived from London taxi drivers with varying years of experience. Long-term memory involves formation of stable synapses and demands structural changes in gray matter. Memory encoding (or learning) is associated with an increased complexity of neuronal processes that can sometimes be appreciated as an increase in the volume of even a macroscopically defined brain region. The brain images show the result of a statistical comparison across the group of taxi drivers. It was assumed that greater numbers of years of experience were associated with the development of more detailed navigational memory for the city. The highlighted right hippocampal formation shows a statistically significant correlation between volume of gray matter and years of London taxi driving experience, whose quantitative relationship is shown in the graph. This finding is consistent with a considerable body of independent data suggesting that the right hippocampus plays an important role in spatial memory formation (see, e.g., figure 5.4).

Images courtesy of Prof. Eleanor A. Maguire, University College, London.

Working Memory

Functional imaging studies have also contributed considerably to elucidat-
ing the different set of distributed brain systems responsible for working
memory. Working memory allows short-term retention of information
just perceived or recalled in ways that facilitate its manipulation or encoding into a longer-term memory trace. The British neuropsychologist Alan
Baddeley emphasized the distinction between declarative and working
memory when he described the latter as an "interface between perception,
long-term memory and action."[18]

Building on the early concept of working memory as a short-term
store, Baddeley proposed modality-specific short-term memory stores of
two types: a visuospatial "scratchpad" for short-term maintenance of visual
percepts and spatial relations and a phonological loop for maintenance
of spoken words or sounds. What makes working memory conceptually
distinct from the simpler idea of a short-term information store is that
the visuospatial scratchpad and the phonological loop are integrated with
a coordinating "central executive," which provides a link between the
maintenance of short-term memories and their application.

fMRI has allowed direct testing of this psychological construct (figure
5.6). Meta-analysis of extant studies (an approach that allows a summary
of consistent observations across different experiments and between different laboratories) establishes a framework for this approach to working
memory studies.[19] Short-term storage of verbal information involves activation of the lateral frontal cortex of the left hemisphere, in particular.
This includes the region defined by the nineteenth-century French neurologist Pierre Paul Broca as selectively subserving functions critical to
spoken language. By contrast, both spatial and object stores are associated
with stronger activation more posteriorly in the brain. A dorsal posterior
region shows greater responses to objects, whereas a more ventral posterior region shows greater responses to information concerning spatial relations (this corresponds to preferential engagement of dorsal and ventral
posterior brain streams in visual processing of "what" versus "where,"
respectively).[20] These observations therefore suggest brain correlates for
Baddeley's concepts of a verbal (left lateral frontal cortex) and a visuospatial scratchpad (occipital-parietal cortex).[21] The observations also highlight
limitations of the model in defining the complexity of visual processes.

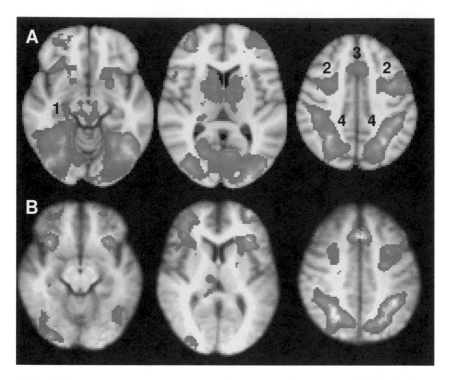

Figure 5.6
Functional magnetic resonance images illustrating localized activation of the brain
during a paired associate learning working memory task. Unnameable visual stimuli
were presented serially to each of 20 subjects at various locations on a computer
screen. Subjects were instructed to learn the locations of the stimuli during an *encoding* phase. Each stimulus was subsequently presented in order in the center of the
screen, cuing the subject to move a joystick to the appropriate location where this
image was first seen during the *recall* phase. The upper panels show brain activations
associated with encoding that include the right hippocampus (1) and the prefrontal
(2), cingulate (3), and parietal (4) cortices. The lower panels show a different pattern
of activation during recall, notably not involving significant hippocampal activation. The images illustrate the highly distributed nature of brain regions mediating
working memory even during a simple working memory task.
Images courtesy of the GlaxoSmithKline Clinical Imaging Centre, Hammersmith
Hospital, London.

The evidence is not consistent with the notion that there are *single* brain subsystems that uniquely correspond to these behaviorally distinguishable functionalities.

This becomes even more apparent when brain correlates of a central executive are explored. Brain activation with executive processing is not tightly localized, but is distributed widely in the brain, with the greatest relative activation in the superior frontal, dorsal lateral prefrontal and medial and lateral parietal cortices. Coordinating the continued *updating* and temporal ordering of information involves the superior frontal and dorsal lateral prefrontal cortices, in particular. Posteriorly, adjacent regions of midline parietal cortex known as the "cuneus" and "precuneus" (which have rich inputs from many regions of the brain) become more active with *manipulation* of information in working memory. The cuneus and precuneus are the metabolically most active regions of the brain, consistent with an especially high rate of local information processing. The anterior tip of the brain also shows greater activity, with more complex manipulations that involve, for example, matching new input against some rule that is being held "online." This distributed executive may be acting primarily to bias output from other brain regions to be consistent with the immediate cognitive objective.

Thus working memory, even more obviously than other forms of memory, cannot be localized meaningfully to a single region of the brain. It is an *emergent* property of functional interactions between highly associative neocortical regions (prefrontal and parietal cortices, cuneus and precuneus) and the rest of the brain.[22]

Why Do We Forget?

With approximately 100 billion neurons in the brain, each having perhaps 10,000 synapses, the brain has a tremendous capacity for the integrated storage of information. Some memories are maintained through most of a lifetime. Does forgetting simply represent a *failure* of effective consolidation or reconsolidation? Evolutionary biology presents an alternative view: because it facilitates selectivity for rapid, efficient recollection, forgetting may be, at least to some extent, adaptive.

The question of why we forget was addressed in a creative imaging study from Anthony Wagner's laboratory at Stanford University.[23] Wagner and colleagues asked subjects to memorize word pairs (each consisting of a cue and a target). The paired word list used the same cue word for multiple targets, creating ambiguity in the pairing with cue presentation alone. Some of the word pairs were practiced to consolidate these memories. They then tested the memories by presenting the cue word with the first letter of the target. Not surprisingly, subjects remembered the practiced pairs better than unpracticed pairs. There also was a clear differentiation between recollection of the targets of unpracticed word pairs. Word pairs that included a cue word unique to the unpracticed set were remembered more reliably. The subjects "selectively forgot" new cue-target associations when the associations were in conflict with a repeated (learned) pairing, which suggests that forgetting may be biased toward information in conflict with previously established memories.

The potential benefits of such selective forgetting for cognitive processing were suggested by the results of brain imaging subjects as they performed the cue-target word pair task. Repetition and stabilization of memory for this type of task are associated with reduced brain activity and more "efficient" cognitive processing (figure 5.7). Competition between target recall for cues was introduced to map brain regions responsible for suppression of conflicting information (active forgetting). fMRI scanning showed greater increases in activity of the anterior cingulate cortex (ACC) and greater reductions of activity in the prefrontal cortex in subjects who, as stronger "suppressors," displayed more selective recall of new pairings (figure 5.8). Knowledge of the kinds of processes that these two brain regions mediate provides clues to what is happening when we selectively forget. The anterior cingulate cortex is activated when cognitive inputs compete or conflict. Processing in the prefrontal cortex contributes to selectivity of response. A key aspect of memory is the selective retrieval of the most relevant information. Wagner and colleagues' study highlights that this retrieval process sets up "mnemonic conflict" during recollection. It suggests that selective forgetting brings benefits of increased efficiency (or reduced "cognitive cost").

From Systems to Molecules: The Basis for a Neuropharmacology of Memory

Cellular and molecular studies of memory provide a foundation for the development of treatments for diseases affecting memory. Most current

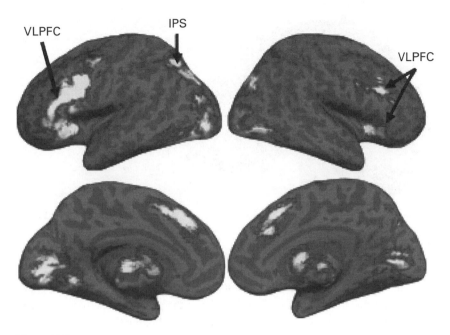

Figure 5.7

Functional magnetic resonance images illustrating how stabilization of an association memory leads to reduced brain activation for the same level of performance during recollection, and thus to greater cognitive "efficiency." Successful recollection improves with practice. For example, recall of the target word with presentation of its cue improves with repetition of paired word associations. With three practice repetitions to strengthen memories for word pairs, brain activity was reduced in several regions highlighted in the images acquired during performance of the task. Brain regions showing greater decreases in activity with repetition are represented as brighter on the gray scale. These images also demonstrate the important role of activity in the prefrontal cortex for selective memory retrieval. VLPFC, ventrolateral prefrontal cortex; IPS, intraparietal sulcus.

Reproduced with permission from Brice A. Kuhl et al., "Decreased Demands on Cognitive Control Reveal the Neural Processing Benefits of Forgetting," *Nature Neuroscience* 10 (2007): figure 2.

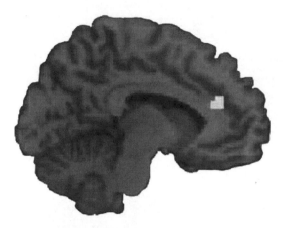

Figure 5.8

Brain image illustrating how recollection of new word pair associations is impaired when they conflict with those previously presented. In an extension of the experiment illustrated in figure 5.7, memories of new word pairings in conflict with previously established associations were suppressed in the paired word association task. This effect varied between subjects. The image here highlights a region of brain known as the "anterior cingulate cortex" (ACC), which has greater activity in subjects who showed greater suppression of conflicting new information (selective "forgetting"). Subjects who were more effective suppressors showed greater decreases of activity in the prefrontal cortex with practice (data not shown), suggesting that specific regions of the brain contribute to forgetting as an active process that facilitates cognitive efficiency for selective memory.

Reproduced with permission from Brice A. Kuhl et al., "Decreased Demands on Cognitive Control Reveal the Neural Processing Benefits of Forgetting," *Nature Neuroscience* 10 (2007): figure 3.

work is based on the premise that memory relies on increasing strengths of connections between key sets of neurons in the brain. Strengthening of *specific* connections between neurons for memory has special characteristics that correspond to what is now known as "Hebbian plasticity," after Donald Hebb, the Canadian neuropsychologist who described this phenomenon theoretically.

Long-term potentiation (LTP) displays properties that make it the best candidate for a correlate to memory at a cellular level.[24] Classical LTP is driven by release of the neurotransmitter glutamate, receptors for which lead to electrophysiological changes only when the postsynaptic cell is already depolarized by other, simultaneous inputs. Set against the glutamate-based facilitatory mechanisms for LTP is an inhibitory system based on release of the neurotransmitter gamma-aminobutyric acid (GABA). Acting through GABA-A receptors and released by a specialized set of interneurons that join with excitatory glutamatergic neurons to form local excitatory-inhibitory circuits, GABA allows local regulation of LTP.

Long-term potentiation provides a useful paradigm for memory formation even at a gross anatomical level. Processes analogous to LTP can be triggered in humans by applying repetitive pulses of small magnetic fields to the surface of the brain using transcranial magnetic stimulation (TMS), a simple, noninvasive, and painless procedure. TMS mimics simultaneous input volleys on accessible sets of neurons. Drugs can also modulate to normal memory processes in ways that can be predicted from studies of long-term potentiation. For example, the anesthetic ketamine (now a drug of abuse because of its curious "dissociative" cognitive effects), which antagonizes the action of the neurotransmitter glutamate, also transiently blocks formation of new memories when administered. Similarly, *agonists* (stimulators) of GABA-A receptors not only block experimental LTP, but also interfere with new memory formation.

Other neurotransmitters also have roles in memory processes, as well. For example, dopamine-containing neurons (whose progressive degeneration lies at the core of Parkinson's disease) likely play central roles in cognitive control processes contributing to working memory.[25] Improper regulation of *phasic* dopamine release may lead to "cognitive discoordination" in ways at least conceptually analogous to the breakdown of smooth movement sequences in Parkinson's disease. Lack of appropriate levels of *tonic* dopamine release may contribute to pathological destabilization of cognitive states.

Finding Drugs to Enhance Memory

A major goal in modern drug development has been to extend current understanding of the cellular and molecular basis for memory in order to identify safe, effective ways of enhancing LTP-like processes for memory in ways that could provide useful treatments for Alzheimer's and related diseases.[26] Unfortunately, drugs directly acting on glutaminergic or GABA-ergic receptors have not proven useful for memory enhancement thus far. It has been difficult to develop chemicals that directly stimulate glutamatergic receptors yet do not also cause undesirable levels of excitation of the brain (which would increase the likelihood of seizures). Flumazanil, a GABA antagonist acting at GABA-A receptors, reverses major effects of benzodiazepines (drugs related to diazepam or valium, once a popular antianxiety medication), as well as some forms of limited, experimentally induced amnesia in humans. There is no evidence that it reverses the major effects of Alzheimer's disease, however.

More emphasis in recent years has been placed on pharmacological approaches targeting neurotransmitters that *modulate* activity in the glutamatergic-GABA-ergic excitatory-inhibitory circuits. A potential advantage of this strategy is that these molecules may interfere less with control mechanisms essential to normal memory formation. There are several neurotransmitter systems that could enhance memory.[27] The monoamine molecules dopamine, noradrenaline, and serotonin (5-hydroxytryptamine) can enhance memory in some animal models, for example. Activation of the dopamine D1 receptor system enhances synaptic plasticity in the hippocampus. Noradrenaline (acting through its β-receptor) contributes to maintaining LTP after its induction, as well as to consolidation of particular forms of memory formation, such as fear conditioning. Blocking some actions of the neurotransmitter histamine, which helps to regulate the release of monoamines through its H3 receptor, can facilitate measures of memory in animal models, and, in particular, reverse the partial amnesia induced by scopolamine, an antagonist of the neurotransmitter acetylcholine, which acts at the muscarinic cholinergic receptor.

Acetylcholine has been the primary focus of memory enhancement strategies for at least three decades. Neurons that release acetylcholine are especially vulnerable in the early stages of Alzheimer's disease. Rivastrigmine and donepazil, both of which are currently marketed for symptomatic treatment of Alzheimer's disease work by inhibiting the breakdown of acetylcholine released at (cholinergic) synapses in the brain, enhancing the actions of cholinergic neurons.

Pathologies of Memory

The story of HM illustrates how much has been learned about memory from studies of patients with focal lesions of the brain. Natural pathologies of the brain also illustrate properties of memory. Conversely, understanding the mechanisms of memory contributes to fuller appreciation of the experience of patients suffering from diseases of memory.

A central tenet of the neurobiological hypothesis for mechanisms of memory is that long-term memories are not established immediately. As discussed from several perspectives in this volume, memories are fragile, especially soon after they are encoded. A striking clinical example of how fragile memories are before consolidation is provided by the behavior of patients with transient global amnesia (TGA). This curious syndrome occurs in otherwise healthy people and involves the transient loss of the ability to form new memories or to recall more recent (up to weeks or years) memories. Its rapid and sometimes dramatic onset can be mistaken for a confusional state, although patients are normally alert and attentive and can undertake even complex tasks. It typically resolves over hours, after which patients, though otherwise well, have a profound memory deficit not only for events during the amnesia, but also for those shortly before its onset, illustrating how vulnerable recently acquired memory traces are to disruption. Because onset of the syndrome cannot be anticipated, studies of TGA patients have been opportunistic.

More controlled data regarding consolidation come from studies of patients treated for depression with electroconvulsive therapy (ECT).[28] Immediately following treatment, these patients may show impairment of declarative memories even from the remote past. Over several months, memory partially recovers, with patients typically showing partial impairment of memories for about a two-year period prior to the ECT. Significantly, however, they show profound impairment of memories encoded within days of the ECT, the period of time when critical processes contributing to consolidation are thought to occur.

Korsakoff's syndrome provides an uncommon, but sobering demonstration of the extent to which proper functioning of even an organ as complex as the brain relies on simple chemicals. The syndrome, in which specific brain midline systems are profoundly damaged but neocortical systems remain intact, arises from a severe deficiency in thiamine (vitamin B_1) in people with, for example, chronic alcoholism or malnutrition. Thiamine is an essential cofactor for cellular metabolism, particularly in the brain. Deficiency leads to injury and death of neurons in the mammillary bodies, a part of the subcortical gray matter just below the base of the cerebrum, and in the middle regions of the thalamus to which these neurons connect.

The syndrome is characterized by severe anterograde and retrograde amnesia. What is most extraordinary is that patients display no insight into the memory loss. They become highly suggestible and can engage in sometimes florid confabulations in which they invent or accept sometimes patently false stories as true "memories." For example, if a researcher is wearing a hospital white coat on meeting a patient with Korsakoff's syndrome, the patient can be prompted not only to falsely recollect the wearer to be his or her doctor, but also to confabulate meeting on multiple occasions before. Unlike Alzheimer's disease, Korsakoff's syndrome does not lead to significant deficits of implicit memories, despite the profound impairment of declarative memory. Sadly, though preventable with good nutrition, the disease cannot be treated.

In his most celebrated novel, *One Hundred Years of Solitude*, Colombian Nobel laureate Gabriel García Márquez describes the consequences of a slowly progressive loss of memory. After a mysterious insomnia plague attacks the South American village of Macondo, villagers first find it difficult to recall less commonly used words. "One day [the village blacksmith] was looking for the small anvil that he used for laminating metals and he could not remember its name. ... This was the first manifestation of a loss of memory, because the object had a difficult name to remember."[29] Semantic memories are then lost to the point where villagers need explicit reminders of how to perform even everyday activities: "This is a cow. She must be milked every morning so she will produce milk and the milk must be boiled."[30] In later stages of the disease, the villagers' personal histories become inaccessible and they cannot recognize even family members as they sink "irrevocably into a quicksand of forgetfulness." Fortunately, a cure is found. We have not yet been so fortunate with real memory loss, whose symptoms Márquez describes so well.

Progressive loss of memory from Alzheimer's disease, the most common dementia syndrome of older age, affects as many as 1 in 4 people over the age of 65. Like Márquez's insomnia plague, the most typical form of Alzheimer's disease begins with impairments of declarative memory, initially manifest as lapses of memory such as forgetting appointments or recent conversations. Over time, this develops into disabling forgetfulness for common day-to-day activities, major events and even names or relationships to friends. Working memory also is affected from the early stages of Alzheimer's. Just as for Márquez's fictional characters, memory loss can be compensated for partially by cues, but such compensation is complicated by an increasing frequency of misattributions and eventually is lost. In later stages, patients suffer from a profound loss of memory, inability to recognize even close family members, and sustained disorientiation to time, place, and personal history.

Distant memories appear better preserved than more recent ones in early to moderate Alzheimer's disease. However, neuropsychologists who have studied this phenomenon closely believe that it is more a reflection of the greater number of early memories or their relative lack of specificity, instead of a selective preservation. In an attempt to test this objectively, recognition of images of people who became well known in different years was tested and shown to decrease similarly across the life-span.[31]

Semantic memory is lost along with episodic memory. In the earlier stages of the disease, patients typically will provide a functional description (e.g., referring to a "comb" as that "hair thing") or use a word for another object of the same type (e.g., "brush" for "comb") when struggling to recall a needed word. Object naming difficulties contribute to the loss of verbal fluency and an increasing poverty of thought. A unique opportunity to chart the progressive sparseness of vocabulary in Alzheimer's patients over time presented itself in the later works of the famous Oxford author Iris Murdoch, who was still writing in the early stages of the disease.[32] An additional curious observation has been that some patients seem to have greater problems in recognizing living things, while naming of nonliving things is more impaired for others.

Implicit memories are not spared. Impairments of coordinated patterns of movement (*dyspraxias*) develop and even well-learned skills are lost. Nonetheless, patients in the earlier stages of Alzheimer's disease can learn motor skills just as fast as healthy people. Forms of perceptual learning also are unaffected.

While symptoms may show some fluctuation, memory loss with Alzheimer's disease is irreversible; patients sink in a "quicksand of forgetfulness." Ultimately, Alzheimer's patients become fully dependent on others and enter a state of inanition—unable to recognize even those close to them and unable to perform even simple tasks for themselves. They appear to lose their identities, as well as their capacity for intelligent response.

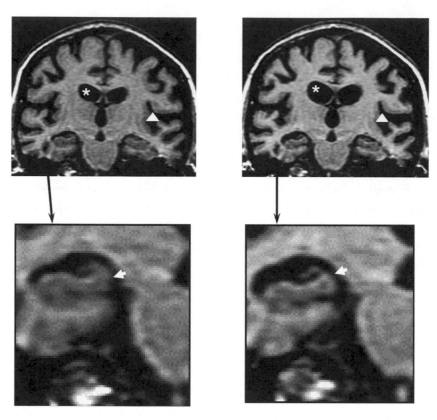

Figure 5.9

Brain images acquired during two examinations of a patient with Alzheimer's disease over a period of eighteen months. Progressive neurodegeneration in Alzheimer's disease is accompanied by loss of brain volume, especially marked in the hippocampus, an early site of pathology in the disease. Between the two examinations, the fluid-filled central *ventricles* of the brain have expanded (the right ventricle is marked with an asterisk), as have the depth and width of the *sulci* (one of which is marked with a white triangle) separating gyral folds on the surface of the brain. The lower images show changes in the right hippocampal formation (identified with an arrowhead) in coronal sections, illustrating how dramatically the two hippocampi atrophied even over this short observation period. Brain atrophy in Alzheimer's disease is related to loss of both neurites and neurons.

Image courtesy of Prof. Nick Fox, University College, London.

The inexorable progression of symptoms is a consequence of progressive neuronal degeneration and death (figure 5.9). Macroscopically, Alzheimer's disease is characterized most obviously by atrophy of the brain. The specific neuropathological hallmark of the disease that can be observed with a microscope is the loss of neurons accompanied by the formation of dense "plaques" of β-amyloid protein and intracellular "tangles" made from the neuronal tau protein. Now that plaques of β-amyloid can now be imaged in the living brain, studies have made clear that the deposition of amyloid can precede the development of disease by many years.[33]

What makes patients with Alzheimer's disease so profoundly impaired in comparison to those with, for example, Korsakoff's syndrome, is that Alzheimer's involves the death not only of hippocampal neurons, but also of neurons in widely interconnecting brain regions, including particularly those in the temporal and parietal lobes (figure 5.10). The latter changes account for the severity of language deficits. By contrast, relative sparing of the motor cortex explains preservation of new motor skill learning.

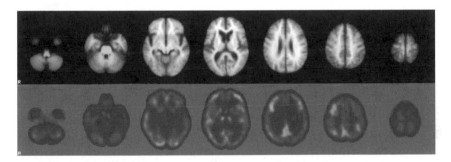

Figure 5.10
Brain images acquired from a population of Alzheimer's patients studied twice over a one-year period. Brain activity decreases progressively over time as dementia worsens in patients with Alzheimer's disease. This decrease in brain activity can be measured using PET imaging as changes in the rate with which the brain metabolizes the glucose analog, fluorodeoxyglucose (FDG). The upper images show composite MRI scans of the brains of the subjects studied. The lower images show corresponding composite PET scans, which represent *changes* in FDG uptake over the one-year period. The gray scale defines the magnitude of the decline in FDG uptake in the gray matter of the brain; brighter areas had greater decreases. Note that these changes are widespread across the cortex.
Images courtesy of the GlaxoSmithKline Clinical Imaging Centre, Hammersmith Hospital, London.

The mechanisms responsible for neurodegeneration in Alzheimer's disease are not well understood. A leading hypothesis is that abnormal expression of the β-amyloid protein, which is toxic for nerve cells, may be responsible. Rare forms of early-onset Alzheimer's disease can be linked to genetic defects in the amyloid protein gene or in enzymes responsible for its processing. Research also has implicated tau aggregation in the genesis of the disease, as other forms of dementia are caused by abnormalities specific to this protein. Additional clues to what is likely to prove to be a very complex, interacting range of mechanisms are coming from epidemiological studies demonstrating an increased incidence of Alzheimer's disease in people with a history of diabetes or vascular disease.

For a more nuanced perspective, let us return to HM, who lost most or all episodic memory and was unable to form new semantic memories, but remained able to communicate and interact at a high level. What were the implications to him of the profound loss of memories of a personal history? The Harvard neuropsychologist Susan Corkin, who was able to work with HM through most of her scientific career, has reflected movingly on this.[34] She describes HM as a person of conscience with high moral standards and a good sense of humor, who had a clear sense of self, despite his deficits. She speculates that this was based on a framework for a self-concept provided by those remote memories that were spared (even if they were "semanticized") and on a clear, personal set of values.

It is worth noting that impairments related to memory need not all arise simply from the *loss* of memory. The Argentinian author Jorge Luis Borges, in his fantastical short story "Funes el memorioso" (translated as "Funes the Memorious" or "Funes, His Memory"), imagines a 19-year-old boy living in South America in the latter part of the nineteenth century who, after a fall from his horse, becomes both bedridden with chronic physical injuries and mentally transformed in a remarkable way: he remembers everything, even the most transient of perceptions: "He knew the forms of clouds in the southern sky on the morning of April 30, 1882, and he could compare them in his memory with the veins in the marbled binding of a book he had seen only once. … Funes remembered not only every leaf of every tree in every patch of forest, but every time he had perceived or imagined that leaf."[35] A friend of Funes, who runs a literary magazine, describes him as "a precursor of a race of supermen." In Borges's view, however, Funes is as crippled mentally as he is physically. He describes Funes lying down at night, reflecting on a new section of town that he has not visited. "He pictured [the new houses] as black, compact, made of homogeneous shadow. ... He was not very good at thinking. To think is to ignore (or forget) differences, to generalize, to abstract."[36] Declarative memory for Funes is precise, but inflexible. He cannot use memories to *imagine*. The Canadian neuropsychologist Endel Tulving has reflected that memory should allow each of us to effortlessly travel in time, relying on memory for the past to project a possible future.[37] This ability is lost to Funes.

Borges's 1942 story has surprisingly close correspondences to a real clinical case that the Soviet neuropsychologist A. R. Luria later described as a study of the "mnemonist S."[38] Luria recounts how S, who started work a newspaper reporter, came to his laboratory in the 1920s. S had been encouraged to seek Luria's help by his editor, who was amazed that S—who never recorded notes as the long list of tasks was assigned to each reporter at the start of each day—could nonetheless effortlessly recount assignments word for word. Luria noted that S did not even need to make a strong conscious effort to remember. He would listen, sometimes closing his eyes in apparent concentration, and, then, after a pause of only a few seconds, be able to repeat what had been presented to him exactly, whether meaningful or not, orally or written, in the order given or in reverse. He could also recall exact details of the context within which he became aware of any information he recalled.

Much of Luria's research with S focused on trying to understand how the memories were formed. S appeared to be able to mentally "see" words or numbers presented or to otherwise transform what he wished to recall into visual images. An extraordinary automatic elaboration of data was apparent in the visual images he created. Luria reports S as saying, "When I hear the word *green*, a green flowerpot appears; with the word *red* I see a man in a red shirt coming toward me. ... Even numbers remind me of images. Take the number 1. This is a proud, well-built man."[39] S showed clear symptoms of *synesthesia*, a syndrome in which information from different sensory pathways becomes mixed in perception, with letters or numbers often perceived as intrinsically colored. He found no distinction between sensations of color and sound or between those of taste and touch: S "walked over to the vendor and asked her what kind of ice cream she had. 'Fruit ice cream,' she said. But she answered back in such a tone that a whole pile of coals, of black cinders, came bursting out of her mouth and I couldn't bring myself to buy any ice cream."[40]

This begins to illustrate the maladaptiveness of the peculiar mind that has this extraordinary memory. Luria explains how S's need to automatically classify information—so helpful for memory—limited his ability to *understand*. S was incapable of appreciating nuanced words or words with multiple meanings, as in a poem, for example. He could not maintain the multiple simultaneous and conflicting mental images that poetry evokes. He complained that poetry created such a jumble of images that he became too distracted to grasp the meaning of a sentence. Complex or abstract relationships were difficult for him in general. In the end, despite his extraordinary memory, the only career S could find was as an entertainer, a "mnemonist," whose prodigious memory was limited to its most literal application.

From our current perspective, it is tempting to speculate that the extraordinary skills of the mnemonist may reflect hyperfunction of the more inflexible memory mechanisms we associate with implicit memory, somehow brought to conscious awareness, with loss of the flexible, relational elements of usual declarative memory. The association with synesthesia is especially intriguing because this syndrome has been hypothesized to reflect abnormal plasticity of connections linking the thalamus and neocortex.[41]

Memory may be the most fundamental of higher cognitive processes. It is through memory that we access the world beyond immediate perception. Memory also provides the foundations for expectations of the future, allowing us to adapt our behaviors to best prepare for what *could* be.

The current scientific understanding of memory is still incomplete. Yet even though we cannot explain how a specific memory is encoded and accessed, we can be confident that a strong framework has been established for revealing the mechanisms of memory. Our recent realization that it is changes in molecular and cellular interactions that allow us to re-create a beautiful sunset or the feeling of first love may have even more profound consequences for humankind than did the realization that the same force that allows an apple to drop also determines the structure of our solar system.

As this and other chapters in this volume attest, memory studies also illustrate how literary imagination, psychology, cognitive neuroscience, and neurobiology, however distinct their modes of inquiry, are all reaching toward consilience with convergent concepts of memory. The complexity of modern neuroimaging tools often obscures the central purpose of cognitive neuroscience, which is simply to ask important questions, image possible outcomes, and test these against close observation and experience. Expressed in this way, much of the perceived divide between neuroscience and the humanities becomes a matter of using different approaches and different tools to achieve the same ends.

Diseases of memory will affect us all in some major way over the course of our lives. Whether we suffer memory loss ourselves or care for a loved one who does, understanding both the mechanisms and the phenomena of memory is important. There is now a well-founded hope that this understanding will lead, if not to full knowledge of memory, then to effective new treatments of its diseases in the near future.

Notes

1. Paul M. Matthews and Peter Jezzard, "Functional Magnetic Resonance Imaging," *Journal of Neurology, Neurosurgery & Psychiatry* 75 (2004): 6–12.

2. Suzanne Corkin, "What's New with the Amnesic Patient H.M?" *Nature Reviews Neuroscience* 3 (2002): 153–160.

3. David H. Salat at al., "Neuroimaging H.M.: A 10-Year Follow-Up Examination," *Hippocampus* 16 (2006): 936–943.

4. Nancy L. Rempel-Clower et al., "Three Cases of Enduring Memory Impairment after Bilateral Damage Limited to the Hippocampal Formation," *Journal of Neuroscience* 16 (1996): 5233–5255.

5. Peter E. Wais, "fMRI Signals Associated with Memory Strength in the Medial Temporal Lobes: A Meta-analysis," *Neuropsychologia* 46 (2008): 3185–3196.

6. Larry R. Squire, Craig E. Stark, and Robert E. Clark, "The Medial Temporal Lobe," *Annual Review of Neuroscience* 27 (2004): 279–306.

7. Christine N. Smith and Larry R. Squire, "Medial Temporal Lobe Activity during Retrieval of Semantic Memory Is Related to the Age of the Memory," *Journal of Neuroscience* 29 (2009): 930–938.

8. James L. McClelland, Bruce L. McNaughton, and Randall C. O'Reilly, "Why There Are Complementary Learning Systems in the Hippocampus and Neocortex: Insights from the Successes and Failures of Connectionist Models of Learning and Memory," *Psychological Review* 102 (1995): 419–457.

9. C. N. Smith and L. R. Squire, "Medial Temporal Lobe Activity during Retrieval of Semantic Memory is Related to the Age of the Memory."

10. Charan Ranganath and Mark D'Esposito, "Medial Temporal Lobe Activity Associated with Active Maintenance of Novel Information," *Neuron* 31 (2001): 865–873.

11. Atsuko Takashima et al., "Shift from Hippocampal to Neocortical Centered Retrieval Network with Consolidation," *Journal of Neuroscience* 29 (2009): 10087–10093.

12. John O'Keefe, "Place Units in the Hippocampus of the Freely Moving Rat," *Experimental Neurology* 51 (1976): 78–109.

13. Eleanor A. Maguire et al., "Knowing Where and Getting There: A Human Navigation Network," *Science* 280 (1998): 921–924.

14. Eleanor A. Maguire et al., "Navigation-Related Structural Change in the Hippocampi of Taxi Drivers," *Proceedings of the National Academy of Sciences USA* 97 (2000): 4398–4403.

15. Claire D. Clelland et al., "A Functional Role for Adult Hippocampal Neurogenesis in Spatial Pattern Separation," *Science* 325 (2009): 210–213.

16. Neil Burgess, Eleanor A. Maguire, and John O'Keefe, "The Human Hippocampus and Spatial and Episodic Memory," *Neuron* 35 (2002): 625–641.

17. N. Burgess, E. A. Maguire, and J. O'Keefe, "The Human Hippocampus and Spatial and Episodic Memory."

18. Alan Baddeley, "Working Memory: Looking Back and Looking Forward," *Nature Reviews Neuroscience* 4 (2003): 829–839.

19. Tor D. Wager and Edward E. Smith, "Neuroimaging Studies of Working Memory: A Meta-analysis," *Cognitive, Affective & Behavioral Neuroscience* 3 (2003): 255–274.

20. Leslie G. Ungerleider and James V. Haxby, "'What' and 'Where' in the Human Brain," *Current Opinion in Neurobiology* 4 (1994): 157–165.

21. A. Baddeley, "Working Memory: Looking Back and Looking Forward."

22. Mark D'Esposito, "From Cognitive to Neural Models of Working Memory," *Philosophical Transactions of the Royal Society of London* B 362 (2007): 761–772.

23. Brice A. Kuhl et al., "Decreased Demands on Cognitive Control Reveal the Neural Processing Benefits of Forgetting," *Nature Neuroscience* 10 (2007): 908–914.

24. S. F. Cooke and T. V. P. Bliss, "Plasticity in the Human Central Nervous System," *Brain* 129 (2006): 1659–1673.

25. Roshan Cools and Trevor W. Robbins, "Chemistry of the Adaptive Mind," *Philosophical Transactions of the Royal Society of London* A 362 (2004): 2871–2888.

26. Iván Izquierdo et al., "Pharmacological Findings on the Biochemical Bases of Memory Processes: A General View," *Neural Plasticity* 11 (2004): 159–189.

27. I. Izquierdo et al., "Pharmacological Findings on the Biochemical Bases of Memory Processes: A General View."

28. Lorena Rami-Gonzalez et al., "Subtypes of Memory Dysfunction Associated with ECT: Characteristics and Neurobiological Bases," *Journal of ECT* 17 (2001): 129–135.

29. Gabriel García Márquez, *One Hundred Years of Solitude,* trans. Gregory Rabassa (London: Picador, 1978).

30. G. G. Márquez, *One Hundred Years of Solitude* (1978): 45.

31. David W. Greene and John R. Hodges, "Identification of Famous Faces and Famous Names in Early Alzheimer's Disease: Relationship to Anterograde and General Semantic Memory," *Brain* 119 (1996): 111–128.

32. Peter Garrard et al., "The Effects of Very Early Alzheimer's Disease on the Characteristics of Writing by a Renowned Author," *Brain* 128 (2005): 250–260.

33. Milos D. Ikonomovic et al., "Post-mortem Correlates of *in Vivo* Pib-PET Amyloid Imaging in a Typical Case of Alzheimer's Disease," *Brain* 131 (2008): 1630–1645.

34. S. Corkin, "What's New with the Amnesic Patient H.M?"

35. Jorge Luis Borges, "Funes, His Memory," *Fictions* (2000): 96–98.

36. J. L. Borges, "Funes, His Memory." *Fictions* (2000): 91

37. R. Shayna Rosenbaum et al., "The Case of K.C.: Contributions of a Memory-Impaired Person to Memory Theory," *Neuropsychologia* 43 (2005): 989–1021.

38. A. R. Luria, *The Mind of a Mnemonist: A Little Book about a Vast Memory,* trans. Lynn Solotaroff (Cambridge, MA: Harvard University Press, 1968).

39. A. R. Luria, *The Mind of a Mnemonist: A Little Book about a Vast Memory.* (1968): 31.

40. A. R. Luria, *The Mind of a Mnemonist: A Little Book about a Vast Memory.* (1968): 82.

41. Tony Ro et al., "Feeling Sounds after a Thalamic Lesion," *Annals of Neurology* 62 (2007): 433–441.

6 Memory as a Constructive Process: The Parallel Distributed Processing Approach

James L. McClelland

In Harold Pinter's play *Old Times*, a husband and wife of many years reminisce about the early days of their relationship while awaiting a visit from the wife's best friend at that time. We learn just how differently two people can remember the same events and the same people—most notably, themselves and the wife's best friend. For each, these reminiscences have become embedded in a complex, inconsistent, and self-serving personal history that does not stand up well to the reminiscences of the other.

When asked to comment on his thoughts while writing the play, Pinter replied, "What interests me a great deal is the mistiness of the past."[1] Cloudlike, forever changing, memories are clearly not like snapshots taken on a day long ago and pulled out years later from the back of a drawer. Indeed, since the work of Frederic Bartlett in 1932, memory researchers have been keenly aware of the constructive nature of memory.[2] Bartlett asked educated people at Cambridge to read and later to recall a story from a native North American culture. Both the structure and the content of the story were unfamiliar to the participants. Their recollections retained elements from the original story but omitted many details or transformed them in ways that seemed to Bartlett to fit better with the cultural context of those recalling them. Repeated attempts at recall by the same individual resulted in the gradual fixing of the elements, but into a story sometimes quite different from the original. Such findings led Bartlett and others to view recollection as a process much like reconstructing a dinosaur from a collection of bones. The final result contains the fragments of possibly several dinosaurs, and many parts are filled in based on the paleontologists' knowledge of other, similar dinosaurs. Close resemblance to any real creature that once lived is far from guaranteed.

The idea of memory as a constructive process, which clearly has its advocates in both science and the humanities, provides a useful bridge between the two worlds. This chapter offers a scientific theory of the nature of human memory that fits this constructive perspective very naturally. This theory, the complementary learning systems theory, is grounded in a broad framework for understanding human cognitive processes called the parallel distributed processing (PDP) framework, a framework I participated in developing with David Rumelhart and others in 1986.[3] The theory of memory was developed in the early 1990s and presented in a 1995 paper by Bruce McNaughton, Randall O'Reilly, and myself.[4] At that time, the focus was on one of the theory's two complementary learning systems, a fast-learning system in the medial temporal lobes of the brain. Subsequent work with Timothy Rogers, presented in *Semantic Cognition* (2004), focused on the other, slow-learning system, located elsewhere in the neocortex.[5]

After introducing the groundwork, this chapter lays out the theory itself, distinguishing it from other researchers' approaches to the neuroscience of memory. It then considers recent developments, as well as questions about the theory and its relevance to the humanities.

Neurons and Synapses: The Physical Substrate for Representation and Memory

The complementary learning systems theory is grounded in a way of thinking about representation and memory in the brain that arose in the 1980s. It started with the crucial physiological building blocks of the brain: neurons and synapses. The human brain contains nearly 100 billion neurons, and each neuron has from 1,000 to 100,000 synapses: points of contact with other neurons. A famous drawing by the nineteenth-century neuroanatomist Santiago Ramón y Cajal, shown in figure 6.1, evokes a sense of the overall structure.[6] The treatment Ramón y Cajal used caused one out of every 100 neurons in a thin slice of brain tissue to turn black, allowing him to clearly see the structure of individual neurons—the pyramid-like blobs in the figure—as he gazed through his microscope. Coming out of each cell body are several branching structures—the dendrites, whose thicker branches reach up and to the sides of the cell body, and the narrow axon, which arises from the bottom of the cell's body and projects downward, with finer branches that turn back up into the tissue. Not

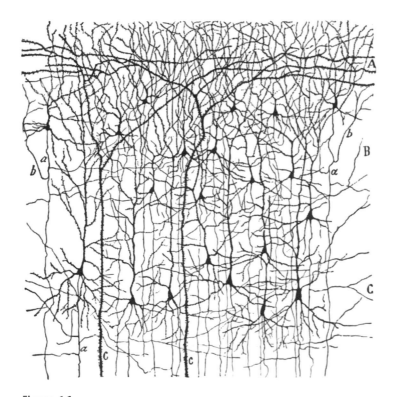

Figure 6.1
Microanatomy of the cerebral cortex, as drawn by the Spanish neuroanatomist
Santiago Ramón y Cajal.
Reproduced from Santiago Ramón y Cajal, *Comparative Study of the Sensory Areas of
the Human Cortex* (Worcester, MA: Clark University, 1899), 325.

shown are the dense branching of these axons into tiny filaments and the
terminals of these axons on the dendrites. The little bumps along the
dendrites, called "synaptic boutons," are the main locations where connections are made between neurons. Envision, if you will, this structure in
its full three-dimensional splendor, with dendrites and axons branching
out to the front and to the back as well as to the sides, and with 100 times
as many neurons packed into the same space. This is just one cubic millimeter of the human brain, only about 1 millionth of its entire volume.

Neurons and synapses constitute the physical substrate for our active
mental states and our memories. An active mental state can arise from
perception, of the sound of a person's name, for example, or the sight of

a person's face, or from thinking, as when we see a cat creeping up on a bird and think that the bird may fly away. In the complementary learning systems theory, these active mental states are patterns of activation over populations of neurons across many regions of the neocortex of our brain. This raises two questions: How are different aspects of mental content localized in different brain regions and within brain regions? And is mental content localized in individual neurons?

We can address the first question with the help of figure 6.2, which shows two views of the left hemisphere of a typical brain. In the upper panel, the hemisphere is seen from its left, outer side; in the lower one, it is tilted onto its flat, inner side, so that we are looking at what is usually its underside. Most of the colored regions (shown in shades of gray) illustrate areas that become active when a person perceives or is asked to bring to mind a particular kind of information about an object. In one valuable experiment, participants were shown a series of words denoting common objects. They were asked to think of the color of each object or of the action performed on or with it. In the first case, activation was found in the region labeled "Color"; in the second, in the region labeled "Action." Other studies have fairly well established that different kinds of information—about faces, for example, or about the sound, articulation, or spelling of words—are represented in different, specialized regions of the brain, some relevant to those illustrated in figure 6.2.

Representations of spoken language—for example, representations of the sounds of spoken words or of the pattern of gestures associated with pronouncing a word—may also be activated. When we hear the sound of a word, or when we think of producing a spoken word, it produces activation in the areas labeled "speech" in figure 6.2. Of the two regions shown, the one more toward the front of the brain appears to be more strongly associated with production of speech, whereas the elongated area below it is more strongly associated with perception or understanding of speech; but activations in these areas are often intercorrelated, suggesting that perceiving and producing speech are strongly integrated.

Localized versus Distributed Representation

The role of individual neurons within each brain region is less settled. One view holds that individual neurons stand for entities or properties of entities we recognize intuitively and can easily label or describe. A

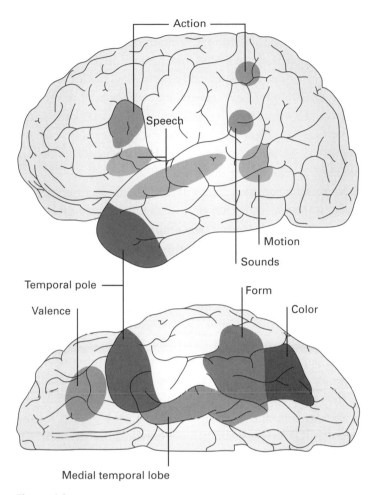

Figure 6.2
Left hemisphere of the human brain as seen from the side (top) and from below (bottom), showing areas that become active when a person processes different kinds of information about an object, including the spoken word form or the object's name.
Adapted from J. L. McClelland and T. T. Rogers, "The Parallel Distributed Processing Approach to Semantic Cognition," *Nature Reviews Neuroscience* 4 (2003): 315.

representation of this type is often called a "local" representations (local to an individual neuron), or sometimes a "grandmother cell" representation because among the things an individual neuron might represent is something as specific as one's grandmother. In this view, upon seeing grandmother, one or perhaps a few neurons have the specialized role of representing the crinkly lines around grandmother's eyes, others the grayish tint of her hair; and most controvertially still other neurons have the specialized role of representing that it is grandmother. This readily comprehensible view is still widely discussed.[7]

The alternative to local representation, distributed representation, has a long history, and was set forth within the parallel distributed processing (PDP) framework by Geoffrey E. Hinton, David Rumelhart, and myself.[8] In distributed representations, the focus is on the pattern of activation as a whole, and not on the individual neuron. In this view, each individual neuron participates in the representation of many different things, and no neurons are dedicated to individual items. What is of the essence here is that the representations of things similar in the kind of information represented (the action performed on or with an object, for example) involve highly overlapping populations of neurons. Among neurons representing the visual appearance of a cheetah, a leopard, and a flamingo, for example, the pattern for the visual appearance of the cheetah and the leopard will have far more units in common than either has with the pattern for the flamingo. The similarities in information represented can be of many different types, including similarities in such abstract domains as activities or even likelihood of extinction.

An Integrative Representation Independent of Any Specific Kind of Content?

As another of its distinctive features, the complementary learning systems theory calls for an area in the neocortex where there is an integrative representation of all sorts of things, encompassing all aspects of their content.[9] Research is ongoing on this issue, but some evidence points to the possibility that such a representation may exist in the anterior temporal cortex, sometimes called the "temporal pole," and labeled as such in figure 6.2. According to the theory, whether we hear the word *dog*, or hear a dog barking, or see a dog, or think about how a dog responds when greeting our houseguests, a representation is initially activated in the regions directly related to the input (e.g., for the spoken word, the receptive language area), and this then gives rise to a pattern of activation in our anterior temporal cortex. These patterns in anterior temporal cortex then give rise to patterns of activation in other areas corresponding to the particular type of content they represent. What this allows is for any type of input—a name, a face, the sound of a voice, or an aroma—to bring back all other aspects of the item cued by the given input. Note that the principle that similar things produce similar patterns still applies. Each particular thought of a particular dog will evoke a slightly different representation, and these will generally be more similar to each other than they are to the representations of other things.

The Knowledge Is in the Connections: Acquisition of Semantic Memory through Connection Adjustment

When a speaker produces the word *dog*, vibrations reach the ear, giving rise to the firing of neurons in the auditory pathway. How can this give rise to a pattern of activation corresponding to the typical color of a dog or of the sound of the dog barking, or of the way the dog wags its tail? According to the complementary learning systems theory, this depends on the pattern of interconnection among neurons. Connections carry signals from neurons in the ear to neurons in primary auditory cortex, and from there to neurons in higher auditory cortex. Perhaps through further intermediaries, connections then carry signals to the neurons that participate in the integrative representation, and still other connections carry signals from these to neurons representing each of the different kinds of content (The reader is invited to envision two-way bundles of nerve fibers, connecting each of the areas labeled with a specific type of content with the anterior temporal lobe; these pathways appear as solid lines in figure 6.4). The connections in the auditory pathway itself are initialized early in development before the eyes open. For our present purposes, we can treat these connections as if they were fixed. But how do we activate the neural pattern for the color, shape, sounds, and movements of a dog from a neural representation of the spoken word *dog*, or conversely how do we activate the sound of the word upon seeing a dog or hearing it bark? Clearly, knowledge acquired from experience is necessary, since the relationship between the word and the objects that it stands for is idiosyncratic and language specific. For this reason, many researchers treat this knowledge as a form of memory—often called "semantic memory." In our theory, memory of this kind and memories of other kinds are stored in connections. The idea that knowledge and memory are stored in connections is sometimes called "connectionism," and theories based on this idea are often called "connectionist theories."

A schematic illustration of this concept is shown in figure 6.3. Let us imagine, for concreteness, that we are considering connections that allow a pattern corresponding to the sound of the name of an object to produce

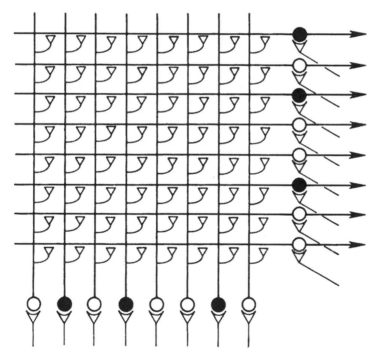

Figure 6.3
Simplified neural network that can learn to associate one kind of information about an object (such as the sound of the word designating its name) with another (such as the object's visual appearance). Each kind of information is represented as a pattern of activation (active units are shown in black; inactive units in white). The learned association depends on strengthened connections from the units active in one representation to the units active in the other.
Adapted from James L. McClelland and David E. Rumelhart, *Explorations in Parallel Distributed Processing: A Handbook of Models, Programs, and Exercises* (Cambridge, MA: MIT Press, 1988), 90.

a pattern corresponding to another kind of information, what the object looks like, for example (this is a simplification of the theory as discussed above, where we noted that the integrative representation actually mediates between the name of an object and other kinds of information about it). At the outset of learning, synaptic connections between the neurons in the auditory representation and those in the visual representation are thought to be weak and nonspecific. In this situation, the activation of the pattern for the sound of a word and the closely following activation of the pattern for the appearance of the object it denotes create the conditions needed for strengthening the connections from the neurons active in the sound representation to the neurons active in the visual representation.

The idea that pre- then post-synaptic activation will lead to the strengthening of connections among neurons is a variant of the famous proposal of Donald Hebb in 1949,[10] widely discussed in other chapters of this volume. Hebb established a starting point for a large number of experimental investigations and computational models of the underlying physical process that provides the substrate for learning and memory. The exact formulation of the details of the "synaptic modification rule" is a subject of considerable ongoing investigation both in computational and experimental investigations.

How the brain achieves its remarkable success in making connection adjustments that successfully form the substrate of learning and memory is still not fully understood. It is assumed that the brain can do so even when intermediate or "hidden" neurons, like those in our integrative layer, are involved. Such a network is illustrated schematically in figure 6.4. Inputs of different kinds specify the patterns of activation representing different kinds of information about a known thing or item, but do not specify what pattern should be used for the item's representation on the integrative layer. Using a sophisticated connection adjustment rule,[11] it is possible for repeated experience with many different known things to produce useful cumulative adjustments to the connections. The presentation of any unique aspect of one of these known things (the aroma of a rose or the prick of its thorns; the bark of a dog or the spoken word *dog*) will give rise to activation of an item-specific pattern on the hidden layer and of the appropriate item-specific patterns across all of the visible layers.[12]

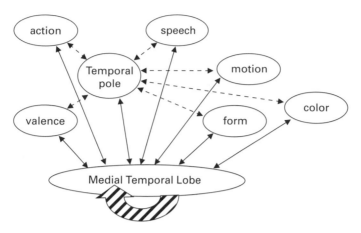

Figure 6.4
Schematic diagram of the brain network thought to underlie memory in the complementary learning systems theory. Ovals represent neuron-rich brain areas that, apart
from the medial temporal lobe, are all thought to be parts of the slow-learning
neocortical system. Dashed, bidirectonal arrows represent projections or bundles of
axons that carry signals between neocortical brain areas. Solid arrows represent
projections or fiber bundles that carry signals between the neocortex and the medial
temporal lobes. The heavy, looping arrow connecting the medial temporal lobe to
itself represents the highly plastic synaptic connections within the medial temporal
lobe. It is changes in these connections that form the initial substrate of a new
arbitrary associative memory.

What Is the Memory Trace of an Experience?

What is most important in the present context is not the exact nature of
the connection adjustment rule, but the more fundamental fact that the
memory trace left behind by a specific experience is *a pattern of connection
adjustments*. Unlike the standard view of the memory trace as a record of
the experience itself that can be separately filed away, somewhat like a
memorandum, for subsequent retrieval, the complementary learning
systems theory holds that memory traces of different experiences are not
kept separate. In the case of words and the objects they denote, each
object's name will be a pattern of activation that overlaps with the patterns
for the names of other objects, and each object's visual representation will
be a pattern that overlaps with the patterns for the visual representations
of other objects. Repeated experiences in which we hear the word *dog* and
see a dog will gradually lead to the buildup of strong connections allowing

the word to activate the visual pattern. Repeated experiences with other similar objects or objects with similar names will, also, affect the same connections.

According to the theory, then, there is no real possibility of retrieving a specific memory. A memory does not exist in its own separate storage location—its residue in the brain is distributed over many synaptic connections, whose values have also been shaped by many other experiences. Thus, for example, remembering what a dog looks like upon hearing the word *dog* is always a constructive process, one that involves the participation of influences arising from many experiences overlapping with each other in various ways and to various degrees. In a nutshell, remembering in a system that uses connection adjustment between neurons participating in distributed representation is intrinsically a constructive process. With this in mind, let us now consider some important facts that have played a key role in shaping the development of the complementary learning systems theory.

Key Discoveries about the Brain Basis of Memory

Our understanding of the brain basis of memory took a quantum leap forward after the surgeon William Scoville removed both left and right medial temporal lobes from the patient HM to treat his intractable epilepsy.[13] Upon waking up after the surgery, HM recognized family members and appeared able to converse normally. In formal testing, his IQ was not diminished, and he performed at least as well as he had previously on tests of general knowledge, vocabulary, and memory of events in the early periods of his life. Moreover, he could carry out attention-demanding tasks at normal levels. As is well known, however, HM exhibited profound and striking deficits. Most notably, he could not form new memories either of people or events. A person not previously known to HM could come into his hospital room and carry on a conversation with him for any length of time; if the person then left the room even for a minute or two and came back in again, HM would neither recognize the person nor remember the conversation they had been engaged in only moments before. This profound deficit in the ability to form new memories has been documented in many other patients with similar patterns of brain damage—indeed, in some whose memory deficit is even more profound than HM's. Further studies of HM and many similar patients underscore three additional important points.[14]

Normal Acquisition of Skills

In one study, HM was repeatedly asked to trace a figure while viewing the figure and his hand in a mirror. Like others, he was initially bad at this, often making movements in the wrong direction. With practice he improved, however, and he appeared to improve at about the same rate as healthy normal individuals. This was so even though he had no recollection of ever having performed the task before. Similar findings have been reported in many other studies.

Normal Levels of Item-Specific Priming Another form of memory that appears to be spared in patients with medial temporal lobe lesions is revealed when they are tested for subtle aftereffects of previous experiences with individual items, such as words or pictures. One such test involved a standardized picture fragments task, where the patient is shown several series of cards, each containing an increasing number of fragments or line segments from a drawing of a familiar object, such as an airplane, and is asked to identify the object. HM's ability to recognize the object improved at about the rate as that seen in normal subjects. For example, he might have needed 70% of the fragments to recognize the airplane the first time through the airplane series, but only 50% of the fragments the second time. Importantly, his performance improved even though he had no recollection of having seen any cards with fragmentary drawings!

Graded Loss of Memories of Experiences before Surgery

HM and other hippocampal removal patients appear to have no memory for events occurring within a period of months or even years before the surgery, even though memory for events from early life appears to be intact. Thus HM had no recollection after the surgery of ever having met Dr. Scoville before his surgery, nor did he recall that he had consented to the operation, although he could recall many events from earlier periods of his life. There is disagreement about how far back the retrograde amnesia can extend. The phenomenon is difficult to study in humans because it is hard to document each individual's prior experiences clearly enough to assess how well they are remembered. There is evidence that the deficit is graded, such that the most recent memories are the most profoundly impaired. In some patients, the deficit may extend over several decades.[15]

The Complementary Learning Systems Theory

Several different explanatory frameworks can help make sense of these findings. Some of these frameworks rely on the idea that there are many separate memory systems in the brain. One notable version of this view, presented by Larry Squire in 1992, is that these memory systems are divided into two types—declarative and nondeclarative.[16] Declarative memories are memories we attest to, whereas nondeclarative memories are memories that affect our behavior even when we are unaware of how these memories were formed. Squire proposed that the medial temporal lobe region is involved in the formation of new explicit memories and the recall of recent declarative memories, but not in the formation of or recall of nondeclarative memories. Following Brenda Milner[17] and others, Squire also suggested that some unspecified process, often labeled "consolidation," occurs after memories are first acquired such that, over time, they become independent of the medial temporal lobe memory system.

The theory developed by my colleagues and me attempts to go beyond this level of description. Drawing ideas from an earlier theory of David Marr,[18] it captures in greater detail the mechanisms involved in the formation and retrieval of all kinds of memories, and it explains why it makes sense to have more than one learning system involved in memory formation.

According to our theory, when someone processes an item—perhaps a fragmentary picture of an airplane—patterns of activation arise in early stages of the visual processing stream, leading up to the visual association areas where the shape or form of the pictured object is represented. If enough fragments are presented, the visual pattern will be close enough to that of previously seen airplanes to give rise to patterns of activation in areas representing many of the different types of information about an airplane, including the pattern on the integrative layer for such an airplane and the pattern in a speech-relevant area corresponding to the spoken word *airplane*. Small adjustments to the strengths of the participating connections will then occur. The consequence of these small adjustments is to slightly facilitate the subsequent processing of the same item, and to make it possible for the learning system to enter the distributed state of recognizing the airplane with slightly fewer fragments than before. In this way, the theory addresses the subtle aftereffects of specific episodes of processing.

An essential element of the complementary learning systems theory is that the connection adjustments are quite small and have only subtle aftereffects. Such adjustments may cumulate over repeated presentations of the same input and corresponding output (for example, the reflected letter *r* in reversed presentations of many different words containing this letter), so that gradually the ability to read the reversed letter *r* correctly will build up. But, according to the theory, these connection adjustments are not large enough to allow an arbitrary new association—for example, between a person's name and the person's face—to be formed after one or just a few exposures.

To allow the rapid formation of such new associations, my colleagues and I proposed that the medial temporal lobes provide a learning system that complements the gradual learning system in the neocortex. This system is diagrammed in figure 6.4, where the medial temporal lobe region is shown sending and receiving connections to and from important representational areas in the neocortex. According to the theory, when we see a person and hear the person's name, patterns of activation arise in the relevant cortical areas. They arise in other areas as well, corresponding to the location in which the person and name are encountered, the emotional state associated with the encounter, the sound of the person's voice, and so on. These in turn are propagated into the medial temporal area via the axons of neurons arising within each of the involved areas. These inputs then set up a pattern in several regions of the hippocampus, deep inside the medial temporal lobe area, corresponding to the entire experience of seeing the person and hearing the person's name. Large connection adjustments then occur among the neurons participating in the hippocampal representation of the encounter, which have the effect of linking together the elements of the encounter so that, if a part of the input is presented again at a later time—for example, we see the person's face a week later— the pattern will tend to be reconstructed. Return connections from the hippocampus to the contributing neocortical areas then allow the corresponding cortical pattern to be reconstructed, giving rise to the experienced memory for the previous event.

It should be clear how the theory can explain why a patient like HM would fail to form new arbitrary associations between a new person's name and face, and would also fail to associate these things with the episode in which that person was encountered. In HM's case, almost the entire medial temporal lobe area, including the hippocampus, was removed on both sides of his brain. Thus the neural substrate for forming such new traces would largely be absent. The theory explains why HM would fail to remember a person or episode encountered shortly before his surgery. The physical substrate of the memory for the episode—the brain areas containing the neurons and connections in which the memory trace of the experience was stored—would no longer be available to construct the distributed neocortical pattern corresponding to the (re) constructed memory.

But why, within this theory, should a memory—say, for the name that goes with a particular face—gradually become less dependent on the presence of the medial temporal lobe area? Although the memory trace (the critical connection weight changes) that are necessary for reconstructing the memory are initially within the hippocampus, this trace provides the basis for the reconstruction of the brain representation of the event through activation of the corresponding pattern in the neocortex. Such occurrences might correspond to waking experiences of recollection, as when one sees someone one has met before and recollects aspects of the previous encounter. These occurrences might correspond to conscious and deliberate recollection of the previous experience, as when one thinks back about the past; or they might correspond to spontaneous reactivations of the hippocampal patterns corresponding to the relevant memory, perhaps arising during sleep. Regardless of what caused it, each such reactivation would give rise to a reactivation in the neocortex, providing the slow-learning neocortical system with another chance to learn. In this way, over many such repetitions, connections within the neocortex could become strong enough to allow a person's face to give rise to the pattern corresponding to the person's name.

In short, the complementary learning systems my colleagues and I proposed—one in the neocortex, which relies on small connection adjustments, and one in the medial temporal lobe, which relies on quite large connection adjustments—work together, over time, to provide an overall mechanism that allows declarative memories to become integrated into neocortical connections, gradually losing their dependence on the medial temporal lobes.

Cooperation of Complementary Learning Systems in Memory for Meaningful Materials

According to the complementary learning systems theory, the neocortex and the medial temporal lobes generally work together in remembering. Associations that already have some preexisting strength (e.g., between the word *dog* and the word *bone*) will benefit from the synergistic contributions of both systems, whereas associations that are completely arbitrary (e.g., *city-ostrich*) will depend almost entirely on the fast-learning medial temporal lobe system. The stronger the preexisting strength of the connections in the cortex, the less important the medial temporal lobe contribution will be. Other studies have shown that preexisting associations can also contribute to false recollection, so that if *dog* and *bone* occur in different sentences we have heard, we may sometimes also recall the words and others they occurred with in the same sentence.[19] Here the cortex and medial temporal lobe are working at cross-purposes, creating a false memory.

Recapitulation: Cooperation of Complementary Learning Systems in the Repeated Recall of an Initially Unfamiliar Story

We can now go back to consider something as complex as the successive recollection of the story Frederic Bartlett presented to the subjects in his experiment. According to the complementary learning systems theory, these subjects initially made connection weight adjustments within their medial temporal lobes at the time of their initial reading of the story. Processes operating at the time of reading the story in the first place may well have distorted their understanding as they took the story in, something very much expected to happen within the overall parallel distributed processing framework.[20] The patterns of activation arising in the neocortex in the course of reading the story would then give rise to patterns in the hippocampus. Fast changes in the strengths of connections among the participating neurons would in turn provide the initial memory trace that contributes to the participants' efforts to reconstruct the story at a later time. This process, however, would also be affected by prior associations of recollected elements of the story with other things known to the participants, giving rise both to the opportunity for selective memory for elements of the story that make sense and to distortion in the recollection in the direction of further sense making. This act of reconstruction would lead to further connections within the medial temporal lobes, as well as to small adjustments to relevant connections within the neocortex. If the process of recollection were repeated often, recall would be expected to gradually strengthen and increase in consistency over time, and to become gradually less dependent on the medial temporal cortex.

Questions for the Complementary Learning Systems Theory

This chapter has presented evidence that there are two complementary learning systems, but has not yet explained why this would be desirable or necessary. Specifically, it has shown that the neocortex makes only small connection adjustments, insufficient to store new arbitrary associations rapidly. But why should this be so? Why shouldn't the size of connection adjustments in the neocortical system be increased so as to allow new information to be stored rapidly? This question lies at the heart of the 1995 article in which my colleagues and I presented the theory. That article made two important points:[21]

First, the ability to generalize what we learn about one thing to other things and to find the statistical regularities underlying a range of related experiences depends on slow learning. If connection adjustments are too large, the idiosyncratic aspects of particular experiences dominate learning too much, and the connection weights fail to capture the common structure underlying a set of related events and experiences.

Second, if a body of knowledge has been gradually built up in a neocortex-like slow-learning system, any attempt to add arbitrary new information into the connection weights at all once will create a phenomenon known as "catastrophic interference."[22] This means that, although the new learning may be possible, it will drastically interfere with what has previously been stored in the system. If a network is forced to learn about a penguin, for example—a bird that can swim but cannot fly—this information interferes with preexisting knowledge about what other birds can do. Crucially, though, catastrophic interference can be overcome if the information is learned in the right way. If presentation of the new information about the penguin is interleaved with ongoing exposure to information about other birds, knowledge that the penguin is a bird that can swim but cannot fly is gradually learned, and the knowledge about what other birds can do is maintained.

These observations explain why we have complementary learning systems. The fast-learning system provides a way to store and remember new arbitrary information quickly but in a separate system from the one containing our preexisting knowledge about other things. Once stored in the fast-learning system, this information can be replayed occasionally, interspersed with ongoing experience or with information about other things. Gradual learning of the new information then occurs in the neo-cortex, without catastrophic interference. The fast-learning medial tempo-ral lobe system, working together with the neocortical system, thus provides a way to eventually knit the newly formed memory into the fabric of what is already known to the slow-learning neocortical system.

Does Neuroscientific Evidence Support the Basic Tenets of the Complementary Learning Systems Theory?

When my colleagues and I initially developed our theory, we sought evidence that would support or refute it in a number of different places. First, we asked whether the necessary long-distance connections exist in the brain, to carry out the necessary long-range interactions with the neocortex. We found that evidence collected by the neuroanatomist David Amaral and colleagues was completely consistent with the theory's requirements.[23] In brief, there are two-way fiber bundles connecting the hippocampus with all relevant areas of the neocortex and with other relevant noncortical brain areas. Second, we found supporting evidence for differences in synaptic plasticity between the hippocampus and neocortex. Thus the phenomenon of *long-term potentiation* (LTP)—in which simultaneous pre- and postsynaptic activation give rise to long-lasting changes in strengths of synaptic connections—was first described in slices taken from the hippocampus.[24] Although long-term potentiation can be produced in the neocortex, a study by Ronald Racine and colleagues showed, as the theory had predicted, that hippocampal LTP reaches maximum levels quickly, whereas in neocortical synapses changes are quite small each time the stimulation is applied and build up gradually with repeated exposures.[25] Finally, my colleagues and I asked whether there was evidence that patterns of activation established during a learning event were reactivated at later times, in particular while an animal was sleeping. In 1992, when we were first developing the theory, there was little known about the matter, but, in 1994, Matthew Wilson and Bruce McNaughton[26] provided the first clear support for the sleep-reactivation idea, now a well-studied phenomenon (see chapter 4 of this volume).

Moreover, there is a vast body of research both on the role of the medial temporal lobes in learning and memory and on the biological processes underlying learning and memory. One line of evidence helping to explain the exact nature of the role of the hippocampus in memory relates to the following question: If connection adjustment is involved in learning in both hippocampus and neocortex, why is interference only a problem in the neocortex? Specifically, why are we able to learn new arbitrary things in the hippocampus without this new learning interfering catastrophically with other information already stored in connections between hippocampal neurons? Since connection adjustment is assumed to be involved in both the hippocampus and the neocortex, why doesn't learning something new rapidly also produce catastrophic interference in the hippocampus? An answer to this question is suggested by observing differences between the activation of neurons in both areas of the brain in response to the same experience. Experiments from many laboratories have shown that a far smaller fraction of the neurons are active at any one time in the hippocampus than in relevant regions of the neocortex.[27] This sparser pattern of activation tends to reduce the extent to which memories for different things are stored in the same connections, drastically reducing the amount of interference in memory. A detailed theory of how sparse representations minimize interference has been developed with contributions from a number of memory researchers.[28]

It should be noted that there are complementary benefits to the use of overlapping representations: When representations overlap, they access some of the same connections, so that what is learned or remembered about one thing transfers to others. To the extent that overlap captures important elements of similarity that support such generalizations, a high degree of overlap of representations can be a good thing. There remains debate about the degree of similarity-based overlap in neocortical representations, but the overlap is clearly greater in many areas of the cortex than in the hippocampus.

Can the Theory Address Recent Discoveries about the Neural Basis of Memory?

The complementary learning systems theory is fifteen years old; since it first appeared, there have certainly been many new developments in memory research. Some of these developments provide striking confirmation of details of the mechanisms my colleagues and I, and others, have proposed, such as a mechanism within the hippocampus for assigning separate, nonoverlapping patterns of activation to very similar experiences.[29]

One intriguing development that was not anticipated in the complementary learning systems theory is discovery of the process of *reconsolidation*,[30] in which memories thought to have already been consolidated can sometimes be put back into a fragile state, if brought to mind by a cue or reminder of the remembered experience. This process suggests that memories can sometimes be erased, or possibly edited, with new information replacing information previously consolidated due to a single reminding/revision episode. If such a process could occur for all information stored in the neocortical learning system, it would pose a severe challenge to our theory. The generality of the process remains unclear, however, and there have been several failures to reproduce it. It is possible that reconsolidation may be occurring, if it occurs at all, when memories are still relatively new and unconsolidated. Memories that have undergone repeated reinstatement appear to be more robust, so that returning them to a more labile state is no longer possible.[31] If reconsolidation can only occur when a memory is new, this would make it more compatible with the complementary learning systems theory.

It should be emphasized, however, that within the theory, the overt recollection of an event can certainly be affected by the content of subsequent experience. This can occur because the adjustments previously made to the strengths of connections can have new adjustments overlaid on top of them, pushing the connections in different directions and affecting the representation of an earlier event that is reconstructed at the time of remembering.

In conclusion, the two main points of this chapter are, first, that memory is a constructive process and, second, that the biological substrate of memory is the pattern of adjustments an experience produces to connections between neurons. The chapter has discussed how these ideas are compatible, and has shown how apparently different forms of knowledge or memory may depend on connection adjustments in two complementary learning systems. Both systems rely on connections to store memory and knowledge; but their different characteristics allow them to perform different roles in our ability to remember and, as Pinter reminded us, to misremember.

Notes

1. Mel Gussow, *Conversations with Pinter* (London: Nick Hearn Books, 1994), 16.

2. Frederic C. Bartlett, *Remembering: A Study in Experimental and Social Psychology* (London: Cambridge University Press, 1932).

3. David E. Rumelhart, James L. McClelland, and the PDP research group, *Parallel Distributed Processing: Explorations in the Microstructure of Cognition,* 2 vols. (Cambridge, MA: MIT Press, 1986).

4. James L. McClelland, Bruce L. McNaughton, and Randall C. O'Reilly, "Why There Are Complementary Learning Systems in the Hippocampus and Neocortex: Insights from the Successes and Failures of Connectionist Models of Learning and Memory," *Psychological Review* 102 (1995): 419–457.

5. Timothy T. Rogers and James L. McClelland, *Semantic Cognition: A Parallel Distributed Processing Approach* (Cambridge, MA: MIT Press, 2004).

6. Santiago Ramón y Cajal, *Comparative Study of the Sensory Areas of the Human Cortex* (Worcester, MA: Clark University, 1899), 325.

7. Jeffrey S. Bowers, "On the Biological Plausibility of Grandmother Cells: Implications for Neural Network Theories in Psychology and Neuroscience," *Psychological Review* 116 (2009): 220–251; Stephen Waydo et al., "Sparse Representation in the Human Medial Temporal Lobe," *Journal of Neuroscience* 26 (2006): 10232–10234; David C. Plaut and James L. McClelland, "Locating Object Knowledge in the Brain: A Critique of Bowers' (2009) Attempt to Revive the Grandmother Cell Hypothesis," *Psychological Review* 117 (2010): 284–288.

8. Geoffrey E. Hinton, James L. McClelland, and David E. Rumelhart, "Distributed Representations," in *Parallel Distributed Processing: Explorations in the Microstructure of Cognition,* 1:77–109; James L. McClelland and David E. Rumelhart, "Distributed Memory and the Representation of General and Specific Information," *Journal of Experimental Psychology: General* 114 (1985): 159–188.

9. James L. McClelland and Timothy T. Rogers, "The Parallel Distributed Processing Approach to Semantic Cognition," *Nature Reviews Neuroscience* 4 (2003): 310–322. A number of other theorists have proposed related ideas. See, for example, Antonio R. Damasio, "The Brain Binds Entities and Events by Multiregional Activation from

Convergence Zones," *Neural Computation* 1 (1989): 123–132. For an alternative perspective, see Alex Martin and Linda L. Chao, "Semantic Memory in the Brain: Structure and Processes," *Current Opinion in Neurobiology* 11 (2001): 194–201.

10. Donald O. Hebb, *The Organization of Behavior: A Neuropsychological Theory* (New York: Wiley, 1949).

11. David E. Rumelhart, Geoffrey E. Hinton, and Ronald J. Williams, "Learning Representations by Backpropagating Errors," *Nature* 323 (1986): 533–536.

12. Timothy T. Rogers et al., "The Structure and Deterioration of Semantic Memory: A Neuropsychological and Computational Investigation," *Psychological Review* 111 (2004): 205–235.

13. William Beecher Scoville and Brenda Milner, "Loss of Recent Memory after Bilateral Hippocampal Lesions," *Journal of Neurology, Neurosurgery, and Psychiatry* 20 (1957): 11–21.

14. Larry R. Squire, "Memory and the Hippocampus: A Synthesis from Findings with Rats, Monkeys, and Humans," *Psychological Review* 99 (1992): 195–231.

15. Dean F. McKinnon and Larry R Squire, "Autobiographical Memory and Amnesia," *Psychobiology* 17 (1989): 247–256.

16. L. R. Squire, "Memory and the Hippocampus: A Synthesis from Findings with Rats, Monkeys, and Humans."

17. B. Milner, "Amnesia Following Operation on the Temporal Lobes," in *Amnesia*, ed. Charles W. M. Whitty and Oliver. L. Zangwill (London: Butterworth, 1966), 109–133.

18. D. Marr, "Simple Memory: A Theory for Archicortex," *Philosophical Transactions of the Royal Society of London* B 262 (1971): 2381.

19. Cynthia Henderson and James L. McClelland, "Semantic Interference during Episodic Recall," in *Proceedings of the Thirty-first Annual Conference of the Cognitive Science Society*, ed. Niels Taatgen and Hedderik van Rijn, Cognitive Science Society, 2009, http://cognitivesciencesociety.org/, 3203.

20. David E. Rumelhart et al., "Parallel Distributed Processing Models of Schemata and Sequential Thought Processes," in *Parallel Distributed Processing: Explorations in the Microstructure of Cognition*, vol. 2, chap. 14.

21. J. L. McClelland, Bruce L. McNaughton, and Randall C. O'Reilly, "Why There Are Complementary Learning Systems in the Hippocampus and Neocortex: Insights from the Successes and Failures of Connectionist Models of Learning and Memory."

22. Michael McCloskey and Neal J. Cohen, "Catastrophic Interference in Connectionist Networks: The Sequential Learning Problem," in *The Psychology of Learning and Motivation*, ed. Gordon H. Bower (New York: Academic Press, 1989), 24, 109–165.

23. Larry R. Squire, Arthur P. Shimamura, and David G. Amaral, "Memory and the Hippocampus," in *Neural Models of Plasticity: Experimental and Theoretical Approaches*, ed. John H. Byrne and William O. Berry (New York: Academic Press, 1989), 208–239.

24. Tim V. P. Bliss and Terje Lømo, "Long-Lasting Potentiation of Synaptic Transmission in the Dentate Area of the Anaesthetized Rabbit Following Stimulation of the Perforant Path," *Journal of Physiology* (London) 232 (1973): 331–356.

25. Ronald J. Racine et al., "Post-activation Potentiation in the Neocortex. 4. Multiple Sessions Required for Induction of Long-Term Potentiation in the Chronic Preparation," *Brain Research* 702 (1995): 87–93.

26. M. A. Wilson and B. L. McNaughton, "Reactivation of Hippocampal Ensemble Memories during Sleep," *Science* 265 (1994): 676–679.

27. Carol A. Barnes et al., "Comparison of Spatial and Temporal Characteristics of Neuronal Activity in Sequential Stages of Hippocampal Processing," *Progress in Brain Research* 83 (1990): 287–300.

28. David Marr, "A Theory of Cerebellar Cortex," *Journal of Physiology* (London), 202 (1969): 437–470; Bruce L. McNaughton and Richard G. M. Morris, "Hippocampal Synaptic Enhancement and Information Storage within a Distributed Memory System," *Trends in Neurosciences* 10 (1987): 408–415; Randall C. O'Reilly and James L. McClelland, "Hippocampal Conjunctive Encoding, Storage, and Recall: Avoiding a Tradeoff," *Hippocampus* 4 (1994): 661–682.

29. Jill K. Leutgeb et al., "Pattern Separation in the Dentate Gyrus and CA3 of the Hippocampus," *Science* 315 (2007): 961–966; Thomas J. McHugh et al., "Dentate Gyrus NMDA Receptors Mediate Rapid Pattern Separation in the Hippocampal Network," *Science* 317 (2007): 94–99.

30. Karim Nader, Glenn E. Schafe, and Joseph E. Le Doux, "Fear Memories Require Protein Synthesis in the Amygdala for Reconsolidation after Retrieval," *Nature* 406 (2000): 722–726.

31. Yadin Dudai, "Reconsolidation: The Advantage of Being Refocused," *Current Opinion in Neurobiology* 16 (2006): 174–178.

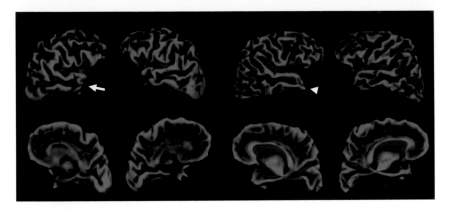

Plate 1 (Figure 5.1)
Magnetic resonance images of HM's brain, scanned in late life. Images on left show a reconstruction of its surface anatomy, with the folds of gyri digitally enhanced as green colors. Images on right show a healthy control brain for comparison (small arrowhead), clearly highlighting bilateral surgical loss of the anterior temporal lobes in images on left (arrow).
Modified with permission from David H. Salat et al., "Neuroimaging H.M.: A 10-Year Follow-Up Examination." *Hippocampus* 16 (2006): figure 3.

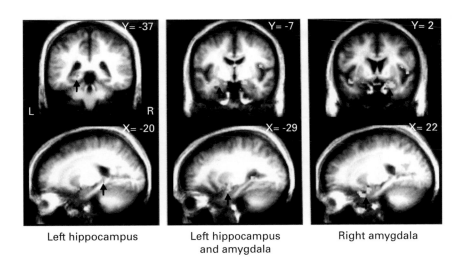

| Left hippocampus | Left hippocampus and amygdala | Right amygdala |

Plate 2 (Figure 5.2)
Functional magnetic resonance images illustrating how activity in the hippocampal formation is greater during recollection of more recent memories. The images (in different views) highlight regions of brain that show greater activity (more yellow along an orange-yellow color spectrum) for more recent memories. Regions with time-dependent recall activity include particularly the left hippocampus.
Reproduced with permission from Christine N. Smith and Larry R. Squire, "Medial Temporal Lobe Activity during Retrieval of Semantic Memory Is Related to the Age of the Memory," *Journal of Neuroscience* 29 (2009): figure 4.

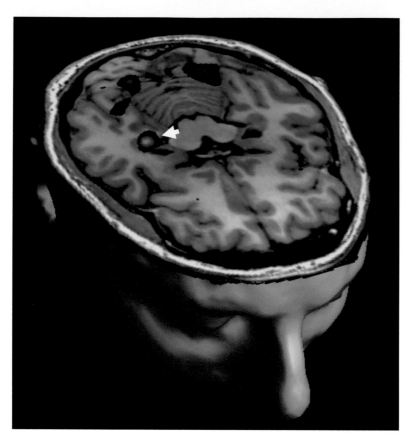

Plate 3 (Figure 5.4)

Three-dimensional reconstruction of the brain at the level of the right hippocampus, representing statistically significant increases in brain activity in subjects performing a virtual reality spatial navigation task. Note the prominent activation (blob in the right hippocampus; arrow), which mediates important processing functions of spatial memory, crucial to navigation. Activations at the back of the brain are related to visual cortex activity with the task.

Images courtesy of Prof. Eleanor A. Maguire, University College, London.

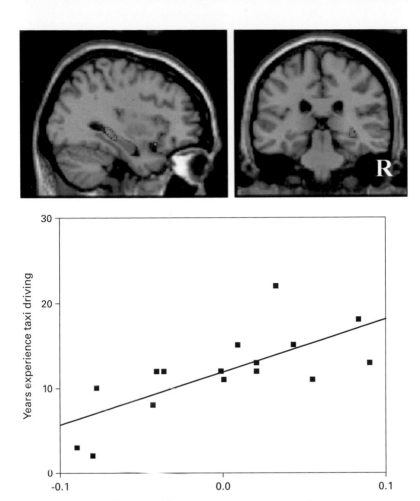

Plate 4 (Figure 5.5)

Functional brain images derived from London taxi drivers with varying years of experience. Long-term memory involves formation of stable synapses and demands structural changes in gray matter. Memory encoding (or learning) is associated with an increased complexity of neuronal processes that can sometimes be appreciated as an increase in the volume of even a macroscopically defined brain region. The brain images show the result of a statistical comparison across the group of taxi drivers. It was assumed that greater numbers of years of experience were associated with the development of more detailed navigational memory for the city. The highlighted right hippocampal formation shows a statistically significant correlation between volume of gray matter and years of London taxi driving experience, whose quantitative relationship is shown in the graph. This finding is consistent with a considerable body of independent data suggesting that the right hippocampus plays an important role in spatial memory formation (see, e.g., figure 5.4).

Images courtesy of Prof. Eleanor A. Maguire, University College, London.

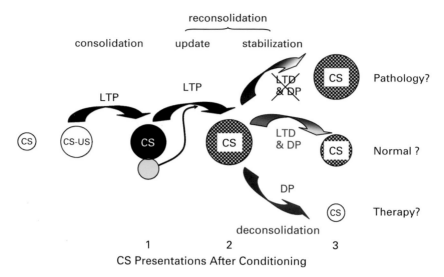

reconsolidation

consolidation   update   stabilization

LTP

LTP

LTP

CS   Pathology?

LTD & DP

CS

CS   CS   LTD & DP   CS   Normal ?

CS-US

DP

CS   Therapy?

deconsolidation

1   2   3

CS Presentations After Conditioning

Plate 5 (Figure 7.1)

Dynamical fear memory trace in the lateral amygdala. This diagram depicts the hypothetical changes that a fear memory trace might undergo after learning and reactivation. The size of the conditioned stimulus (CS) circle represents its fear potency, as reflected in the magnitude of the fear response it elicits. After fear conditioning, that is, conditioned-unconditioned stimulus (CS-US) pairing, the lateral amygdala's cellular responses and freezing behavior to the conditioned stimulus are potentiated via a long-term-potentiation-like mechanism. This potentiation is stabilized over 24 hours (consolidation). After consolidation, the first presentation of the conditioned stimulus triggers an update of the fear memory, and produces a further potentiation in the lateral amygdala, presumably updating the information (yellow circle) and incorporating it in the old memory trace, via again an LTP-like mechanism. It is speculated that in a normal situation, long-term depression (LTD) and depotentiation (DP) mechanisms (red-shaded yellow arrow) are at play during the reconsolidation of this newly formed memory (black and yellow circle), in order to reduce the fear attached to it and maintain homeostatic balance of potentiation. When these mechanisms are dysfunctional (black-shaded white arrow), the new fear memory remains potentiated. Therapy is presumed to produce a depotentiation, so that fear memory in the lateral amygdala is erased and goes back to its initial level (deconsolidation). Whether pharmacological and behavioral therapeutical tools act in similar ways is not yet clear.

7 Emotional Memory Processing: Synaptic Connectivity

Joseph E. LeDoux and Valérie Doyère

Emotions play an important role in mental life, coloring our perceptions, thoughts, and memories. Most of the objects and events that elicit emotions do so based on memories formed through life experiences. When implicit and not consciously accessible, such memories can be thought of as "emotional memories," but when explicit and conscious, they are better referred to as "memories about emotions."

Work on the neural basis of emotion, and the relation between emotion and memory, has focused mainly on negative emotions. The study of fear in carefully controlled laboratory experiments with animals, for example, has shed considerable light on the neural circuits of emotional memory. Fear has been the most frequently studied emotion both because of its robustness and generality across species and because of its essential role in survival and maintaining well-being. Research on fear memories, whether in humans or (nonhuman) animals, falls largely in the category of implicit emotional memories as opposed to explicit, conscious memories about emotion. Fear memories are rapidly acquired, involving changes in synaptic transmission, and persistence, with stabilization of those changes.

Much has been learned about the neural circuits and the cellular and molecular mechanisms that underlie the acquisition (learning) and persistence (memory) of fear. Recently, interest has grown in the counterintuitive hypothesis that, after use or retrieval, a persistent memory is destabilized and must be re-stored through additional cellular and molecular mechanisms in order to persist.

Called "consolidation," the process of making memories persist after initial learning involves establishing a short-term memory (STM) during acquisition and converting this temporary trace into a persistent, long-term memory (LTM) through the synthesis of new proteins that stabilize synapses modified during acquisition. During memory retrieval, the consolidated trace is destabilized and must be restabilized through an active process involving new protein synthesis in order to persist, a process referred to as "reconsolidation."

This chapter reviews what is known about the neural basis of fear memory, emphasizing implicit, unconscious emotional memory. It discusses how fear memories are acquired, consolidated, and reconsolidated. And it considers broader implications of reconsolidation research, in particular, that after retrieval, while the memory is destabilized and before it is reconsolidated, a brief window of opportunity exists for memory dampening, and possibly even erasure.

Pavlovian Conditioning as a Tool for Studying Fear

In the laboratory, fear memories can be created using the paradigm of Pavlovian fear conditioning. After being associated with a biologically salient *unconditioned stimulus*, an initially neutral stimulus acquires the ability to control conditioned responding and becomes a *conditioned stimulus*. In Pavlov's earlier studies of dogs, the conditioned stimulus was sound (often said to be the ringing of a bell, but more likely the ringing of a tuning fork) and the unconditioned stimulus was food. After the sound and food were presented together repeatedly, the sound alone produced salivation in anticipation of the food.

This paradigm was adapted subsequently to focus on aversive conditioning, in which the unconditioned stimulus is an unpleasant, fearful, or even painful stimulus. This provides a model for posttraumatic stress disorder. Use of the aversive conditioning model has increased immensely over the last decade. In a rodent model of fear conditioning, the unconditioned stimulus is typically an electric shock, which can be paired with a variety of possible conditioned stimuli (lights, odors, tones, the apparatuses or contexts in which conditioning occurs). Most studies have involved an auditory conditioned stimulus paired with a foot shock. When presented alone, the conditioned stimulus comes to elicit behavioral and physiological responses normally elicited only by predators or other natural threats. Not surprisingly, fear conditioning is a highly conserved form of learning that is observed in a wide range of species. Although the term *fear* implies a conscious state, fear conditioning, as noted, is an implicit form of learning that occurs independent of awareness. And although *defensive conditioning* is a more neutral term with respect to conscious experience and reflects the protective nature of the resulting responses, we use the more pertinent term *fear conditioning* for our discussion.

Neural Circuits Mediating Fear Conditioning

The amygdala is critical to fear memory; without it, neither animals nor humans can learn to fear the conditioned stimulus. The anatomical structure and connectivity of the amygdala, which contains a dozen functionally specialized clusters of neurons or *nuclei* located deep inside the medial part of the temporal lobe, are well conserved across species, albeit with slight differences in size and organization of the nuclei. Here we review findings on connections between the amygdala and other brain regions that are particularly relevant to fear conditioning.

The amygdala is a key information integration or association system in the service of controlling emotional responses. It receives inputs from all sensory modalities (auditory, visual, olfactory, somatosensory, gustatory, and visceral), as well as connections from higher-order processing structures such as the prefrontal cortex, the perirhinal cortex, and the hippocampal formation. Of the many outputs of the amygdala, particularly relevant to our concerns are connections to brainstem areas involved in the control of species-typical defense responses (freezing, flight) and physiological homeostatic systems (the autonomic nervous system and networks controlling the release of stress hormones). Internal connections allow the amygdala to integrate converging sensory and higher information, to process it internally within its networks, and then to generate outputs that affect behavioral and physiological responses in threatening situations.

At the neuronal level, conditioned and unconditioned stimulus information can become associated when the separate stimulus processing pathways converge on common neurons. The primary site of convergence for auditory fear conditioning (pairing a tone conditioned stimulus with a shock unconditioned stimulus, for example) is the lateral nucleus of the amygdala, or lateral amygdala for short, whose cells receive both auditory and somatosensory (including nociceptive, or pain-sensing) information. Recordings of single cells in the lateral amygdala have confirmed that even individual cells there receive convergent signals from conditioned and unconditioned stimulus pathways.

The shortest route by which auditory information reaches the lateral amygdala is via synaptic pathways through medial areas of the auditory thalamus. Highly processed auditory information also reaches the lateral amygdala as projections from auditory associative cortices via the auditory thalamus. Fear conditioning to a simple auditory conditioned stimulus can be mediated by either of these pathways, but the cortical route is more likely involved when two complex or subtle auditory stimuli must be distinguished. The somatosensory information about the uncondi-tioned stimulus also reaches the lateral amygdala either by a short route from the sensory thalamic complex or by a longer cortical route through the somatosensory cortex.

The lateral amygdala itself can be partitioned into dorsal, ventromedial, and ventrolateral subnuclei. Electrophysiological studies have highlighted that the dorsal division is the main site of conditioned-unconditioned stimulus convergence, where plasticity during learning occurs and persis-tent fear memories are stored. A micronetwork within the dorsal division of the lateral amygdala, with feedforward and feedback connections, may maintain activity within the lateral amygdala and process (e.g., store, filter) information. Single-cell recordings also have shown that the superior and inferior parts of the dorsal division respond in different ways over the course of fear conditioning: the superior part shows conditioned cellular responses transiently early in training, and the inferior part, sustained conditioned responses late in learning. Although repeated presentation of the conditioned stimulus alone—without the unconditioned stimulus—extinguishes behavioral responses, late responses in the inferior part of the dorsal lateral amygdala persist. These extinction-resistant cellular responses may represent stable fear memories and may be responsible for the poten-tial resurgence of those memories under conditions of stress or after specific triggers. Fear memories may therefore be differentially stored in two kinds of local networks within the dorsal division of the lateral amygdala: a flex-ible network for learning and updating processes; and a more stable network for long-term storage and memory persistence.

It is commonly assumed that, in processing fear memories, information so processed is sent from the lateral to the central amygdala both directly and via intra-amygdala connections. These connections are numerous and reciprocal, except in the central amygdala, which receives inputs from other amygdala nuclei but does not project back to them. The central amygdala serves as the main output of the amygdala to the hypothalamus and to those areas of the brainstem involved in autonomic, hormonal, and defensive behavioral responses.

Whereas connections from the lateral amygdala to the central amygdala produce autonomic nervous system responses and emotional reactions such as freezing, connections from the lateral amygdala to the basal amygdala are involved in active instrumental behaviors such as avoidance. Instrumental responses, in contrast to Pavlovian responses, allow an animal to gain control over the delivery of the unconditioned response by acting (e.g., to avoid the unconditioned stimulus by moving to another compartment). Connections from the basal amygdala to the striatum may be responsible for these instrumental responses.

The amygdala also plays a significant role in the processing of positive emotions. There is growing evidence, for example, that it may be critical to certain aspects of appetitive or reward learning in rats, where food, water, or sex is used as an unconditioned stimulus, although available data do not generally isolate the possible differential roles of the lateral, basal, and accessory basal nuclei within the amygdala's basolateral complex. So-called stimulus-reward learning has also been studied using devaluation procedures that permit the current value of a reinforcer to be reduced and its impact on the behavioral conditioned responses to be observed, a procedure difficult to apply in aversive situations. The available data suggest that the basolateral amygdala may be critically involved in representing or performing the rapid updating of the current value of the rewards according to their sensory properties. Based on these studies, it has recently been suggested that the basolateral complex and the central nuclei of the amygdala process information in parallel and serve different functions. Thus stimulus-specific conditioned-unconditioned stimulus associations in the basolateral amygdala may elicit unconditioned stimulus–specific conditioned responses (such as consummatory responses), while general conditioned stimulus–affective associations in the central amygdala may generate behavior based on unconditioned stimulus valence. This concept may not apply to aversive situations since, as part of the basolateral amygdala, the lateral amygdala is required for conditioned-unconditioned stimulus convergence and plasticity in fear conditioning. On the other hand, recent data suggest that plasticity in the central amygdala may also be critically involved in fear conditioning, although its specific role beyond that of the lateral amygdala remains to be defined. Nevertheless, on the output side, the parallel motivation model may apply to aversive conditioning, with the pathway from the lateral amygdala to the central nucleus being involved in general aspects of motivation and the pathway from the lateral amygdala to the basal amygdala, in more specifically oriented or goal-directed behaviors.

Functional magnetic resonance imaging (fMRI) in humans has revealed activation of the amygdala in response to stimuli associated with both positive and negative emotions. To date, however, human studies have not been informative about the role of specific nuclei.

Cellular Foundations of Fear Conditioning

Neurons communicate in general by means of chemical transmitters that bridge the synaptic junctions where the terminal axon (sending element) of one neuron meets with a dendrite (receiving element) of another. Synaptic plasticity, which refers to the modification of transmission between neurons across synaptic junctions, is believed to support learning at the cellular level. In long-term potentiation (LTP), a widely accepted model of synaptic plasticity, the patterns of electrical stimulation of sending neurons facilitate transmission between sending and receiving neurons by altering their physiological and molecular properties. Studies of synaptic plasticity in the amygdala during fear conditioning provide some of the most convincing evidence that links LTP to memory.

The convergence of conditioned and unconditioned stimulus sensory information in the amygdala constitutes the condition required for long-term potentiation to occur. Recordings from single cells in the lateral amygdala have shown that conditioned-unconditioned stimulus convergence leads to learning-related modifications in synaptic transmission in the affected neurons, although, in most experimental situations, the unconditioned stimulus reaches the amygdala after the initial cellular responses elicited by the conditioned stimulus have subsided. Processing through both cortical networks as well as intra-amygdala reverberating feedback loops may permit the temporal coincidence necessary for inducing plasticity mechanisms.[1] Triggered oscillations may participate in the sustained cellular activity as well, increasing the likelihood of coincidence between conditioned and unconditioned stimulus cellular responses. Some of these changes may take place at a level of activation insufficient to trigger full-blown action potentials, possibly explaining how the arrival of the unconditioned stimulus at a time when the conditioned stimulus is no longer eliciting action potentials might lead to plasticity.

The study of long-term potentiation in the lateral amygdala of awake freely moving rats has suggested that plasticity at thalamic afferents may be stable for more than a week, whereas plasticity at cortical afferents decays more rapidly. Fear memory, though long-lasting, loses precision as time passes, tending to facilitate fear generalization. Functionally, nondecremental plasticity at auditory thalamic afferents to the lateral amygdala may underlie more rigid, sustained encoding of "crude" aspects of fear memories and may account for the persistence of some aspects of learned fear. Plasticity at cortical afferents may lead to synaptic changes that more rapidly decay over time, perhaps accounting for the loss of detailed, precise encoded information with time, but also providing some flexibility for adjustments in fear memory as situations change. Whether the sustained, extinction-resistant conditioned cellular responses in the inferior part of the dorsal lateral amygdala reflect thalamically induced, nondecremented long-term potentiation, and thus represent poorly detailed fear memory, has not yet been tested.

Molecular Mechanisms

Having seen how fear associations are acquired through synaptic plasticity of the lateral amygdala, we can turn to the molecular mechanisms that underlie the conversion of short- to long-term memory. It is widely accepted that persistent synaptic plasticity underlying long-term memory requires de novo protein synthesis. This has been determined through behavioral studies using a wide variety of paradigms and studies of long-term potentiation in areas like the hippocampus and amygdala. LTP studies have been especially fruitful in identifying a cascade of intracellular events that are activated following strong depolarization and that ultimately lead to protein synthesis and memory consolidation. Many of the same molecular events have been implicated in fear memory formation.

During fear acquisition, the binding of glutamate released from the pre-synaptic side of thalamic or cortical afferents in the lateral amygdala onto AMPA and NMDA receptors at the postsynaptic side triggers the entrance of Ca^{++} into the spine. This activity-dependent increase in intracellular Ca^{++} in the lateral amygdala neurons leads, directly or indirectly, to the activation of both protein kinase A (PKA) and the extracellular signal-regulated kinase / mitogen-activated protein kinase (ERK/MAPK). ERK then activates transcription factors, including the cAMP-response-element binding protein (CREB) and CREB-mediated immediate-early genes that ultimately lead to protein and RNA synthesis.

Fear conditioning has been shown to induce the expression of several immediate-early and downstream genes in the lateral amygdala. Although the specific contributions of these genes to fear memory remain unclear, it is believed that learning-induced gene expression ultimately contributes to changes in cell structure that stabilize memory. Recent data suggest that morphological changes of spines may well be the support of a synaptic fear memory in the lateral amygdala.[2] The integration into the synaptic membrane of newly synthesized proteins may serve to incorporate new receptors, thus increasing synaptic transmission in already implicated synapses, but also possibly unsilencing synapses that lacked AMPA receptors, needed to participate in the synaptic transmission. Apart from Ca^{++} signaling triggered by glutamate binding, neurotrophins such as the brain-derived neurotrophic factor (BDNF) may also promote the activation of protein kinases such as ERK. The activation of beta-adrenergic receptors by noradrenaline may also affect this cascade of events, possibly through the activation of protein kinase A. Finally, stressors may also affect CREB mechanisms. Changes at the presynaptic level may also support long-term memory, but research on this matter is still in its infancy.

Any interactive intervention at any level of these intracellular cascades of molecular events, such as antagonism of ERK phosphorylation or inhibition of protein synthesis, should modulate the transformation of short-term into long-term memory. Such interventions could in turn disrupt the consolidation of fear memory in the lateral amygdala. Targeting specific structures with vector-inducible toxins or pharmacological agents makes it possible to specify the role of a given structure or even a population of neurons in the long-term memory for fear. By infusing an inhibitor of ERK activation in the lateral amygdala, for example, we have shown that long-term fear memory was correlated with the magnitude of plasticity developed in the lateral amygdala. Recent results indicate that some plasticity may also occur in the central amygdala, likely in conjunction with plasticity occurring first in the lateral amygdala.

How those changes remain selective and specific to the activated synapses is a challenging question. Research on long-term potentiation in the hippocampus has led to the hypothesis of a synaptic "tag" that would serve as a marker of recent synaptic activity. This marker would thus constitute a "synaptic short-term memory," which would also provide a tool for keeping the specificity of modifications. The tag is transient, setting a time window during which the newly synthesized plasticity-related proteins can be captured by the tagged synapse, synaptic plasticity can be transformed from short- to long-term, and the "synaptic long-term memory" consolidated. The physical molecule that constitutes the tag is unknown, but data thus far suggest that specific proteins may mediate the tagging process in a structure-specific manner. As appealing as it is, however, the hypothesis of a synaptic tag has not yet been convincingly validated in relation to plasticity in the amygdala, much less in relation to fear memory.

Retrieval: A Window for Selective Weakening or Enhancement of Memory

Having considered how memory is formed when a conditioned and an unconditioned stimulus occur together, we can turn our attention to the consequences of retrieving a consolidated long-term memory. We find that there is a selective time window after retrieval during which memories can be either strengthened or weakened depending on how the memory is manipulated, whether by pharmacological, electrophysiological, or behavioral means.

The longstanding view that emerged from research on memory consolidation was that, once stabilized or consolidated through protein syntheses, memories are permanently engraved and left in a dormant, stable state. When retrieved, the original memory formed during the initial experience is dredged up. By contrast, the reconsolidation view holds that, upon retrieval (reactivation), memories are returned to a labile state, becoming sensitive to disruption or enhancement, and must be restabilized (reconsolidated). Each time we retrieve a memory we thus retrieve the last memory stored rather than the original trace. Something like this is probably at work when a witness testifying in court about a crime includes information read in newspaper accounts. Thus the simple act of remembering renders memory subject to change. Both consolidation and reconsolidation processes take time, the exact duration being subject to variation depending on the task, the amount of training, and presumably other parameters yet to be defined. In general, fear memories are thought to be stabilized within a six-hour time window after training or reactivation.

In real life, memories are complex and comprise multiple associations, with higher-order relations. In his famous account of the complex characteristics of memories (*Remembrance of Things Past*), Marcel Proust describes how a stimulus related to the memory, a retrieval cue or reminder such as an odor, a taste, or a touch, may produce the recall of many of related elements initially formed as part of the memory. Such cues can trigger the remembrance not only of scenes and facts, but also of the emotional meanings attached to the memory. This raises the question of what exactly is dampened when memories are disrupted after their retrieval, for example, following pharmacological manipulations. Can emotions associated with memories be blunted selectively? Or will the associated cognitive memories also be lost?

The study of the reconsolidation phenomenon during fear conditioning has recently begun to yield answers to these questions.[3] The accumulated findings on synaptic and cellular reconsolidation in localized neural networks have shown that reconsolidation of fear memory depends on the amygdala. If protein synthesis or the molecular cascades contributing to it are disrupted in the lateral amygdala after retrieval of the fear memory, the conditioned stimulus no longer elicits fear responses. The reconsolidation of the retrieved memory can also be disrupted using behavioral methods, such as interference training (including extinction protocols).

Does retrieval trigger the reconsolidation of all memories, from the most recent to the earliest? To test whether this is so in animals, a second-order conditioning paradigm can be used: to acquire fear, the first-order conditioned stimulus is paired with the unconditioned stimulus, and another, second-order conditioned stimulus is paired with the first-order conditioned stimulus. As a consequence, the fear of the second-order conditioned stimulus serves as a reminder of the fear evoked by the first-order one. Data show that the reactivation of the memory by the second-order conditioned stimulus produces the reconsolidation of the fear memory of that stimulus, but not of the first-order one. In other words, the first-order conditioned stimulus memory is not rendered labile; it remains intact and still elicits fear, whereas the second-order conditioned stimulus has been disrupted. Several experiments have thus far confirmed that reconsolidation processes in the lateral amygdala are highly selective and involve only directly associated reactivated memories, not remotely associated ones.[4] Studies in animals have shown that the reconsolidation process permits some memories to be strengthened, rather than weakened, pharmacologically. Whether this strengthening proceeds in a selective manner, as the weakening does, remains to be tested.

Does the reconsolidation process affect only the emotional aspect of the memory? Recent findings in humans show that propanolol reduces the emotional aspect of a reactivated fear memory, but leaves intact its declarative, cognitive component (i.e., knowing what is associated with what).[5] This does not imply, however, either that only emotional aspects of memories or that only amygdala-dependent memories are reconsolidated. For example, reconsolidation of contextual fear memories in rats also depends on the hippocampus, in addition to the amygdala. Research in rats and in humans has shown that spatial memory, procedural memory of a motor skill task, and declarative memory of paired associates also undergo reconsolidation. Why are declarative memories put in a labile state, whereas the declarative aspect of fear memories is not? Are the distributed memory traces not equal in their susceptibility to reconsolidation? Is there a primary storage site related to the kind of memory (e.g., the amygdala for amygdala-dependent memories) that would be solely at risk when that memory is reactivated? These questions will need to be addressed in further studies.

One important issue concerns the physiological mechanism responsible for retrieval-related forgetting when reconsolidation is disrupted. Are fear memories forgotten because they have been erased, or simply because they are inaccessible? This question has been hotly debated since the first description in the late 1960s of consolidation and reconsolidation and their disruption by various manipulations. In effect, behaviorally, amnesia due to a retrieval failure (inaccessible memory trace) may not be distinguishable from amnesia due to a memory erasure. Recently, recordings of neurophysiological markers of fear memory in the lateral amygdala have tended to validate the "erasure" hypothesis. In effect, recordings of cellular responses evoked by the conditioned stimulus in the lateral amygdala in rats have shown that, in parallel with the selective loss of the reactivated fear memory when reconsolidation was pharmacologically prevented, the synaptic potentiation associated with the initial fear memory was also reduced. Behavioral forgetting was thus correlated with a "depotentiation" in the lateral amygdala, an erasure mechanism at the synaptic level.

That reactivated memory traces in different neural networks may be disrupted independently of each other raises the interesting possibility that in some particular cases a "local erasure" might be responsible for the retrieval failure of the entire initial memory trace. Mechanisms at the micronetwork level could also be responsible for a retrieval failure. The exact mechanism of the disruption of reconsolidation at the cellular level is not known. Although the data suggest that the "deconsolidation" of the fear memory is due to a depotentiation of the initial learning-induced synaptic changes, it is conceivable that this erasure mechanism affects some, but not all, synaptic nodes, resulting in the failure to locally reactivate the whole micronetwork.

Clearly, more studies are needed to understand the precise conditions that could initiate reconsolidation processes and the rules that govern their selectivity. One implication arising from all these findings is that the dichotomous view that the memory trace must be in either an active or an inactive state of memory representation may not suffice, and that "labile" or "nonlabile" labels may have to be added to characterize different active states.[6]

Remembering Fear Memories May Strengthen Them

Reconsolidation is defined by its lability, that is, by its rendering the initial memory trace fragile and sensitive to disruption. The question of what function reconsolidation serves normally in nondisrupted conditions is difficult to assess. Does recall of memories leave these memories intact, or does it modify them? And, if it modifies them, how? Does it incorporate new information in the original memory trace?

The act of remembering not only renders certain aspects of our memory fragile but does indeed modify them, at least at the cellular level. The retrieval may induce insertion of new receptors into the postsynaptic membrane, unsilencing synapses, and therefore producing the strengthening of synaptic plasticity, adding further potentiation. This plasticity, though not observed in every brain region involved in the remembered memory, is clearly observed in the amygdala in the case of fear memory. Our own recent data have shown that the strengthening of plasticity in the amygdala induced by retrieval is selective to the reactivated memory, and may also concern only emotional aspects of the memory rather than other aspects. Here the emotional component of the reactivated conditioned stimulus— but not the one attached to nonreactivated memories—is updated in the lateral amygdala, whereas the sensory component of the association is not updated in the auditory thalamus. The further potentiation thus does not represent a general affective emotional strengthening, but rather an adjustment of the emotional component of the reactivated memory, which might be the most important part of the memory that needs to be updated. More experiments will be needed to characterize the boundaries for this *emotional updating*.

How this plasticity is triggered is not known either. Why reactivating memory with a single conditioned stimulus (unpaired with any unconditioned stimulus) triggers the strengthening of the memory at the cellular level, whereas repeating that same stimulus triggers its weakening and extinction is a puzzling issue. Extinction is a form of new learning that may involve populations of cells in the amygdala different from those encoding learning during conditioning. Whether the extinction process eliminates or prevents the strengthening of the memory trace due to its first reactivation, or whether both phenomena (i.e., extinction and strengthening) are at play in parallel in different cell populations is an open question. Recent data suggest that the presentation of a conditioned stimulus alone has a different impact at the cellular level depending on when the memory has been reactivated.[7] This result supports the hypothesis that extinction and strengthening are competing processes at the cellular level, although clearly more experiments are needed to unravel all the detailed mechanisms triggered by memory reactivation. As mentioned earlier, coincidence and convergence between conditioned and unconditioned stimulus activations at the cellular level are thought to be the key for the initial plasticity during learning. How can the conditioned stimulus alone trigger the same mechanism at the cellular level? Does the conditioned stimulus reactivate an unconditioned stimulus representation within the amygdala? Does the reverberation of both traces provide opportunities for strengthening when neural activities coincide? Stress-related modulators triggered by the emotional reactivation may facilitate this potentiation as well, but they must do so in a way that is selective to the reactivated memory.

The question arises whether the mechanisms responsible for the strengthening of the trace after reactivation and for the destabilization of the initial trace are mechanistically independent processes or whether one leads to the other. Should the term *reconsolidation* encompass both related phenomena, or does retrieval trigger two independent processes, one that destabilizes the initial memory, and another that strengthens it? It seems that the memory is destabilized when additional information is acquired. This, in turn, suggests that the updating process may be necessary to trigger the trace lability mechanism. On the other hand, when reconsolidation is disrupted, retrieval-induced potentiation does not seem necessary for depotentiation of the initial learning-related plasticity. Both processes might thus be independent, once initiated by the reactivating retrieval cue. A better understanding of the cellular mechanisms that underlie the updating and destabilization processes will certainly shed more light on this issue. Whereas protein synthesis is necessary for reconsolidation of updated memories following their reactivation, recent data suggest that synaptic protein degradation might be responsible for memory destabilization. Whatever the mechanisms, they have to allow for a high level of selectivity. One possibility is that the two processes may involve different dendritic compartments or synaptic populations of the same cell, allowing interaction at the level of a single amygdala cell. This would suggest that a tag at the synaptic level serves as a transient memory of the recently activated synapses during the retrieval. Conceivably, presynaptic activations might also serve to maintain specificity.

Does strengthening of the emotional cellular trace upon reactivation of a fear memory represent the creation of a new trace, with new cells and synapses recruited as in the multiple-trace hypothesis of Lynn Nadel and Morris Moscovitch?[8] Or does it represent increased efficacy at the level of the synapses originally involved in the initial memory trace? In either case, the reactivated memory would be stronger in the amygdala because the initial trace would be strengthened and because the creation of multiple traces would render it easier to retrieve. Substantial advances have been made recently in enumerating the different elements in the molecular machinery that are involved in both consolidation (after training) and reconsolidation (after reactivation) processes. It is now clear that reconsolidation caused by memory reactivation is not a simple repeat of consolidation. Interestingly, a 2008 study on contextual fear conditioning has shown that, as long as a first association has been acquired and consolidated, even a second training trial of the same kind will trigger the strengthening of the trace using a reconsolidation, rather than consolidation, mechanism.[9] The 2008 study also showed the hippocampus to be the critical site in contextual fear conditioning. If the same applies to the amygdala, it would suggest that the mechanisms at play during reconsolidation may update the original fear memory trace rather than create a new one. It remains possible however, that new elements or additional retrieval routes may also be incorporated in the initial memory trace. Notably, both the strengthening of original memory and the addition of multiple traces to the amygdala would render the fear memory easier to retrieve, and therefore less forgettable.

Despite the substantial advances made in the last decade and reviewed here, numerous enigmas remain. To date, it is clear that amygdala networks store fear memories in a sensory-specific manner that is far more sophisticated than once thought. Once a fear memory is stored and consolidated, its reactivation initiates a "reconsolidation" process that is not a simple unitary event (figure 7.1, plate 5) and opens a window for its emotional blunting. Several processes may be at play, at the level of brain structures, local micronetworks, and, potentially, single cells. The precise conditions under which these multiple processes are triggered in a parceled memory trace remain to be elucidated. One challenging question is to understand precisely the mechanisms at the synaptic and cellular level that are responsible for both the lability and the high selectivity of the fear memory trace. It seems that several tags have to be invoked in order to reconcile consolidation, selective "erasure," and selective strengthening following retrieval.

Do the processes triggered by the reactivation of memory happen only once, or every time the memory is reactivated? Although our data show that associated fear memories differ from directly reactivated ones, because these associated memories are not put into a labile state, the recall of associated memories may actually strengthen them. If true, self-elicited remembering and mental rehearsal may trigger the same phenomenon. Our brain's capacity to retrieve memories from pieces of information is

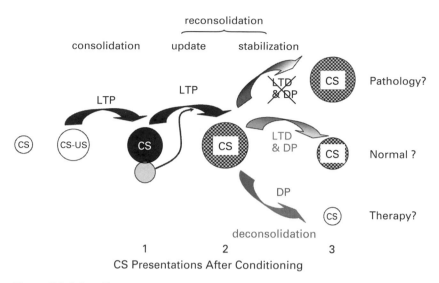

Figure 7.1 (plate 5)

Dynamical fear memory trace in the lateral amygdala. This diagram depicts the hypothetical changes that a fear memory trace might undergo after learning and reactivation. The size of the conditioned stimulus (CS) circle represents its fear potency, as reflected in the magnitude of the fear response it elicits. After fear conditioning, that is, conditioned-unconditioned stimulus (CS-US) pairing, the lateral amygdala's cellular responses and freezing behavior to the conditioned stimulus are potentiated via a long-term-potentiation-like mechanism. This potentiation is stabilized over 24 hours (consolidation). After consolidation, the first presentation of the conditioned stimulus triggers an update of the fear memory, and produces a further potentiation in the lateral amygdala, presumably updating the information (yellow circle) and incorporating it in the old memory trace, via again an LTP-like mechanism. It is speculated that in a normal situation, long-term depression (LTD) and depotentiation (DP) mechanisms (red-shaded yellow arrow) are at play during the reconsolidation of this newly formed memory (black and yellow circle), in order to reduce the fear attached to it and maintain homeostatic balance of potentiation. When these mechanisms are dysfunctional (black-shaded white arrow), the new fear memory remains potentiated. Therapy is presumed to produce a depotentiation, so that fear memory in the lateral amygdala is erased and goes back to its initial level (deconsolidation). Whether pharmacological and behavioral therapeutical tools act in similar ways is not yet clear.

quite advantageous in normal situations. The possibility that memory can be strengthened by retrieval, instead of weakened, as the lack of predicted reinforcer would logically predict, may explain in part why fear memories are so hard to forget. On the other hand, in normal conditions, the labile characteristic of the reactivated fear trace may open a window for active repression mechanisms or interfering processes (triggering a natural depotentiation) that would prevent the overstrengthening of emotional remembered memories. If the potentiation/depotentiation mechanism becomes dysfunctional and unbalanced, the amygdala's synaptic machinery provides the basis of a vicious circle of self-perpetuating remembering. Unsolicited flashbacks or reminders in patients with posttraumatic stress disorder may therefore result in a strengthening of the initial fear, rather than an update and reevaluation of the memory in the new safe situation.

The accumulated findings about the amygdala's connectivity and its synaptic mechanisms have unraveled its critical role in the dynamic processing of fear memories during storage and updating in long-term memory. Despite much progress, however, we are far from fully understanding how our normal memory functions and how we remember or forget our fears. Can fear memories decay with time and be forgotten on their own, or must they be recalled in order to be actively repressed or erased? It is true that fear memories, though among the most durable memories, are also modifiable when reactivated, that they can in some circumstances be weakened using pharmacological or behavioral tools. This capability to be at once stable and labile resides in the molecular machinery controlling plasticity at the amygdala's synapses. The dual strengthening and weakening capabilities of the amygdala memory trace when retrieved may be responsible for its "permanent" quality: when not disturbed, retrieval may strengthen the original fear memory, incorporate new elements, and create new access to the memory trace. Further understanding of the complexity of fear memories may also provide a window for cure of posttraumatic stress disorder. It is likely that several molecular tags are at play in these strengthening/weakening processes, the parameters of which remain to be discovered.

Notes

1. Donald O. Hebb, in *The Organization of Behavior: A Neuropsychological Theory* (New York: Wiley, 1949), has argued that, for learning to happen at the cellular level,

activated ensembles of neurons must reverberate to provide temporal coordination of different neural signals, and thereby facilitate coincidence detection. Recently, Luke R. Johnson et al., "A Recurrent Network in the Lateral Amygdala: A Mechanism for Coincidence Detection," *Frontiers in Neural Circuits* 2 (2008): 3, have shown that recurrent microcircuits may allow reverberatory activity in the lateral amygdala, with a temporal structure that would facilitate coincidence detection between cortical and subcortical afferent information.

2. Raphael Lamprecht et al., "Fear Conditioning Drives Profilin into Amygdala Dendritic Spines," *Nature Neuroscience* 9 (2006): 481–483. This study shows that fear conditioning in rats produces changes in spine morphology in the lateral amygdala, such as enlargements in their postsynaptic densities (PSDs) where glutamate receptors are located. The literature on the morphological correlates of plasticity has interpreted the enlargement of PSDs as possibly reflecting the insertion of certain types of glutamate receptors (e.g., AMPA) into the postsynaptic membrane, resulting in the unsilencing of synapses and increased synaptic efficacy. Those changes are believed to require protein synthesis for making new receptors.

3. The study of reconsolidation began in the 1960s, only to fall out of favor in the face of an impressive body of research supporting the consolidation theory and its thesis that the same memory is retrieved each time a retrieval cue is present. The reconsolidation hypothesis was revived by Susan J. Sara, in "Reconsolidation: Strengthening the Shaky Trace through Retrieval," *Nature Reviews Neuroscience* 1 (2000): 212–214. In this review, Sara summarizes her own recent data and reviews the literature showing that memory reactivation opens an opportunity to strengthen the memory trace with pharmacological tools. See also Karim Nader, Glenn E. Schafe, and Joseph E. LeDoux, "Fear Memories Require Protein Synthesis in the Amygdala for Reconsolidation after Retrieval," *Nature* 406 (2000): 722–726, whose study was the first to demonstrate that fear memory reconsolidation depended on protein synthesis in the amygdala.

4. Jacek Debiec et al., "Directly Reactivated, but Not Indirectly Reactivated, Memories Undergo Reconsolidation in the Amygdala," *Proceedings of the National Academy of Sciences USA* 103 (2006): 3428–3433; Valérie Doyère et al., "Synapse-Specific Reconsolidation of Distinct Fear Memories in the Lateral Amygdala,"*Nature Neuroscience* 10 (2007): 414–416. These studies showed that the lateral amygdala stores fear memories based on the sensory features of the stimuli, allowing it to reconsolidate a particular conditioned-unconditioned stimulus association (e.g., a pure tone associated with a foot shock), while leaving intact other conditioned-unconditioned stimulus associations (e.g., an FM tone associated with the same foot shock).

5. Merel Kindt, Marieke Soeter, and Bram Vervliet, "Beyond Extinction: Erasing Human Fear Responses and Preventing the Return of Fear," *Nature Neuroscience* 12 (2009): 256–258. This study is the first controlled experiment in humans to demonstrate that the disruption of fear memory reconsolidation by propanolol, a blocker

of beta-adrenergic receptors, targets specifically the emotional component of the memory as observed through skin conductance changes. This component, which is dependent on the amygdala, leaves intact the declarative (the knowing what) component, which is dependent on the hippocampus. Importantly, the study showed that fear memory could not be reinstated, suggesting a real forgetting of the fear memory.

6. Donald J. Lewis, "The Psychobiology of Active and Inactive Memory," *Psychological Bulletin* 86 (1979): 1054–1083. Lewis proposed that the memory trace can be in either of two states, an active state (composed of new and reactivated memories) or an inactive state (composed of consolidated memories in a stable form).

7. Marie-H. Monfils et al., "Extinction-Reconsolidation Boundaries: Key to Persistent Attenuation of Fear Memories," *Science* 324 (2009): 951–955. Monfils and colleagues showed that, if a conditioned stimulus is presented within a specific time window (1 hour, but not 3 minutes) after reactivation, a behavioral interference procedure (extinction) may disrupt the reconsolidation of fear memory by producing a dephosphorylation of glutamate receptors in the lateral amygdala. This suggests that erasure rather than extinction mechanisms are determined by precise temporal rules at the synaptic level.

8. Lynn Nadel and Morris Moscovitch, "Memory Consolidation, Retrograde Amnesia and the Hippocampal Complex," *Current Opinion in Neurobiology* 7 (1997): 217–227. Nadel and Moscovitch defend a countertheory to the trace transfer theory, according to which the memory trace "migrates" from the hippocampus to the cortex to account for the temporal gradient of retrograde amnesia after hippocampal damage. They propose instead that each reactivated memory builds a new trace in the hippocampus and its corresponding index to a stored trace in the cortex, creating multiple, related traces of an episode, and therefore facilitating its retrieval, making it more resistant to amnesia.

9. Jonathan L. C. Lee, "Memory Reconsolidation Mediates the Strengthening of Memories by Additional Learning," *Nature Neuroscience* 11 (2008): 1264–1266. Using pharmacological tools in a fear conditioning paradigm to specifically target consolidation rather than reconsolidation mechanisms, Lee demonstrates that, with the context serving as a conditioned stimulus, as long as a first training trial has been consolidated over 24 hours, a second identical training trial will trigger reconsolidation rather than consolidation (i.e., learning-related) mechanisms at the cellular level. This is a clear demonstration that training may involve not only a de novo learning mechanism but also updating processes (modification of already consolidated information).

8 Functions of Human Emotional Memory: The Brain and Emotion

Edmund T. Rolls

This chapter's approach to human emotion and memory takes into account different types of emotional memory and considers how conscious, rational (explicit) and unconscious (implicit) processing both take part in emotion, as two separate processing systems for different types of emotional memory. With different goals, the systems have somewhat different perspectives on emotional events. Moreover, the implicit system may influence the explicit system without awareness of that influence and with confabulation occurring. Such memory phenomena provide fertile ground for imaginative literature. The chapter also shows how "noise" in the brain caused by the random spike timing of neuronal firings leads the brain to be a nondeterministic system. This new theory generates hypotheses on recall decisions in memory processing, which help reveal underlying aspects of both scientific and literary creativity.

Emotions as States

A useful operational definition of *emotions* would be "states elicited by rewards and punishers that have particular functions."[1] A reward is anything for which an animal (which includes humans) will work; a punisher, anything that an animal will escape from or avoid. The functions, as defined below, include working to obtain rewards and to avoid punishers. An emotion might thus be the happiness produced by being given a particular reward, such as a pleasant touch, praise, or a large sum of money. Or it might be fear produced by the sound of a rapidly approaching bus or the sight of an angry expression on someone's face. We work to avoid such stimuli, which are punishing. It might be frustration, anger, or sadness produced by the omission of an expected reward or the termination of a reward, such as the death of a loved one. Or it might be relief produced by the omission or termination of a punishing stimulus, such as the removal of a painful stimulus or sailing out of danger. These examples indicate how emotions can be produced by the delivery, omission, or termination of rewarding or punishing stimuli, and go some way to indicate how different emotions might be produced and classified in terms of the rewards and punishers received, omitted, or terminated. A diagram summarizing some of the emotions associated with the delivery or omission of a reward or punisher or a stimulus associated with them is shown in figure 8.1.

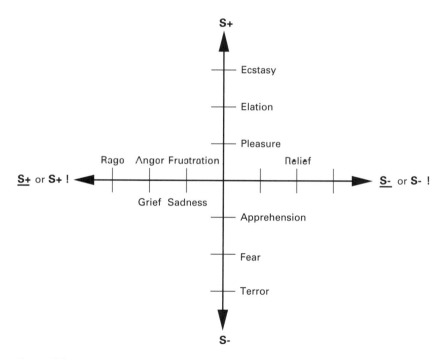

Figure 8.1
Emotions associated with different reinforcement contingencies. Intensity increases away from the center of the diagram, on a continuous scale. The classification scheme created by the different reinforcement contingencies consists of (1) the presentation of a positive reinforcer (S+); (2) the presentation of a negative reinforcer (S-); (3) the omission of a positive reinforcer (<u>S+</u>) or the termination of a positive reinforcer (S+!); and (4) the omission of a negative reinforcer (<u>S-</u>) or the termination of a negative reinforcer (S-!).

Before proceeding further, we should consider whether there are any exceptions to the proposed definition. Are there any emotions caused by stimuli, events, or remembered events that are not rewarding or punishing? Do any rewarding or punishing stimuli not cause emotions? These questions will be considered in greater detail below. If there are no major exceptions, or if any exceptions can be clearly accounted for, then we may have a good working definition of at least what causes emotions. Here it is worth pointing out that many approaches to or theories of emotion involve "appraisal," assessing whether something is rewarding or punishing.[2] The description in terms of reward or punishment presented here seems more tightly and operationally specified.

My book *Emotion Explained* considers a slightly more formal definition that beyond rewards or punishers introduces the concept of reinforcers.[3] It shows that emotions can be usefully seen as states produced by instrumental reinforcing stimuli, which, if their occurrence, termination, or omission is made contingent on a response, alter the future probability of making that response. Some stimuli are unlearned, primary reinforcers (e.g., the taste of food if the animal is hungry), whereas others are learned because of their association with such primary reinforcers, thereby becoming "secondary reinforcers."

This foundation has been laid to show how the operation of a number of factors, including the following, can account for a wide range of emotions:

1. *Reinforcement contingency* (whether reward or punishment is given or withheld).

2. *Intensity of the reinforcer.*

3. *Reinforcement association*   Any environmental stimulus might have a number of different reinforcement associations. A stimulus might be associated with the presentation of both a reward and a punisher, allowing states such as conflict and guilt to arise.

4. *Different primary reinforcers*   Emotions elicited by stimuli associated with different primary reinforcers will be different.

5. *Different secondary reinforcers*   Emotions elicited by different secondary reinforcers will be different (even if the primary reinforcer is the same).

6. *Active or passive nature of the behavioral response*   If an active behavioral response to the omission of a positive reinforcer is possible, then anger

might be produced, but if only a passive response is possible, then sadness, depression, or grief might occur.

It is also worth noting that emotions can be produced as much by the recall of reinforcing events as by external reinforcing stimuli. Indeed, emotions normally consist of complex cognitive processing that analyzes the stimulus, determines its reinforcing valence, and then elicits a mood change if the valence is positive or negative. A mood or affective state may occur in the absence of an external stimulus, as in some types of depression. Normally, however, the mood or affective state is produced by an external stimulus, with the whole process of stimulus representation, evaluation in terms of reward or punishment, and the resulting mood or affect being referred to as "emotion."

The Functions of Emotion

The functions of emotion also provide insight into the nature of emotion, Leading to the discussion of memory storage and recall, these functions of emotion can be summarized as follows:

1. *Elicitation of autonomic and endocrine responses.* By eliciting a rise in the heart rate and the release of adrenaline, for example, emotion prepares the body for action.

2. *Flexibility of behavioral responses to reinforcing stimuli.* Emotional states allow a simple interface between sensory inputs and action systems. Goals for behavior are specified by evaluation of rewards and punishments. When an environmental stimulus has been decoded as a primary reward or punishment or (after previous stimulus-reinforcer association learning) as a secondary reward or punishment, it becomes a goal for action. A human can then perform any (instrumental) action to obtain the reward or to avoid the punisher. Thus there is flexibility of action, in contrast to stimulus-response learning, in which a particular response to a particular stimulus is learned. The emotional route to action is flexible not only because any action can be performed to obtain the reward or avoid the punishment, but also because the human subject can learn in as little as one trial that a reward or punishment is associated with a particular stimulus, in what is termed *stimulus-reinforcer association learning.*

Accordingly, two processes are involved in the actions being described. The first is stimulus-reinforcer association learning, and the second is instrumental learning of an operant response made to approach and obtain the reward or to avoid or escape from the punisher. Emotion is an integral part of this, for it is the state elicited in the motivating first stage, by stimuli that are decoded as rewards or punishers. The motivation is to obtain the reward or avoid the punisher (the goals for the action). Animals must be built to obtain certain rewards and avoid certain punishers; indeed, the genes that specify primary or unlearned rewards and punishers effectively specify the goals for action. This is the solution that natural selection has found for how genes can influence behavior to promote their fitness (as measured by reproductive success), and for how the brain can interface sensory with action systems—an important part of my theory of emotion.

To select between obtaining available rewards and avoiding punishers, each with its associated costs, is a process that can take place both implicitly (unconsciously) and explicitly using a language system to enable long-term plans to be made.[4] Many different brain systems, some involving implicit evaluation of rewards, and others explicit, verbal, conscious evaluation of rewards and planned long-term goals, must enter into the selection of behavior (figure 8.2).

The implication is that using reward and punishment systems built by genes and tuned to dimensions of the environment that increase fitness provides a workable mode of operation for organisms that evolve by natural selection. That such systems gain their adaptive value by being tuned to a goal for action offers a deep insight into how natural selection has shaped many brain systems and is a fascinating outcome of Darwinian thought.[5]

3. *Motivation of actions* For example, fear learned by stimulus-reinforcement association motivates actions to avoid noxious stimuli.

4. *Communication of intentions* Monkeys, for example, may communicate their emotional state by making an open-mouth threat to indicate the extent to which they are willing to compete for resources; in doing so, they may influence the behavior of other animals. This aspect of emotion was emphasized by Darwin; it has been studied more recently by Paul Ekman and, in terms of the brain mechanisms, by me.[6]

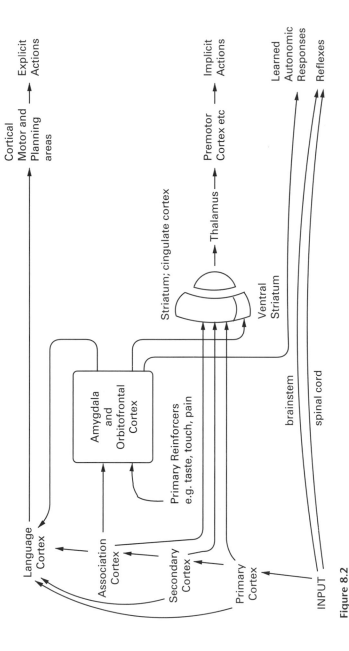

Figure 8.2

Dual routes to the initiation of action in response to rewarding and punishing stimuli. The different sensory inputs enable evaluations of incoming or remembered stimuli within the orbitofrontal cortex and amygdala based mainly on primary (unlearned) reinforcement for taste, touch, and smell stimuli and on secondary (learned) reinforcement for sight and sound stimuli. In the case of vision, the inferior temporal visual cortex is the "association cortex" that outputs representations of objects to the amygdala and orbitofrontal cortex. One route for the outputs from these evaluative brain structures is via projections directly to structures such as the basal ganglia (including the striatum and ventral striatum) to enable implicit, direct behavioral responses based on the reward- or punishment-related evaluation of the stimuli to be made. A second route is via the language systems of the brain, which allow explicit decisions involving multistep syntactic planning to be implemented.

5. *Social bonding* Examples are the emotions associated with the attachment of the parents to their young and vice versa.

6. *Memory* Our current mood state can affect the cognitive evaluation of events or memories.[7] Thus we are more likely to recall happy memories when we are happy and depressing memories when we are depressed. The recall of depressing memories, in turn, can have the effect of perpetuating depression, a factor relevant to its etiology and treatment.

A normal function of the effects of mood state on memory recall might be to facilitate continuity in the interpretation of the reinforcing value of events in the environment or of an individual's behavior by others, or simply to keep behavior motivated to a particular goal. Another possibility, and one I have repeatedly raised, is that the effects of mood state on memory have no adaptive value, but are a consequence of having a general cortical architecture with backprojections. Simon Stringer and I have analyzed the interactions between mood state and memory systems using neural networks that capture this connectivity, as shown in figure 8.3.[8]

What, indeed, are the mechanisms by which mood state affects memory? It is thought that, whenever memories are stored, part of the context is stored with the memory. This is quite likely to happen in associative neuronal networks such as those in the hippocampus.[9] The CA3 part of the hippocampus may operate as a single autoassociative memory capable of linking together almost arbitrary co-occurrences of inputs, including inputs about emotional state that reach the entorhinal cortex from, for example, the amygdala. Recall of a memory occurs best in such networks when the input key to the memory is nearest to the original input pattern of activity that was stored. It thus follows that a memory of, for example, a happy episode is recalled best when in a happy mood state. This is a special case of a general theory of how context is stored with a memory and how it influences recall.

7. *Facilitation of the storage of memories by emotion* The current emotional state may be stored with episodic memories, providing a mechanism for it to affect which memories are recalled. Or it may guide the cerebral cortex in the representations of the world that are set up using backprojections of the type illustrated in figure 8.3.

8. *Facilitation of persistent and continuing motivation and direction of behavior* By enduring for minutes or longer after a reinforcing stimulus has

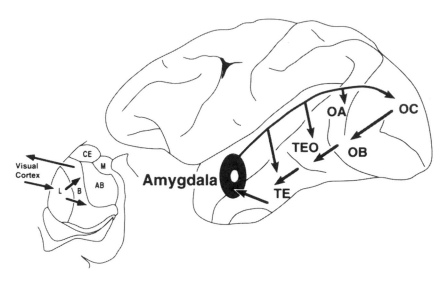

Figure 8.3

Backprojections from the primate amygdala to visual cortical areas in the temporal lobe. Here areas of the inferior temporal visual cortex (TE and TEO) that receive their inputs from prestriate areas (OB) in turn receive inputs from the primary visual cortex (OC). The insert to the left shows a coronal section of the primate amygdala, indicating that many of the visual cortical afferents reach its lateral nucleus (L) and that many of the backprojections arise from its basal nucleus (B). AB, accessory basal nucleus; CE, central nucleus; M, medial nucleus.

Reproduced with permission from David G. Amaral et al. "Anatomical Organization of the Primate Amygdaloid Complex," in *The Amygdala: Neurobiological Aspects of Emotion, Memory, and Mental Dysfunction*, ed. J. Aggleton (New York: Wiley-Liss, 1992), figure 8.

occurred, emotion may continue to motivate behavior, to help achieve a goal or goals.

9. *Triggering the recall of memories* Amygdala backprojections to the neocortex (figure 8.3) could enable emotion to retrieve representations stored there in much the same way the hippocampus retrieves recent episodic memories in the neocortex.

Different Systems for Emotional Learning and Memory

When stimuli are paired with primary reinforcers, associations that perform many types of function are formed. Many processes take place during emotion, all contributing to the richness and sometimes the inconsistency of what happens during emotional behavior. Understanding the diversity of these processes provides a foundation for analyses and descriptions of emotional behavior, including those found in literary works.

Classical (Pavlovian) conditioning, in which a stimulus is paired with another stimulus or response, and where the actions have no influence on the pairing, has the potential to create multiple associative representations in the brain, as next described.[10]

1. *Stimulus-response association* The conditioned stimulus (CS) may become directly associated with the unconditioned response (UR), a simple stimulus-response (S-R) association that carries no information about the identity of the unconditioned stimulus (pathway 1 in figure 8.4). Such unconditioned stimulus–elicited responses include both preparatory responses that are not specific to the type of unconditioned stimulus involved, such as orienting to a stimulus or increased arousal, and "consummatory" responses that are, such as salivating to food, blinking to an air puff applied to the eye, or approach to a food. A single unconditioned stimulus may elicit both preparatory and consummatory responses, and thus the conditioned stimulus may enter into simple S-R associations with several types of response.

2. *Representation of affect* The conditioned stimulus can evoke a representation of affect, that is, an emotional state, such as fear or the expectation of reward (pathway 2 in figure 8.4), a phenomenon demonstrated operationally by transreinforcer blocking. Normally, however, at least in humans, affective states have content, that is, they are about particular reinforcers (such as feeling happy when seeing a friend, or feeling happy when receiving a gift), and these states are better described by the third type of association, described next.

3. *Conditioned stimulus–unconditioned stimulus associations* The conditioned stimulus can become associated with the specific sensory properties of the unconditioned stimulus including its visual appearance, sound, and smell and its "consummatory" (primary reinforcing) properties such as its taste, nutritive value, and feel (pathway 3 in figure 8.4).

Different pathways in the brain are involved in the Pavlovian learned autonomic and skeletal responses to a conditioned stimulus, and in the affective representation or emotional state (e.g., fear), which may itself enter into associations and influence choice.

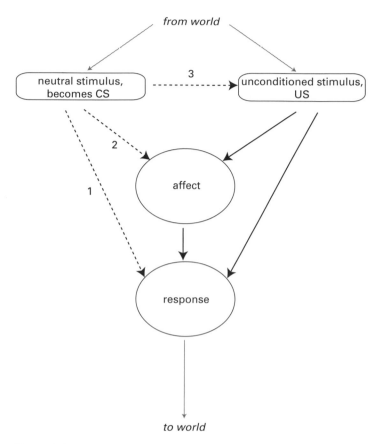

Figure 8.4
Pavlovian conditioning. Dashed arrows represent associatively learned links. Several different types of response may be involved, including preparatory responses that are not specific to the type of unconditioned stimulus (US) involved, such as orienting to a stimulus or increased arousal, and "consummatory" responses that are specific, such as salivating to food or blinking to an air puff applied to the eye.
Adapted from Rudolf N. Cardinal et al., "Emotion and Motivation: The Role of the Amygdala, Ventral Striatum, and Prefrontal Cortex," *Neuroscience and Biobehavioral Reviews* 26 (2002): figure1.

In instrumental learning, there is a contingency between the behavior and the reinforcing outcome. A number of different learning processes may operate during this procedure, which, it turns out, may have somewhat different brain implementations. One key process is action-outcome learning, where the outcome is represented as reward or affective value, implemented by the firing of orbitofrontal cortex neurons that respond, for example, to the taste of food only if hunger is present. Other processes that influence instrumental learning include Pavlovian processes that can facilitate performance, such as Pavlovian-instrumental transfer. Furthermore, approach to a food may be under Pavlovian rather than instrumental control. Finally, we must keep in mind that, after overtraining, responses may become inflexibly linked to stimuli, and that the goals and their reward value may no longer be directly influencing behavior in an ongoing way.

There are many different brain processes and two principal systems involved in learning emotional responses; different brain regions are involved in different types of learning. What is learned in one system may be somewhat independent of what is learned in other. It is important to recognize that emotion is *not* a single unified process, but may comprise many different underlying and not always consistent ones.

Masterworks of poetry or fiction have explored the rich complexity and inconsistency of many of the processes involved in emotion and their effects, which can now be at least partly analyzed systematically and scientifically. This complexity is further enriched when we add the effects of the rational (reasoning) processing system described next, whose outcomes do not always match those generated by the gene-based, implicit, and often unconscious processing system described above.

A Separate, Rational, Reasoning, Conscious System for Identifying Emotional Goals

I have proposed elsewhere that, in addition to the gene-based processing system for emotion described above, there is a separate rational (reasoning) processing system that can plan ahead and work for what are sometimes different, long-term goals.[11] This system involves multistep trains of first-order thought, as might be required to formulate a plan with many steps. I have argued that, when we correct such multistep plans or trains of thought, we need to think about these first-order thoughts; the system that does so is thus a higher-order thought system.[12] Because each step has its own symbols, syntactic linking is needed between the symbols within each step, and some syntactic (relational) links must be made between symbols in different steps. This arbitrary symbol manipulation using important aspects of language processing to plan (but not to initiate all types of behavior) is close to what consciousness is about. In particular, consciousness may *be* the state that arises in a system that can think about (or reflect on) its own (or other people's) thoughts, that is, a system capable of second- or higher-order thoughts.[13]

It is worth considering the role of emotion in the evolution of a system for flexible planning. Take grief, which may occur when a reward is terminated and no immediate action is possible.[14] It may be adaptive by leading to a cessation of the formerly rewarded behavior and thus facilitating the possible identification of other positive reinforcers in the environment. In humans, grief may be particularly and especially potent because it becomes represented in a system that can plan ahead and understand the enduring implications of the loss. This may in part explain why emotion and emotional memory, in particular, are such an important force in poetry and fiction.

An interesting question arises as to how decisions are made in humans having both implicit and explicit processing systems for emotional memory (figure 8.2). The first, implicit system may be especially useful when rapid reactions to stimuli with reward or punishment value must be made (for which the direct connections from structures such as the orbitofrontal cortex to the basal ganglia may allow rapid actions). The implicit system is also important in guiding actions when there may be too many factors to be taken into account easily by the explicit, rational, planning system. In contrast, when the implicit system continually makes errors, it would be beneficial to switch to the explicit conscious control system, which can evaluate with its long-term planning algorithms what action should be performed next. Indeed, it would be optimally adaptive for the explicit system to regularly assess performance using the more automatic implicit system, and to intervene to control behavior quite frequently, as needed. There may also be a flow of influence from the explicit, verbal system to the implicit system, in that the explicit system may decide on a plan of action or strategy, and exert an influence on the implicit system that will alter the reinforcement evaluations made and the signals produced by the implicit system.

Not surprisingly, the two processing systems may often conflict, in that the implicit system guides behavior to obtain the greatest immediate reinforcement, whereas the explicit system defers immediate rewards when longer-term, multistep plans need to be formed. This type of conflict occurs in animals with a syntactic planning ability, that is, in humans and any other animals with the ability to process a series of "if ... then" stages of planning. Such conflict may be an important aspect of the operation of at least the human mind because it is so essential for humans to correctly decide, at every moment, whether to invest in a relationship or a group that may offer long-term benefits or to directly pursue immediate benefits.

As we have seen, much complex animal (including human) behavior can take place using the implicit, unconscious route to action. We should therefore be careful not to postulate intentional states (intentions, beliefs, and desires), for which, it seems to me, a flexible, one-time linguistic processing system is needed, unless the evidence for them is strong.

The two routes for making decisions, an emotional route that can operate unconsciously, and a rational, conscious route, produce separate processing systems for different types of emotional memory. Sometimes decisions may be made by one system, sometimes by the other. When the decisions are made by the unconscious emotional system, the rational, conscious system may confabulate an explanation for the decision having little to do with the original causes of the behavior. Furthermore, the decisions may be taken by these two systems on a somewhat probabilistic basis (as described below), and thus may be different on different occasions even if the circumstances are somewhat similar. Also, factors that may be manipulated in the environment can have effects on whether the rational or emotional system takes control on a particular occasion. Alcohol, for example, by reducing emotional restraint and inhibition, can induce the emotional system to produce an extra strong output for an action that might overcome the rational system. These foundations provide for a scientific understanding of many observations about memory in works of literature and their evolutionary and computational origins.[15]

Effects of Emotion on Cognitive Processing

Thus far, we have been concerned primarily with how stimuli are decoded to produce emotional states, and with how these states can influence behavior. Moreover, it has been recognized that current mood state can affect the cognitive evaluation of events or memories. For example, happy memories are more likely to be recalled when happy. Why does this occur?

It is thought that, whenever a memory is stored, part of the context is stored with the memory. This is most likely to happen in associative neuronal networks such as those in the hippocampus. The CA3 part of the hippocampus may operate as a single autoassociative memory capable of linking together almost arbitrary co-occurrences of inputs, including inputs about emotional state that reach the entorhinal cortex from, for example, the amygdala. Recall of a memory occurs best in such networks when the input key to the memory is nearest to the original input pattern of activity that was stored, and this effect is now well understood. It thus follows that our memory of, for example, a happy episode is recalled best when we are in a happy mood state. This is a special case of a general theory of how context is stored with a memory, and of how it influences recall. The effect of emotional state on cognitive processing and memory is thus thought to be a particular case of the more general way that context can affect cognitive processing and the storage and retrieval of memories.

Another brain system where emotional states affect storage and recall of memories is the backprojection system from the amygdala and orbitofrontal cortex (structures important in emotion) to the inferior visual temporal cortex (important in the representation of objects). It is thought that coactivity between forward and backprojecting inputs to strongly activated cortical pyramidal cells may lead to both sets of synapses being modified. This could facilitate recall of cortical representations (of particular faces, for example) that had become associated with emotional states, represented by activity in the amygdala.

Emotional states may affect whether or how strongly memories are stored using the cholinergic basal forebrain system; stored as part of many memories, they may influence both the recall of such memories and the operation of cognitive processing. For example, when pleasant events are being described, or memories of them are being recalled, there will be top-down influences from the cognitive level at which words are represented onto emotional processing systems (such as those in the orbitofrontal cortex) to produce or influence emotional feelings.[16]

Noise in the Brain, Memory Recall, Nondeterministic Decision-Making, and Creativity

A theoretical framework for understanding decision making in the brain has recently emerged, with interesting implications for the study of memory.[17] At its center is a neural network having positive internal feedback between its neurons that can fall into a number of states. Each state corresponds to a decision and consists of one winning population of neurons firing at a high rate and inhibiting the other populations. Each is called an "attractor state" because, once its high firing rate state starts up, it takes off with the other neurons in that population, all of which then remain in a stable state of high firing. When the decision process starts, the inputs for each decision state push the system around, but if the inputs are relatively equal, the state that is reached is influenced by the "noisy," that is random spike timings of the firings of the neurons in the different populations. If, by chance, many of the neurons in one of the possible attractors happen to fire close together in a short time period, that attractor is more likely to win the competition on that trial or occasion, and thus also the decision to be reached. This probabilistic method of reaching a decision, with an element of randomness on each occasion, lends great richness to behavior and to situations explored in literary works.

Furthermore, as introduced above, this type of noise in decision-making processes may operate at many different stages of brain processing. It may even affect the way decisions are influenced on different occasions—between the unconscious emotional system and the rational (reasoning) decision-making system.[18] The same type of noise that influences which memory is recalled influences which thought follows any one thought. This, it is argued, is what makes our thought processes nondeterministic, thereby greatly contributing to *creativity*.[19] Indeed, it may be that when noise in this system for thoughts has too much effect, it leads to associations between thoughts that are both particularly loose and particularly creative, as in James Joyce's *Finnegans Wake*. In a more extreme case, this noise effect could lead to thoughts that are so loose that they become bizarre and even schizophrenic.[20] At the other end of the continuum, if the thoughts are too stable, this might result in great perseverance in thoughts, aims, and actions, and, toward the end of the continuum, in obsessive-compulsive disorder, in which thoughts and behavior are too fixed and stable, and too little influenced by noise in the system.[21] Thus, we can see a broad distribution of stability versus the ability to be influenced by noise in the human population. There are different advantages to being in different parts of the distribution, with major disadvantages being incurred only at its extremes. This may be typical of how Darwinian evolution operates, with considerable variation in a population being useful, and selection within that population based (in the end) on reproductive success.[22]

Interestingly, some such probabilistic, nondeterministic, mental processing may be useful in the stages of the creative process of literature. Different degrees of this noise may be useful in different forms of creativity as opposed to rational processing. The creative process may itself be biased by top-down cognition to emphasize processing in the more rational system, or in the more emotional system, or perhaps in the more visual area of processing which is especially relevant to visual art such as painting and sculpture.

In sum, we have pointed to some of the ways in which brain processing with respect to emotional memory might actually help to generate interesting future imaginative literature. This chapter has shown how random effects within the brain caused by neuronal spike timing help to generate creative and nondeterministic thoughts, important in producing different behavior in people on different occasions, and providing a basis for much of the rich tapestry woven by literature in its exploration of people's emotional states, situations, and decisions. Scientific progress in understanding how the memory and emotional systems in the brain work has implications for interpreting literature. New insights into both human behavior and the creative process itself may foster not only deeper understanding of how the brain works, but also prompt the creation of more great literature.

Notes

1. See Edmund T. Rolls, *Emotion Explained* (Oxford: Oxford University Press, 2005); E. T. Rolls, *The Brain and Emotion* (Oxford: Oxford University Press, 1999).

2. On theories of emotions, see Kenneth T. Strongman, *The Psychology of Emotion*, 4th ed. (London: Wiley, 1996). On the role of appraisal in emotion, see Nico H. Frijda, *The Emotions* (Cambridge: Cambridge University Press, 1986); Richard S. Lazarus, *Emotion and Adaptation* (New York: Oxford University Press, 1991); Keith Oatley and Jennifer M. Jenkins, *Understanding Emotions* (Oxford: Blackwell, 1996).

3. See E. T. Rolls, *Emotion Explained*. Many other insights in the current chapter derive from this book.

4. See E. T. Rolls, *Memory, Attention, and Decision-Making: A Unifying Computational Neuroscience Approach* (Oxford: Oxford University Press, 2008).

5. E. T. Rolls, "A Neurobiological Basis for Affective Feelings and Aesthetics," in *Philosophy and Aesthetic Psychology*, ed. Elisabeth Schellekens and Peter Goldie (Oxford: Oxford University Press, 2010).

6. Charles Darwin, *The Expression of the Emotions in Man and Animals*, 3rd ed. (Chicago: University of Chicago Press, 1872); Paul Ekman, "Facial Expression and Emotion," *American Psychologist* 48 (1993): 384–392. Also see E. T., Rolls *Emotion Explained*; E. T. Rolls and Fabian Grabenhorst, "The Orbitofrontal Cortex and Beyond: From Affect to Decision-Making," *Progress in Neurobiology* 86: 216–244.

7. K. Oatley and J. M. Jenkins, *Understanding Emotions*; Paul H. Blaney, "Affect and Memory: A Review," *Psychological Bulletin* 99 (1986): 229–246.

8. E. T. Rolls and S. M. Stringer, "A Model of the Interaction between Mood and Memory," *Network: Computation in Neural Systems* 12 (2001): 111–129.

9. See E. T. Rolls, *Memory, Attention, and Decision-Making: A Unifying Computational Neuroscience Approach*. Many of the insights in the discussions of memory in this section are derived from this book. See also E. T. Rolls and Raymond P. Kesner, "A Computational Theory of Hippocampal Function, and Empirical Tests of the Theory," *Progress in Neurobiology* 79 (2006): 1–48.

10. See Rudolf N. Cardinal et al., "Emotion and Motivation: The Role of the Amygdala, Ventral Striatum, and Prefrontal Cortex," *Neuroscience and Biobehavioral Reviews* 26 (2002): 321–352.

11. E. T. Rolls, "Consciousness in Neural Networks?" *Neural Networks* 10 (1997): 1227–1240; E. T. Rolls, "Consciousness Absent and Present: A Neurophysiological Exploration," *Progress in Brain Research* 144 (2003): 95–106; E. T. Rolls, "A Higher Order Syntactic Thought (Host) Theory of Consciousness," in *Higher-Order Theories of Consciousness: An Anthology*, ed. Rocco J. Gennaro (Amsterdam: John Benjamins, 2004), 137–172; E. T. Rolls, "The Affective Neuroscience of Consciousness: Higher Order Linguistic Thoughts, Dual Routes to Emotion and Action, and Consciousness," in *Cambridge Handbook of Consciousness*, ed. Philip David Zelazo, Morris Moscovitch, and Evan Thompson (Cambridge: Cambridge

University Press, 2007), 831–859; Edmund T. Rolls, "Consciousness Absent or Present: A Neurophysiological Exploration of Masking," in *The First Half Second: The Microgenesis and Temporal Dynamics of Unconscious and Conscious Visual Processes*, ed. Haluk Ogmen and Bruno G. Breitmeyer (Cambridge, MA: MIT Press, 2005), 89–108; E. T. Rolls, "A Computational Neuroscience Approach to Consciousness," *Neural Networks* 20 (2007): 962–982; E. T. Rolls, "Emotion, Higher Order Syntactic Thoughts, and Consciousness," in *Frontiers of Consciousness*, ed. Lawrence Weiskrantz and Martin K. Davies (Oxford: Oxford University Press, 2008): 131–167.

12. There is a fundamentally important distinction here. Working for a gene-specified reward, as in many emotions, is performed in the interests of the "selfish" genes, whereas working for rationally planned rewards may be performed in the interests of the phenotype or the particular individual, which may not always be in the interests of the genotype. See E. T. Rolls, "Consciousness, Decision-Making, and Neural Computation," in *Perception-Reason-Action Cycle: Models, Algorithms and Systems*, ed. Vassilis Cutsuridis et al. (Berlin: Springer, 2010).

13. See E. T. Rolls, "Consciousness in Neural Networks?"; E. T. Rolls, "A Higher Order Syntactic Thought (Host) Theory of Consciousness"; E. T. Rolls, "The Affective Neuroscience of Consciousness: Higher Order Linguistic Thoughts, Dual Routes to Emotion and Action, and Consciousness"; David M. Rosenthal, "Two Concepts of Consciousness," *Philosophical Studies* 49 (1986): 329–359; David M. Rosenthal, "A Theory of Consciousness," Report 40 (Bielefeld, Germany: Center for Interdisciplinary Research, 1990); David M. Rosenthal, "Thinking That One Thinks," in *Consciousness*, ed. Martin Davies and Glyn W. Humphreys (Oxford: Blackwell, 1993), 197–223; David M. Rosenthal, "Varieties of Higher-Order Theory," in *Higher Order Theories of Consciousness*, ed. Rocco J. Gennaro (Amsterdam: John Benjamins, 2004), 17–44; David M. Rosenthal, *Consciousness and Mind* (Oxford: Oxford University Press, 2005); Peter Carruthers, *Language, Thought and Consciousness* (Cambridge: Cambridge University Press, 1996). Daniel C. Dennett, *Consciousness Explained* (London: Penguin, 1991); Rocco J. Gennaro, ed., *Higher Order Theories of Consciousness* (Amsterdam: John Benjamins, 2004); Edmund T. Rolls, "A Theory of Emotion and Consciousness, and Its Application to Understanding the Neural Basis of Emotion," in *The Cognitive Neurosciences*, ed. Michael S. Gazzaniga (Cambridge, MA: MIT Press, 1995), 1091–1106; Edmund T. Rolls, "Brain Mechanisms of Vision, Memory, and Consciousness," in *Cognition, Computation, and Consciousness*, ed. Masao Ito, Yasushi Miyashita, and Edmund T. Rolls (Oxford: Oxford University Press, 1997), 81–120.

14. See E. T. Rolls, "A Theory of Emotion, and Its Application to Understanding the Neural Basis of Emotion."

15. See E. T. Rolls, "A Neurobiological Basis for Affective Feelings and Aesthetics."

16. Fabian Grabenhorst, E. T. Rolls, and Amy Bilderbeck, "How Cognition Modulates Affective Responses to Taste and Flavor: Top-Down Influences on the

Orbitofrontal and Pregenual Cingulate Cortices," *Cerebral Cortex* 18 (2008): 1549–1559; E. T. Rolls and Fabian Grabenhorst, "The Orbitofrontal Cortex and Beyond: From Affect to Decision-Making," *Progress in Neurobiology* 86 (2008): 216–244.

17. See E. T. Rolls and Gustavo Deco, *The Noisy Brain: Stochastic Dynamics as a Principle of Brain Function* (Oxford: Oxford University Press, 2010); Gustavo Deco, Edmund T. Rolls, and Ranulfo Romo, "Stochastic Dynamics as a Principle of Brain Function," *Progress in Neurobiology* 88 (2009): 1–16.

18. E. T. Rolls, "A Higher Order Syntactic Thought (Host) Theory of Consciousness"; E. T. Rolls, "The Affective Neuroscience of Consciousness: Higher Order Linguistic Thoughts, Dual Routes to Emotion and Action, and Consciousness"; E. T. Rolls, "Consciousness Absent or Present: A Neurophysiological Exploration of Masking"; E. T. Rolls, "A Computational Neuroscience Approach to Consciousness"; E. T. Rolls, "Emotion, Higher Order Syntactic Thoughts, and Consciousness."

19. See E. T. Rolls and G. Deco, *The Noisy Brain: Stochastic Dynamics as a Principle of Brain Function*.

20. Marco Loh, E. T. Rolls, and Gustavo Deco, "A Dynamical Systems Hypothesis of Schizophrenia," *PLoS Computational Biology* 3 (2007): 11; Edmund T. Rolls et al., "Computational Models of Schizophrenia and Dopamine Modulation in the Prefrontal Cortex," *Nature Reviews Neuroscience* 9 (2008): 696–709.

21. E. T. Rolls, Marco Loh, and Gustavo Deco, "An Attractor Hypothesis of Obsessive-Compulsive Disorder," *European Journal of Neuroscience* 28 (2008): 782–793.

22. See E. T. Rolls, "A Neurobiological Basis for Affective Feelings and Aesthetics."

III Crossroads to the Humanities

9 Memory and Neurophilosophy

John Bickle

Neuroscientific findings about *learning and memory* have been central to neurophilosophy since its inception as an academic specialization in the mid-1980s. Mostly, this is because of the depth and richness of these scientific results. Early on, neuroscientists recognized that memory is a genuine cognitive function suitable for a variety of their investigative methods. And since neurophilosophy demands a strong empirical focus, it is no wonder that it is peppered with case studies drawn from memory research. This chapter illuminates some ways that such research has been featured in landmark work in neurophilosophy. Precisely because it is so suitable for neuroscientific investigation and explanation, memory lends itself to neurophilosophical reflections on, for example, the status of folk psychology, methodology in neuroscience, scientific reductionism, causal-mechanistic explanations, and multiple realization. The hope is that these reflections might guide us toward a greater philosophical understanding of cognitive functions whose neural underpinnings are less obvious, such as perception, consciousness, decision-making, and normative judgment, to name a few that have garnered recent attention.

Memory and 1980s-Style Eliminative Materialism

In the fourth chapter of her 1986 landmark book *Neurophilosophy*, Patricia Churchland introduces the neuroscience of memory, claiming that "some data discovered by neuropsychologists are so remarkable, and so contrary to customary assumptions, that they suggest that some basic assumptions about memory may be in need of radical revision."[1] The data she reviews come from work done three to five decades ago with human global amnesics. Because of extensive bilateral damage to their brains, usually in the medial temporal lobes, these patients had virtually no capacity to recall daily life events and semantically presented information beyond a short time span (a few minutes). For example, their doctors and nurses typically had to reintroduce themselves to them with each daily visit. Yet, remarkably, these patients could still learn and remember particular tasks, including motor, perceptual-motor, perceptual, and some cognitive tasks. Early studies with the famous global amnesic patient HM showed that he could perform a mirror-tracing task, in which subjects must learn to trace a mirror-inverted image of a figure, with the speed and accuracy of age- and sex-matched nonamnesic controls. A group of amnesics, including patient NA, Korsakoff amnesics, and patients who underwent electroconvulsive therapy for severe depression six to nine days before testing, were able to acquire a mirror-reading skill at a rate statistically identical to age- and sex-matched nonamnesic controls, although their performance fell off from control performance levels in a version of the test that exploited explicit memories of previously encountered mirror-inverted words. Global amnesics can be classically conditioned and are just as susceptible as non-amnesics to priming effects when the test phase doesn't require or exploit explicit recall of the primed stimuli.[2]

The preserved memory capacities in global amnesics turned out to be many and varied in kind; it what other capacities were preserved could not be readily predicted from the ones already known, "which entails," Churchland notes, "that we do not yet know what the capacities are."[3] "Learning and memory," she goes on to observe, "are at the dead center of cognition, if anything is, and as their categories are revised and redrawn, the theoretical landscape of higher functions is undergoing tremendous transformations."[4]

Many readers will recognize the *eliminative materialism* implicit in these comments. Some neurophilosophers—Patricia and Paul Churchland, most notably—have insisted that the data and theoretic explanations emerging from contemporary neuroscience seem poised to radically revise our "folk-psychological" concepts and kinds, indeed, to show that folk-psychological properties and events are empty and that folk psychology's explanatory generalizations about the actual causes of human behavior are simply false. In contrast, the states and dynamics of human cognition as described by neuroscientists are not only unrecognized by common sense but also antithetical to it.

Neurophilosophers did not invent eliminative materialism. Philosophers Paul Feyerabend and Richard Rorty had advocated the "disappearance theory of mind" since the mid-1960s.[5] And some well-known identity theorists of that era, in particular J. J. C. Smart and Herbert Feigl, were tempted by it.[6] But it fell to neurophilosophers to put empirical flesh on the eliminativist skeleton, which up until then had relied entirely on suggestive historical eliminations—caloric fluid, the heavenly crystal sphere of medieval astronomy, phlogiston, witches, and demonic possession— and not at all on any actual neuroscientific findings. By the late 1980s, the Churchlands were championing "connectionism" as the detailed neuroscientific basis for eliminative materialism, especially its geometric "phase space" interpretation, with representational content characterized as points in multidimensional vector spaces and computations over those contents characterized as vector transformations.[7] Still, as Patricia Churchland made clear in the early chapters of *Neurophilosophy*, the neuropsychology of human learning and memory paved the way to an eliminative materialism based on real neuroscientific detail.

Memory and the Coevolutionary Research Ideology

The ninth chapter of *Neurophilosophy* gives extended treatment to memory research, focusing on methodology in the mind/brain sciences. Functionalism was still the orthodox view in both philosophy of mind and psychology in the mid-1980s. Based primarily on intuitions about the massive multiple realization of psychological on physical states and events, functionalists insisted on studying the "cognitive economy," abstracted away from the physical "hardware" of the mammalian brain—the latter being only one of its myriad possible physical "realizations." Psychological states (wanting to drink a cold beer, for example) were to be characterized in terms of their typical causes and effects, including sensory inputs (seeing a tavern sign), behavioral outputs (moving up to the tavern's bar), and other internal states (believing that to drink the beer you must bring the mug to your lips). Any physical system composed of any components and processes capable of realizing or instantiating the full panoply of inputs, outputs, and internal states mediating the causes and effects of the target state will likewise want to drink a cold beer—no matter how different those realizing physical states are compared to yours. The implicit methodology in the functionalist program for developing a science of mind therefore ignores the "engineering level" details of the human brain, and focuses instead on getting the abstract specifications articulated and justified. In other words, the methodology is decidedly top-down: you start by getting the abstract characterization correct, and then if you wish—perhaps if you happen to be concerned with clinical human neuropsychology or neurology—you can go looking for the physical mechanisms that realize this abstract cause-and-effect economy in human brains. Functionalism's top-down methodology was not merely the idle speculations of philosophers. Real cognitive psychologists and computational scientists articulated related methodologies.[8]

Patricia Churchland would have none of this. Not only did she defend a mind-brain "reductionism" that functionalism eschews, but she also advocated a "coevolutionary research ideology" on both normative and metascientific grounds, basing her latter argument on the neuroscience of memory. (Interestingly, memory research per se was not a great concern among orthodox computational cognitive scientists.) Coevolution, as opposed to both the top-down methodology of functionalism and the exclusively bottom-up methodology of philosophical reductionism, insisted that scientific research at any single "level" was capable of informing and guiding research at any other "level" below or above it. To show that coevolution was a matter of actual neuroscientific practice, Churchland canvassed scientific research from the 1970s through the mid-1980s. Her chosen area was learning and memory.[9] Her wide-ranging examples were drawn from studies at four distinct levels:

1. The "cellular and molecular level," as presented in work by Eric Kandel and colleagues on habituation, sensitization, and classical conditioning in the sea slug *Aplysia*, by William Quinn and colleagues with engineered *Drosophila* memory mutants, and by Gary Lynch and colleagues with mammalian hippocampus slice preparations.

2. The "anatomical level," as revealed in work on the mammalian hippocampus, inspired by the early research on surgically induced global amnesics such as HM.

3. The "neuropsychological level," as shown in work with patients displaying a variety of memory deficits that led to the multiple memory system hypotheses of Larry Squire and Daniel Schacter.

4. The "behavioral level," as demonstrated in work with animal models of human memory deficits, with early parallel distributed processing (PDP; "connectionist") models of memory, and with the earliest functional neuroimaging techniques.

Churchland stressed the many ways that work at each of these levels inspired, suggested, and guided work at *all other* levels, just as the coevolutionary research methodology recommended. "The memory and learning field has in the last twenty-odd years become a classical exhibit of productive research on a nervous system capacity at many levels at once," she observed, and "research influences go up and down and all over the map."[10] "It is simply not rewarding to sort out this research in terms of the trilevel computer analogy, nor is there any useful purpose to be served by trying to force a fit."[11]

In the end, argued Churchland, the very integrity of psychology as a science was at stake in this debate. The "isolation" of psychology from neuroscientific disconfirmation, as advocated by the strictly top-down methodology of functionalism and classic cognitive psychology, "would be a mistake, because in general, it is such susceptibility that keeps a science honest."[12] Among the philosophical consequences of the coevolutionary research methodology, climinativism about folk categories and explanatory posits was one: "As neuroscience and psychology coevolve, both will need folk psychology less and less."[13] And a sophisticated intertheoretic reductionism within the mind-brain sciences was another: "The coevolutionary development of neuroscience and psychology means that establishing points of reductive contact is more or less inevitable."[14] Thus, at bottom, these deep philosophical conclusions, so central to philosophy of mind in the late twentieth century, rested squarely on empirical details from the neuroscience of memory.

Subsequently, in the mid-1990s, philosophers of mind became reenamored with consciousness, and discussions of state-of-the-science memory research fell away from philosophical discussions. Fortunately, mainstream neuroscience persevered with its work on memory. These later discoveries set the stage for the next round of philosophical debates about the neuroscience of memory, under the guise of "new mechanism" versus what I have termed *ruthless reductionism*.[15]

Neuroscience of Memory in the New Mechanism–Ruthless Reductionism Debate

In 2000, Peter Machamer, Lindley Darden, and Carl Craver coauthored a paper that will certainly be remembered as a classic and the starting point of the "new mechanism" movement, which promised to radically change the way most of the issues dominating the philosophy of science throughout the twentieth century are viewed.[16] The movement sees explanations, not as arguments from covering laws, statistical generalizations, or initial conditions, not as answers to "why" questions dependent on context, but rather as mechanisms—accounts of the components of a system, their dynamics, and their organization, which generate the system's input-output profile. The exact definition of *mechanism* differs across new mechanists, as do the favored illustrations (scientific and commonsensical). In 1993, William Bechtel and Robert Richardson's prescient book *Discovering Complexity* anticipated many features of this movement, and ultimately many of its ideas can be traced back to William Wimsatt's richly difficult essays from the 1970s and 1980s.[17]

Carl Craver and William Bechtel have most comprehensively articulated the new mechanistic view within the philosophy of neuroscience.[18] Craver draws on case studies from learning and memory research, discussing both the detailed history of *long-term potentiation* (LTP) as a hypothesized mechanism of memory and research seeking to discover the mechanisms of spatial memory in rodents (figure 9.1).[19] The phenomenon of spatial memory at any given level of biological organization—the mouse navigating the water maze, the mouse's hippocampus generating a spatial map of the maze environment, the hippocampus neurons inducing long-term potentiation, or the postsynaptic NMDA receptor proteins changing their three-dimensional configurations to permit Ca^{++} influx—results from mechanisms constructed out of the active components at the next level down. The mouse's improved performance in the water maze over a dozen trials, for example, is explained by the stability of the place cells generated over the trials by hippocampus activity, which in turn is explained by those neurons inducing late LTP, and so on down the line. At each step, the mechanistic explanation that current neuroscience provides meets the new mechanists' definition of *mechanism*: S's Ψ-ing is explained by its components $(X_1, X_2, \ldots, X_m)$, their activities $(\Phi_1, \Phi_2, \ldots, \Phi_n)$, and their organization (figure 9.2).

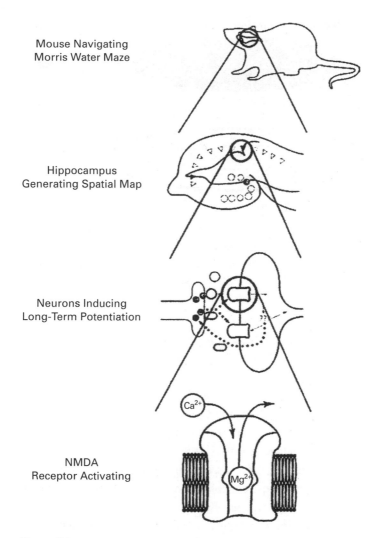

Mouse Navigating
Morris Water Maze

Hippocampus
Generating Spatial Map

Neurons Inducing
Long-Term Potentiation

NMDA
Receptor Activating

Figure 9.1

Levels of spatial memory.

Reproduced from Carl F. Craver, *Explaining the Brain: Mechanisms and the Mosaic Unity of Neuroscience* (New York: Oxford University Press, 2007), figure 5.1.

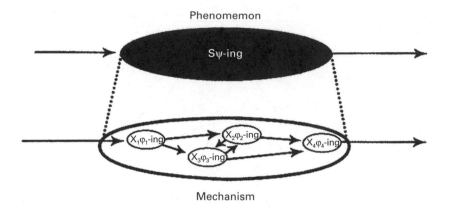

Figure 9.2

Cognitive phenomenon and its mechanism.

Reproduced from Carl F. Craver, *Explaining the Brain: Mechanisms and the Mosaic Unity of Neuroscience* (New York: Oxford University Press, 2007), figure 1.1.

At first glance, Craver's diagram and case study compare favorably with the classical psychoneural reductionist view (figure 9.3). But Craver is quick to point out the contrasts. His is explicitly an "alternative" to the reductionists' view of scientific explanation, including an alternate set of norms by which explanations should be assessed.[20] The new mechanists' "upward-looking trends," in addition to the "downward-looking" ones they share with classical reductionists, suggest a "mosaic unity" for neuroscience, not a "reductionist unity" still mired in 1950s-style logical empiricism.[21] Most important, Craver's account recognizes the very existence of "multilevel mechanistic explanations"—the kinds he claims dominate neuroscience, and the kinds that reductionists force into a mold that entirely misses their multilevel character. For the reductionists, no matter how "liberalized" or "reformed," the higher-level *causal* mechanisms can't be acknowledged. Indeed, the higher level is "nothing but" the components, their activities, and their organization at the next level down, and down, and down ... until we hit rock bottom and lose all claims to real causal mechanisms. For the reductionists, the mouse navigating the water maze is nothing but its hippocampus forming spatial maps (along with the rest of its biological features described at that level of organization), which is nothing but its hippocampus neurons inducing long-term potentiation, which is nothing but their postsynaptic NMDA

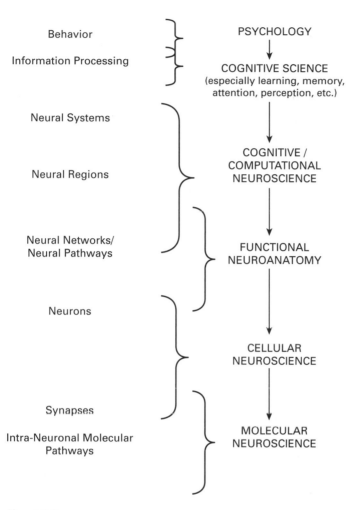

Figure 9.3

Classical reductionist schema of levels of organization within the nervous system, relationships to higher levels of organization, and the scopes of the mind-brain sciences addressing these levels. Downward arrows represent the step-by-step picture of classical intertheoretic reduction.

Reproduced from John Bickle, "Reducing Mind to Molecular Pathways: Explicating the Reductionism Implicit in Current Mainstream Neuroscience," *Synthese* 152 (2006): figure 1.

receptors activating to permit Ca^{++} influx, which is nothing but ... But such reductionism, says Craver, is not what current neuroscientists are offering. Instead, their explanations abound with causal mechanisms that seamlessly engage multiple levels of biological organization.

One interesting feature of this debate is the agreement between new mechanists and die-hard reductionists that a correct *descriptive metascience* is crucial to sound neurophilosophical reflection. Remarkably, Craver and I also agree that, among recent neuroscience initiatives, his spatial memory case study is the one most worthy of philosophical (and, in Craver's case, historical) reflection. In advocating "ruthless reductionism," I have relied on recent work on the mechanisms of memory consolidation and have emphasized the experimental practices that have dominated neuroscientific investigations into memory phenomena over the past two decades.[22] These practices depend especially on the use of genetically engineered mice, typically those in which the genetic material for a specific intracellular signaling protein has either been knocked out or overexpressed, with the mutants' performances on particular well-accepted measures of memory consolidation then compared with wild types' performances (typically littermate control animals that didn't undergo the engineered genetic mutation).

The actual experimental details quickly become daunting for nonspecialists, but a simplified example is readily grasped. Cyclic AMP-responsive-element-binding protein, or CREB, is a DNA transcriptional protein that binds to cyclic AMP-responsive elements (CRE sites) in the promoter regions on a variety of genes. Some isoforms of CREB induce (enhance) gene transcription at that site; some block (repress) it. Knocking out the gene for the CREB enhancer isoforms generates a mutant mouse whose neurons cannot induce late LTP, the protein synthesis-dependent form that maintains for hours to days (and beyond), although they can induce early LTP, a protein synthesis-independent form that lasts for around one hour. Behaviorally, these mutants tend to be intact (compared to wild-type littermate controls) on short-term tests of various memory phenomena, but deficient on long-term tests.[23] Interestingly, these experimentalists speak of finding "molecular mechanisms of long-term declarative memory" and of contributing to "a molecular biology of cognition,"[24] whereas, in my view, current neuroscience, especially its "molecular and cellular cognition" core, is ruthlessly reductionistic. But unlike the classical reductionist picture and the new mechanistic one contrasted with it, neuroscience seeks direct explanations of cognitive phenomena at increasingly lower levels of biological explanation. This is "explanation in a single bound" of cognitive phenomena, as indicated by the specific performance measures used on well-accepted behavioral tests and by the cellular and molecular mechanisms experimentalists now present at increasingly lower levels of biological organization (figure 9.4). Philosophers and cognitive scientists might gape in disbelief at the very idea of such a project, but cellular and molecular neuroscientists are successfully performing the experiments in their laboratories. And learning and memory research serves as a showpiece for their work.

Recently, William Bechtel has given the new mechanist–ruthless reductionist scuffle an interesting new twist.[25] He does not deny that a "ruthless reductionism" informs experimental research in the cellular and molecular core of contemporary neuroscience. But he insists that another form of reductionism, "mechanistic reduction," also informs current neuroscience, especially the cognitive neuroscience that made a historical break four decades ago with the programs that went on to coalesce into the current Society for Neuroscience. The metascientific descriptions of the current neuroscience of memory are two broad programs at work, with distinct accounts of reduction, experimental techniques, and even historical antecedents. Having said that, Bechtel comes down firmly on the side of mechanistic reductionism, at least as a general method for developing a neuroscience of cognition.[26] That approach doesn't disregard the results streaming in from ruthlessly reductive neuroscience, but rather locates those results within multilevel causal mechanisms.[27] Thus the recent neuroscience of memory is once again at the forefront of a spirited debate in the philosophy of neuroscience.

Multiple Realizability Redux

Some findings from the current neuroscience of learning and memory have also surfaced in a recent attempt to redefend the old multiple realization premise about psychological and neurobiological properties, states, and events. In the heyday of functionalism, a straightforward argument held sway: psychological properties (states, events) are multiply realized in distinct physical properties (states, events). Multiple realization of potentially

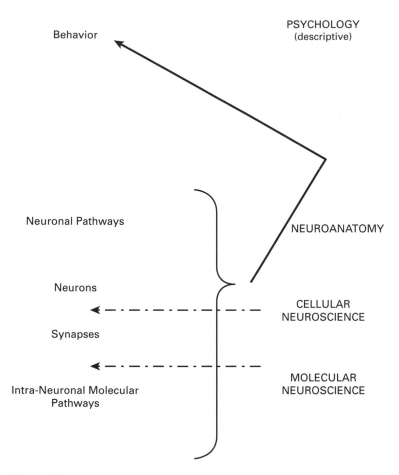

Figure 9.4
Ruthless reductionist schema of cellular and molecular cognition. Dashed arrows represent levels of experimental interventions; solid arrow represents the level at which the effects of these interventions are measured. Psychology is a descriptive endeavor generating behavioral data rather than an explanatory science.
Reproduced from John Bickle, "Reducing Mind to Molecular Pathways: Explicating the Reductionism Implicit in Current Mainstream Neuroscience," *Synthese* 152 (2006): figure 8.

reducible on reducing properties is inconsistent with the demands of reduction or identity theories. This is to say, psychological properties (states, events) can't be reduced to or are not identical with physical properties (states, events), such as those of the functioning mammalian brain. Hilary Putnam pointed out the species-dependent nature of the neural realizers of psychological properties; Jerry Fodor and Ned Block were first to stress the multiple realizability of psychological on neural states in individuals over time, based on some simple facts about neural plasticity.[28] Functionalists used this critical argument as the basis for their alternative account of the nature of mind, touched on above. Interestingly, the nonreductive physicalists, whose views came to dominate philosophy of mind from the early 1990s to the present, adopted the functionalists' multiple realization critique against reductive physicalism without alteration.[29]

Initially, the few psychoneural reductionists whose voices could be heard took on the second premise of the multiple realization argument. Historical scientific case studies were mustered to show that multiple realization of reduced on reducing kinds can be found in some widely accepted examples of actual intertheoretic reduction. Even if multiple realization, in itself, didn't rule out reductionism, it might warrant some important changes to the account of intertheoretic reduction widely accepted at the time, namely, Ernest Nagel's logical empiricist account.[30] Hardly any critic took on the first premise of the basic multiple realization argument (as presented above). The only exception was Nick Zangwill, who, in a little-cited 1992 paper, argued that multiple realization of psychological on physical kinds wasn't "proven."[31]

Then, a decade ago, the tide changed. The multiple realization premise itself, now part of the nonreductive physicalists' arsenal, became the target of sustained attack. Bechtel and Jennifer Mundale appealed to the findings of functional neuroanatomy; I appealed to the cellular and molecular neuroscience of memory consolidation, and to arguments scientists were themselves making about the "evolutionary conservatism" of these basic mechanisms. The comparative biochemistry of these intracellular signaling molecules revealed similarities across a wide range of species, from fruit flies and sea slugs to mice and humans—and down to the level of identical amino acid sequences in the proteins' functional units and in the nucleotide base pairs of the genes whose transcription started the process of protein synthesis. The evolutionary argument for biochemical conservatism was straightforward. These key proteins—CREB, protein kinase A (PKA, the kinase that attaches a phosphate group to the CREB molecule to activate it as a transcriptional enhancer), and cyclic adenosine monophosphate (cAMP, the second messenger that binds to regulatory subunits of PKA to start the cascade)—are basic cell-metabolic and housekeeping proteins. Changes to their amino acid sequences, or changes in the genes that code for them, would generate proteins incapable of performing these basic cellular functions and quickly lead to a nonviable organism.

As insect biologists Josh Dubnau and Tim Tully explained in 1998:

In all systems studied, the cAMP signaling cascade has been identified as one of the major biochemical pathways involved in modulating both neuronal and behavioral plasticity. … More recently, elucidation of the role of CREB-mediated transcription in long-term memory in flies, LTP and long-term memory in vertebrates, and long-term facilitation in [the sea slug] *A. californica* suggest that CREB may constitute a universally conserved molecular switch for long-term memory.[32]

This evolutionary argument against the multiple realization premise, widely accepted among cellular and molecular cognitivists, seems conclusive. Multiple realization of psychological on physical kinds might appear to be obvious from the perspective of comparative functional neuroanatomy. After all, the neuroanatomies of fruit flies, sea slugs, mice, and humans differ vastly. But when we probe into the underlying molecular processes that drive neuron activity, including the synaptic plasticity that has dominated learning and memory research within neuroscience for decades, we find unity, not multiplicity. Practically speaking, when it comes to the mechanisms of experience-driven synaptic plasticity, a fruit fly neuron is a sea slug neuron is a mouse neuron is a human neuron. Multiple realizability vanishes with the evolution of molecular and cellular cognition.[33]

The philosopher Ken Aizawa finds reductionistic arguments such as these less than persuasive.[34] Biochemical similarity isn't *identity*, Aizawa insists—despite the amino acid sequence identities in the functional domains of the key protein components of the cAMP-PKA-CREB–new gene expression–new protein synthesis pathway, and despite the comparative cases across genera and even phyla that biologists make for evolutionary conservation of the key molecular and genetic components. If the amino acid sequences making up, for example, the PKA protein across species differ at a single residue, that's multiple realization. If key protein constituents within neurons differ biochemically, that's likewise multiple realization. But this massive multiple realization need not concern reduction-minded philosophers, Aizawa argues: their scientific counterparts routinely acknowledge it and deal with it in their experimental design and interpretation. Interestingly, he agrees that the biochemistry and molecular biology of memory consolidation make excellent food for philosophical reflection on long-standing questions about multiple realization and its consequences for our views about both mind and science.

Memory and First Steps toward a "Science of Research"

Recently, neurobiologist Alcino Silva, who coined the term *molecular and cellular cognition*, neurophilosopher Anthony Landreth, and I have teamed up to develop the most basic principles of a "science of research," derived from scientific case studies on the molecular and cellular mechanisms of memory.[35] To explain any specific cognitive phenomenon, we offer four principles—the "convergent four"—to gather what practicing neuroscientists take to be sufficient evidence for a hypothesized cellular or molecular mechanism.[36] "Convergent" refers here to the joint satisfaction of causal criteria established by all four principles. The principles call for positive and negative manipulation experiments, in which the hypothesized mechanism is either elicited or blocked in vivo and the resulting behaviors used to indicate the occurrence of the cognitive phenomenon are tracked; a correlation experiment, in which occurrences of the hypothesized mechanism are correlated with occurrences of the indicating behaviors; and integration, in which the hypothesized causal mechanism is conjoined with discoveries about all the related causal phenomena that mediate between it and the behaviors. Importantly, integration includes accounting for inconsistent experimental evidence emerging across laboratories. The most interesting feature of memory research from the perspective of the convergent four is that, for at least two intracellular signaling molecules—CREB (mentioned above) and α-calcium-calmodulin kinase II (αCaMKII)—the causal criteria of all four convergent principles have been met in published experimental results. These results directly tie activity of these signaling molecules to the induction or maintenance of long-term potentiation and to the occurrence of a variety of forms of memory consolidation using a variety of well-accepted behavioral protocols. When, for example, the CREB gene has been knocked out in mice, these mice typically show intact early LTP but deficient late LTP, and intact short-term memory but deficient long-term memory on a variety of behavioral tests. When the CREB gene has been inserted into neurons in specific regions, using microinjections of virus vectors, long-term memory behavior has been recovered in CREB knockout mice and increased in wild-type mice. CREB activity in neurons in specific brain regions has long been correlated with memory consolidation behavior. And CREB activity has been integrated into the signaling pathway in neurons involving cAMP, protein kinase A, and a variety of gene targets coding for proteins now known to increase long-term synaptic efficacy through the activation of "hidden" AMPA receptors and even the growth of new synapses.[37]

Building on the Prominence of Memory Research in Neurophilosophy

Why, then, has memory research been so central to neurophilosophy since the beginning? In a superficial sense, this question is easy to answer. Neurophilosophy relies heavily on established neuroscience findings, and learning and memory research has provided neuroscience's greatest accomplishments in finding neural mechanisms for explaining genuine cognitive functions. But let's dig deeper.

Learning and memory are perhaps unique among cognitive functions in that the neurobiological building blocks of their mechanistic explanations are *obvious*. Whatever the ensuing details turn out to be, the neuroscience of learning and memory will rest on facts about synaptic plasticity, their resulting effects in individual neuronal and organized circuit activities, and transmission, and about processes out to the behavioral periphery where neural meets muscle tissue. Unlike the neuroscience of other cognitive functions, memory research was anchored from the start; neuroscientists could move quickly up and down from this anchor: up to neural regions, systems, and behavior, and down to molecular biology and biochemistry. The same can hardly be said for other cognitive functions that interest neurophilosophers. Where exactly within the levels of neural organization does neuroscience anchor key features of sensory experience, for example? Or decision-making, ethical judgment, phenomenal consciousness, awareness, and attention, for that matter?

Long before anything of significance was known about synaptic plasticity, neuroscientists were already speculating about it as a hypothetical mechanism for information storage in the brain. The neuropsychologist Larry Squire and the neurobiologist Eric Kandel report that, as early as 1890, the great Spanish neuroanatomist Santiago Ramón y Cajal had proposed:

Learning might cause existing nerve cells to strengthen their connections with other nerve cells so as to be able to communicate more effectively with them. In order to store long-term memories, nerve cells might grow more branches and thereby form new or stronger connections. As memory fades, the nerve cells might lose these branches and thereby weaken their connections.[38]

Note that Ramón y Cajal was speculating at a time when the empirical evidence wasn't yet conclusive for the existence of neurons as discrete cells, much less for the plasticity of their myriad "connections." Donald Hebb hypothesized a rule for synaptic strengthening, its subsequent effects on "cell assemblies," and their roles in various psychological capacities, memory included, a quarter century before the first systematic study of synaptic long-lasting facilitation was published by Timothy Bliss and Terje Lømo.[39] In fact, the term *long-term potentiation* wasn't coined until 1975, two years after publication of Bliss and Lømo's paper. Even Karl Lashley, who so famously despaired after his thirty-year experimental "search for the engram," by stating, "I sometimes feel, in reviewing the evidence on the localization of the memory trace, that the necessary conclusion is that learning just is not possible,"[40] nevertheless introduced his 1950 paper by reflecting on a quote from Descartes: "His theory has in fact a remarkably modern sound. Substitute nerve impulse for animal spirits, synapse for pore and the result is the doctrine of learning as change in resistance of synapses."[41]

Perhaps the neuroscientific experimental literature on learning and memory is so rich and detailed, and hence so worthy of neurophilosophical reflection, because its neural anchor has been so evident. If we want to know what state-of-the-art neuroscience can teach us about the status of our commonsense conception of the mental, about methodology in the cognitive and brain sciences, about the scope and limits of scientific reductionism, about the nature of causal-mechanistic explanations and their place in science more generally, about multiple realization and its lessons, and about the conditions on sufficient evidence for establishing a cellular or molecular mechanism for a cognitive function, we are well advised to look to neuroscience's best cases. The conceptual tie that learning and memory enjoy with synaptic plasticity virtually guarantees that they will provide such cases. That assurance should guide us when we seek to expand neurophilosophical reflections to cognitive functions whose underlying neural mechanisms are less obvious. Thus guided, perhaps neurophilosophy can return the favor, and help push actual neuroscience farther along.

Notes

1. Patricia Smith Churchland, *Neurophilosophy: Toward a Unified Science of the Mind-Brain* (Cambridge, MA: MIT Press, 1986), 150.

2. For an excellent review of memory research, with extensive references to the primary experimental literature, see Larry R. Squire, "Memory and the Hippocampus: A Synthesis from Findings with Rats, Monkeys, and Humans, *Psychological Review* 99 (1992): 195–231.

3. P. S. Churchland, *Neurophilosophy: Toward a Unified Science of the Mind-Brain*, 151.

4. P. S. Churchland, *Neurophilosophy: Toward a Unified Science of the Mind-Brain*, 151.

5. For an excellent review of eliminative materialism with references to the primary literature, see William Ramsey, "Eliminative Materialism," *Stanford Encyclopedia of Philosophy*, October 9, 2007; at http://plato.stanford.edu/entries/materialism-eliminative/.

6. For a discussion of identity theorists' views of eliminative materialism, see John Bickle, *Philosophy and Neuroscience: A Ruthlessly Reductive Account* (New York: Springer, 2003), chap. 1.

7. See especially the essays in Paul M. Churchland, *A Neurocomputational Perspective* (Cambridge, MA: MIT Press, 1989), part II.

8. See Zenon Pylyshyn, *Computation and Cognition* (Cambridge, MA: MIT Press, 1984); David Marr, *Vision* (New York: Freeman, 1982).

9. P. S. Churchland, *Neurophilosophy: Toward a Unified Science of the Mind-Brain*, 368–373.

10. P. S. Churchland, *Neurophilosophy: Toward a Unified Science of the Mind-Brain*, 368.

11. P. S. Churchland, *Neurophilosophy: Toward a Unified Science of the Mind-Brain*, 360.

12. P. S. Churchland, *Neurophilosophy: Toward a Unified Science of the Mind-Brain*, 376.

13. P. S. Churchland, *Neurophilosophy: Toward a Unified Science of the Mind-Brain*, 374.

14. P. S. Churchland, *Neurophilosophy: Toward a Unified Science of the Mind-Brain*, 374.

15. J. Bickle, *Philosophy and Neuroscience: A Ruthlessly Reductive Account*.

16. Peter K. Machamer, Lindley Darden, and Carl F. Craver, "Thinking about Mechanisms," *Philosophy of Science* 57 (2000): 1–25.

17. William Bechtel and Robert C. Richardson, *Discovering Complexity: Decomposition and Localization as Strategies in Scientific Research* (Princeton, NJ: Princeton University Press, 1993). William Wimsett, "Reductionism, Levels of Organization and the Mind-Body Problem," in *Consciousness and the Brain*, ed. G. Globus, I. Savodnik, and G. Maxwell, eds. (New York: Plenum Press, 1976), 199–267.

18. Carl F. Craver, *Explaining the Brain: Mechanisms and the Mosaic Unity of Neuroscience* (New York: Oxford University Press, 2007); William Bechtel, *Mental Mechanisms: Philosophical Perspectives on Cognitive Neuroscience* (London: Routledge, 2008); William Bechtel, "Molecules, Systems, and Behavior: Another View of Memory Consolidation," in *Oxford Handbook of Philosophy and Neuroscience*, ed. John Bickle (New York: Oxford University Press, 2009), 13–40.

19. C. F. Craver, "The Making of a Memory Mechanism," *Journal of the History of Biology* 36 (2003): 153–195; C. F. Craver, *Explaining the Brain: Mechanisms and the Mosaic Unity of Neuroscience*, chap. 5.

20. C. F. Craver, *Explaining the Brain: Mechanisms and the Mosaic Unity of Neuroscience*, 111.

21. C. F. Craver, *Explaining the Brain: Mechanisms and the Mosaic Unity of Neuroscience*, 246–252.

22. *Consolidation* is the process by which labile, easily disrupted short-term memories are converted into long-term memories with similar content. Craver doesn't always use the term, but a quick review of the science he appeals to in discussing, for example, rodent spatial memory, shows that he has mechanistic explanations of exactly this feature in his sights. On experimental practices that have dominated neuroscientific memory research, see John Bickle, *Philosophy and Neuroscience: A Ruthlessly Reductive Account*, chaps. 2 and 3; J. Bickle, "Reducing Mind to Molecular Pathways: Explicating the Reductionism Implicit in Current Mainstream Neuroscience," *Synthese* 152 (2006): 411–434.

23. For a description of the experimental details of cellular and molecular neuroscience research, written especially for nonspecialists, see J. Bickle, *Philosophy and Neuroscience: A Ruthlessly Reductive Account*, chap. 2, and J. Bickle, "Reducing Mind to Molecular Pathways."

24. For numerous direct quotations from cellular and molecular experimentalists, see J. Bickle, *Philosophy and Neuroscience: A Ruthlessly Reductive Account*, chap. 3.

25. See W. Bechtel, "Molecules, Systems, and Behavior: Another View of Memory Consolidation."

26. See W. Bechtel, "Molecules, Systems, and Behavior: Another View of Memory Consolidation."

27. See especially Carl F. Craver and William Bechtel, "Top-Down Causation without Top-Down Causes," *Biology and Philosophy* 22 (2007): 547–563, for their account of multilevel mechanisms that avoid invoking images of "top-down causation."

28. For a review of the research on multiple realization with references to the principal publications, see John Bickle, "Multiple Realizability," *Stanford Encyclopedia of Philosophy* (July 27, 2006), http://plato.stanford.edu/entries/multiple-realizability/.

29. Terence Horgan, "Nonreductive Materialism and the Explanatory Autonomy of Psychology," in *Naturalism: A Critical Appraisal*, ed. Steven J. Wagner and Richard Warner (Notre Dame, IN; University of Notre Dame Press, 1993), 295–320.

30. Robert Richardson provides a careful reading of Nagel's actual account, applied critically to functionalists' appeals to multiple realization. See J. Bickle, "Reducing Mind to Molecular Pathways: Explicating the Reductionism Implicit in Current Mainstream Neuroscience," for a review and citations.

31. Nick Zangwill, "Variable Realization: Not Proven," *Philosophical Quarterly* (1992). For a detailed review of reductionist responses, with references to the principal publications, see J. Bickle, "Multiple Realizability."

32. Josh Dubnau and Tim Tully, "Gene Discovery in *Drosophila*: New Insights for Learning and Memory," *Annual Review of Neuroscience* 21 (1998): 438.

33. With one very interesting, evolutionarily significant difference: these same basic molecular mechanisms do most of their work presynaptically in invertebrates, and both pre- and postsynaptically in vertebrates.

34. Kenneth Aizawa, "The Biochemistry of Memory Consolidation: A Model System for the Philosophy of Mind," *Synthese* 155 (2007): 65–98. I am not the only opponent of the classic multiple realizability argument whose work has been challenged by Aizawa. In collaboration with philosopher Carl Gillett, Aizawa has been arguing against every significant attempt over the past decade to challenge the multiple realization premise.

35. Alcino J. Silva and John Bickle, "The Science of Research and the Search for Molecular Mechanisms of Cognitive Functions," in *Oxford Handbook of Philosophy and Neuroscience*, ed. John Bickle (New York: Oxford University Press, 2009), 92–126; Alcino Silva, John Bickle, and Anthony Landreth, *Engineering the Next Revolution in Neuroscience* (New York: Oxford University Press, 2010).

36. These causal criteria defy brief presentation. In A. Silva, J. Bickle, and A. Landreth, *Engineering the Next Revolution in Neuroscience,* the presentation occupies two chapters. One chapter alone is dedicated to the integration criterion.

37. Appeals to examples of memory research in neuroscience occupy six of the twenty-four chapters of the recently published *Oxford Handbook of Philosophy and Neuroscience,* edited by John Bickle. In addition to the chapters by Bechtel, Silva, and Bickle already discussed, there are those by behavioral neuroscientists Anthony Chemero and Charles Heyser, philosophers Alexander Rosenberg, Peter Machamer, and Colin Allen and neuroscientists Jim Grau and Mary Meagher. Memory's place in neurophilosophy remains as central to this day as it was in Churchland's 1986 groundbreaking book, *Neurophilosophy: Toward a Unified Science of the Mind-Brain.* For a brief presentation of cognitive experiments involving CREB, cAMP, protein kinase A, and AMPA receptors, with extensive references to the key papers in the literature, see A. J. Silva and J. Bickle, "The Science of Research and the Search for Molecular Mechanisms of Cognitive Functions."

38. Santiago Ramón y Cajal, as quoted in Larry R. Squire and Eric R. Kandel, *Memory: From Mind to Molecules* (New York: Holt, 1999), 16.

39. Donald O. Hebb, *The Organization of Behavior: A Neuropsychological Theory* (New York: Wiley, 1949); T. W. Bliss and T. Lømo, "Long-Lasting Potentiation of Synaptic Transmission in the Dentate Area of the Anaesthetized Rabbit Following Stimulation of the Perforant Path," *Journal of Physiology* (London) 232 (1973): 331–356

40. Karl S. Lashley, "In Search of the Engram," *Society of Experimental Biology Symposium* 4 (1950): 474.

41. K. S. Lashley, "In Search of the Engram," 454.

10 Confabulations about Personal Memories, Normal and Abnormal

William Hirstein

Certain types of neurological patients, and normal people in certain situations, will confabulate—sincerely claim to remember events that did not actually happen. The word *confabulate* is derived from the Latin verb *confabulari*, meaning "to talk with," derived in turn from the Latin noun *fabula*, meaning "tale" or "fable." It was perhaps this original root that the German neurologists Karl Bonhoeffer, Arnold Pick, and Carl Wernicke had in mind when they began referring to false memory reports made by their amnesic patients as *"Konfabulationen."* Most of these patients suffered from what later came to be known as "Korsakoff's syndrome." When asked what they did the day before, typical Korsakoff's patients have no memory at all but, instead of admitting ignorance, will confidently report events that either did not happen (at least not to them) or happened to them long ago. A male patient, for example, might claim that he was finishing up the year-end inventory at his supermarket, when in fact he had been in bed at the hospital the whole time. This chapter examines two neurological syndromes that gave rise to the concept of confabulation: Korsakoff's syndrome and aneurysm of the anterior communicating artery. These syndromes will then be compared with false memory syndrome, which can affect normal children and adults. The connections between the neurological phenomenon of confabulation and normal memory errors can provide insights into the complex functions of memory.

A full understanding of confabulation in both normal people and neurological patients will require contributions from psychology, neuroscience, and philosophy as well as classical neurology. Recently, the psychological investigation of the functional dynamics of memory has merged with the neuroscientific investigation of the brain processes responsible for them in the new field of cognitive neuropsychology. Philosophy can also play a helpful role here in several ways. Epistemology, the philosophical investigation of knowledge, contains detailed theories of what formally constitutes knowledge and how to assess knowledge claims. Confabulations about memories are flawed knowledge claims generated by brain processes that are malfunctioning (temporarily in the case of normal people; chronically in the neurological patients). There is also a long tradition in philosophical thought, dating back at least to Locke, on the relationship between our memory and our identity over time. Confabulation may be an attempt to maintain a coherent identity over time by linking our current self to previous actions or events, to present our self to others as a unified being, aware of and responsible for our past actions.

Implicit and Explicit Memory

The brain's many memory systems can be divided into two main types: implicit and explicit. Explicit memory presents information to consciousness in the form of thoughts or images, whereas implicit memory largely bypasses consciousness. Procedural memory, a type of implicit memory, allows us to acquire skills, such as how to play the piano or ski. It functions largely without consciousness; indeed, conscious awareness can interfere with its workings, as in the case of the trick sometimes played on fellow golfers: asking them whether they inhale or exhale when they swing. Simply considering the answer can cause the intricate pattern of muscle activations to fall completely apart. Classical conditioning, of the type discovered by Pavlov, is also a form of implicit memory. The focus here will be on a type of explicit memory known as "episodic" or "autobiographical memory."

Can you remember what you had for breakfast this morning? To do this, you need to employ your *autobiographical memory*. A record of our personal experiences, usually from our point of view, autobiographical memory is fragmentary—we can forget whole hours, days, weeks, and even years. It is an especially individual form of memory, not only because it records most indelibly those things of greatest importance to us, but also because losing it means losing a sense of our self, as anyone who has ever watched someone succumb to Alzheimer's can testify. The Alzheimer's patient eventually forgets you and may claim that you are someone else, or a stranger. This calls to mind another function of autobiographical memory: it records information about other people, places, and things that are significant to us and thus allows us to build lasting social relationships.

With some of the things we know, the knowledge of when and where we first acquired that information is long gone. We know that cats have claws, but we most likely have no idea when or where we learned this. Other information brings with it what researchers call "source memory": a type of episodic memory about when and where a memory was acquired. Source memory is a fragile thing, and we are all prone to characteristic errors in source memory tasks. We may remember an interesting medical fact but misremember which television program we learned it from, or we may remember a mildly interesting piece of gossip, but misremember whom we learned it from. The prefrontal lobes are important for retrieving source memories. In one study, normal people and hospital patients with frontal cortical lesions learned the answers to a set of trivia questions. When they were tested a week later, the frontal patients had normal memory of the answers themselves, but showed poor source memory, often claiming they had learned the answer at some earlier point in life.[1]

Another type of explicit memory, one that most often comes without a source memory tag, is called "semantic memory" and involves knowledge of impersonal facts, such as that the Eiffel Tower is in Paris, that Truman was a U.S. president, and so on. Thus far, researchers have been unable to clearly separate the neural loci of semantic and episodic memory, and perhaps for good reason: the two memory systems interact in several ways, and some have suggested they are merely different levels of categorization in the same memory store.[2] Autobiographical memories do seem to aggregate into semantic memories, as when we learn on several occasions that Lincoln gave the Gettysburg Address. We forget the occasions, but remember the core fact. Semantic and autobiographical memories would also need to interact when confabulations are produced about autobiographical events that also involve semantic knowledge, such as a "memory" of being present at some historical event. Such interactions might lead to wholesale changes in the memory system and the creation of a type of fictional autobiography, complete with surrounding (fictional) history.

Autobiographical memory is a function of the medial temporal lobe memory system, which includes the hippocampus and the adjacent para-hippocampal and perirhinal cortices. The hippocampus is not where the content itself of memories is stored, but rather appears to contain a set of neural links to the content, which is distributed widely throughout the cortex. Memories of an episode in our life typically contain information from more than one modality: sight, hearing, and even taste, touch, and smell. Each of these components is stored in a unimodal sensory area; for example, the visual components of an episodic memory are stored in the visual cortices in the occipital and inferior temporal lobes whereas the auditory components are stored in the auditory cortex in the superior temporal lobes. These distributed representations are linked to a central index in the hippocampus. When recent episodes are retrieved, the index is reactivated, causing activation to spread to each of the associated unimodal areas. Once a representation of an episode has been fully consolidated, activation can spread between the separate features themselves, so that hippocampal activation is no longer needed.

Neuroscientists are beginning to understand which brain areas make up the frontal components of the medial temporal lobe memory system. The medial temporal and hippocampal regions tend to be more involved in spatial context memory, whereas the frontocortical region, the diencephalon, and the temporal lobes are involved in temporal context memory. Much has also been learned about the neural bases of short-term memory systems located in the frontal lobes. Psychologists have not been able, however, to determine whether there is one type of short-term memory or several and exactly what time span is involved, although "short term" is typically thought to mean several seconds. In the 1980s, neuroscientists began exploring a large area in the dorsolateral portion of the prefrontal lobes that seems to be responsible for what has been called "working memory," which at least overlaps with the psychologist's concept of short-term memory.[3] This prefrontal area appears to monitor and manipulate representations contained in posterior cortical areas.[4]

In the late 1950s, surgeons removed much of a man's temporal lobes (including most of the hippocampus, the parahippocampal gyrus, and the amygdala) in an attempt to reduce the severity of his epileptic seizures.[5] This patient, known as "HM," developed a severe amnesia for autobiographical events, but retained his basic intelligence and his personality. Researchers also observed that HM could retain information for a short time and could also acquire new motor skills such as mirror writing, solving puzzles, or tracing mazes, without knowing that he was doing so, a form of procedural memory.

Korsakoff's Syndrome

Confabulation was among the symptoms Sergei Korsakoff observed in a group of alcoholic patients he was treating in 1887. Other symptoms included memory loss, anxiety, fear, depression, and general irritability. It has since been learned that the syndrome is caused by a lack of vitamin B_1, or thiamine, and not directly by alcohol itself. Korsakoff's syndrome can come on quickly, after an alcoholic coma, or it can progress slowly over many years. And although it occurs primarily in alcoholics, it may also occur in nonalcoholic patients whose digestive systems fail to absorb B_1 for other reasons (malabsorption syndrome, regional enteritis, cancer of the stomach).[6] Alcohol is known to interfere with transport of thiamine in the gastrointestinal tract, and chronic liver disease, a common consequence of alcoholism, can affect the liver's ability to store thiamine. Because chemicals derived from it are involved in the synthesis of neurotransmitters, particularly acetylcholine, as well as GABA, thiamine plays an important role in the proper functioning of the brain.

Memory loss in Korsakoff's is anterograde—patients are unable to form new memories. As with HM, their procedural memories are left intact (they can still drive a car, for example). Korsakoff's patients tend to underestimate both the time they have spent in the hospital and their own ages. Korsakoff himself successfully traced the memory reports of his patients to actual experiences but found that the memories had been displaced in time by the patients. In the early phase of their illness, the confabulations of Korsakoff's patients are typically internally consistent accounts about themselves. The contents of these accounts are drawn fully or principally from the patients' recollections of their actual experiences, including their thoughts in the past.

Aneurysm of the Anterior Communicating Artery

Confabulation can also result from aneurysm of a critical brain artery—the anterior communicating artery (ACoA), which distributes blood to portions of the ventromedial lobe (including parts of the orbitofrontal lobes) and related structures. Aneurysms occur when the walls of blood vessels, weakened by infection or degenerative illness, bulge abnormally. Unless properly treated, the aneurysm may rupture, causing a hemorrhage and destruction of the surrounding tissue. Although small, the anterior communicating artery feeds a variety of brain areas and organs (portions of the ventromedial frontal lobes, the basal forebrain, fornix, septum, anterior cingulate gyrus, and corpus callosum), and damage to it may also seriously affect blood flow in one or both of the anterior cerebral arteries.

The important cognitive features of the classical ACoA syndrome are:

1. *Memory loss* Patients show both anterograde and retrograde amnesia, the latter often for several years preceding the aneurysm. As in Korsakoff's, short-term memory appears to be intact. In tests of recognition memory, patients can often correctly recognize famous people, for example, at a normal level, but they can exhibit something called "pathological false recognition," that is, cases where they claim to recognize a stimulus they are actually seeing for the first time.

2. *Changes in personality* Like Korsakoff's patients, ACoA aneurysm patients undergo personality changes—manifested as impulsivity, impatience, disinhibition, emotional lability, depression, problems in decision making, and poor judgment in social situations—that compromise their ability to socially interact.

3. *Executive deficits* These include perseveration, poor concept formation, problems with set shifting, reduced verbal fluency, and impairments in cognitive estimation.

4. *Confabulation* Appearing as implausible and "spontaneous" in the acute phase right after the aneurysm, confabulation quite often persists, only as more plausible and "provoked," in the chronic phase.[7]

The memory deficits caused by aneurysm of the anterior communicating artery and by lifelong drinking in Korsakoff's syndrome hold a special interest for memory researchers, indicating as they do important frontal components to the memory system. Neuroanatomists have confirmed that the areas constituting the medial temporal lobe memory system have strong, reciprocal connections to at least two frontal areas. The sites of lesion in Korsakoff's and ACoA amnesia are clearly different from those involved in medial temporal lobe amnesia. There are corresponding differences between the temporal and frontal amnesic patients, the most important being that medial temporal lobe amnesics do not confabulate, will admit their memory deficits, and will pursue compensatory strategies. Indeed, medial temporal lobe amnesics have been found to be *less* likely than normal people to produce false memories on tasks specifically designed to elicit them (see below). They show much higher latencies in giving their answers and make many more self-corrections than confabulating frontal memory patients in memory tasks, which suggests that their intact executive processes are struggling to correct degraded memories.

False Memories in Normal People

Many of the memory and confabulation problems seen in neurological patients are simply extreme versions of those affecting all of us every day. We sometimes remember what we intended to say or do, rather than what we actually said or did. We frequently displace events in time upon recalling them. And we mistake events that we merely dreamed of for real events or, less often, vice versa. Recent trends in memory research have strongly confirmed what memory researchers have always known, that memorizing something is not at all like recording it and that recalling something is not at all like replaying a recording. Memory is a selective and reconstructive process, which can go wrong in several ways.

The phrase "false memory" is somewhat of a contradiction in terms, given that we cannot be said to truly remember something that never happened, but the phrase's meaning is clear enough. False memories can easily be produced in children by asking them leading questions. In one telling experiment, children were presented with a deck of cards, each of which described an event. Some of the events had actually happened to the children, whereas others had not. When they were repeatedly asked whether the false events had happened to them, a majority of the children eventually agreed that they had, and many of them embellished the events with confabulated details.[8] Apparently, our memory systems have a baseline accuracy level, and we use different frontal checking procedures to increase this level. As already noted, our normal correct memories are rational reconstructions, in that the reconstruction process is guided by what seems rational to us. This can be seen in certain patterns of error in false memories, where we misremember something odd in an event as something more normal or rational.

It is interesting that young children exhibit some of the same memory problems that frontal patients show. This may be because the frontal lobes are among the last cortical areas to mature. Most of the development of the frontal lobes occurs between ages 5 and 10, and they do not fully mature until the teenage years. Perhaps nature's plan is that the checking processes described above will be instilled after birth, during the long training period we humans require, principally by our parents. What begins as an external loop is made internal: children naturally confabulate, parents correct, and the children change what they said. As we mature, we internalize these corrections, so that the loop runs completely within our brains, although it shares some of the same dynamics: there is still a candidate claim, and there is still a check that has the power to correct the claim or inhibit it from being made.

Adults are also prone to false memories in certain circumstances. The "misinformation effect" is a way to induce false memories in adults in laboratory settings. In a typical experiment, subjects will be first shown a video depicting a staged crime, and then exposed to false information designed to interfere with their memories of the event. When asked later to recount the event, subjects show a strong tendency to incorporate this false information. A number of researchers including Elizabeth Loftus and colleagues have also shown that exposure to prejudicial information after having witnessed an event can influence the subject's later recall of that event.[9] Maryanne Garry's research group has found that both imagining events that never happened and paraphrasing descriptions of such events can make us more likely to later report that those events actually happened.[10] In another type of experiment, normal subjects were presented with a list of words related to sleep, excluding the word *sleep* itself: *bed*, *rest*, *awake*, *tired*, *dream*, *wake*, *snooze*, and so on. When they were later tested, between 30% and 40% of the subjects claimed that they had seen the word *sleep*.[11] Researchers who observed the brains of normal subjects using PET as they performed tasks in which they first heard a list of related words, then were tested for memory of the words were able to successfully differentiate correct from incorrect memories by their different patterns of activation.[12] Subjects of hypnosis may also confabulate when they are asked to recall information associated with crimes, causing researchers to warn criminologists about the dangers of obtaining information from hypnotized subjects. There are also anecdotal reports of hypnotized subjects confabulating when asked why they did something in accord with their hypnotic suggestion. For instance, a hypnotized man is given the suggestion that he will wave his hands whenever he hears the word *money*.

When asked later why is he is waving his hands, he replies, "Oh, I just felt like stretching."

Studying patients with brain damage may be an easier route to understanding confabulation than studying normal people since the patients' site of damage and the known functions of that area provide an obvious starting point. When resulting from frontal brain injuries (such as aneurysms or strokes), confabulations are about past events in patients' lives that either did not happen (or not to them) or did not happen to them when the patients believe they did. With the increasing information available about how our memory systems work, the discussion of memory-based confabulation has grown increasingly sophisticated. One theme of great interest that comes up frequently in the literature is that these types of confabulations might be caused by two separate malfunctions. First, frontal lobe patients have a memory problem, which they share with medial temporal lobe patients. And second, the patients have what is typically referred to as an "executive problem," which is responsible for the failure to realize that the memories they are reporting are fictitious. In a particular case of confabulation, the two problems manifest as two *phases*: first, a false memory is produced, but then, frontal areas fail to perform functions that would allow the person to realize the falsity of the memory. This succession implies that the thoughts that give rise to confabulations exist as genuine beliefs in the patients' mind, as opposed to the patients merely finding certain claims coming out of their mouths, without their actually believing them. It seems, therefore, that the patients' confabulations are accurately reporting their (disordered or ill-grounded) conscious experiences.

We can now turn to a definition of *confabulation,* which involves six individually testable criteria. A subject (S) confabulates in claiming that a proposition (p) is true if and only if (1) S claims that p is true; (2) S thinks that p is true; (3) S's thought that p is true is ill-grounded; (4) S does not know that S's thought is ill-grounded; (5) S should know that S's thought is ill-grounded; and (6) S is confident that p is true.[13] The concept of *claiming* (rather than, for instance, *saying* or *asserting*) is broad enough to cover a wide variety of responses by subjects, including nonverbal responses, such as drawing and pointing. The second criterion captures the sincerity of confabulators. If explicitly asked, "Do you think that p is true?" they invariably answer yes. The third criterion refers to the problem that caused the flawed response to be generated: processes within the relevant knowledge domain were malfunctioning. The fourth criterion refers to a cognitive failure at a second executive phase, the failure to check and reject the flawed response. The fifth criterion captures a normative element in our concept of confabulation: if the confabulator's brain were functioning properly, the confabulator would know that the claim is ill-grounded, and not make it. The claims made are about things any normal person would easily get right. The sixth and last criterion refers to another important characteristic of confabulators observed in the clinic, the serene certainty they have in their claims, even in the face of obvious disbelief by their listeners. This epistemic approach eliminates a problem endemic to the falsity criterion in the original definition, proposed by memory researchers such as Korsakoff, according to which confabulations are false memory reports: Subjects might answer correctly out of luck. The problem is not so much the falsity of the subjects' claims but rather their ill-groundedness and consequent unreliability, at least in the affected domain, for example, autobiographical memory. In short then, in this epistemic view, to confabulate is to confidently make an ill-grounded claim that we should, but do not, know is ill grounded.

Theories about memory confabulation divide into two categories, depending on which of the two problems is emphasized:

1. *Retrieval theories*   Confabulation is caused by a deficit in the "strategic retrieval" of memories, which in turn causes a loss of our sense of the temporal order of our memories, and of their *sources*—the places and times they represent. Theories of this type can be traced all the way back to Korsakoff.

2. *Executive theories*   Confabulating amnesics are to be differentiated from their nonconfabulating counterparts by their additional frontal damage. Confabulation reflects two different damaged processes: a memory process and an executive or "monitoring" process. The executive process fails to correct the false memory.

Cognition requires both representations and executive processes for manipulating those representations. Representations are expensive to produce, update, and maintain. Their primary purpose is to allow us to understand and affect the things they represent. Executive processes in the brain's prefrontal lobes perform different operations on our

representations when we decide, weigh, reason, infer, examine, resolve—
processes we commonly call by the collective name "thinking." Our
memory is itself an immense collection of representations. Executive
processes, typically centered in the prefrontal lobes, must control the
search and reconstruction processes that take place when we remember.
As an example of an executive theory, Marcia Johnson attributes confabulation to a deficit in a more general executive function she calls
"reality monitoring," the ability to distinguish real from imagined
events.[14] Normal people are able to differentiate real from imagined
information at high rates of success. This seems to be a learned, or
at least a developed, ability. Real memories, according to Johnson, can
often be distinguished from mere imaginings by the amount of perceptual detail they contain and by the presence of supporting memories—source memories—about where and when the remembered event
occurred. It may be, however, that retrieval theories and executive
theories are merely directed at different parts of the confabulation
process, whose first phase involves the production of a false memory,
and whose second phase involves failure to notice and correct the
falsity. Retrieval theories focus on the failure to access the correct
memories; executive theories, on the failure to correct false ones. Executive theorists typically attribute confabulation to a failure in what they
call "self-monitoring" or "self-awareness."

Reality Monitoring

Confabulation may be due to a broader failure to test representations,
whether they are from memory or not. According to Johnson, episodic
memories of an event bind together elements of several different types,
some of which represent impersonal features of the event, while others
represent personal features, for example, our thoughts or emotions in
reaction to witnessing the event. These different features include colors,
sounds, tastes, emotions, objects, and locations, as well as information
contained in semantic memory. Recall of any one of these features is
often enough to draw the entire autobiographical memory back into our
awareness. When thoughts presenting themselves as memories are so rich
in detail often they are regarded as being genuine. Because of this, if we
have a vivid and detailed imagination, we can mistake memories of our

imaginings for memories of actual events, for example, when we believe we did something we only imagined doing.

In reality monitoring, there are further checks we can make to separate real from imagined memories. We can check the consistency of the candidate memory with our set of beliefs, noting any inconsistencies between representations currently in our consciousness or between those and our long-term knowledge. Confabulation patients tend not to notice or worry when they contradict themselves. One male patient, for example, contradicted himself in the same sentence, saying first that he had just visited a store he formerly owned, then that the store no longer existed. As early as 1915, Arnold Pick noted that Korsakoff's patients also feel no need to correct their contradictions.

We can intentionally tighten our monitoring standards when motivated to do so. Researchers often report that simply admonishing memory patients to be more careful can work to increase the accuracy level of their reported memories. It is interesting to note that we tend not to consciously or intentionally loosen our standards; rather, we do so unconsciously and spontaneously. Johnson and her colleagues distinguish between *heuristic* checking of candidate memories, which usually operates automatically when we are remembering, and *systematic* checking, which is intentional. Heuristic processing consists of fewer component processes and uses readily available information, such as familiarity, perceptual detail, and schemas (e.g., world knowledge, stereotypes), typically activated by a cue. Systematic processing is made up of more component processes and may also involve the retrieval of other memories and knowledge that are not initially activated.

Systematic processing requires selective attention: we must explicitly attend to the candidate memory. It also includes self-provided memory cues. We often cue our own memories: when we want to remember someone's name, for example, we may imagine that person's face, producing a cue for our memory system to use in retrieving the name. We can then monitor any representations the cue gives rise to. We may need to use other information to reject candidate names that come up. Often, we may need to use this cuing process several times to reconstruct the memory correctly. As to the neural locus of these monitoring processes, researchers point to bifrontal areas.

The Suppression of Irrelevant Memories

Armin Schnider's research group has advanced a similar hypothesis: memory confabulation results from the orbitofrontal cortex and its limbic connections not performing their function of suppressing or inhibiting recalled memories irrelevant to the current task.[15] Schnider and colleagues argue that the posterior medial orbitofrontal cortex sorts out the mental associations that pertain to ongoing reality by suppressing memory traces that have no current relevance. Schnider claims that lesion of an orbito-frontal-mediodorsal-amygdala circuit produces spontaneous confabula-tion, which appears to emanate from interruption of the loop connecting the posterior orbitofrontal cortex directly and indirectly (via the medio-dorsal thalamus) with the amygdala. Connecting confabulation in ACoA patients with that found in Korsakoff's patients, Schnider points out that the basal forebrain lesions seen in the former group often include damage to the posterior medial orbitofrontal cortex, present in the latter. Schnider's localization is supported by two of his findings. First, patients with lesions involving the posterior medial orbitofrontal cortex and basal forebrain confabulate for much longer periods (several months) than patients with anterior medial orbitofrontal lesions. And, second, there is posterior medial orbitofrontal cortex activation in normal sub-jects performing a memory task that requires them to carefully separate relevant from similar but irrelevant memories.

If memory confabulation results from two independent lesions, this indicates that there are two types of patients:

1. Those who sustained the memory system lesion first. Such patients should admit their memory deficit until the executive deficit develops, at which point he should deny it and commence confabulating.

2. Those who sustained the executive system lesion first. The course of the disease among such patients may be rather subtle. We also need to allow for people who simply do not develop the executive processes needed to check memory reports——who make do with their memories alone and tolerate a high rate of errors. Thus some Korsakoff's patients are confabulatory, having lost the ability to check their thoughts or candidate memories, *before* losing their memory. Their deficit may pass unnoticed

because they are substantially correct in what they say. But once the amnesia sets in, the problem becomes painfully obvious.

The brain's many types of different memory systems testify to the value evolutionary development places on learning from the past. Several questions remain. Do memory confabulations belong to the larger set of completion phenomena, such as the filling in of the visual blind spot? The brain's executive processes, located in the prefrontal lobes, require clear, unambiguous information in order to achieve their primary task, the creation of effective actions. We typically do not have the time to spend examining gaps in our perceptions and memories. Quite often in real life, when memories occur, we make a quick plausibility check, sort out any obvious contradictions or impossibilities in the memory, and move forward with the belief that the memory is correct. Thus confabulation might be seen as a type of completion phenomenon occurring at a higher social level. We respond to a question about our past with a coherent, reasonable answer, in order to create a coherent, gap-free account of our own life, and present it to others.

The philosopher Daniel Dennett sees confabulation as a type of self-creating activity, in which our confabulations—stories—tend to depict us in favorable ways. Taken together, they constitute a narrative we create and tell to others, about the sort of person we are.[16] Typically the stories that make up this narrative depict us as intelligent, in command of the situation and its relevant facts, and fully aware of the reasons and intentions behind our actions. The stories are all about the same person, the one referred to with that special word *I*. But if we collect all the I-claims, do we find a unified brain system playing a crucial causal role in the making such claims? Perhaps not, since some of the claims will be about our bodies, some about our current actions, others about our past experiences, while still others will be about our semantic knowledge of ourselves. Each of these types of knowledge is accomplished by a different brain system. This can tend to make our sense of self look as if it is produced by a motley collection of processes, cobbled together for various motives and conveniences, and then—protected and patched up by confabulation—presented to others.

Confabulation may be telling us something important about the human mind and about human nature. The ability to create narratives and the ability to check them for truth or at least plausibility seem to be separate in the human brain—confabulatory patients retain the first ability, but have lost the second. One of the characters in their inner dialogue has fallen silent, and the other prattles on unchecked. Without this second character, however, they have lost the ability to admit ignorance. We see mild versions of this in normal people. We are all familiar with people who seem unable to say, "I don't know," and who will quickly produce some sort of plausible-sounding response to whatever they are asked. A friend once described such a person as "a know-it-all who doesn't know anything."

Those who have lost both their memories and their awareness that they once possessed those memories are untroubled by the loss and move forward in life with what mental abilities remain. They may confabulate when asked about their pasts, and these confabulations are satisfying to them—but not to their friends, relatives, and doctors. Each false claim they make causes us to doubt whether they can continue to relate to us in a normal way. Perhaps one reason why clinical confabulation is so fascinating is that we see a bit of ourselves in the neurological patients. We are aware, at some level, that the difference between us and them is only a matter of degree.

Notes

1. Arthur P. Shimamura, Jeri S. Janowsky, and Larry R. Squire, "Memory for the Temporal Order of Events in Patients with Frontal Lobe Lesions," *Neuropsychologia* 28 (1990): 801–813.

2. See Joaquin M. Fuster, *Memory in the Cerebral Cortex* (Cambridge, MA: MIT Press, 1995).

3. Patricia S. Goldman-Rakic, "Circuitry of Primate Prefrontal Cortex and Regulation of Behavior by Representational Memory," in *Handbook of Physiology: The Nervous System: Higher Functions of the Brain*, ed. Fred Plum (Bethesda, MD: American Physiological Society, 1987), 5: 373–417.

4. Michael Petrides, "Lateral Prefrontal Cortex: Architectonic and Functional Organization," *Philosophical Transactions of the Royal Society* B 360 (2005): 781–795.

5. William B. Scoville and Brenda Milner, "Loss of Recent Memory after Bilateral Hippocampal Lesions," *Journal of Neurology, Neurosurgery, and Psychiatry* 20 (1957): 11–21.

6. See Alan Parkin and Nicholas R. C. Leng, *Neuropsychology of the Amnesic Syndrome* (Hove, UK: Erlbaum, 1993).

7. John DeLuca and Bruce J. Diamond, "Aneurysm of the Anterior Communicating Artery: A Review of the Neuroanatomical and Neuropsychological Sequelae, "*Journal of Clinical and Experimental Neuropsychology* 17 (1995): 100–121.

8. Stephen J. Ceci, Mary Lyn Huffman, and Edward Smith, "Repeatedly Thinking about a Non-event: Source Misattributions among Preschoolers," *Consciousness and Cognition* 3 (1994): 388–407.

9. Elizabeth F. Loftus, "Made in Memory: Distortions in Recollection after Misleading Information," in *The Psychology of Learning and Motivation: Advances in Research and Theory*, ed. Gordon H. Bower (San Diego: Academic Press, 1991), 187–198.

10. Maryanne Garry, Charles G. Manning, and Elizabeth F. Loftus, "Imagination Inflation: Imagining a Childhood Event Inflates Confidence That It Occurred," *Psychonomic Bulletin and Review* 12 (1996): 359–366.

11. James Deese, "On the Prediction of Occurrence of Particular Verbal Intrusions in Immediate Recall," *Journal of Experimental Psychology* 58 (1959): 17–22.

12. Daniel L. Schacter et al., "Neuroanatomical Correlates of Veridical and Illusory Recognition Memory: Evidence from Positron Emission Tomography," *Neuron* 17 (1996): 267–274.

13. William Hirstein, *Brain Fiction: Self-Deception and the Riddle of Confabulation*. (Cambridge, MA: MIT Press, 2005). See chapter 8.

14. See Marcia K. Johnson and Carol L. Raye, "False Memories and Confabulation," *Trends in Cognitive Sciences* 2 (1998): 137–145. See also Marcia K. Johnson, "Reality Monitoring: Evidence from Confabulation in Organic Brain Disease Patients," in *Awareness of Deficit after Brain Injury: Clinical and Theoretical Issues,* ed. George P. Prigatano and Daniel L. Schacter (Oxford: Oxford University Press, 1991), 176–197.

15. See Armin Schnider, "Spontaneous Confabulation, Reality Monitoring, and the Limbic System: A Review," *Brain Research Reviews* 36 (2001): 150–160.

16. See Daniel C. Dennett, *Consciousness Explained* (Boston: Little, Brown, 1991).

11 The Neuroethics of Memory

Walter Glannon

Research into the molecular mechanisms of different memory systems has revealed promising interventions for both therapy and enhancement. Memory is essential to human survival, enabling us to recognize and respond appropriately to external threats. In linking the past to the present and future, memory is also essential to personal identity and the experience of persisting through time. Further, memory is a critical component of our moral sensibility by generating emotions such as shame and regret for past misdeeds. This chapter considers the actual and potential ways in which manipulating memory can affect these critical functions of our capacity to recall the past.

A number of ethical issues can be raised regarding both the pharmacological modification of memory and diagnostic brain imaging in cases of criminal negligence. Although modifying pathological memory by certain drugs that weaken its emotional content may be an acceptable trade-off in severe cases of posttraumatic stress disorder, doing so can have untoward effects on autobiographical memory. And although neuroimaging might be used to test the capacity for recall in certain legal cases, there is considerable ambiguity in interpreting images of the brain and questions about the inferences we can draw from them about guilty states of mind.

Dampening Pathological Memories

Let's first consider posttraumatic stress disorder (PTSD). When one experiences a traumatic event, such as an automobile accident or a military attack, the adrenal glands release adrenaline (epinephrine) into the bloodstream as part of the body's fight-or-flight response. This hormone in turn activates noradrenaline (norepinephrine) in the amygdala, which promotes the consolidation of unconscious emotionally charged memories of such an event. As a main structure of the limbic system, the amygdala mediates primitive emotions such as fear and is critical in avoiding threats and surviving in the natural environment. If, however, the release of adrenaline and noradrenaline embeds emotional memory too strongly in the amygdala, it can generate a heightened fear response that is out of proportion to the actual nature of external events. The result can be posttraumatic stress disorder, a pathological condition characterized by nightmares and uncontrolled flashbacks that cause one to mentally return to the setting in which the trauma first occurred. Memories of a traumatic experience are more emotionally charged, and better remembered, than emotionally neutralones.[1] Indeed, memories causing PTSD are so emotionally charged that patients suffering from the disorder cannot rid themselves of them.

Ideally, a drug blocking the release of adrenaline could prevent the consolidation of an emotionally charged memory in the amygdala. Or at least it could modulate one's emotional response to the memory. Researchers in a number of studies have used the beta-adrenergic antagonist propranolol (Inderal) to achieve the second goal with some degree of success. Initially developed as an antihypertensive and antiarrhythmic drug that modulates the excitatory cardiovascular response, propranolol was also found to influence beta-adrenergic receptors in the brain. A pilot study conducted by psychiatrist Roger Pitman and colleagues at the Massachusetts General Hospital involved patients admitted to the emergency room. Half were given propranolol and half a placebo for ten days immediately after a traumatic injury.[2] One month later, those who had taken propranolol had fewer flashbacks and nightmares and more moderate responses to stimuli resembling the initial traumatic event than those who had taken the placebo. This manipulation of emotionally charged memory could have therapeutic effects for a significant number of people. In particular, it could benefit many soldiers returning from combat with PTSD by controlling the symptoms of the disorder. More recent studies have replicated some of the results of the Pitman study, showing that the emotional content of a memory could be separated to some extent from the memory itself.[3]

Because chronic use of propranolol might blunt one's normal response to fear-inducing stimuli, causing one to underreact rather than overreact to stimuli, one could become vulnerable to real threats. Moreover, chronic manipulation of the neural mechanisms mediating emotional responses to the natural and social environment might weaken or even destroy inhibitory mechanisms controlling harmful behavior and thus also the capacity to conform to social norms. This is symptomatic of psychopathy, which is associated with dysfunction in the pathway between the amygdala to the prefrontal cortex. The possibility of adverse effects on the brain and central nervous system from too much propranolol, though unproven, should not be dismissed out of hand.[4] It should also be noted that not all people who experience traumatic events go on to develop PTSD. In some cases, a traumatized individual who would not have developed the disorder might be given such a drug and be unnecessarily exposed to its risks.[5]

If the emotional content of a memory could be dampened, whether with propranolol or with some other drug, then one could recall a traumatic or fearful event without reexperiencing the trauma or fear.[6] One could, in effect, become emotionally disengaged from the context in which one experienced the event. Yet we need to be careful in manipulating memory in this way. There are extensive projections from the amygdala to the hippocampus, and vice versa, and considerable overlap between the memory functions they mediate.[7] Both of these limbic structures influence how one recalls the events in one's life. Dampening the content of unconscious emotionally charged memories might also dampen the content of conscious episodic memories, taking the sting out of recalling a traumatic event. But it might, at the same time, remove some of the positive emotional aspects of one's autobiographical memories.

On the other hand, some cases of amnesia suggest that the declarative memory system mediated by the medial temporal lobes and prefrontal cortex can function independently of the nondeclarative memory system mediated by the cerebellum and striatum. Whereas the declarative system consists of semantic and episodic memory enabling us to consciously recall facts and events, the nondeclarative system consists of procedural memory enabling us to unconsciously know how to do things such as ride a bicycle or drive a car. HM (Henry Molaison), who died in December 2008 at age 82, was perhaps the best-known amnesic patient. He developed a severe seizure disorder in his late teens and twenties. Surgery that bilaterally removed the hippocampus and adjacent structures from his medial temporal lobes resolved the seizures but left him with profound anterograde amnesia. Although HM could recall some events from the time before his surgery, he lost all autobiographical memory and was unable to form new long-term memories. He retained his procedural memory, which enabled him to perform daily tasks.[8] HM's case seems to confirm the thesis that memory systems function independently of each other.

Yet recent advances in cognitive neuroscience have shown that recollection of personal episodes from the past depends on activation and reactivation of latent emotional associations with these episodes.[9] This process appears to involve distinct but interacting memory systems. If the amygdala and hippocampus function interdependently in enabling these associations, then weakening the emotional response to unconscious pathological memory might also weaken the emotional response to conscious episodic memory. Studies have indicated that an amygdalar-hippocampal network supports emotional arousal, while a prefrontal-hippocampal network supports emotional valence. Yet because the hippocampus is active in both networks and both types of emotion, it seems plausible that altering one circuit could affect the other and that altering emotional arousal could alter emotional valence. Insofar as emotion is critical to the meaningful recall of experience, this could impair the ability to make sense of the past.

Losing some of the content of our autobiography may be an acceptable price to pay for modulating an emotionally charged memory, but only if that memory has a significant negative impact on our quality of life. Weakening or neutralizing the emotional content of memory could impair our ability to place experienced events within a unified and meaningful narrative of our lives. We might be left with the capacity to recall particular events without being able to understand how they relate to each other or how they shape our autobiographies. The physical and social context in which we experience an event is a critical component of the emotional content of our memory of that event. And this emotional content is an essential component of the experience of recalling the event. The connection between context and content in episodic memory is part of the basic spatial and temporal structure of our mental life. Removing the emotional content of memory from the context in which we experienced the recalled event could disrupt this structure and the narrative continuity of our autobiographies.[10] Pharmacological therapies targeting memory systems need to be sensitive to how spatial and temporal features of the environment in which we act shape the meaning of memory for us.

In a 2003 working paper, the U.S. President's Council on Bioethics expressed concern that pharmacological modification of memory could have untoward consequences.[11] Erasing or dampening emotionally charged memories could erode much of our moral sensibility by making us lose our sense of shame and regret. It could remove psychological inhibitory mechanisms against doing things we would not otherwise do. Given the essential role of memory in shaping our personal identity and moral responsibility, memory modification could reshape who we are in ways that might not be beneficial or benign. But the Council failed to distinguish between memories that are unpleasant or disturbing and memories that are pathological. The aim of using propranolol for posttraumatic stress disorder is not to reshape a normal self but to restore a dysfunctional self to normal functioning. Indeed, the Council acknowledged that some memories are so severely traumatic they can destroy the lives of those who suffer from them; in such cases, pharmacological intervention would be defensible. Thus, when PTSD severely affects our ability to function in daily life, the use of propranolol to attenuate the emotional content of memory can be justified, despite the risk of altering some of our affective capacities.

Therapeutic Forgetting

The Council's general concern about manipulating unpleasant memories would be warranted, however, if it caused us to lose our capacity to respond to moral emotions. These emotions are essential to our capacity to take responsibility for our actions and their consequences, as well as to our practices of holding others morally and legally responsible. In particular, regret is necessary for the counterfactual reasoning we engage in when considering alternative courses of action and making decisions about how to act.[12] It plays a crucial role in our capacity to respond to prudential and moral reasons for and against different actions. If erasing an unpleasant memory or removing its emotional content resulted in the loss of our moral emotions, then it could have significant negative impact on the normative content of our thought and behavior. It could impair our capacity to respond to moral reasons and conform to social norms.

Yet there may be some instances in which preventing or erasing a disturbing memory would benefit a person without weakening the influence of moral emotions on the person's general thought and behavior.

Therapeutic forgetting may be defensible in some cases. In a hypothetical case, a certain Ann Smith, a young academic, gives a lecture in which she makes a glaring factual error, mistaken inference, or fails miserably in response to questions from the audience. Smith is embarrassed by the experience and internalizes it to such a degree that it weakens her self-confidence and self-esteem. Although the memory of this event may not put her at risk of developing a psychiatric condition such as generalized anxiety disorder or major depression, it can have harmful psychological effects on her. If a drug could erase this memory by interfering with the process of reconsolidation, then taking it would eliminate the persistent feeling of embarrassment and insecurity and make Smith better off psychologically. Manipulating the memory in this way would not necessarily undermine Smith's capacity for moral emotions. It would not incline Smith to perform harmful or wrongful acts she would not otherwise perform.

Whereas erasing a memory of a wrongful or harmful act we performed may desensitize us to an appropriate emotional response to that act or to future circumstances and have an adverse effect on our behavior, erasing an unpleasant memory of an act that was neither harmful nor wrongful is unlikely to have any such effect. Deleting one unpleasant episode from our autobiography would not weaken our moral sensibility.

Still, some might object that therapeutic forgetting would undermine our authenticity. According to philosopher Charles Taylor, authenticity means that it is up to each of us as a human being to find our own way in the world, to flourish, and to be true to our authentic self. "If I am not true to myself, I miss the point of my life. I miss what being human is for me."[13] We come to have authentic selves by identifying with the mental states that constitute our selves. This identification results from a process of critical self-reflection on our desires, beliefs, intentions, and emotions. It is through this reflection that we reinforce or reject these states as the springs of our actions. The philosopher Harry Frankfurt argues that being a free and authentic agent consists in having the general reflective capacity to control that particular mental states issue in our actions.[14] Insofar as agency is a necessary condition of selfhood, being an authentic agent is a necessary condition of having an authentic self. Altering the process of critical reflection and the mental states that result from it with psychotropic drugs presumably would alienate us from our true selves. We could not identify with these altered states and would not have authentic selves because something alien to us would be the agent of change. Leon Kass and other members of the President's Council raise this as a possible consequence of manipulating the mind in general and memory in particular: "As the power to transform our native powers increases both in magnitude and refinement, so does the possibility for 'self-alienation'—for losing, confounding, or abandoning our identity."[15]

Yet it does not necessarily follow that the voluntary use of a drug to dampen or erase a memory would make us inauthentic. If Tim Jones, as an individual with the capacity for critical self-reflection and prudential reasoning, freely decides to take a memory-modifying drug, then he is the agent of any change in his mental states. The drug is merely the means through which Jones effects the change. If Jones has the capacity to weigh the reasons for and against manipulating memory and to act on these reasons, and if this is what he desires, intends, and freely decides to do, the change would be of his own doing. Thus erasing a memory may be consistent with our authenticity by reflecting the set of experiences that we want to have as our autobiography. It would be one way of editing or rewriting a part of our life narrative while retaining the integrity of the whole. It is useful to distinguish between therapy and enhancement. *Therapy* is defined as any intervention that sustains or restores good physical or mental health. *Enhancement* is defined as any intervention designed to improve human form or functioning beyond what is necessary to sustain or restore good human health.[16] In some cases, the boundary between therapy and enhancement is poorly defined. Although I referred to memory erasure as "therapeutic forgetting" in the discussion above, it may also be understood as an example of an intervention that lies in the gray area on the continuum from therapy to enhancement. In one sense, erasure of memory can be described as therapy because it reduces psychological harm to the individual. In another sense, it can be described as enhancement because, by eliminating a disturbing memory, it increases the net positive set of memories for the individual. An actual case, reported in an article published in *Time* magazine on October 15, 2007,[17] illustrates how erasing a disturbing memory may be described both as therapy and prevention. More important, it raises the question of whether it can be ethical for one person to erase another person's memory.

In 1997, the orthopedic surgeon Dr. Scott Haig was performing a biopsy on a suspicious-looking lump near the end of a female patient's collarbone. The patient consented to receive local rather than general anesthesia for the procedure. Dr. Haig and the patient agreed that some sedation might be given if it became necessary, and an anesthesiologist was in the surgical suite for this purpose. The surgeon removed the tissue sample and sent it to the hospital pathologist. Over the intercom, Dr. Haig asked the pathologist to discuss the pathology report privately with him on the phone in a separate room. Saying that he could barely hear Dr. Haig, the pathologist blurted out: "This is a wildly pleomorphic tumor, very anaplastic. I can't tell what cell type it is, but it's really, really bad ... cancer." Upon hearing this, the patient, who was not sedated, screamed, "Oh my God, my God! My kids!" Then, shortly after that, she cried, "Oh, my arm ... my arm ..." The burning pain in her arm was due to an infusion of propofol, a white liquid medication that is sometimes called "milk of amnesia." This drug not only induces sedation but also prevents the consolidation or reconsolidation of new memories of very recent events. It induces short-term anterograde amnesia rather than retrograde amnesia. After the patient woke up, Dr. Haig said that the procedure had gone smoothly but that they would have to wait for the final pathology report. The patient had no memory of hearing the pathologist's comment. Dr. Haig admitted in the *Time* article that he did not tell her the whole truth and that he was not sure that he had done the right thing.

At first blush, the surgeon's decision to give propofol to his patient and the anesthesiologist's action of infusing it into her arm seem unethical. Because the patient did not consent to receive the drug, the anesthesiologist and the surgeon could have been legally charged with battery. They could also be held ethically accountable for failing to respect her right to know what occurred by not informing her after the incident. Before a procedure, a surgeon and patient may discuss the possibility of unanticipated events requiring interventions other than the procedure to which the patient explicitly consents. A patient may implicitly consent to an intervention deemed necessary to prevent or control any adverse effects of the procedure. The patient in this case agreed to receive sedation, though its presumed purpose was to control any pain or discomfort during the surgery. The patient did not implicitly consent to sedation for the purpose of preventing or erasing a memory.

Upon reflection, Dr. Haig's actions can be defended for the following three reasons. First, he was not withholding medically relevant information from the patient before the procedure. He did not have this information at this time because he could not have foreseen the pathologist blurting out the grave diagnosis over the intercom. Second, although the propofol infusion was not primarily intended to sedate the patient, it was an intervention necessary to prevent an adverse psychological effect on the patient from the pathologist's negligence. It prevented harm to her by blocking the formation of a disturbing memory of what the pathologist said. Third, Dr. Haig was not obligated to tell the patient about the pathologist's remark and the propofol infusion at any time after the incident. Physicians are obligated to disclose medical errors and any corrective measures to patients when those same physicians—or others working under them—commit errors resulting in harm to the patients. Neither of these conditions was present in this case. The error was committed by the pathologist, and Dr. Haig was not obligated to take responsibility for it because the pathologist was not working under his authority. Moreover, the propofol that Dr. Haig ordered to correct the pathologist's error did not cause but prevented harm to the patient.

The malignant tumor was a recurrence of a cancer the patient had some years earlier. She died six years after the propofol incident, without Dr. Haig ever telling her about it. Still, the main medical and ethical issue was that the patient be informed of the pathology report on the biopsy in a timely manner. Dr. Haig informed her of this once he had the final report. There was no compelling reason to inform her that she had heard the diagnosis during the procedure and that he and the anesthesiologist intervened to prevent her from recalling it. The infusion of propofol to prevent a bad memory and psychological harm, and Dr. Haig's decision not to inform the patient of this action, were ethically justified.

Enhancing Long-Term Memory

Let's now turn to "smart" drugs used for memory enhancement, outside of pathological and therapeutic considerations. By expediting the process of long-term potentiation (LTP), these drugs may enhance memory reconsolidation, the process through which a memory is formed and stored in the brain.[18] In LTP, molecular changes in the synapse strengthen connections between neurons. Long-term memory needs to be reconsolidated through LTP in order not to be removed from storage sites in the cerebral cortex. Ampakines, such as CX-516 (Ampalex), are one class of drugs that can strengthen long-term potentiation as well as memory reconsolidation by activating the excitatory neurotransmitter glutamate through the AMPA receptor.[19] This promotes better communication between synapses and may increase the capacity for memory formation in the hippocampus and memory storage in different regions of the cortex. These drugs can improve the encoding and organization of information in the brain. Other drugs can increase the amount of the transcription factor cAMP-responsive element-binding protein (CREB).[20] The PDE4 inhibitor rolipram is one drug that can produce this effect. Like ampakines, drugs targeting CREB may facilitate the synthesis of new proteins, strengthen communication between synapses, and enhance memory consolidation. Insofar as it would be used by people with a normal capacity for storing and retrieving long-term memory, this type of enhancement would be different from the therapeutic use of drugs such as the cholinesterase inhibitor donepezil (Aricept) and the glutamate antagonist memantine (Namenda) to retard memory loss in Alzheimer's disease. Of the drugs designed to enhance memory, ampakines appear to be the furthest along in development and may have the most promise. As Martha Farah and others have noted, studies of drugs used to enhance memory and other cognitive functions have shown that the short-term enhancing effects are moderate or marginal for individuals with a higher functional baseline and more pronounced for those with a lower baseline.[21] Yet, because there have not been a sufficient number of longitudinal studies on healthy human volunteers, the long-term effects of these drugs are not well known.

Increasing our capacity to store more episodic and semantic memory would not necessarily benefit us in all relevant respects. There may be a trade-off between enhanced long-term memory and impaired short-term working memory. Beyond a certain point, recalling more facts and events might interfere with our capacity to attend to immediate cognitive tasks. An increase in memory storage might overload the brain and make it more difficult to learn new things.[22] This idea is based on the established view that learning new things depends on a certain degree of forgetting. As an adaptive mechanism in human organisms, there is an optimal balance between formation of new memories and extinction of old.[23] In theory, drugs could be designed to avoid the adverse effect of an overload problem by enhancing the storage and retrieval of recent memory while allowing a normal rate of forgetting of remote memory. But even recent memory can include many trivial details that can clutter the mind and interfere with learning. It is unclear how ampakines or drugs targeting CREB could weed out recent memory of trivial facts and events from recent memory of useful facts and events. It is also unclear how increasing memory storage might affect memory retrieval, or how retrieval of more stored memories might affect the capacity to form new memories. Too much storage or retrieval of memory may be more burdensome than beneficial.

Consider the case of Jill Price, a 44-year-old Californian working as an assistant at a religious school. At age 14, she noticed that she had an exceptional autobiographical memory, being able to recall events she had experienced in almost perfect detail. Although her memories were beneficial to her when she worked as an administrative assistant in a law firm, most of them were filled with trivial and intrusive details. More significantly, her recall was involuntary: "I don't make any effort to call memories up; they just fill my mind. In fact, they're not under my conscious control, and as much as I'd like to, I can't stop them." Price describes her autobiographical memories as "a horrible distraction." Autobiographical memory is essential for each of us to construct a narrative of our life. But some degree of forgetting of events we have experienced is also necessary to project our self into the future as part of that narrative. This can be a challenge when so much of an individual's thought consists in involuntarily recalling the past, as noted by Price: "Whereas people generally create narratives of their lives that are fashioned by a process of selective remembering and an enormous amount of forgetting and continuously recrafting that narrative through the course of life, I have not been able to do so." Further, "I've come to understand that there is real value in being able to forget a good deal about our lives." Instead, "I remember all the clutter."

Jill Price was diagnosed with hyperthymestic syndrome, a condition also referred to as "autobiographical memory syndrome," where a patient recalls an inordinate number of events from the patient's past in great detail. The excessive recall interferes with the ability to focus on the present and project oneself into the future. It can also cause impairment in other types of memory. Price has below-normal capacity to memorize facts ("I'm horrible at memorizing").[24] This suggests that too much retrieval of episodic memory can interfere with one's capacity to form new memories and process new information. Increased activity in the parahippocampal gyrus and the region of the prefrontal cortex mediating retrieval of episodic memory might result in decreased activity in the region of the prefrontal cortex mediating working memory. In the case of Jill Price, an abnormally large and hyperactive brain region involved in retrieval of long-term memory comes at the cost of impairment in short-term memory.

The prominent memory researcher James McGaugh and colleagues examined Price and made a diagnosis.[25] Price cannot turn off retrieval mechanisms in her brain that would ordinarily limit the amount of memory available for recall. Brain scans have shown that the structures in her brain mediating episodic memory retrieval are enlarged, which partly explains her syndrome. That Price's syndrome involves autobiographical memory distinguishes it from the case of Russian neuropsychologist Aleksander Luria's patient, Solomon Shereshevsky, whose exceptional capacity for recall consisted mainly of semantic memory of facts without any particular autobiographical quality.[26] The Price case shows that retrieving a considerable volume of memory can be more of a curse than a blessing. It tells us that we should avoid inferring that if a certain amount of memory retrieval is good, then more retrieval is better.[27] As drugs to enhance the neural mechanisms of memory are further developed, researchers need to ensure that none of these mechanisms becomes hyperactive and that the optimal balance between remembering and forgetting is retained. Although it may be rare, those who are intent on enhancing memory should look to hyperthymestic syndrome as the type of condition they would want to avoid.

Long-term memory involves critical mechanisms other than those for storage and retrieval. It is not known what effects drugs designed to enhance these mechanisms might have on the qualitative features of our capacity for recall. A study by Demis Hassabis and colleagues compared subjects with amnesia caused by bilateral damage to their hippocampus with subjects whose episodic memory was intact.[28] Whatever episodic memory the amnesics retained consisted mainly in recalling isolated trivial details of events. Unable to contextualize more significant details as part of a continuous narrative in time and space, they were unable to express the general meaning of these events. Nor were they able to imagine new experiences. HM had this same problem with his profound amnesia. This supports the hypothesis that remembering the past and imagining the future are interrelated mental capacities, indeed, mirror images of one another. The fact that none of the amnesics was able to capture the gist of the past suggests that what matters is not only *how much* we can recall but also *how* we recall it. The ability to meaningfully recall the past and anticipate the future appears to depend as much on qualitative as on quantitative aspects of our episodic memory. Hassabis's study suggests that increasing the quantity of memory might interfere with the qualitative capacity to make sense of past experience and simulate future experience. This dual constructive capacity enables us to have a unified set of psychological properties necessary for our experience as subjects persisting through time. Although this requires a certain amount of memory storage and retrieval, it is more than a function of how many memories of facts and events our brains can store or how efficiently our brains can retrieve them.

As Daniel L. Schacter and Donna Rose Addis point out, "Remembering the gist of what happened is an economical way of storing the most important aspects of our experiences without cluttering memory with trivial details."[29] They also note that "information about the past is useful only to the extent that it allows us to anticipate what may happen in the future."[30] The extent to which we can learn new things is a function of the meaning we can construct from what we have experienced. In addition to the hippocampus in the temporal lobe, regions in the frontal and parietal lobes play a role in the dual capacity to remember the past and anticipate the future. All of these brain regions provide a holistic representation of the environmental setting in which we can meaningfully recall past experience and simulate or imagine future experience. Increasing our capacity to store and retrieve memories might leave us too focused on the past, which might alter our phenomenological experience of persisting through time. As Jill Price's hyperthymestic syndrome illustrates, too much storage or retrieval of long-term memory could also impair our short-term working memory and our ability to form new memories. Our cognitive capacities could be diminished by our ability to recall more facts and events that had little or no meaning or purpose for us. Too much memory may impair our capacity to construct a narrative that unifies the experiences in our lives. Before we pharmacologically tinker with memory systems, we need to consider how this might affect the neurological and mental capacities that mediate the content and meaning of our memory.

Images of Forgetting

Finally, there is the issue of the role of memory in the legal system, particularly with respect to criminal law. Images of the brain produced by positron-emission tomography (PET) and functional magnetic resonance imaging (fMRI) display increased metabolic activity and blood flow in the parahippocampal gyrus and a region of the prefrontal cortex when subjects are asked to recall events. The images provide a glimpse of what occurs in the brain during memory retrieval. They could shed new light on the reliability of eyewitness testimony and the recovery of repressed memories.[31] Could brain imaging support a charge of criminal negligence for failing to remember an event, when that failure results in serious harm?

Consider the case of Carie Engholm, a hospital administrator in Texas.[32] She drove to work one extremely hot summer day with her young son and daughter in the backseat of her van. She was not accustomed to taking her daughter with her. After dropping off her son at day care, she drove to work and parked in an exposed lot, forgetting that her daughter was still in the van. The daughter was found dead from hyperthermia later that day—a day on which the temperature had risen to over 100 degrees Fahrenheit. Was Carie responsible for forgetting? Though she was initially charged with negligent homicide, a judge ruled that Carie was not responsible because forgetting is involuntary and not within our conscious control. But if a functional brain scan could show that her capacity to recall leaving her daughter in the van was intact, could the case be made and upheld that she was legally responsible for her daughter's death?

There are four main problems with using brain imaging to support a legal judgment of this sort. First, brain images of increased blood flow and glucose metabolism are not identical to events and processes occurring at the neuronal level. They are visualizations of statistical analyses based on a large number of images and are more accurately described as scientific constructs than actual images of the brain. Second, neuroimaging provides correlations between brain states and mental states. But correlation is not causation, and any claim that a person was responsible for forgetting would have to be based on a causal connection between a brain state and the mental state of forgetting. Third, neuroimaging by itself cannot tell us whether a person lacked the capacity to retrieve a memory, or had the capacity but failed to exercise it. Data that would allow us to draw this distinction would only be available from group studies. We would have to average data from images of the brains of many people before a particular image, or set of images, could have any statistical significance. Fourth, whereas claims about brain structure and processes are empirical, claims about criminal negligence are normative and are based on social expectations about how people ought to act. Empirical data can and should inform normative judgments about moral and criminal responsibility. But these judgments are more than just a function of such data.[33]

There is one scenario in which a brain scan might support an argument for the claim that the mother was not responsible for the omission resulting in her daughter's death. Carie Engholm's failure to remember leaving her daughter in the van may have been one instance in a pattern of similar behavior over a period of time. On the basis of this behavior, a scan showing significant damage to her medial temporal lobes might suggest she was suffering from anterograde amnesia. The damage might have prevented her from forming new memories and might have explained her inability to recall the critical event. The combination of the brain scan and her pattern of behavior might indicate that she could not be held responsible for forgetting something she could not have remembered. This scenario suggests that more refined brain imaging may go some way toward a better understanding of criminal responsibility for omissions. Nevertheless, the fact that neuroimaging provides only correlations between brain states and mental states and does not establish a causal connection between the brain and the mind shows the limitations of this technique as a tool in the criminal law.

Although the mental states that constitute personhood and the capacity for agency are generated and sustained by the brain, they are not only a function of the brain. Normative claims about how people can be expected to act are not reducible to the activity of neurons, synapses, and neurotransmitters. Our thought, behavior, and our brains are influenced by the social and natural environment in which we live and act. Given its limitations in reflecting the content of our mental states, neuroimaging should complement and not replace behavioral criteria of normative judgments of negligence and responsibility. Because it is still an imprecise technology, it will be some time before diagnostic brain imaging becomes a useful tool in informing these judgments. If it does, then it most likely will be used to support mitigation of or exoneration from responsibility for harmful acts of negligence by revealing significant brain dysfunction that interferes with the mechanisms of memory. Even so, it will not be just neuroscientists and legal theorists but society as a whole that will decide how information about the brain should be used in determining moral and legal responsibility.

Since antiquity, humans have been intrigued by the possibility of manipulating memory. In classical mythology, those who drank from or crossed the river Lethe in the underworld would lose all memory of their past lives when they became reincarnated, whereas those who drank from the river Mnemosyne would remember everything and become omniscient. Instead of drinking from or crossing mythical rivers, we can now alter memory through pharmacological means. This alteration may come in the form of dampening the emotional response to a memory of a traumatic event, preventing the formation of or erasing a memory, or enhancing the ability to form, store, and retrieve new memories. NeuroImaging has provided us with a better understanding of the effects of drugs on memory systems in general and on the brain regions involved in memory retrieval in particular. Although studies have not shown any significant short-term adverse effects of memory modification, its long-term benefits and risks are not known. Given what we now know about how different brain regions mediate different memory systems, we need to anticipate what the full effects of memory modification might be. This can lead to the formulation of ethical principles that will guide memory researchers so that any intervention in these systems will maximize benefit and minimize harm. The actual and possible ways of pharmacologically altering memory need to be complemented by ethical discussion of the reasons for or against these interventions.

Notes

1. James L. McGaugh, "The Amygdala Modulates the Consolidation of Memories of Emotionally Arousing Experiences," *Annual Review of Neuroscience* 27 (2004): 1–28; James L. McGaugh, "Make Mild Moments Memorable: Add a Little Arousal," *Trends in Cognitive Sciences* 10 (2006): 345–347; and James L. McGaugh, *Memory and Emotion: The Making of Lasting Memories* (New York: Columbia University Press, 2003).

2. Roger K. Pitman et al., "Pilot Study of Secondary Prevention of Posttraumatic Stress Disorder with Propranolol," *Biological Psychiatry* 51 (2002): 189–192.

3. Alain Brunet et al., "Effect of Post-retrieval Propranolol on Psychophysiologic Responding during Subsequent Script-Driven Traumatic Imagery in Post-traumatic Stress Disorder," *Journal of Psychiatric Research* 42 (2008): 503–506; Kevin LaBar and Roberto Cabeza, "Cognitive Neuroscience of Emotional Memory," *Nature Reviews Neuroscience* 7 (2006): 54–64.

4. Nor should propranolol's potentially harmful metabolic effects be overlooked. In 2006, after chronic use of beta-adrenergic antagonists was associated with the development of metabolic disorders such as type 2 diabetes, the United Kingdom downgraded propranolol from a first- to a fourth-line drug in the treatment of hypertension and arrhythmia.

5. Sharon Gill et al., "Does Memory of a Traumatic Event Increase the Risk for Posttraumatic Stress Disorder in Patients with Traumatic Brain Injury? A Prospective Study," *American Journal of Psychiatry* 162 (2005): 963–969.

6. Nicholas Medford et al., "Emotional Memory: Separating Content and Context," *Psychiatry Research: Neuroimaging* 138 (2005): 247–258.

7. Mark Richardson, Bryan A. Strange, and Raymond J. Dolan, "Encoding of Emotional Memories Depends on Amygdala and Hippocampus and Their Interactions," *Nature Neuroscience* 7 (2004): 278–285.

8. Daniel Schacter discusses HM and other famous cases of profound amnesia in *Searching for Memory: The Brain, the Mind, and the Past* (New York: Basic Books, 1996), chap. 5.

9. K. LaBar and R. Cabeza, "Cognitive Neuroscience of Emotional Memory."

10. Marya Schechtman calls the integrated and unified set of one's experiences one's "narrative identity," in *The Constitution of Selves* (Ithaca, NY: Cornell University Press, 1997). See also David DeGrazia, *Human Identity and Bioethics* (New York: Cambridge University Press, 2005).

11. U. S. President's Council on Bioethics, Staff Working Paper, "Better Memories? The Promise and Perils of Pharmacological Interventions," March 6, 2003, session 4; at http://www.bioethics.gov/transcripts/mar03.html/. President George W. Bush formed the council in August 2001 with the primary purpose of establishing ethical guidelines for stem-cell research. See also Leon Kass and U.S. President's Council on Bioethics, *Beyond Therapy: Biotechnology and the Pursuit of Happiness* (New York: Dana Press, 2003). Neil Levy discusses these and related issues in *Neuroethics: Challenges for the 21st Century* (Cambridge: Cambridge University Press, 2007), chap. 5.

12. Nathalie Camille, "The Involvement of the Orbitofrontal Cortex in the Experience of Regret," *Science* 304 (2004): 1167–1170.

13. Charles Taylor, *The Ethics of Authenticity* (Cambridge, MA: Harvard University Press, 1991), 29. See also Erik Parens, "Authenticity and Ambivalence: Toward Understanding the Enhancement Debate," *Hastings Center Report* 35 (May–June 2005): 34–41.

14. Harry Frankfurt, "Freedom of the Will and the Concept of a Person" and "Identification and Externality," both in *The Importance of What We Care About*, ed. Harry G. Frankfurt (New York: Cambridge University Press, 1988), 11–25, 58–68.

15. L. Kass and U. S. President's Council on Bioethics, *Beyond Therapy: Biotechnology and the Pursuit of Happiness*, 294.

16. For discussion of the therapy-enhancement distinction, see the papers in *Enhancing Human Traits: Ethical and Social Implications*, ed. Erik Parens (Washington, DC: Georgetown University Press, 1998).

17. "The Ethics of Erasing a Bad Memory," *Time* (online edition, October 15, 2007); at http://www.time.com/time/health/article/0,8599,1671492,00.html/. Adam Kolber discusses some of the ethical and legal implications of this case in "Freedom of Memory Today," *Neuroethics* 1 (2008): 145–148.

18. Steven Rose, "How Smart Are Smart Drugs?" *Lancet* 372 (2008): 198–199.

19. Gary Lynch, "Memory Enhancement: The Search for Mechanism-Based Drugs," *Nature Neuroscience* 5 (2002): 1035–1038; and Gary Lynch, "Glutamate-Based Therapeutic Approaches: Ampakines," *Current Opinion in Pharmacology* 6 (2006): 82–88. See also Gary Lynch and Christine Gall, "Ampakines and the Threefold Path to Cognitive Enhancement," *Trends in Neurosciences* 29 (2006): 554–562.

20. Tim Tully et al., "Targeting the CREB Pathway for Memory Enhancers," *Nature Reviews: Drug Discovery* 2 (2003): 266–277.

21. Martha Farah et al., "Neurocognitive Enhancement: What Can We Do and What Should We Do?" *Nature Reviews Neuroscience* 5 (2004): 421–425.

22. Torkel Klingberg proposes ways of avoiding the problem of overloading the brain with increased memory storage in *The Overflowing Brain: Information Overload and the Limits of Working Memory* (Oxford: Oxford University Press, 2008).

23. Martha Farah discusses the concept of an optimal balance between memory formation and extinction in "Emerging Ethical Issues in Neuroscience," *Nature Neuroscience* 5 (2002): 1123–1129.

24. Jill Price with Bart Davis, *The Woman Who Can't Forget: A Memoir* (New York: Free Press, 2008), 2, 38, 6, 45, and 24.

25. Elizabeth S. Parker, Larry Cahill, and James L. McGaugh, "Case of Unusual Autobiographical Remembering," *Neurocase* 12 (2006): 35–49.

26. See A. R. Luria, *The Mind of a Mnemonist: A Little Book about a Vast Memory*, trans. Lynn Solotaroff (Cambridge, MA: Harvard University Press, 1968).

27. As noted by James McGaugh in his testimony to the U. S. President's Council on Bioethics, seventh meeting, October 17, 2002, session 3; "Remembering and Forgetting: Physiological and Pharmacological Aspects."

28. Demis Hassabis et al., "Patients with Hippocampal Amnesia Cannot Imagine New Experiences," *Proceedings of the National Academy of Sciences USA* 104 (2007): 1726–1731.

29. Daniel L. Schacter and Donna Rose Addis, "The Ghosts of Past and Future," *Nature* 445 (2007): 27.

30. D. Schacter and D. R. Addis, "The Ghosts of Past and Future," 27. See also Eric R. Kandel, *The Search for Memory—The Emergence of a New Science of Mind* (New York: Norton, 2007).

31. Elizabeth Loftus, "Our Changeable Memories: Legal and Practical Implications," *Nature Reviews Neuroscience* 4 (2003): 231–234.

32. Daniel Schacter presented this case to the U.S. President's Council on Bioethics, seventh meeting, October 17, 2002, session 4: "Remembering and Forgetting: Psychological Aspects."

33. Dean Mobbs and colleagues give a more complete list of the limitations of brain imaging for use in the criminal law in "Law, Responsibility, and the Brain," *PLoS Biology* 5 (2007): e103.

IV Literary Data for Memory Studies

12   Autobiographical Memory in Modernist Literature and Neuroscience

Suzanne Nalbantian

Modern autobiographical literature of the twentieth century can be used virtually as a laboratory for the study of the encoding, storage, and retrieval of episodic memory. Masterworks of the Western tradition—notably those by Virginia Woolf, Marcel Proust, James Joyce, William Faulkner, Anaïs Nin, André Breton, Octavio Paz, Jorge Luis Borges, as well as the painter Salvador Dalí—provide a new kind of empirical data for understanding memory in its phenomenological expressions. I have classified the memory experiences of healthy, human subjects as enacted dynamically in modern fiction according to distinct typologies. These case studies are distinctly applicable to established viewpoints in memory research, corroborating some and predating others. They also demonstrate a variety of human memory processes, instead of remaining confined to any single scientifically based theory. The descriptive interpretations presented in this chapter help to illuminate certain intricate interactions and selectivity in human memory processing. My ongoing interdisciplinary analysis of major twentieth-century writers has led me to an overriding hypothesis that human memory can be understood as a dynamic process, often working with fixed elements that become transformed in the crucible of creative construction.

For many scientific researchers, landmark cases of impaired or diseased patients such as Phineas Gage (with frontal lobe damage) and Henry Molaison (or HM; with medial temporal lobe damage) have opened up an understanding of neural activity.[1] But from a humanistic angle we can derive striking evidence from the study of subjects who are *outliers* in a different way—writers with brilliant, creative powers who enact their memory experiences in their art. In their autobiographical literature, the authors under consideration here have recorded and enacted memory experiences that heighten, through the magnification of art, certain normal brain processes. Their "lived data" or "lived biology," conveyed through selective and synthetic verbal expressions, sheds light on various types of memory processing. Major autobiographical writers of the twentieth century are extraordinary subjects for the study of memory because of their heightened sensitivity, acute perception, and astute ability to communicate memory experiences. In this capacity, they provide evidence of the subjective experiences that some present-day neuroscientists are seeking to correlate with objective experimental findings.

The literary works under scrutiny here not only have autobiographical memory as their key subject matter, but being "modernist," they are also metacognitive or *process*-oriented. That is to say, these aesthetic autobiographical works reveal how memory is constructed, helping us to understand different kinds of memory processing. Their autobiographical basis gives a factual frame of reference against which to judge the authenticity or veracity of the memory episodes whose truth is embedded in their fictional rendition.[2] Such artistic works from the modern period contain subjects, revelatory metaphors, and dramatic scenes that bring to life in vivid, specific terms the workings of physiological memory in different phases of encoding, consolidation, and retrieval. The experiences felt and described by the novelist, poet, or even painter have interacted with the circuitry of the brain to affect the biochemistry that has created synaptic growth and long-term memory. The value of the literary text lies in the parsimony[3] with which it captures the complex memory phenomena as they are conjoined through dynamic interactions between component and system-level functioning.

Neuroscientific hypotheses regarding the emotional brain, sensory trigger mechanisms, memory traces, confabulation, consolidation and reconsolidation theory, and that most intricate field of implicit or unconscious memory can be further understood through the modernist literary expression of memory experiences. The literary case studies presented here demonstrate different kinds of memory: consolidated memory (Virginia Woolf), sensory memory (Marcel Proust), associative cued retrieval (James Joyce), time-dependent associative memory (William Faulkner), emotional memory involving the amygdala (Anaïs Nin), reactivated memory involving the hippocampus (Salvador Dalí), and unconscious memory involving a wide range of cortical networks for dream input and word activation (poets André Breton, Guillaume Apollinaire, Robert Desnos, and Octavio Paz).

The Stability of Memory

Virginia Woolf's quintessential memory novel *To the Lighthouse* (1927) with its tripartite structure offers a comprehensive view of conscious, voluntary, episodic memory processing in the traditional phases of encoding, storage, and retrieval. This autobiographical novel was prompted by the writer's desire to retrieve the memory of her mother, Julia Stephen, who had died when Virginia was only thirteen years old. Vivid memories of her mother were associated with the Godrevy lighthouse, as seen from the family summer home in St. Ives, Cornwall. Spanning the decade from 1910 to 1920, the novel is divided into three parts, which effectively chart three successive stages of memory processing: "The Window," "Time Passes," and "The Lighthouse." In the first section of the novel, "The Window," the memory of the mother figure, Mrs. Ramsay, is encoded in the brains of the family and friends by her association with the guiding light of the lighthouse whose "long steady stroke, was her stroke."[4] This lighthouse "stark and straight" becomes the stable embodiment of a memory that will persist over time.

The central section "Time Passes" of this remarkably inclusive novel (in which Mrs. Ramsay has died) presents in both literal and metaphoric terms the consolidation of memory over a ten-year period of sleep and darkness. As those years pass in the novel, we are shown not only that memory consolidates over time, but also that the sleep state participates in the consolidation of memory.[5] During this period of consolidation, under the seeming guise of forgetting in a place (the abandoned family house) where there are significantly no remembering subjects memory is converted from short- to long-term. This transformation appears to reflect the standard systems theories of memory consolidation, which implicate the interactions of several brain regions.[6] Interesting questions come to mind. Is the prefrontal cortex deactivated in this sleep mode? Is the hippocampus processing the amygdala-mediated emotional memories to the long-term memory that arises "ten years later" in the daylight of the cortical remembering? As we proceed to the third section of the novel, "The Lighthouse," we find that the remembering subjects reemerge. They are emotionally

charged in an anticipatory way. In the early morning hours they are especially "alert" and "vigilant." This last part of the novel lends credence to
emerging scientific evidence that during sleep, in particular, emotional
episodic scene memories can be stored as units.[7] The subjects in the novel
are able to retrieve the memory of the important mother figure when they
return to the site of a lighthouse that serves as the predominant, visual
retrieval cue for the resuscitated, stabilized memory. They include not only
three family members who take a trip to the lighthouse in memory of the
deceased mother, but also the artist Lily Briscoe, who completes a painting
of her.

Lily Briscoe's memory painting of Mrs. Ramsay could represent the kind
of top-down executive control of memory that emerges from the neuro-
aesthetic dimension that Jean-Pierre Changeux has brought to the global
workspace model. Proceeding from that neuronal model of fast connectional epigenesis (which is described in chapter 3 of this volume), Changeux has hypothesized that the broad interconnectivity of the neuronal
workspace would be the privileged seat for the "synthetic" aesthetic experience. From a pharmacological viewpoint, the workspace neurons in the
prefrontal cortex are themselves targets of ascending modulatory neurotransmitters, such as acetylcholine, noradrenaline and serotonin, which
are associated with attention, vigilance and memory. For Changeux, the
work of art requires the voluntary and conscious retrieval of long-term
memories with emotional resonances often unconscious and registered as
fragmentary traces in the limbic system. Changeux has proposed that a
painting mobilizes memory in this manner for artistic purposes.[8]

With its memory painting, Woolf's novel demonstrates how explicit
declarative memory involving the conscious retrieval of life facts and
events can be closely linked to the artistic process. The visual and topographic context is significant for this type of episodic memory. There is
similarity between conditions of encoding (engraphy) and conditions of
retrieval (ecphory) in the cuing process. Demonstrably in the novel, the
encoding, which originally established the links of association of memories
and material objects, thereby storing part of the context as well, is the basis
for the retrieval of memory in the same environment. Woolf shows how,
once an experience is stored, simple visual cues can stimulate the recall of
those old memories. This type of recall is particularly pertinent to her,
since she had written elsewhere that she was endowed with a memory that

preserved visual scenes in her mind. The wide-ranging brain activity of the process would clearly involve the hippocampal network, as memory is consolidated and interacts with the association areas of the neocortex. This type of contextual memory processing relates to the work of the French neuroscientist Alain Berthoz and colleagues on the integrative role of the hippocampal-parietal system, whose processing of spatial and topographic memory, in conjunction with inputs from emotion-related limbic responses, implicates several brain structures.[9] In her novel Woolf herself also seems to have also forged a pathway from emotional encoding (related to limbic neurons of the amygdala that "sealed" those memories for her) to cognitive retrieval of the memory of the emotion even though later in life she continued to ponder this issue stating: "I feel that strong emotion must leave its trace; and it is only a question of discovering how we can get ourselves again attached to it."[10]

In contrast to the globalized memory process revealed by Woolf, a more localized memory process can be demonstrated in the opus of Marcel Proust, *Remembrance of Things Past*. Proust is the supreme case of involuntary, sensory memory, associated with the rudimentary engram or fixed, encoded memory trace that appears to enjoy a privileged stability. It is ironic that this most sophisticated of writers may have in fact been displaying the most primitive, instinctive form of sensory memory in what is considered phylogenetically to be the oldest part of the brain. Proust starts off by presenting somatic memory in the narrator's recall of the past from the position of his reclining, aging body down to the position of his limbs. But the most commonly cited literary memory episode from *Swann's Way*, the first volume of *Remembrance of Things Past*, involves the middle-aged narrator's tasting of a madeleine dipped in tea, which instantly brings him back to his childhood vacations in Combray at the home of his Aunt Léonie: "the whole of Combray and its surroundings, taking shape and solidity, sprang into being, town and gardens alike, from my cup of tea."[11]

Proust made it clear that smell and taste (*l'odeur et la saveur*) alone are gateways to the vast structure of recollection. In his insistence on the specificity, intensity, and selectivity of the sensory sources, Proust is a good subject for further investigation of the neurological pathways from sensation to cognition. His visceral memory experiences are in line with what the neurologist Marsel Mesulam has called "sensory-fugal" processing, a hierarchical kind of linear sensory processing with forward pathways into cortical circuitry.[12] Proust emphasizes that it is taste, not sight, that is the trigger mechanism for such reminiscence because it reenacts the specific sensory relation that the child had experienced in his first contact with the madeleine. Seeing madeleines in pastry shop windows in later years therefore neither elicits nor contaminates the original reminiscence, which seems impervious to interference. Here it is a case of encoding specificity rather than condition-dependent retrieval, especially since Proust insists that the context of the retrieval is not involved. Quite simply, the recall of the original stimulus, occurring involuntarily in a Paris apartment, productively takes the narrator back to a scene in the distant past in which he feels fully immersed. Could this unadulterated form of memory also reflect the fact that Proust, during the last period of his life (his writing years), sequestered himself in a soundproof cork-lined room of his apartment on the Boulevard Hausmann in Paris?

Of the some twelve instances of involuntary memory throughout the eight-volume *Remembrance of Things Past*, the madeleine episode is the only literary memory experience considered by current neuroscientists. There is, however, a specificity to the Proustian stimulus-based memory process linking sensation to cognition that merits further exploration.[13] Proust, who was no Romantic, judged emotional memory to be a weak form of memory. In the novel's fourth volume, *Sodom and Gomorrah*, Proust's narrator emphasizes that it is the involuntary physical trigger of unbuttoning his boot, not the emotion of remorse he feels over having ridiculed his late grandmother that calls up the vivid memory of her. Similarly, in the last volume, *Time Regained*, the narrator's physical contact with a particular book, a novel by George Sand, serendipitously taken from a shelf, provokes the second remembrance of his mother. The book's reddish binding and what neuropsychologists would call the "musical image" of the sound of its title, not the content of the book, elicit the vivid episodic memory of his mother reading this book to him as a child.[14] Consistently, Proust's work identifies and reenacts involuntary sensory trigger mechanism in the memory process. That spontaneous involuntary memory, for him the most supreme kind of memory, is the trigger for voluntary memory which enables him to reconstruct the past in this novel. This "bottom up" memory process is the basis of his conscious art-making.[15]

Another classification of memory is that of the purely associative kind, exemplified in the fiction of James Joyce and William Faulkner, as well as

Virginia Woolf, in their stream-of-consciousness novels. In fact, each of these three writers highlights a different aspect of the associative process. In contrast to Proust, these writers allow for the cognitive environment of the present to enter into the retrieval of memory. This approach to associative memory, first elaborated by William James in his classic *Principles of Psychology* (1890), has been taken in modern times, most notably by the Canadian neuropsychologist Endel Tulving since he defined *episodic memory* in 1972. Over his entire career, Tulving has focused on the physical and cognitive environments that initiate retrieval, where a cue may have symbolic form—"a word, a phrase, a question, a spoken hint."[16] He has found memory retrieval to be most effective when it involves the same cues and context as those of the original information. Also, highly pertinent here is Edmund Rolls's seminal theory that partial memory cues or fragmentary clues in the autoassociative network of the hippocampus can contribute to the formation of long-term, context-dependent episodic memories.[17]

This associative cuing activity clearly relates to James Joyce. Specifically, gifted in languages and music, Joyce positioned sound at the forefront of such cues. Notably, his memory story "The Dead" (1907) helps to situate him within the context of the neuroscience of music. This celebrated story from the *Dubliners* collection reflects Joyce's own struggle, through his persona Gabriel Conroy, with the past of his native Ireland in the throes of transition to the modern world of the early twentieth century. In that story it is an old Gaelic folk song, "The Lass of Aughrim," heard by Gabriel's wife Gretta at a party they attend, that resurrects the long-term memory of her deceased Irish lover, a memory that she tearfully shares with Gabriel. Here, therefore, music sets off an epiphany linked with a personal memory that is also symbolic of Joyce's recollection of Ireland's past. Dramatically, Joyce demonstrates the retrieval of autobiographical memory from music by way of the emotion connected to a familiar tune.[18] This painful memory episode accords with the view of Isabelle Peretz and Robert Zatorre that "music may serve as an excellent paradigm to explore the interactions between neocortically mediated cognitive processes and subcortically mediated affective responses."[19]

Sound also figures prominently as a sensory memory cue in Joyce's autobiographical novel *A Portrait of the Artist as a Young Man* (1916), where music and the sound of Irish place-names such as Clongowes, Clane, and

Cork propel the succession of associations that constitute the fictional recollection of Joyce's early life. Through his distanced persona Stephen Dedalus in this typical stream-of-consciousness novel, Joyce virtually reconstructs his past (up to the age of twenty) by the successive retrieval of memory experiences through environmental cues of place and locale in his native Ireland. The stream of associations provides the links and fills any gaps in the linear narrative of the remembrances, reenacting the author's own logical retrieval of memory. This device mimics the actual workings of the mind and represents an aspect of what Alain Berthoz calls *remplissage*, or the brain's capacity for "filling in."[20] Joyce's use of both music and the sound of words as memory cues brings to life what recent neuroimaging data and cognitive theory have led the researcher Aniruddh Patel to propose: "a specific point of convergence between syntactic processing in language and music."[21] The sound of language is a prime impetus for Joyce's memory retrieval, suggesting a possible neural relationship between language and music. The auditory memory images of song and language may also account for the semipermanence of Joyce's memories. Sounds appear in his earliest infant recollections of the voices of his mother and father, who mingled storytelling, the singing of Irish tunes, and piano playing. Later, the "naughty" and crude words uttered by the schoolmates of the young Stephen Dedalus bring back the vivid episodic long-term memory of his parents leaving him at the Clongowes Wood College boarding school at the tender age of six-and-a-half.

The Variability of Memory

Turning to the American writer William Faulkner, who likewise struggles with his own deep national roots, we find that his work features the dimension of time as a factor in the analysis of the associative memory process. His renowned novel *The Sound and the Fury* (1929) is replete with references to the decayed past of the American South in the author's native Mississippi setting through the varying perspectives of members of an erstwhile aristocratic family in decline. In crystallizing confrontations with this cultural past in individual memory events the novel powerfully contrasts continuous (Bergsonian) with relativistic (Einsteinian) time frames that shape the personal memory process. Whereas the mentally retarded "idiot" character Benjy Compson lives in the continuous past of *duration*, his evidently intelligent brother, Quentin, a Harvard student, cannot fully escape to that fixed past and thereby gain a sense of much needed stability and solace.

Accordingly, contrasting temporal orientations toward memory in the novel produce distinctly contrasting identities and mindsets. For example, at the very beginning, Benjy's clothing is caught by a nail in a fence—a simple sensation that instantly triggers his stream of recollection of his distant childhood twenty-six years before when he was seven in rural Mississippi. Here the fence is not an isolated trigger but an integral part of the past, connecting many significant scenes of family life in which Benjy becomes immersed to the point of reexperiencing actual sights and smells of his childhood. The experiences of Quentin, an autobiographical character who reflects Faulkner's own obsession with matters of memory and time, prove to be quite different. Throughout his peregrinations in Boston on June 2, 1910, the day of his suicide, Quentin is haunted by watches, clock chimes, and natural signs of time such as shifting shadows. He chances upon a jewelry shop window display of a dozen watches showing a dozen different hours. In the midst of such relativistic, mathematical time, Quentin intermittently experiences memories—fragments of human time—which pass fleetingly through his mind, compromised by the invasive present. In an earlier short story, "That Evening Sun," Faulkner had shown the Quentin character existing as both boy and adult, and reexperiencing the boy's view of the past from the perspective of the adult's present. For Faulkner, memory is altered according to his subjects' negotiation with time. This updating and editing of memory can be understood in the neurocognitive framework of subjective time and consciousness of self—"autonoetic awareness"—that Endel Tulving has described.[22] It also reflects Antonio Damasio's concept of "mind time," according to which "the process of time and certain types of memory must share some common neurological pathways."[23] In The Sound and the Fury and in his other literary works, Faulkner was introducing the notion of the relativity of memory that results from the subjective experience of time.

With the modern, cosmopolitan writer-diarist Anaïs Nin, we move from associative, logical stream of consciousness (conscious, explicit memory) to deeply embedded traumatic memory (unconscious, implicit memory), often presumed to be modulated by the amygdala, which engages in the processing of unconscious emotional memories. Nin shows memory retrieval through chain reactions, triggered by emotionally arousing experiences, whereby short-term memories are supplanted by long-term ones. This writer was haunted all her life by the memory of her father, the Cuban musician Joaquín Nin, who abandoned her and her family when she was only eleven in Europe. She was reunited with her father twenty years later, but then rejected him purportedly after a brief but deeply wounding incestuous affair. In Nin's fiction, the imprints of such deep emotional memories are suggested by images of splinters, grooves, and tattoos. Nin perceives that such memory traces are permanent and indelible because they seem to be engraved repeatedly and continuously on the brain in analogous or parallel patterns over a lifetime. Thus their recovery from different neural networks can be of special interest here.

Nin transferred her personal traumatic memories to her fiction in *Cities of the Interior*. The predicaments of her female personae in the five volumes of Nin's "continuous novel" can shed light on aspects of what Edmund Rolls and Joseph LeDoux have envisaged as the "emotional brain." In the 1990s, the two neuroscientists initiated the study of the neural basis of emotions, which has since proliferated, with multiple versions of emotional tagging theory. As seen in chapters 7 and 8 of this volume, useful distinctions continue to be drawn between explicit and implicit memory processing, between memories about emotions and emotional memories. With his systems-level approach, Rolls has probed the emotional component in contextual episodic memory storage and retrieval, involving backprojection pathways to the neocortex from both the hippocampus and the amygdala.[24] Nin's literary material may help to illuminate discriminations and interactions between these two brain structures in their mediation of emotional memory in human subjects. LeDoux has undertaken a more localized investigation of the neural basis of emotions as cellular and molecular events on the synaptic level. In concentrating on fear as modeled in animal studies, he has focused on conditioned memory processing in the amygdala.[25] Nin's traumatic, implicit emotional memory transfixed in the frightening image of the minotaur in her striking fifth book of *Cities of the Interior* may serve to translate LeDoux's findings into human terms.

In Nin's novel *Seduction of the Minotaur* (1961) the ubiquitous labyrinth image suggests an archaeology of the mind, where passageways such as tunnels and corridors are networks through which memories flow in the internal sites of the unconscious. Nin thereby portrayed through metaphor this new "brain space" for the recovery of memory. The title evokes the mythic minotaur locked in a labyrinth on the isle of Crete. In the novel, the 1950s autobiographical persona Lillian Beye from White Plains, New York, spends three months as a jazz musician in a Mexican city of her childhood that harbored remembrances of her father. During her flight back to New York, Lillian confronts the image of a minotaur in the plane window that represents the traumatic memory of her abusive father from that distant past and that also reflects Nin's own recollections of her real father. Nin had likened Lillian's journey to a mining expedition with symbolic resonances of a trip through a labyrinth to unlock the imprisoned minotaur. This extended metaphor could help us better understand what have been scientifically termed *nested structures*, placing autobiographical memory in layers of complex stratification that require a multistage process of retrieval.[26]

But this explicit quest for the memory of an emotion in *Seduction of the Minotaur* soon leads more significantly to Nin's emotional memories of the unconscious kind. Such implicit memories might be encoded and tagged in the amygdala,[27] where synapses are formed and modified with the help of powerful neurotransmitters, such as serotonin and acetylcholine, that are known to be memory enhancers. It is striking that Nin's persona even searches for a "chemical compound"[28] as an equivalent for the remembered love of her father. Also she shows us that, when some aspect of the stimulus situation for a memory—whether place, cue, emotion, or image—recurs, the memory is reinforced. Nin's portrayals are strikingly in line with those who study the synaptic transmission of memory and the neuromodulatory influences that can govern its consolidation. The Nin example can help to illustrate James McGaugh's long-standing view that emotionally arousing experiences release stress-related hormones (such as epinephrine) that activate the amygdala in consolidating lasting memory traces in other brain regions.[29] Nin's work shows how highly emotional memories can be among the most permanent types of memory that remain stored.

Whereas in the early 1930s Nin first sought psychotherapy from analysts such as Otto Rank and René Allendy, she eventually rejected their Freudian approach with its theory of repressed long-term memory. Nin's lifelong diary from age eleven lent credence to her early memories, which were not disguised, Freudian "screen memories" but real, uncovered ones

that were documented and accurately described. In rejecting psychotherapy, she may have been instinctively trying to prevent the memory
distortion that psychoanalytic intrusion can provoke, as certain current
neuropsychologists have since explained.[30] Successfully using both her
diary and her novelistic art as active means of memory retrieval, Nin
moved from short- to long-term memory and gained psychological libera-
tion from the symptomatic, neurobiological effects that traumatic, hidden
memory events could have engendered.

The Lability of Memory

In contrast to such relatively permanent experiences of consolidated
memory, the surrealist painter Salvador Dalí visually presents what is
known neuroscientifically in our time as "reactivated memory," that is to
say, memory that is conceived to be labile and ever-changing. Reconsolidation theory has been qualifying the notion of permanent long-term
memory by showing that previously consolidated memory can be modified
when it returns to a labile, destabilized state upon retrieval.[31] Unlike some
of the modernist writers considered above, Dalí vividly suggested that
memory is mutable, that it changes over time, and that it is subject to the
influences of dream, hallucination, and automatism that the Surrealists
exploited for artistic purposes.

In his autobiography *The Secret Life of Salvador Dalí* (1942), the artist
explains the genesis of his famous 1931 painting *The Persistence of Memory*,
giving us insight into his concept of memory.[32] In that painting, Dalí
recaptures the authentic past of his early childhood through a luminous
rendition of the rocks and coastline of his native Catalan landscape, which
he puts into a kind of twilight zone. His long-term memory was converted
to a setting of *fourth dimension space-time* for some new insight. Upon his
return to Paris from a three-month stay at his childhood home of Port
Lligat on Spain's Costa Brava, Dalí's vision of the distant past had been
resuscitated and reactivated by a short-term memory of his recent visit. In
Paris, far from the remembered site in Spain, he had been in the process
of painting a literal rendition of the landscape of his childhood. But he
explains how on one particular evening, in a fringe state of consciousness
between wakefulness and sleep, he is struck by the sight on his dinner table

of melting camembert. This image suggests to Dalí the malleability of memory, of remembered time, which he was then to incarnate in the soft, limp watches in the foreground of the painting.

Dalí thereby disassociated his childhood memory from the confines of a fixed past and the alleged veridicality of hippocampally mediated memory. Dalí's "hypervisuality" demonstrates what some neuroscientists have observed, that unconscious memories of the dream or hallucinatory state present their own scheme of interpretation in which connectivity is different from that of the waking state. Associations occur without a connecting thread. Such memories, which an artist like Dalí consciously integrates in his art, demonstrate the heightened role of the imagination in securing memory through creative appropriation. With the juxtaposition of the two landscapes in his painting, Dalí vividly portrayed the modification of memory. Instead of representing a specific instance of memory retrieval, *The Persistence of Memory* is self-reflexive—theoretically, about the memory process itself. The painting graphically reveals that reactivated memory can turn a previously consolidated memory back into a productively fragile and labile state again.

It is important to note that Dalí's hypervision of the camembert on the dinner table is not at all a Proustian episode. It is not the taste or smell of the cheese that is the involuntary trigger for memory in a conscious state of hippocampal processing. Nor is the memory resuscitated through the environmental cues of place or through the consolidation of sleep, as in the case of Virginia Woolf. The painting is completed in Paris, not on the Costa Brava during Dalí's brief return there. Moreover, Dalí's type of mentation involves the processing of sensory stimuli in an artistic state of altered consciousness sustained by the enabling neurotransmitters of both dream and hallucinatory states.

For Dalí and modernist poets such as André Breton, Guillaume Apollinaire, and Robert Desnos, the specifically surrealist imagination secures memory through the creative modification that occurs with the biochemical and cognitive resources of the dream state. For the surrealists, the poet is the "watchman" (*guetteur* in French) in preconscious waters with another kind of vigilance than that of the waking state. This designation by Breton and his fellow poet-dreamers, uncanny and prescient as it was, seems to conform with Changeux's speculation regarding the paradoxical effects of acetylcholine, namely, that the sudden imbalance of the acetylcholine/ noradrenaline ratio in certain phases of REM sleep affects the alertness of the dream state. It is all the more intriguing that for over half a century the French have used the catchy and revelatory term *sommeil paradoxal* (paradoxical sleep) for REM sleep.[33] Breton's concept of "arborescent recollections" (*souvenirs arborescents*) suggests that implicit memory emerging spontaneously and from dreams creates tributaries that are in turn sources for artistic appropriation in the conscious state.[34] Breton was redirecting the memory process to achieve a larger recuperation from its unconscious state. He was less interested in the contents of his own childhood memory (as Proust would have been) than in the mental process that those memories elicit in activating the mind. In Guillaume Apollinaire's strange story "La Fiancée posthume" (The Posthumous Fiancée; 1911), a couple, bereaved by the tragic loss of their five-year-old daughter, delude themselves into creating an imaginary wedding for her years later from the memories that evolved into the future. This phenomenon, corroborated by Breton's arresting phrase "the memory of the future" (*le souvenir du futur*),[35] might well be an example of what is being called "prospective memory." We can also consider Robert Desnos's notion of erotic memory derived from his French poem "Erotisme de la mémoire," in which the word *erotic* in surrealist usage suggests the unanticipated coupling of retrieved images and objects in the memory process. With "erotic" memory, traces are not triggers to a specific scene in the past but memory-fragments of a dreamscape that are dislodged from past associations and integrated into present perceptions as components of episodic memory that the artist amalgamates in his work.

From a neurocognitive standpoint, J. Allan Hobson and Robert Stickgold have explained how in dream states there is a relaxation or loosening up of the standard associative memory networks with their connecting threads. The hyperassociativity within REM sleep yields higher level conceptual associations of heightened cholinergic activity.[36] Reactivation can turn a previously consolidated memory back into a productively fragile and labile state, rendering it susceptible to interference and to some sort of confabulation in stages of dissociation—which, arguably, artists recuperate for the art of their paintings. According to Stickgold, "creativity can be thought of as the process of identifying new and useful associations among pre-existing memories":[37] Memory traces that had been flagged in the amygdala by emotion—not from episodic memory already consolidated in the hippocampus—are replayed in the dream environment and rolled like dice through the associative networks for reactivation. With striking prescience, such aleatory, oneiric material is what surrealists experienced and experimented with almost a century ago.

Linked to surrealist art, modernist poetry offers a dense language imagery that can be studied in relation to implicit memory and contextual priming. For some modernist poets, language becomes another trigger mechanism for memory. Words themselves are stimuli that can prompt the assembling of different memory traces distributed throughout the brain. For example, Octavio Paz, in his long poem "Pasado en claro" ("The Past Clarified"; 1972), is able as a poet to retrieve, through the catalytic power of poetic language, his distant past in Mixcoac, Mexico:

Heard by the soul, footsteps
In the mind, more than shadows
Shadows of thought more than footsteps
Through the path of echoes
That memory invents and erases.[38]

Mirrors and echoes in this poem suggest the reflective and resonant power of words and their multiple associations, not to replicate, but to re-create the past. Paz's language shapes, refashions, and virtually embodies the confused and volatile remembrances. As he "travels toward himself" through his poetry into the past of his childhood, Paz encounters the sound image of a patio as the conduit for memory. But soon this "patio" image "dissolves" with other objects into the form of a lake, so that the poet declares that his memory is "a puddle" or a "muddy mirror," meaning that it is also confused and transitory. In saying that "words are my eyes," Paz contends that it is language that shapes and contains the volatile reminiscences. Paz concludes with the sun as the ultimate metaphor for the clarification and transformation of memory by language, stating, "The sun, in my writing, drinks the shadows." The shadowy draft becomes the clear copy of memory. For Paz, memory with its erasures and additions is in a constant state of reconstruction, not unlike current versions of reconsolidation theory, which even employ similar language to describe memory lability.

Hence, poets such as Octavio Paz and his French predecessor André Breton fall in line with the connectionist systems modeling of memory, which rejects the notion of fixed memory storage or fixed memory traces, as witnessed in Proust and Woolf. That is to say, these poets suggest that the evocation of memory is dependent on a network of connections and associative contingencies that bring in new associations of words and images. This modernist poetic perspective is in tandem with the complementary learning systems theory of James McClelland and colleagues, which construes memory not simply as retrieval but as a synthetic construction often dependent on the strength of connections, known as "connection weights," between neurons in the brain.[39] In McClelland's theory of constructive memory, the synaptic connections among the neurons store associative relationships between aspects of content. The connections involved in storing an experience poetically with one item such as a word, face, landscape, or even event would be altered due to exposures to other experiences over a lifetime. Therefore, the resulting memory becomes a "synthesis of contributions from many different sources of information."[40] The richly layered terrain of the neocortex is the site of interweaved operations that allow for such cumulative, active construction.

Memory as Approximation

The neurocognitive concept of constructive memory is captured most fully in the synthetic view of ultramodernist poet Jorge Luis Borges. This poet held that, amid the transient flow of time and disintegration, only an approximation of a memory experience could be reached, and then only in "privileged" heightened or critical moments of concentration and fixation. Borges speaks of crossing a "threshold" to arrive at these selected transcendent moments through language that is created, not stored. For example, the fixation on the "Zahir" coin in the haunting story of that title reifies and enlarges the subject's memory of a deceased loved one. According to Borges, forgetting is also necessary for the constructive power of the imagination to come into play. His famous memory story entitled "Funes el memorioso" (Funes the Memorious; 1942) presents the case of a young man, who, having fallen from a horse and injured his brain, is overwhelmed by a boundless memory. He remembers the minutest details of his past, such as the forms of clouds on a certain day in 1882 or every detail of every dream he has ever had. This fictional case study suggests that the mind, in a chaotic state of uncontrolled memory, without the organization and selection of the artistic imagination integral to what Borges regards as the "true" memory process, can become like a garbage heap.[41] Borges thus provides one more instance supporting the notion that the operations of creativity, far from being ornamental or distorting, are endemic to human memory.

The autobiographical literary data presented above vividly demonstrate that the artistic modification involved in the literary rendering of memory reenacts the sophisticated constructionist component inherent in the biological workings of memory itself. This approach is based on the scientifically proven malleability of memory. The literary cases show that creativity does not necessarily undermine the veracity of the original memory, but transforms it and, with characteristic parsimony, embodies it in metaphor, metonymy, analogy, and other devices of literary expression. When memory is productively "distorted,"[42] its component of creativity becomes more visible for analysis. My thesis is in accord with the contention by neural Darwinists Jean-Pierre Changeux and Gerald Edelman that memory is not simply replicative, because it involves synaptic selection, incorporation of ongoing experience, and recategorization. Moreover, autobiographical literary data support my further claim that memory is *inherently* a *creative* process, amplified by the artist but also operative that way in the ordinary human brain.

Notes

1. For the case of Phineas Gage, see Antonio Damasio, *Descartes' Error: Emotion, Reason, and the Human Brain* (New York: Putnam's, 1994); for the case of HM, see Brenda Milner, "The Medial Temporal–Lobe Amnesic Syndrome," *Psychiatric Clinics of North America* 28 (2005): 599–611.

2. In analyzing the transformation of fact into fiction by autobiographical writers of the twentieth century in my book *Aesthetic Autobiography: From Life to Art in Marcel Proust, James Joyce, Virginia Woolf and Anaïs Nin* (London: Palgrave Macmillan, 1994), I discovered that the truth about their lives could often be found in their fiction. It was thus that I began to connect the memory process with the artistic process that governs this particular type of fiction writing. This led to my interdisciplinary analysis of memory in my subsequent book *Memory in Literature: From Rousseau to Neuroscience* (London: Palgrave Macmillan, 2003).

3. Here I am applying *parsimony* to literature in the scientific sense used by the economist Herbert A. Simon, who defined the term as the human brain's ability to extract and represent simple patterns in the midst of apparently complex distributions and disorder. See Herbert A. Simon, "Science Seeks Parsimony Not Simplicity: Searching for Pattern in Phenomena," in *Simplicity, Inference and Modeling: Keeping It Sophisticatedly Simple*, ed. Arnold Zellner, Hugo A. Keuzenkamp, and Michael McAleer (New York: Cambridge University Press, 2001), 32–69.

4. Virginia Woolf, *To the Lighthouse* (1927; reprint, New York: Harcourt Brace, 1981), 63.

5. The widely held view that sleep participates in the consolidation of memories has involved study of the neuromodulatory contexts of the sleeping brain over many years and by many memory researchers, including James L. McGaugh, Robert Stickgold, Matthew Walker, Bruce L. McNaughton, and Michael E. Hasselmo, to name just a few.

6. Woolf demonstrates a number of memory system theories in *To the Lighthouse*. Here, in "Time Passes," she seems to be demonstrating aspects of both classic "trace-transfer consolidation" theory, which is time dependent, and "modulation-of-consolidation" theory, which involves sleep. These theories are clearly described by Karim Nader, Glenn E. Schafe, and Joseph LeDoux, in "The Labile Nature of Consolidation Theory," *Nature* 1 (2000): 216–219.

7. Jessica D. Payne et al., "Sleep Preferentially Enhances Memory for Emotional Components of Scenes," *Psychological Science* 19 (2008): 781–788.

8. See Jean-Pierre Changeux, *The Physiology of Truth* (Cambridge, MA: Harvard University Press, 2004), chap. 3. See also J. P. Changeux, "Art and Neuroscience," *Leonardo* 27 (1994): .189–201.

9. See Sidney I. Weiner, Alain Berthoz, and Michael B. Zugaro, "Multisensory Processing in the Elaboration of Place and Head Direction Responses by Limbic System Neurons," *Cognitive Brain Research* 14 (2002): 75–90.

10. Virginia Woolf, "A Sketch of the Past," in *Moments of Being*, ed. Jeanne Schulkind (New York: Harcourt Brace, 1976), 67.

11. Marcel Proust, *Swann's Way*, in *Remembrance of Things Past*, trans. C. K. Scott Moncrieff and Terence Kilmartin (New York: Random House, 1981), 1:51.

12. See Marsel Mesulam "Representation, Inference and Transcendent Encoding in Neurocognitive Networks of the Human Brain," *Annals of Neurology* 64 (2008): 367–377.

13. Joseph LeDoux and Valérie Doyère are among those who describe complex memory traces whose components (emotional or sensory, for example) can be separated during acts of retrieval and reconsolidation (see chapter 7 in this volume). It

would seem that Proust experienced sensory conditioning that was enhanced by repetition and that did not allow for any updating upon retrieval and therefore could remain intact. It also brings up the question that the stability of the memory might depend on where and how the memory is initially encoded. Careful analysis of Proust can generate many more questions for neuroscientists relating sensory, emotional, and cognitive memory processes.

14. In recounting this memory episode of his mother reading aloud to him, Proust might well have been influenced by the French philosopher Henri Bergson, whom Proust heard lecture at the Sorbonne. Bergson in *Matter and Memory* (1896) had distinguished between "the memory of the reading of a book" and the "memory of the lesson" or the content of the book—an early distinction of what later has come to be known as "episodic" vs. "semantic memory." For detailed analyses of Proust's memory episodes, see S. Nalbantian, *Memory in Literature: From Rousseau to Neuroscience*, 61–76.

15. Literary critics have simplistically equated involuntary memory with unconscious memory. The large design of Proust's work seems to represents conscious memory of the hippocampus.

16. Endel Tulving, *Elements of Episodic Memory* (New York: Oxford University Press, 1983), 171.

17. See Edmund Rolls, "A Theory of Hippocampal Function in Memory," *Hippocampus* 6 (1996). 601–620.

18. A similar memory "epiphany" is experienced by Swann/Proust on hearing Vinteuil's sonata in the second section ("Combray") of *Swann's Way*. For a neuroscientific analysis of this kind of memory processing, see Matthew D. Schulkind, Laura K. Hennis, and David C. R. Rubin, "Music, Emotion and Autobiographical Memory: They're Playing Your Song," *Memory and Cognition* 27 (1999); 948–955.

19. Isabelle Peretz and Robert J. Zatorre, "Brain Organization for Musical Processing," *Annual Review of Psychology* 56 (2005): 99.

20. See Alain Berthoz, *Le sens du mouvement* (Paris: Odile Jacob, 1997), 143.

21. Aniruddh D. Patel, "Language, Music, Syntax and the Brain," *Nature Neuroscience* 6 (2003): 674.

22. See Endel Tulving, "Episodic Memory: From Mind to Brain," *Annual Review of Psychology* 53 (2002): 2.

23. Antonio R. Damasio, "Remembering When," *Scientific American* 287 (September 2002): 68. Damasio holds that "mind time" is determined by the attention and chronology we give to events and by the emotions we feel when they occur.

24. See Edmund T. Rolls, *The Brain and Emotion* (New York: Oxford University Press, 1999), 144.

25. Although LeDoux has concentrated on animal studies, he has suggested that "important studies of rare human cases" might enable us to understand "how memory systems are operating in parallel to give rise to independent memory functions." See Joseph LeDoux, *The Emotional Brain* (New York: Simon & Schuster, 1996), 202

26. Paul W. Burgess and Tim Shallice, "Confabulation and the Control of Recollection," *Memory* 4 (1996): 367.

27. Nin would seem to fall in line with the emotional tagging hypothesis, as discussed by Gal Richter-Levin and Iris Akirav in "Emotional Tagging of Memory Formation," *Brain Research Reviews* 43 (2003): 247–256.

28. Anais Nin, *Seduction of the Minotaur* (Athens: Ohio University Press, 1961), 113.

29. See James L. McGaugh, "The Amygdala Modulates the Consolidation of Memories of Emotionally Arousing Experiences," *Annual Review of Neuroscience* 27 (2004): 1–28.

30. See Elizabeth Loftus and Katherine Ketchan, *The Myth of Repressed Memory* (New York: St. Martin's Press, 1994).

31. Dalí's juxtaposition of consolidated with reconsolidated memory is in accordance with theories of reconsolidation, including Karim Nader's longstanding view that the consolidation of memory is an ongoing process reiterated by reactivation. Karim Nader writes that "post-retrieval memory reflects processes akin to those that stabilized the memory following acquisition." See Karim Nader, "A Single Standard for Memory: The Case for Reconsolidation" *Nature Reviews Neuroscience* 10 (2009): 224. See also chapter 2 by Alcino J. Silva and chapter 7 by Joseph LeDoux and Valérie Doyère in this volume. Current fashionable labels such as "tags," "updating," and "erasures" of memory can be used to describe this kind of memory processing evidenced in some modernist fiction and art.

32. See Salvador Dalí, *The Secret Life of Salvador Dalí*, trans. Haakon M. Chevalier (New York: Dover, 1993), 317.

33. Neurophysiologist Michel Jouvet from the University of Lyon coined the term *sommeil paradoxal* in 1959.

34. See André Breton, "Les champs magnétiques," in *Oeuvres complètes* (Paris: Gallimard, 1988), 1:64.

35. See frontispiece to André Breton, *Introduction au discours sur le peu de réalité* (Paris: Gallimard, 1927). In a different context, for a discussion of "prospective memory" processing, see chapter 13 by Alan Richardson in this volume.

36. This heightened cholingeric activity in REM sleep is in contrast to the aminergic activity of opposing neurotransmitters, such as serotonin, dopamine (for attention), and norepinephrine or noradrenaline, in waking states. See J. Alan Hobson and R.

Stickgold, "The Conscious State Paradigm: A Neurocognitive Approach to Waking, Sleeping, and Dreaming," in *The Cognitive Neurosciences*, ed. Michael S. Gazzaniga et al. (Cambridge, MA: MIT Press, 1995), 1373–1389.

37. Robert Stickgold, "Memory, Cognition and Dreams," in *Sleep and Brain Plasticity*, ed. P. Maquet, C. Smith, and R. Stickgold (New York: Oxford University Press, 2003), 19.

38. Octavio Paz, "The Past Clarified," in *A Draft of Shadows,* ed. and trans. Eliot Weinberger (New York: New Directions, 1972), 123.

39. James L. McClelland, Bruce L. McNaughton, and Randall C. O'Reilly, "Why There Are Complementary Learning Systems in the Hippocampus and Neocortex: Insights from the Successes and Failures of Connectionist Models of Learning and Memory," *Psychological Review* 102 (1995): 419–457. Steven Pinker makes a point of equating "connection weights" with synapses in his description of connectionism in *How the Mind Works* (New York: Norton, 1997), 114.

40. James L. McClelland, "Constructive Memory and Memory Distortions: A Parallel Distributed Processing Approach," *Memory Distortion*, ed. Daniel Schacter (Cambridge, MA: Harvard University Press, 1995), 88. McClelland's neural network model of parallel distributed processing establishes long-term memory as arising from the interaction between the medial temporal region (implicating but not limited to the hippocampus) and the neocortex.

41. Borges's view is in accord with theories of cortical "top-down" executive control proposed by Jean-Pierre Changeux and by William Hirstein (see chapters 3 and 10 in this volume).

42. My view of creative memory is to be distinguished from the largely clinical view of episodic memory distortion and falsification through confabulation that has overtaken a branch of scientific psychology. On the other hand, Daniel Schacter, in *The Seven Sins of Memory* (New York: Houghton Mifflin, 2001), has admitted that distortions of memory by different kinds of interference might in turn reveal important aspects of memory functioning, and William Hirstein, in *Brain Fiction* (Cambridge, MA: MIT Press, 2005), has suggested that confabulation in patients with neurological disorders might be an extreme version of some basic feature of the normal human mind. Further support for my view comes from Edmund Rolls's finding, in *The Brain and Emotion* (Oxford: Oxford University Press, 1999), 144, that a mood state can affect the retrieval of memory; from Tim Shallice's finding, in "Confabulation and the Control of Recollection," *Memory* 4 (1996): 359–411, that, with regard to normal, healthy autobiographical memory, the subject is in a retrieval mode, adding ecphoric information (the product of the encoding process and the retrieval cue) to the engram; and possibly also from J.-P. Changeux's view, in *The Physiology of Truth*, 102, that the distortions might be natural selections.

13 Memory and Imagination in Romantic Fiction

Alan Richardson

Memory and *imagination* might seem to name markedly different human capacities concerned with distinct areas of mental activity. Memory takes the factual as its province: it functions to preserve matters of autobiographical and historical record. Few today would want to claim that memory, whether individual or collective, accurately preserves objective and immutable truths about nature and the world. Memories are widely viewed as subject to inevitable biases in perspective when being formed and to various sorts of degradation and distortion when they are stored and retrieved. Still, we expect memory at least to aspire to truthfulness. Personal memories that stray too far from this standard are labeled "false memories," and collective memories that suffer too much distortion become known as "propaganda" or "myth." Imagination, on the other hand, deals with the nonfactual and even the counterfactual. The Romantic imagination, in particular, functions to model or simulate possible future events that might never come to pass and to create fictional scenarios that are not expected to correspond point by point with the lived world, past, present, or future. Imagination can propose and delineate entities that could not possibly exist, such as flying horses, or events that could not be realized according to current knowledge and understanding, such as faster-than-light ("warp speed") space travel.

Despite the apparent disconnect between memory and imagination, however, recent work in cognitive neuroscience suggests that remembering the past and imagining the future may in fact be closely related functions of a single cognitive system or, at the very least, kindred functions that overlap significantly and share many of the same neural mechanisms. What has been called the "Janus hypothesis"—that retrospection into the past and prospection into the future are "closely linked in mind and brain"—can be traced to speculative work on memory in the 1980s and has recently provoked a veritable "explosion" of theoretical interest and empirical investigation.[1] Converging data from neuropathology, cognitive developmental psychology, psychiatry, and neuroimaging support a growing consensus among cognitive neuroscientists that "memory—especially episodic memory—is crucially involved in our ability to imagine nonexistent events and simulate future happenings."[2] Some researchers have adopted the term *mental time travel* to describe the human cognitive ability to project oneself mentally back into the past, through recollection, or imaginatively forward into the future.[3] The close links postulated between remembering and imagining may also help account for the well-known fragility and error-proneness of episodic (autobiographical and richly detailed) memory, which may be adaptively designed less for accurately recollecting the past than for creatively modeling the future.

The current interest in mental time travel revives a discourse regarding the intimate connections between memory and imagination that goes back at least to the associationist psychology of the seventeenth and eighteenth centuries, significantly revised and extended in Romantic theories of the imagination. The return to these connections in recent neuroscience opens up a new appreciation of how Romantic literary works celebrating memory—such as William Wordsworth's "Tintern Abbey" poem—also show a pronounced and unexpected orientation toward the future. Recent neuroscientific work on mental time travel also sheds new light on Samuel Taylor Coleridge's notion of the "secondary Imagination," perhaps the single most influential literary discussion of the creative imagination to date, and even seems to offer empirical validation for Coleridge's famous distinction between imagination and "Fancy," a weaker form of creative activity. Finally, early representations of mental time travel in Romantic-era novels (here represented by Jane Austen's *Emma* and Walter Scott's *Waverley*) bring out the pronounced relevance of imaginative fiction to emergent theories of memory and imagination. These fictional portrayals also suggest that any straightforward claim for the "adaptive" value of mental time travel—its alleged contribution to human survival and reproductive success—may stand in need of significant qualification.

The recent surge of scientific work on mental time travel began in earnest in 2007, with a flood of important publications appearing in major venues in the wake of a prescient essay, "The Janus Face of Mnemosyne" by Yadin Dudai and Mary Carruthers, published two years earlier in *Nature*. These include "The Ghosts of Past and Future," a "concepts" piece (also in *Nature*) by Daniel L. Schacter and Donna Rose Addis, substantial articles by Schacter and his colleagues in *Philosophical Transactions of the Royal Society* and *Neuropsychologia*, and a hefty "target article" on evolution and mental time travel by Thomas Suddendorf and Michael C. Corballis in *Behavioral and Brain Sciences*, followed by twenty-three response pieces by other leading researchers from a variety of disciplines.[4] Earlier formulations of the Janus hypothesis have been traced to work published in the mid-1980s by Ernest Tulving and D. H. Ingvar; the notion of a future-oriented or "prospective memory" has been traced back still further, to a 1977 article by John A. Meacham and John Singer.[5]

What sorts of empirical evidence have prompted memory researchers to begin taking as much interest in the future as in the past? In terms of neuropathology, as yet another group publishing in 2007 noted, amnesic patients suffering from damage to the hippocampus show a greatly diminished capacity to construct "imaginary" future scenarios.[6] Normal aging has also been associated with a diminished ability to generate "episode-specific details" relating both to memories of past events and imagined events in the future. Developmental studies have shown that children begin to form and retain episodic memories at the same age (between 3 and 5 years) as when they begin thinking about the future. Studies of severely depressed adults, as well as of schizophrenics, have also linked a diminished capacity to recall specific events from the past with an impoverished ability to imagine events that they might experience in the future.[7]

The close relationship suggested by this converging evidence between remembering the past and imagining the future has inspired a series of investigations using neuroimaging techniques specifically aimed at identifying common brain areas active in both retrospective and prospective thinking. A positron-emission tomography (PET) study reported by Jiro Okuda and colleagues in 2005 found increased activation in the frontal and medial temporal lobes when test subjects were either reminiscing or projecting themselves into the future, which suggests that "thinking of the future and past share common cerebral bases."[8] Functional magnetic resonance imaging (fMRI) studies carried out by Schacter and his coinvestigators found a "striking overlap" in remembering specific events from the personal past or imagining such events in the future, especially in the prefrontal and medial temporal regions. The medial temporal lobes in particular (the site of the hippocampus) seem crucial to a "core brain system" supporting both episodic memory and what Schacter's group calls "episodic thought about the future."[9] An fMRI study that teased apart the phase of constructing past or future scenarios and a later phase of detailed elaboration found "extensive overlap" in neural regions showing increased activation during the past and future elaboration tasks in particular.[10] Taken all together, neuroimaging studies have provided strong support for the growing scientific consensus that brain regions already associated with the episodic memory system are equally important for supporting "episodic future thinking."

One intriguing implication of the Janus hypothesis, especially as developed by Schacter and his colleagues, concerns the very design of the episodic memory system. Episodic memories, which tend to reflect personal experience rather than general knowledge or implicit skills and feature phenomenologically rich, detailed, and specific scenarios, are also known for their "fragmentary and fragile" character and have been widely seen as "unreliable and subject to distortion."[11] As Schacter explains, episodic memory is "reconstructive" rather than "reproductive," involving a "constructive process of putting together bits and pieces of information" rather than storing "exact replicas of past experience" such as a mechanical recording device might provide.[12] Episodic memories need to be maintained, refreshed, and periodically re-created in the mind and—if they avoid fading away altogether in the process—they can lose key details, become fused with thematically related or temporally adjacent memories, suffer distortion via suggestion or new biases introduced at the time of retrieval, or otherwise erode in any number of ways. If its function were solely to recapture the personal past as reliably as possible, episodic memory would look flawed to say the least. But if memory serves equally to help one imagine possible futures, the seeming design flaws of episodic memory might instead prove to be adaptive advantages. Once we assume that a "crucial function of memory is to make information available for the simulation of future events," then the provisional nature of episodic memory and its susceptibility to decomposition would serve to make its contents more readily available for creative recombination in the interests of "episodic future thinking."[13] Or, as Suddendorf and Corballis provocatively state, the "primary role of mental time travel into the past is to provide raw material from which to construct and imagine possible futures."[14]

The coalescence of memory and imagination in recent cognitive neuroscience has far-reaching implications, though at this stage researchers disagree about how best to understand it within the larger picture of mental behavior. Suddendorf and Corballis place mental time travel at the center of a whole "suite of cognitive abilities" that includes folk psychology or "theory of mind" (our capacity to recognize and interpret the intentions and emotional states of others) and "metacognition" (the ability to think about thoughts).[15] Randy Buckner and Daniel Carroll have proposed grouping episodic memory, prospective thinking about the future, theory of mind, and navigation together as cognitive activities involving "self-projection," a propensity to project oneself into other times, places, and perspectives that may even turn out to be the human mind's "default" tendency.[16] Literary scholars will instantly recognize a closely related set of capacities missing from Buckner's list: the ability to imagine fictional worlds and to project oneself into the fictional worlds created by others. Mental time travel and theory of mind have also been viewed in terms of a more general capacity for "mental traveling" or, alternatively, a central cognitive "mechanism" for shifting among various "frames of reference."[17] Despite disagreement on the larger picture, however, scientific investigators have reached "almost unanimous agreement" on the core hypothesis of "fundamental links between mental time travel into the past and the future."[18]

Memory researchers have presented the interrelationship between remembering and imagining as a fundamentally new idea: a "function of memory that has been largely overlooked until recently," Schacter, Addis, and Buckner write, "is its role in allowing individuals to imagine possible future events."[19] In fact, the close alliance between memory and imagination made a key element of the associationist tradition in psychology running from Thomas Hobbes in the seventeenth century through later associationist thinkers such as John Locke and David Hartley in the eighteenth century. Hobbes famously defines imagination as "decaying sense," the persistence of sensory images in the mind after their initial presentation to the external senses. These images (whether as originally perceived or as rearranged in novel combinations) remain available to cognitive manipulation in the present only if they are retained in memory, such that, Hobbes continues, "imagination and memory are but one thing."[20] Locke has less to say explicitly about imagination (or, as he calls it, "Fancy"), but retains Hobbes's notion of "decaying sense"—the "pictures drawn in our Minds, are laid in fading Colours"—and implicitly attributes our capacity for prospective thinking to the memory. "We in our Thoughts, Reasonings, Knowledge, could not proceed beyond present Objects, were it not for the persistence of our Memories." Which is to say that "Invention" or "Fancy" is in fact the capacity of the memory to provide the conscious subject with the "dormant Ideas" it stores up.[21] For Hobbes and Locke, in other words, the conjunction if not identity of memory and imagination is axiomatic.

Romantic theories of imagination might initially be seen as decisively departing from this associationist linkage, seeking instead to liberate the imagination from what Coleridge calls the "senseless and passive memory" implied by associationist psychology in order to posit instead a more dynamically creative imaginative faculty. Coleridge does link memory to what he calls "Fancy," but he is careful to distinguish and "desynonymize" *fancy* from its rival term, *imagination*. Fancy, an inferior form of creative activity, functions merely to summon up images stored in memory and represent them or mechanically combine them in a cut-and-paste manner—again, the image of a winged horse comes to mind, or the image of a centaur cited by both Hobbes and Locke. Coleridge considers fancy "no other than a mode of Memory," "emancipated" from the constraints of time and space (hence a horse seen on one occasion and a bird, or man, seen on another can be welded together) and guided by choice. But fancy cannot create anything fundamentally new; it can only manipulate the fixed "counters" supplied to it by memory.[22]

In contrast, what Coleridge calls the "secondary Imagination" is genuinely creative, capable of producing original ideas and images and the shaping force behind all truly great works of art. Rather than working with the "fixities and definites" supplied by memory, in the way of fancy, the secondary imagination "dissolves, diffuses, dissipates, in order to re-create."[23] But however much they are creatively deconstructed and reconstructed, where do the secondary imagination's materials come from? The obvious answer is from the "primary Imagination"—the creative imagination is "secondary" in precisely the sense of depending on the primary imagination for its materials. As James Engell writes, in his lucid overview of Coleridge's somewhat cryptic theory of imagination, the "primary imagination is the agency of perceiving and learning," Coleridgean shorthand for understanding perception as itself a creative activity, involving the interplay of external impressions with various powers of mind, rather than a mechanical registration of sense data on a passive blank slate of a mental apparatus.[24] This notion of perception as active and creative was widely shared by Romantic-era poets and brain scientists alike, and has also become something of a truism in the contemporary neuroscience of perception.

Coleridge does not specify, however, where the materials supplied by the primary imagination are held in waiting for creative disassembling and reassembling by the secondary imagination. It would seem that the secondary imagination, no less than fancy, relies for its materials on memory, only in a remarkably different way, dynamic rather than passive, "vital" (as Coleridge puts it) rather than mechanical. In its commerce with imagination, that is, memory must itself be a good deal more flexible and pliant than what the "decaying sense" model of memory informing the associationist tradition would suggest.

Although Coleridge does not himself supply such an account of memory, we can find one in the new neuroscientific thinking on memory and imagination discussed above. Indeed, the flexibility of episodic memory in particular proves to be, as we have seen, the reverse of its susceptibility to various kinds of distortion and degradation. If the memory system is oriented at least as much toward imagining possible futures as toward recalling past experiences, then the reconstructive (rather than reproductive) character of the episodic memory fits perfectly with its future-oriented task. "A system built according to constructive principles," Schacter and Addis explain, "can draw on the elements and gist of the past, recombine and reassemble them into imaginary events that never occurred in that exact form."[25] In other words, it "dissolves, diffuses, dissipates, in order to re-create," precisely in the manner of Coleridge's secondary imagination. Writing with Buckner, Schacter and Addis also note a difference in the imaginary output of amnesic patients (with "bilateral hippocampal damage") and control subjects that corresponds strikingly to Coleridge's distinction between the secondary imagination and fancy. Not only did the imaginary scenarios of the amnesics lack "richness" of detail and content in comparison to those of control subjects, but the "constructions of the amnesiac patients tended to consist of isolated fragments, rather than connected scenes."[26] Coleridge's classic examples of poetry produced by fancy feature just such "isolated fragments": "Lutes, lobsters, seas of milk, and ships of amber."[27] No one is likely to propose searching for a neural substrate for Coleridge's secondary imagination, but if anyone were, the hippocampus, as a brain region critical for both episodic memory and episodic future thinking, would certainly be the place to start.

Literary theorists from the Romantics to the present have usually spoken of the imagination in relation to the creation of fictive scenarios and original artworks rather than as a faculty for simulating possible courses of action or otherwise "prospecting" into the future. It functions "to break down what has been perceived in order to re-create by an autonomous, willful act of mind that which has no analogue in the natural world," as Engell characterizes Coleridge's secondary imagination.[28] Given, however, that prospective thinking is by definition concerned with the nonactual—even in cases where the simulated events are extremely likely to come about—it would seem quite uneconomical to posit separate cognitive systems for modeling the future and for creating fictions. Rather, imagining possible future events and imagining altogether fictive ones would seem to represent different uses to which the same system might be put. More than that, there seems to be a large area of overlap where prospective thinking and modeling fictional scenarios blend into each other, such as mentally simulating what you will do when you win the multimillion-dollar lottery, with your odds at winning recently calculated at one in 135,145,920.[29]

Recent work in cognitive neuroscience, then, helps elicit a missing element in Coleridge's influential account of the imagination—a memory system "that can draw on the past in a manner that flexibly extracts and recombines elements of previous experiences."[30] In turn, considering literary theories of the imagination from Coleridge to the present might inspire neuroscientists to pay greater attention to the fictive element of prospective thinking and to begin including mental time travel to fictional worlds in their accounts of self-projection. The Janus hypothesis can also enhance our appreciation for the surprisingly prospective or future-oriented character of Romantic literary treatments of memory, here briefly exemplified by William Wordsworth's "Lines Composed a Few Miles above Tintern Abbey."

Wordsworth's poem "Tintern Abbey," whose "very subject is memory" according to Suzanne Nalbantian,[31] begins by juxtaposing a present scene, as the poet drinks in and poetically re-creates the picturesque landscape before him, with the same scene as remembered from an earlier visit five years past. The reminiscing speaker emphasizes continuity more than change: "and again I hear," "Once again / Do I behold," "I again repose / Here," "Once again I see."[32] Any significant change lies more in the perceiver than in the scene perceived, for the poet is not only five years older, five years that have taken him from the end of his "thoughtless" youth to a more "serene" period of greater maturity, but his pleasure in the scene is now also supercharged with the pleasures of recollection. The scene thus features, as Nalbantian writes, "simultaneous encoding and retrieval."[33] Beth Lau, another literary critic who has brought cognitive neuroscientific work on memory to bear on the poem, describes how it develops into a subtle meditation on the relation of memory to personal identity, enacting the maturational process by which the vivid and richly detailed memories of youth begin to give way to a more generalized, abstracted, and (Wordsworth's term) *philosophic* relation to the past.[34]

What emerges with new clarity in light of the recent work on mental time travel is how "Tintern Abbey" looks forward into the future even as it looks backward into the past. Early on, at the beginning of the verse paragraph that gives us glimpses of the poet's youth and further back to his "boyish days," Wordsworth imagines a future that will include the memories being encoded at the very moment of his speaking:

While here I stand, not only with the sense
Of present pleasure, but with pleasing thoughts
That in this moment there is life and food
For future years.

This imagined future visit to Tintern Abbey will again leave the poet with rich memories that will nourish him—emotionally, spiritually, and ethically. The last section of the poem, especially its final thirty lines or so, becomes predominantly if not entirely prospective in character. Turning to his younger sister, who has apparently been standing beside him, silent and unheralded, throughout the poem, the poetic speaker first subordinates her presence to his past: "Oh! yet a little while / May I behold in thee what I was once," a version of self-projection that strikes many critics as narcissistic. Soon, though, the poet begins imagining his sister as she, too, will inevitably grow and mature in "after years," when the "wild ecstasies" of youthful commune with nature "shall be matured / Into a sober pleasure." She in turn will find nourishment in remembered natural scenes and sensations:

> ... when thy mind
> Shall be a mansion for all lovely forms,
> Thy memory be as a dwelling-place
> For all sweet sounds and harmonies.

Finally, the grammatical tense of the poem itself changes to the future conditional, as the poet imagines a future for his sister, who might well survive his own death, "If I should be, where I no more can hear / Thy voice." Corresponding to the series of "again" statements that opens the poem, three "then" phrases, all answering to that suppositious "If," serve to close it. "Oh! then ... wilt thou remember me," he adjures his sister, certain that she will not "then forget" him, and concluding (in the same key), "Nor wilt thou then forget":

> That after many wanderings, many years
> Of absence, these steep woods and lofty cliffs,
> And this green pastoral landscape, were to me
> More dear, both for themselves, and for thy sake.

For Wordsworth, not only does memory prospectively support the future; when at last that future arrives, it will also be characterized by affective and compensatory acts of memory.

If one turns from Romantic poetry to the prose fiction of the same period, it becomes evident that the imagination can prove not only redemptive but also potentially compromising and even hazardous, precisely because of its links to a memory system notoriously susceptible to distortion. These fictions suggest that the "adaptive significance" of a flexible, future-oriented, and fragile memory system can readily be over-stated.[35] Much as humanist scholars may find the notion of "selection-for-imagination" appealing—and there is certainly a great deal to be said for such a conception—we should keep in mind that adaptive arguments demand special critical scrutiny.[36] In this case, several respondents to Suddendorf and Corballis have already noted the "design problem" inherent in episodic future thinking, which may involve maladaptive "prospective fantasy" no less than adaptive future planning.[37] Compulsively betting on lotteries with infinitesimal chances of winning, obsessive sexual fantasies and hopeless erotic pursuits, daydreaming about career success rather than working to achieve it all serve as familiar examples of how prospective thinking can encourage unproductive behaviors. A small segment of the human population known as the "fantasy-prone," who reportedly "enjoy imagining food as much as eating it" and can reach orgasm "without physical stimulation," may constitute only the most obvious group liable to make less than "evolutionarily advantageous" use of prospective episodic thinking. At the very least, arguments for the adaptive significance of a future-oriented memory system need to take "new motivational complexities" into account.[38]

The lucid portrayal of "motivational complexities" has long been the special province of the novelist, and few novels can compete in this regard with Jane Austen's brilliant comedy of manners *Emma*. The title heroine, Emma, embodies a more common form of the "fantasy-prone" condition, although Austen's own term is *imaginist*. Famously "clever" (one of the first words used to describe her) in solving verbal puzzles and making witty conversation, Emma is repeatedly misled by her own "errors of imagination" when it comes to the crucial social task of interpreting the courtship behaviors and identifying the marital goals of the eligible young men around her. Her various marriage schemes for her protégée Harriet, for example, not only misfire badly but also consistently prevent Emma from seeing the obvious, "too eager and busy in her own previous conceptions to hear" a given suitor "impartially, or to see him with clear vision." Emma's prospective thinking on her younger friend's behalf, as she lets "her imagination range and work at Harriet's fortune," functions to block out accurate perception in the present, leading to a series of social disasters and near-disasters that may be comical to the reader but cause Harriet and Emma herself a great deal of emotional torment.[39]

Significantly, Emma's obsessive matchmaking, as good an example of prospective thinking as one could want, is rooted in an equally classic example of a distorted memory. Misled by what memory researchers call "retrospective bias," Emma has convinced herself, in the absence of any supporting evidence whatsoever, that she has been responsible for the favorable match of her former governess, Miss Taylor, and a well-off local widower, Mr. Weston.[40] "I made the match myself," she announces to her neighbor Mr. Knightley, the novel's sharpest social observer, who will have nothing to do with it: "You made a lucky guess; and that is *all* that can be said." Yet it is Emma's distorted memory of having brought the marriage about that fuels her inept and hurtful schemes for Harriet. "When such success has blessed me in this instance," she explains to her pliant father, "you cannot think that I shall leave off matchmaking."[41] Eventually, Emma becomes convinced that her ill-starred matchmaking attempts have ruined her *own* chances for marriage, with a man (the same Mr. Knightley) she comes to see as essential to her future happiness. Here retrospective bias leads to what we might call "prospective bias," jeopardizing a key test of "fitness" (winning at the mating game) in a blatantly maladaptive manner.

Emma exemplifies the vagaries of a future-oriented memory system, showing how the distorted memories of an "imaginist" can help give rise to highly unrealistic future scenarios and encourage maladroit and even harmful social behavior. The potential for such malfunctions in prospective thinking is greatly magnified by the way a given individual's memory may be enhanced—or compromised—by suggestions, communications, even whole scenarios reflecting the experiences, real or imagined, of others. Suddendorf and Corballis view the communication or "broadcasting" of others' remembered experiences as a means for greatly magnifying the utility of mental time travel: "This *broadcasting* of one's mental time travel can indeed be extremely adaptive, in that it allows people to learn from others' mistakes and successes without ever having to experience the events themselves."[42] But if we can be misled (as in Emma's case) by our *own* distorted memories, the potential for mistaken action becomes exponentially greater with the acknowledgment of our reliance on the mental time travel of others. Experiences recounted by others may prove distorted, intentionally or unintentionally misleading, or altogether imaginary and highly unrealistic.[43] Hobbes recognized the potential for a memory system compromised by fictional contamination long ago: "So when a man compoundeth the image of his own person with the image of the actions of another man, as when a man imagines himself a Hercules or an Alexander, which happeneth often to them that are much taken with reading of romances, it is a compounded imagination, and properly but a fiction of the mind."[44] *Don Quixote* is only the first of a long series of novels featuring protagonists whose judgments have been warped, and prospective thinking addled, by too much reading of romances and other fictions. Jane Austen's first published novel, *Northanger Abbey*, belongs squarely in this tradition.

Cognitive science has only begun to explore the effects of fiction on thinking and behavior in the lived world, but an initial consensus is emerging on several key issues. Summarizing research in cognitive psychology and cognitive social psychology on the "power of fiction," Melanie Green, Jennifer Garst, and Timothy Brock emphasize that "individuals regularly alter their real-world beliefs and attitudes in response to fictional communications." This is especially true of "transported readers," those who become "lost in a book," lose track of their immediate physical environment and instead "see the action of the story world unfolding before them." These readers are likely to produce "vivid mental images" tied to the story, and the more the reading experience involves such "concreteness and vivid detail," the more likely the fictional events are later to be "misremembered as real," for the very reason that in their vivid imagery and concrete detail they resemble episodic memories. "Stories are especially influential," Green, Garst, and Brock conclude, when "our cognitive resources, our emotions, and our mental imagery faculties are engaged."[45]

Cognitive literary critics, most notably Elaine Scarry in *Dreaming by the Book*,[46] have already begun to study the ways certain imaginative works call forth rich and detailed images in the minds of their readers. But writers themselves have long been aware of how alternate worlds can be vividly summoned up in the mind's eye of readers or daydreamers. In *Waverley*, the first of his series of historical novels set in Scotland, Walter Scott describes the titular hero spending hours on end engaged in "that internal sorcery, by which past or imaginary events are presented in action, as it were, to the eye of the muser." Note the equivalence here of "past" and "imaginary" events, which in Edward Waverley's case have become almost indistinguishable. Like Austen's Emma, Edward could well be described as an "imaginist" if not altogether fantasy prone: the "imagination" is the "predominant faculty of his mind" and he tends to live in an "ideal world" modeled more on fictions and half-fictionalized family legends than on the characters, objects, and events around him. Edward's prospective imagination, in other words, remains on overdrive throughout most of the novel. He regularly projects the romantic scenarios and situations so often rehearsed in his episodic memory onto the present and draws on these unlikely models in choosing among future courses of action—leading him into a series of "hair-brained" [*sic*] adventures from which he barely escapes with his life.[47]

The highly visual character of Edward's "mental sorcery" serves both to soften any distinction between remembered fact and remembered fiction and to facilitate his frequent (and nearly fatal) indulgence of prospective thinking fueled by memories of such dubious provenance. Neuroscientific research on "episodic future thinking" has shown that greater "vividness of mental imagery" intensifies prospective thinking and renders it more emotionally salient. Experimental subjects with a "higher capacity for visual imagery" imagined future "events that were more important and more intense, and they felt more emotions than participants with less vivid mental imagery." As we would now guess from work on mental time travel, subjects who produced more "visual and sensory details" in imagining the future were just as likely to retain richer and more vivid episodic memories.[48] Some two hundred years ago, Walter Scott had posited the very same connections between episodic memory, prospective thinking, vividness of mental imagery, and the enhanced cognitive and affective salience of imaginary scenarios in his portrayal of Edward Waverley. What Scott adds to our understanding of highly visual, highly imaginative individuals is a further propensity to confound fact with fiction and to project an idealized, romanticized sense of the past onto unrealistic and blatantly maladaptive scenarios for future behavior.

Waverley could in fact be read as a cautionary tale warning against the dangers of basing future plans too uncritically on glorified memories of the past. Edward is the most notable of a number of characters who stubbornly cling to stories, icons, and ideologies that are swiftly becoming, or have already become, archaic. Personal and collective memories, obsessively rehearsed and nurtured over generations, pit these characters against the inevitable progress of modernity, which can be creatively modified but not airily wished away. Most strikingly, Edward becomes caught up in the Jacobite uprising of 1745, portrayed as a neofeudal and nostalgic movement that threatens (though without a chance of success) to restore absolute monarchy at the national level and aristocratic and "squirarchical" domination at the local level. Whatever Scott's reservations regarding modernity, he clearly finds no viable alternative in a return to royal absolutism and feudalistic institutions.

Yet it is just such a reactionary, if romantic, cause that Edward signs on to, despite having accepted a commission in the British army and thus pledged his allegiance to the sitting government. An obsessive reader of romances and other chivalric lore in his youth, Edward also absorbs the oral traditions of his aristocratic family, all of them emphasizing loyalty to "legitimate" rulers in the face of change and innovation. Thanks to his gifts for creative visualization or "mental sorcery," fact, fiction, and family legend have become thoroughly mingled in his memory, rendering him "rather the creature of imagination than of reason." When he visits Scotland, then an exotic locale, and encounters scenes and characters that vaguely fit the scenarios in his mental storehouse, Edward begins to envision a future that would recapture the imaginary glories of the past, launching himself into a series of escapades that result in treason, public humiliation, acts of war against his own former regiment, two incapacitating injuries, several near brushes with death, and the threat of execution after Bonnie Prince Charlie's cause inevitably founders and the rebellion is put down. Fortunately for Edward, the British powers-that-be prove merciful toward certain youthful enthusiasts "misled by wild visions of chivalry and imaginary loyalty."[49] Although Edward's mental time travel has not proved fatal, he survives his adventures mainly thanks to extremely good luck and well-positioned family friends. The moral in this case is clear: vivid memories of the past, especially when idealized and fictionalized, can provide the *worst* possible guide to future behavior.

Emma Woodhouse and Edward Waverley may appear to be unlikely characters, altogether fictional constructs who might have some relevance to the "fantasy-prone" but little bearing on standard-issue minds and brains. Imaginative subjects like Emma, however, who base improbable schemes and risky behaviors on distorted and self-aggrandizing memories of past "successes," seem common enough to merit inclusion among the motivational complexities that further study of mental time travel will need to take into account. *Waverley*, for its part, has never seemed more relevant and prescient, at a time when global politics have been dominated by resurgent nationalisms, ethnic rivalries, sectarian conflict, and separatist movements, nearly always fueled by collective memories of past injuries or former greatness, and personal memories of oppression and shattered hopes. Although cognitive neuroscience provides crucial resources for those seeking to align literary studies more closely with the most persuasive and productive accounts of the human mind and mental behavior currently available, Scott and Austen remind us that the insights of great novelists have much to offer.

Why should neuroscientific researchers begin to learn from literary scholars and theorists? If, as Suddendorf and Corballis bluntly put it, "the past is fact and the future is fiction," then the door has already been opened to collaboration with literary researchers whose careers have been spent studying the fictive mind, including the role of fiction in the way we construct the "facts" of the past.[50] Further research on mental time travel not only invites but demands interdisciplinary engagement with those areas of literary study explicitly devoted to these issues, including possible worlds theory, theories of fictional immersion and identification with fictional characters, narrative theories of persuasion, and cognitive literary criticism in general.[51] If mental time travel proves closely linked to theory of mind under a larger rubric like self-projection or frame shifting, then interdisciplinary studies of fiction and theory of mind, such as Lisa Zunshine's *Why We Read Fiction*,[52] will also come into play. As the example of *Waverley* suggests, work on cognition and ideology will also need to be brought to bear on the ways that imagining the future involve both collective and individual memories. Now that neuroscientific researchers on memory have begun broaching issues of fiction and imagination, active interdisciplinary collaboration with literary scholars and theorists seems less a collegial gesture of goodwill than a necessary next step.

Notes

1. Yadin Dudai and Mary Carruthers, "The Janus Face of Mnemosyne," *Nature* 434 (March 2005): 567. On the "explosion" of neuroscientific research in this area, see Thomas Suddendorf and Michael C. Corballis, "The Evolution of Foresight: What Is Mental Time Travel, and Is It Unique to Humans?" *Behavioral and Brain Sciences* 30 (2007): 335.

2. Daniel L. Schacter, Donna Rose Addis, and Randy L. Buckner, "Remembering the Past to Imagine the Future: The Prospective Brain," *Nature Reviews: Neuroscience* 8 (September 2007): 657

3. Thomas Suddendorf and Michael Corballis claim to have coined the term *mental time travel* in 1997. See T. Suddendorf and M. C. Corballis, "The Evolution of Foresight: What Is Mental Time Travel, and Is It Unique to Humans?" 299.

4. Daniel L. Schacter and Donna Rose Addis, "The Ghosts of Past and Future," *Nature* 445 (2007): 27; Daniel L. Schacter and Donna Rose Addis, "The Cognitive Neuroscience of Constructive Memory: Remembering the Past and Imagining the Future," *Philosophical Transactions of the Royal Society* B 362 (2007): 773–786; Donna Rose

Addis, Alana T. Wong, and Daniel L. Schacter, "Remembering the Past and Imagining the Future: Common and Distinct Neural Substrates during Event Construction and Elaboration," *Neuropsychologia* 45 (2007): 1363–1377. See also Y. Dudai and M. Carruthers, "The Janus Face of Mnemosyne"; T. Suddendorf and M. C. Corballis, "The Evolution of Foresight: What Is Mental Time Travel, and Is It Unique to Humans?"

5. Ernest Tulving, "Memory and Consciousness," *Canadian Journal of Psychology* 26 (1985): 1–12; D. H. Ingvar, "Memory of the Future: An Essay on the Temporal Organization of Conscious Awareness," *Human Neurobiology* 4 (1985): 127–136; John A. Meacham and John A. Singer, "Incentive Effects in Prospective Remembering," *Journal of Psychology* 97 (1977): 191–197.

6. Demis Hassabis et al., "Patients with Hippocampal Amnesia Cannot Imagine New Experiences," *Proceedings of the National Academy of Sciences USA* 104 (2007): 1726–1731, cited and discussed in D. L. Schacter, D. R. Addis, and R. L. Buckner, "Remembering the Past to Imagine the Future: The Prospective Brain," 657.

7. The psychiatric, developmental, and aging studies are summarized by D. L. Schacter, D. R. Addis, and R. L. Buckner, "Remembering the Past to Imagine the Future: The Prospective Brain," 657–658.

8. Jiro Okuda et al., "Thinking of the Future and Past: The Roles of the Frontal Pole and the Medial Temporal Lobes," *NeuroImage* 19 (2003): 1374.

9. D. L. Schacter, D. R. Addis, and R. L. Buckner, "Remembering the Past to Imagine the Future: The Prospective Brain," 658–659.

10. D. R. Addis, A. T. Wong, and, D. L. Schacter, "Remembering the Past and Imagining the Future: Common and Distinct Neural Substrates during Event Construction and Elaboration," 1373.

11. T. Suddendorf and M. C. Corballis, "The Evolution of Foresight: What Is Mental Time Travel, and Is It Unique to Humans?" 302.

12. D. L. Schacter and D. R. Addis, "The Cognitive Neuroscience of Constructive Memory: Remembering the Past and Imagining the Future," 773.

13. D. L. Schacter, D. R. Addis, and R. L. Buckner, "Remembering the Past to Imagine the Future: The Prospective Brain," 659.

14. T. Suddendorf and M. C. Corballis, "The Evolution of Foresight: What Is Mental Time Travel, and Is It Unique to Humans?" 302.

15. T. Suddendorf and M. C. Corballis, "The Evolution of Foresight: What Is Mental Time Travel, and Is It Unique to Humans?" 307–310.

16. Randy L. Buckner and Daniel C. Carroll, "Self-Projection and the Brain," *Trends in Cognitive Neuroscience* 11 (2007): 49–57.

17. Jiro Okuda, "Prospection or Projection: Neurobiological Basis of Stimulus-Independent Mental Traveling," *Behavioral and Brain Sciences* 30 (2007): 328–329; Doris Bischof-Köhler and Norbert Bischof. "Is Mental Time Travel a Frame-of-Reference Issue?" *Behavioral and Brain Sciences* 30 (2007): 316–317.

18. T. Suddendorf and M. C. Corballis, "The Evolution of Foresight: What Is Mental Time Travel, and Is It Unique to Humans?" 335.

19. D. L. Schacter, D. R. Addis, and R. L. Buckner, "Remembering the Past to Imagine the Future: The Prospective Brain," 657.

20. Thomas Hobbes, *Leviathan: Or the Matter, Form and Power of a Commonwealth Ecclesiasticall and Civil*, ed. Michael Oakeshott (New York: Collier, 1962), 23–24.

21. John Locke, *An Essay Concerning Human Understanding*, ed. Peter H. Nidditch (Oxford: Clarendon Press, 1975), 152–153.

22. Samuel Taylor Coleridge, *Biographia Literaria, or, Biographical Sketches of My Literary Life and Opinions*, ed. James Engell and W. Jackson Bate (Princeton, NJ: Princeton University Press, 1983), 1:111, 82, 305.

23. S. T. Coleridge, *Biographia Literaria, or, Biographical Sketches of My Literary Life and Opinions*, 1:304.

24. James Engell, *The Creative Imagination: Enlightenment to Romanticism* (Cambridge, MA: Harvard University Press, 1981), 343.

25. D. L. Schacter and D. R. Addis, "The Ghosts of Past and Future," 27.

26. D. L. Schacter, D. R. Addis, and R. L. Buckner, "The Evolution of Foresight: What Is Mental Time Travel, and Is It Unique to Humans?" 657.

27. S. T. Coleridge, *Biographia Literaria, or, Biographical Sketches of My Literary Life and Opinions*, 1:84.

28. J. Engell, *The Creative Imagination: Enlightenment to Romanticism*, 344.

29. Christopher Solomon, "Why Poor People Win the Lottery," *MSN Money*, May 9, 2008 and February 1, 2009, at http://articles.moneycentral.msn.com/RetirementandWills/RetireEarly/WhyPoorPeopleWinTheLottery.aspx/.

30. D. L. Schacter and D. R. Addis, "The Cognitive Neuroscience of Constructive Memory: Remembering the Past and Imagining the Future," 774.

31. Suzanne Nalbantian, *Memory in Literature: From Rousseau to Neuroscience* (Basingstoke, UK: Palgrave Macmillan, 2003), 35.

32. Citations from the poem "Tintern Abbey" follow the text in William Wordsworth and Samuel Taylor Coleridge, *Lyrical Ballads and Related Writings*, ed. William Richey and Daniel Robinson (Boston: Houghton Mifflin, 2002).

33. S. Nalbantian, *Memory in Literature: From Rousseau to Neuroscience*, 36.

34. Beth Lau, "Wordsworth and Current Memory Research," *SEL* 42 (2002): 682–684.

35. D. R. Addis, A. T. Wong, and, D. L. Schacter, "Remembering the Past and Imagining the Future: Common and Distinct Neural Substrates during Event Construction and Elaboration," 1374.

36. Y. Dudai and M. Carruthers, "The Janus Face of Mnemosyne," 567.

37. George Ainslee, "Foresight Has to Pay Off in the Present Moment," *Behavioral and Brain Sciences* 30 (2007): 313–314; Bjorn Merker, "Memory, Imagination, and the Asymmetry between Past and Future," *Behavioral and Brain Sciences* 30 (2007): 325–326.

38. G. Ainslee, "Foresight Has to Pay Off in the Present Moment," 313.

39. Jane Austen, *Emma*, ed. Fiona Stafford (Harmondsworth, UK: Penguin, 1996), 277, 284, 93, 60.

40. Daniel L. Schacter, Kenneth A. Norman, and Wilma Koutstaal, "The Cognitive Neuroscience of Constructive Memory," *Annual Review of Psychology* 49 (1998): 306.

41. J. Austen, *Emma*, 12–13.

42. T. Suddendorf and M. C. Corballis, "The Evolution of Foresight: What Is Mental Time Travel, and Is It Unique to Humans?" 337.

43. J. Locke, *An Essay Concerning Human Understanding*, 374.

44. T. Hobbes, *Leviathan: Or the Matter, Form and Power of a Commonwealth Ecclesiasticall and Civil*, 24.

45. Melanie C. Green, Jennifer Garst and Timothy C. Brock, "The Power of Fiction: Persuasion via Imagination and Narrative," in *The Psychology of Entertainment Media: Blurring the Lines between Entertainment and Persuasion*, ed. L. J. Shrum (Mahwah, NJ: Erlbaum, 2004), 167–169, 173–174.

46. Elaine Scarry, *Dreaming by the Book* (New York: Farrar, Strauss, and Giroux, 1999).

47. Walter Scott, *Waverley*, ed. Andrew Hook (Harmondsworth, UK: Penguin, 1972), 51–54, 259.

48. Arnaud D'Argambeau and Martial van der Linden, "Individual Differences in the Phenomenology of Mental Time Travel: The Effect of Vivid Visual Imagery and Emotion Regulation Strategies," *Consciousness and Cognition* 15 (2006): 343, 348.

49. W. Scott, *Waverley*, 208, 252.

50. T. Suddendorf and M. C. Corballis, "The Evolution of Foresight: What Is Mental Time Travel, and Is It Unique to Humans?" 302.

51. For overviews of some of the issues and literary subfields involved in cognitive literary criticism, see Alan Palmer, *Fictional Minds* (Lincoln: University of Nebraska Press, 2004); Alan Richardson, "Studies in Literature and Cognition: A Field Map," *The Work of Fiction: Cognition, Culture, and Complexity*, ed. Richardson and Ellen Spolsky (Aldershot, UK: Ashgate, 2004), 1–29.

52. Lisa Zunshine, *Why We Read Fiction: Theory of Mind and the Novel* (Columbus: Ohio State University Press, 2006).

14 Memory in the Literary Memoir

John Burt Foster, Jr.

The literary memoir's very name proclaims its close association with memory. Achieving new heights of popularity in recent decades, this subgenre of life writing focuses with special intensity on its authors' capacity to remember.[1] Indeed, as a current memoirist affirms, "unlike autobiography, memoir relies almost solely on memory."[2]

The literary memoir thus offers fertile ground for evaluating the nature and accuracy of long-term personal memory—the "episodic memory" of neuroscientists—over periods of time that far exceed those of typical psychology experiments. With that opportunity in mind, this chapter considers a range of specimen passages, written in the early and mid-twentieth century, from memoirs by poet and playwright William Butler Yeats and by novelists Vladimir Nabokov and Mary McCarthy. All three were gifted writers who became fascinated with memoir writing, not only to record a variety of vivid and important memories, but also to revisit and refine them later on.

The variations and self-commentary to be found in such unusually expressive "double-exposure" memory writing provide striking insights into the continuities as well as the vicissitudes of long-term, episodic memory. Among the factors that work to sharpen or distort written memories are the memoirist's mood at the time of writing, the audience for whom the memoir is intended, the strength of the memoirist's commitment to scientific standards of accuracy, and the impact of the memoirist's own tastes, of conflicting testimony from other witnesses, of later events, and even of the language in which the memoir is written. The passages presented below also raise questions about the outer limits of human memory and about its interaction, fusion, or confusion with creativity and imagination.

William Butler Yeats: Memory and Mood

We have two accounts of Yeats's life from age twenty-two to thirty-three (1887 to 1898): a private manuscript, written in deep discouragement in 1915 and 1916, and his *Autobiography* of 1922, undertaken in a lighter mood of personal satisfaction. Late in the manuscript, Yeats describes his role in the lead-up to a demonstration against British rule in Ireland: "I have a memory, full of self-mockery, of the Jubilee riot of 1897. Maud Gonne had promised a then small Labour leader, James Connolly, since executed for his part in the rebellion of 1916, to speak at his Socialist society, meaning one of the small regular meetings." On learning that she would be addressing a large crowd, however, Gonne changed her mind. "I was with her when Connolly called," Yeats continues. "If she refused, he was ruined, for nobody would believe that he had ever had a promise. She was firm and he went away, but his despair was so deep that I softened her heart afterwards."[3] Having turned fifty in 1915, Yeats rightly felt discouraged due to major failures in politics, literature, and love. World War I had made Irish independence seem even more remote, while hostile publicity, and even riots, had targeted the Irish theater he had cofounded. Worst of all, he finally realized that winning the love of his life was utterly hopeless. In these circumstances, Yeats wrote a private memoir whose overall mood was one of wasted effort. The quoted passage comes where, no longer capable of sustaining the momentum of an ongoing life story, Yeats simply starts recording a series of vivid but random memories.

The memory has a witness-to-history quality, both because it evokes a protest that disrupted a celebration of Queen Victoria's sixty years of rule and because (at the time of its writing nearly twenty years later) Connolly had been executed for his part in the 1916 Easter Rebellion. Maud Gonne also took part in these struggles as a hotheaded orator, but she is more than just a historical figure. An obliquely confessional mood enters the episode with "a memory, full of self-mockery." What accounts for this expression of shame in it?

Yeats can feel this way because Maud Gonne was his great, unrequited love. Thus, when he recalls softening her heart, he must confront the irony that he could do so only for another man, and in politics rather than love. He had never been so effective on his own behalf. The two final sentences stand out in this regard. They could refer either to what Connolly had said, carrying over from "Connolly called," or to what Yeats had concluded about the meeting, in which case "she refused" becomes a loaded phrase. Not only does it resonate with Maud Gonne's several refusals of his marriage proposals, but later words like "ruined" and "promise" also have personal relevance. So do references to Maud Gonne's firmness and Connolly's "despair" in the next sentence, despite more evident connections with people other than Yeats.

Thus an eyewitness account of a woman patriot's meeting with a future Irish martyr reveals Yeats's personal feelings alongside its contribution to the historical record. The public retelling six years later occurs in very different circumstances: Ireland had its independence and Yeats had made major breakthroughs as a poet, had married someone else entirely, and was a father. His despondency now recedes further into the background: "I find Maud Gonne at her hotel talking to a young working man who looks very melancholy. ... She has refused to speak, and he says that her refusal will be his ruin, as nobody will ever believe that he had any promise at all. ... I can think of nothing but the young man and his look of melancholy. He has left his address, and presently at my persuasion, she drives to his tenement ... The young man is James Connolly."[4]

In the retelling, Yeats's intervention on Connolly's behalf still surfaces as a random memory, and many previous details reappear. But the bitter insistence on "self-mockery" has vanished. In addition, the narrating voice is more distant from the scene since the introduction of "he says" removes the ambiguity about whether the thoughts are Yeats's or Connolly's. Only the repetition of "melancholy" hints at a coalescence between the outer, observed reality and the writer's memories of his own inner state, though "melancholy" softens "despair" and better fits Connolly's situation. A coalescence clearly appears, however, in "I can think of nothing but the young man and his look of melancholy." The present tense here enlivens the memory: the writer's mental activity in the present has fused with the remembered event. On the other hand, phrases like "his look" and "young man" maintain distance. In general, Yeats now appears like a sympathetic man of the world, someone who may have known severe disappointments in his twenties, not in his famous and settled fifties.

Bringing these two passages together shows how sense of audience and especially current mood can affect the articulation of a memory, even when many facts remain unchanged. Such side-by-side comparison differs from neuroscience research on memory and emotion that focuses more on how clearly people can recall past emotions than on how their present mood affects their memories.[5] The Yeats passages also illustrate just how much a few well-chosen words by skilled writers can disclose about the workings of memory.

For a simpler, more graphic example of how mood frames memory, let us turn to a vivid moment in the speech Yeats prevailed on Maud Gonne to give, when she describes being refused access to the graves of Irish leaders executed after the Rebellion of 1798. "She said then," Yeats's earlier memoir reads, "speaking slowly in a low voice that yet seemed to go through the whole crowd, 'Must the graves of our dead go undecorated because Victoria has her Jubilee?' and the whole crowd went wild."[6] In the autobiography, the moment reads: "Then she pauses, and after that her voice rises to a cry, 'Must the graves of our dead go undecorated because Victoria has her Jubilee?'"[7] Both versions quote Maud Gonne word for word, suggesting total recall, but, given the sharp contrast between "speaking slowly in a low voice" and "her voice rises to a cry," how accurate can this memory be?

Certainly, a poet's verbal memory ought to be very exact, and Yeats chose his words extremely carefully. But, for that very reason, he might have given greater force to language that he in fact recalled less precisely or that may not have been spoken quite as pointedly. Still, it is striking that, after six years, Gonne's words as Yeats quotes them stay exactly the same, even though, according to the manuscript's editor, he did not consult the first passage while writing the second.[8] How to account for the major discrepancy between the two in their description of Maud Gonne's voice? Both accounts are dramatic, but in opposite ways: the constraint of grief versus a defiant shout. Yet, as we shall see, each memory might be true, with the difference stemming from Yeats's mood while writing.

Since Maud Gonne had acted in Yeats's plays, on each occasion he could have superimposed a different stage memory onto her words. But the discrepancy could also reaffirm memory's dependence on the writer's mood, given that both accounts could be partly right. If, as seems entirely plausible, "Must the graves of our dead go undecorated" was uttered in grief, whereas "because Victoria has her Jubilee" was a cry of defiance, then the changes in Yeats's situation while writing can account for the discrepancy. For, with the seeming hopelessness of the Irish cause in 1916 and its unexpected success by 1922, it would be natural to recall a grieving voice the first time he wrote, and proud defiance the second.

Vladimir Nabokov: Precision and Commemoration

Unlike Yeats, who was hostile to science, Nabokov embraced it. Indeed, while earning his living as a Russian teacher and working on the first full version of his memoir, he spent several happy years in the 1940s as an unpaid expert with Harvard's Museum of Comparative Zoology, an outgrowth of his lifelong hobby of collecting butterflies and moths. During this period Nabokov published several papers in entomological journals which stand out for their precision in identifying the distinguishing features of new species through patient observation with a microscope. This concern for accuracy carries over to his memory writing. Thus he states, in an author's note to the first version of his memoir, that he saw the book as an experiment in self-observation that will be "as truthful as he could possibly make it."[9] A letter even calls the memoir "a scientific attempt to unravel and trace back all the tangled threads of one's personality."[10]

Of crucial assistance in this aim of precise observation was Nabokov's use of three different languages in his memory writing. In the mid-1930s, in an effort to become better known in France, he wrote a short but spirited memoir about his French teacher in prerevolutionary Russia. He then incorporated an English rewriting of this sketch into an account of his life up to leaving Europe for the United States in 1940, published first as a series of magazine pieces in the late 1940s then as a book, entitled *Conclusive Evidence*, in 1951. Nabokov went on to translate this book into Russian; it appeared in 1954 under the title *Drugie Berega* [*Other Shores*], and in 1967, he published a revised English-language version as *Speak, Memory*. In the foreword to the 1967 book, Nabokov explained that these writings and rewritings in different languages had sharpened his memory in three ways. First, beyond the initial effort to be precise, there were the added bursts of concentration that he brought to bear when he reread his texts at various stages in the publication process, both in 1951 and 1967. Thus, in an extreme case of what researchers might refer to as "repeated cuing leading eventually to memory retrieval,"[11] Nabokov relates how a pair of spectacles that he invented as a chance item in a remembered landscape eventually gave way to the clear and totally factual memory of a cigarette case: "An object, which had been a mere dummy chosen at random and of no factual significance in the account of an important event, kept bothering me every time I reread that passage in the course of correcting the proofs of various editions, until finally I made a great effort, and the arbitrary spectacles ... were metamorphosed into a clearly recalled oystershell-shaped cigarette case, gleaming in the wet grass at the foot of an aspen."[12]

Nabokov found translating this book into Russian to be a second aid to memory, which gains added significance in light of clear evidence that putting a memory into words serves to further its long-term preservation.[13] Translation seems to have spurred even greater efforts to combat imprecision or vagueness since now Nabokov wasn't just rereading his original formulations, he was actively rewording them into Russian: "I tried to do something about the amnesic defects of the original—blank spots, blurry areas, domains of dimness. I discovered that sometimes, by means of intense concentration, the neutral smudge might be forced to come into beautiful focus."[14] A third, less explicit factor surfaces when Nabokov sums up the entire composition process as "This re-Englishing of a Russian re-version of what been an English re-telling of Russian memories in the first place."[15] He omits the initial French link in the interlingual chain, but "Russian memories in the first place" implies that being able to write in the language spoken at the time of the remembered events further stimulated his memory.

We can observe these sharpening processes in two successive versions of an incident involving Nabokov's father and a rare peacock butterfly. Both versions open with the evocative phrase "patch of the past," which crystallizes Nabokov's distinctive approach to memory. The words are a variation on the phrase "pans de mon passé," which had appeared in the French memoir of the 1930s in a reference to episodic memory in general. The word *pan* was also important for Proust, whom Nabokov had been reading at the time. But for Nabokov, who stresses the conscious effort required to bring ever more precise memories to the surface, "pan" as "patch" signals a preference for the "pan lumineux" or "illuminated patch" of voluntary memories. It was just these memories, centered on his mother's good-night kiss, that Proust had scorned in formulating his doctrine of involuntary memory. For Nabokov in his memoirs, however, memory depends on the concentrated power of the will.[16]

To present the passages that elaborate on this opening phrase, the initial treatment in *Conclusive Evidence* is set in roman (regular) typeface and the two later additions in *Speak, Memory* are set in italics. Nabokov's characteristic process of mnemonic focusing will thus become clearly visible:

The act of vividly recalling a patch of the past is something that I seem to have been performing with the utmost zest all my life, and I have reason to believe that this almost pathological keenness of the retrospective faculty is a hereditary trait. There was a certain spot in the forest, a foot bridge across a brown brook, where my father would piously pause to recall the rare butterfly that, on the seventeenth of August, 1883, his German tutor had netted for him. The thirty-year-old scene would be gone through again. He and his brothers had stopped short in helpless excitement at the sight of the coveted insect poised on a log *and moving up and down, as though in alert respiration, its four cherry-red wings with a pavonian eyespot on each. ... My cabinet inherited that specimen a quarter of a century later. One touching detail: its wings had "sprung" because it had been removed from the setting board too early, too eagerly.*[17]

In the first addition, what was once merely a "coveted insect" gets a more precise description, in the manner of Nabokov's entomological research. Indeed, it is so precise that readers might forget that this incident was a boyhood experience of his father's, thus of course never witnessed by Nabokov. For memory researchers, this passage might be taken to illustrate the phenomenon of group memory as it appears within a family circle.[18] This it certainly does, but for Nabokov's own "science of memory" the overlap between the person writing and the one being written about is meant to give further support to his thesis of a "hereditary" connection between father and son, based on their unusual ability to remember. At the recollected moment, the father undoubtedly did not describe the insect in as much detail, but some such image must have formed in his mind when he told the story, just as the son now shows that he can reproduce that inner visualization in language, based on his own observations of these insects. Nabokov joins hands with his father, so to speak, across the gap in time, going back even before the father's story to the original event.

In the movement that this passage implicitly chronicles, from a vivid visual experience to one that only gradually achieves fuller verbal expression, Nabokov may illustrate the primacy assigned by some theorists to a visual memory system over one that processes language.[19] Nabokov himself uses the incident to bring out the temporal ambiguity of memory, to reveal its status both as mental activity in the present and as a record of the past. The passage does so by doubling the ambiguity, thereby emphasizing memory's layered temporality even more forcefully than in the passages from Yeats. Past fuses with present, both in Nabokov's own relation as a memoirist to his father's story and in his father's connection as storyteller to the original event. In the process, Nabokov exploits that ambiguity to create an illusion of time travel, one that is possible in mind and words, if not physically and in fact.

A different gap in time underlies the second revision. We gather that some five years before his father's story, Nabokov's boyhood hobby had advanced to where he could take possession of his father's butterfly collection. The collection itself must have been unavailable at the time of writing, due to the family's haste in fleeing the October Revolution. So the "touching detail" of the butterfly's "sprung wings" is not a direct observation but itself a long-term memory. It allows Nabokov to glimpse, more concretely than anything else in the passage, how important the original capture must have been for his father. For his "helpless excitement" at netting the butterfly had persisted, to be seen in the carelessly mounted specimen. But this extra detail also reveals Nabokov's own zeal as a lepidopterist. Only someone who needed to remind himself not to remove a catch prematurely from the setting board would understand what the "sprung" wings meant. Thus this memory of his father is also a revelation of himself and a sign of their affinity.

The contribution of Nabokov's multilingualism to his powers of memory emerges in the massively reworked 1954 Russian version of this passage. My translation italicizes the parts that appear uniquely in the Russian version, while the parts that Nabokov continued to use in the 1967 portrayal of the butterfly anecdote are underlined as well as italicized:

There was a certain spot in the forest *on one of the old paths on the Batovo estate, and there was* a small bridge across a brook, *and there was a rotting log at the side, and there was* a point on this log, where *on the fifth of August by the old calendar* there suddenly alighted, opening its *silky, crimson <u>wings with pavonian eyespots</u>*, a *Vanessa* butterfly, *extremely* rarely *found in our parts,* which was caught by the *adroit* German tutor of these previous Nabokov boys. *My father somehow even got excited when we stopped with him on this little bridge,* and he would go through and *perform the whole scene from the beginning, how <u>the butterfly sat breathing</u>*...[20]

Several of the passages uniquely in the Russian version suggest that the language used at the time of the memory worked to sharpen Nabokov's sense of time and place: thus he dates the scene with Imperial Russia's old-style Julian calendar, and he qualifies the alleged rarity of the butterfly by conceding that it was hard to find only in that locale. Also, the details evoked by certain adjectives either come into focus or fade away: the tutor is "adroit," the butterfly has "silky" wings, the log on which it is perched is "rotting," but the brook is no longer "brown."

Two innovations are especially notable. One involves how the father shows his excitement at capturing the butterfly. Because in the Russian version he acts out his boyhood feelings right before us rather than having them revealed in the "touching detail," this way of confirming "helpless excitement" misses the opportunity seized in 1967. To mirror the father's enthusiasm in the son's memory of the "sprung" wings personalizes the more distanced account of the father's anecdote provided here. Even more striking is the expansion and displacement of the adverb *piously* applied to the father's repeated narration. That ritualistic sense is conveyed by Nabokov's own prose in 1954, in the fourfold "there was" that brings the reader ever closer to where the butterfly was sighted. As with "sprung wings" in 1967, here too Nabokov has deepened the link with his father, perhaps by imitating his very manner of speech as they neared the special spot. Still, I would contend that the "touching detail" is even more effective, due mainly to Nabokov's eloquence of understatement, which draws the attentive reader more fully into the writing. As already mentioned, could its status as a visual rather than a verbal memory also play a role?

The step-by-step buildup just noted exemplifies a mnemonic technique that Nabokov practiced himself. He liked to follow in memory the woodland paths near his family's country estate, pushing himself to recall as many details as possible until the scene was finally re-created in his mind. This setting, or "ecological niche" as he called it,[21] was one that he could know with such precision because that was where he had hunted butterflies; his mother, who loved to gather mushrooms in those same woods, knew them equally well. After leaving Russia, if we can trust a passage in a Nabokov novel, his mother and he would play a memory game in which they would silently imagine walking along one of those paths with the aim of discovering, on comparing their impressions, that they had ended up at the same spot.[22]

Whatever the truth of this story, Nabokov's famous memoir *Speak, Memory* emphasizes the same memory technique: "I witness with pleasure *the supreme achievement of memory*, which is the masterly use it makes of *innate harmonies* when gathering to its fold the suspended and wandering tonalities of the past. ... I see the tablecloth and the faces of seated people sharing in the animation of light and shade beneath *a moving, a fabulous foliage*, exaggerated, no doubt, by *the same faculty of impassioned commemoration*, of *ceaseless return*, that makes me always approach that banquet table from the outside, from the depth of the park—not from the house—as if the mind, in order to go back thither, had to do so with the silent steps of a prodigal, faint with excitement."[23] Here I have italicized the key phrases in this packed passage: the author, guided by a "faculty of impassioned commemoration" that enables "the supreme achievement of memory," imagines an impossible homecoming. In it he approaches the old family home along the paths and through the woods that he has called to memory so often, in a spirit of "ceaseless return." If we combine this sense of ceaseless return with the anecdote of remembering his father repeatedly remembering, we see that, for Nabokov, "commemoration" must have meant "remembering with" or "co-memoration" in addition to practicing his own memory rituals. Although these experiences have emerged in the more complex circumstances of adulthood and also involve the added pressures of exile and loss, they also call to mind findings on how the interaction between parents and small children promotes a "socialization" of memory.[24]

Nabokov's own practice of ritualistic repetition, the passage also emphasizes, can culminate in the creation of a composite memory. Rather than focusing on a single, dated event like his father's story of netting the butterfly, such a memory assembles scattered details from the family's many outdoor gatherings over the years. The result, though full of facts, is not itself entirely factual, as Nabokov concedes when he stresses the "fabulous" foliage of the trees. This "supreme" memory possesses an inventive and essentially artistic component, one that seizes on "innate harmonies" to create a whole, one that has the capacity to uphold the writer's psychic integrity throughout the "prodigal" wanderings of his later life. Thus the emphasis on "impassioned commemoration" and the second, figurative meaning of exceptional emotional power that attaches to the adjectives "moving" and "fabulous" which are applied to the remembered foliage.

Mary McCarthy: The Failure of Memory

In addition to its vivid re-creations of a purportedly factual past, memory writing can also showcase the ultimate vicissitude of long-term memory— its failures. Such failures usually come out after publication, when authors obtain conflicting information from people with knowledge about matters treated in the memoir, to which they respond if they can return to the memoir later on. Yeats seems to have read his manuscript memoir aloud to Maud Gonne herself and to have taken her reactions very much into account: "I am using Maud Gonne's memory as well as my own."[25] The memories that he kept, like the ones discussed above, have presumably passed this verification test.

For *Conclusive Evidence*, Nabokov had provided this description of a family insignia: "The Nabokov coat of arms displays two bears holding between them what looks like a checkerboard. It is a charming crest, inviting one, as it were, to a quiet game of chess after a day of hunting in the manorial forest."[26] He later had to issue a correction in *Speak, Memory*, after hearing the truth about the long-lost emblem from a relative: "An inexperienced heraldist resembles a medieval traveler who brings back from the East the faunal fantasies influenced by the domestic bestiary he possessed all along rather than by the results of direct zoological exploration. Thus, in the first version of this chapter, when describing the Nabokovs' coat of arms (carelessly glimpsed among some familial trivia many years before), I somehow managed to twist it into the fireside wonder of two bears posing with a great chessboard propped up between them."[27] This demonstration of memory's fallibility does not, of course, prevent readers from surmising other truths about the author, for example a love of chess and of rambles through the woods in the offending passage or a commitment to painstaking observation and an ambivalence about family escutcheons in the rewrite. Indeed, the phrase "carelessly glimpsed among some family trivia" actually serves to validate many other memories in *Speak, Memory*, whose emphasis on touching details recalled with tenacious precision pays tribute to valued persons and cherished places and objects.

Mary McCarthy provides a fuller account of failed memories in *Memories of a Catholic Girlhood*, characterized in her foreword to the reader as a series of "memoirs."[28] McCarthy and Nabokov were acquainted and admired each other's work. During the late 1940s and early 1950s, the two of them authored seventeen short memoirs for *The New Yorker* that later became chapters in their respective books. However, because McCarthy's siblings lived in the United States, unlike Nabokov's, who stayed in Europe, she could get their responses to her sketches before her book appeared. As a result, *Memories of a Catholic Girlhood* can feature so-called interchapters after each of the original sketches in which McCarthy discusses their objections, records her own doubts about the validity of her memories, and adds some afterthoughts.

The following passage by McCarthy appeared in *The New Yorker* two and a half years after Nabokov published a chapter-to-be in his memoir, with the title "Butterflies." Nabokov's tone is ebullient, even euphoric as he records his "incredibly happy memories" as a lepidopterist. When he closes by exclaiming, "This is ecstasy,"[29] most readers would agree. In this context, the very title of McCarthy's sketch, "A Tin Butterfly," sounds a dissonant note; and though her traumatic memories of childhood abuse needed no outside push to revive them, one feels that Nabokov's piece had helped to motivate her. Whatever the case, the two sketches serve to contrast not just happy with harsh memories, but Nabokov's focused effort at total recall with McCarthy's uncertain knowledge of the full truth.

The situation in "A Tin Butterfly" is a painful one. As McCarthy explained in her foreword and her previous chapter, she and her three brothers were orphaned in the 1918 flu epidemic. Now they have become the wards of an erstwhile spinster aunt who has just married the repellent Uncle Myers. This man treats the children badly—to the point they try escaping to an orphanage. When ten-year-old Mary wins an essay contest, she is whipped as a precaution "lest I become stuck-up."[30] In a crowning indignity, the youngest brother's prize possession, a tin butterfly from a Cracker Jack box, goes missing. Mary is accused of stealing it and denies the accusation, but the toy turns up at her place at the dining table, pinned beneath a protective pad. Again she is whipped and, despite her innocence, confesses under duress to her aunt; but when she refuses to confess to Uncle Myers, she is whipped some more. The sketch ends with a passage that discloses something McCarthy claims to have learned only during a reunion with her brothers in 1929, after being separated for years: "Six or seven years later, … my brother Preston told me that on the famous night of the butterfly, he had seen Uncle Myers steal into the dining room from the den and lift the tablecloth, with the tin butterfly in his hand."[31]

The interchapter, however, calls this recollection into question. McCarthy describes rereading her sketch, paralleling the practice that had sharpened Nabokov's memories. But here rereading brings uncertainty: "About the tin butterfly episode, … An awful suspicion occurred to me as I was reading it over the other day. I suddenly remembered that in college I had started writing a play on this subject. Could the idea that Uncle Myers put the butterfly at my place have been suggested to me by my teacher? I can almost hear her voice saying to me excitedly: 'Your uncle must have done it!'"[32] Two decades later, in what memory researchers call "retroactive interference,"[33] had McCarthy projected her teacher's suggestion back onto her brother when she wrote "The Tin Butterfly"?

Plagued by doubt, she consults her brothers, only to learn there had been no revelation in 1929 and no eyewitness to Uncle Myers's crime: "I sent for Kevin ... He remembers the butterfly episode itself and the terrible whipping. ... But he does not remember Preston's saying that Uncle Myers put the butterfly there. Preston, consulted by long-distance telephone, does not remember either saying it or seeing it."[34] The event that seemed so conclusive in the original sketch slips back into conjecture, subject to the traffic between memory and imagination in a creative writer's mind, not to mention the concerns that readers might have about accuracy in recalling such painful events.[35]

Despite these reflections, however, McCarthy still suspects that Uncle Myers had framed her, though uncertainty ironically persists in her struggle to recall her teacher's words. They are now cited somewhat differently, unlike the situation of Yeats with Maud Gonne: "But who did put the butterfly by my place? It may have been Uncle Myers after all. Even if no one saw him, he remains a suspect: he had motive and opportunity. 'I'll bet your uncle did it!'—was that what she said?"[36] The impression lingers that her teacher's words, whatever they were, might easily have scrambled McCarthy's memory.

Not conjectural, however, is the response of McCarthy's grandfather from the other side of her family, a lawyer who terminated Uncle Myers's guardianship. As McCarthy points out, her grandfather gave special credence to an abuse he had witnessed, while apparently dismissing the children's clamor about the tin butterfly and other abuses as mere hearsay: "It was not the tale of the butterfly or the other atrocities that chiefly impressed him as he followed our narration with precise legal eyes, but the fact that I was not wearing my glasses. I was being punished for breaking them in a fall on the school playground by having to go without."[37] Presenting this stern exponent of a strictly factual approach, of relying on what might well be called "conclusive evidence," may be McCarthy's gesture toward Nabokov's program for memory writing. Still, she does confront the reader with uglier memories than Nabokov generally does, except in understated asides about his father's murder or his own exile as an undocumented alien. Given the barriers to clearly recalling traumatic experiences, McCarthy deserves credit for facing them even if she must ultimately remain uncertain whether the apparent key to this sorry episode ever really occurred.

Recent scandals over memoirs have demonstrated that not all writers can be trusted to be as painstaking as Nabokov or as scrupulous as McCarthy.[38] Thus the specimens presented here, selected with an eye to their usefulness and reliability, have special importance. They involve long-term, episodic memories recorded by authors with an exceptional mastery of language and a genuine interest in how memory works, memories that they revisited, deepened, or corrected, at times even in different languages. They represent especially illuminating examples in the spirit of the thought-provoking accounts of mental experience to which memory researchers sometimes turn for illustration or even guidance in pursuing new lines of inquiry. Thus we have Alan Baddeley's "Sebastian" anecdote, on how he identified someone who looked strangely familiar, as discussed in the chapter on recollection and familiarity in *The Oxford Handbook of Memory*, or Raymond S. Nickerson's description of the associative chain that allowed him to retrieve the name of a nearby street, as discussed in the handbook's chapter on control processes in remembering.[39] In the context of such testimonies to the complexities of human memory, the memoirs of Yeats, McCarthy, and especially Nabokov function not only as true literature but also as richly informative experiments in writing with and about memories.

Notes

1. *Life writing* is the umbrella term for the many varieties of nonfictional writing, from biography and autobiography to letters, diaries, travel narratives, and even annotated photograph albums, that have become a major new topic for literary research—as evidenced by the Modern Language Association's having established a Division on Autobiography, Biography, and Life Writing.

2. Sue William Silverman, "An Overview of the Subgenres of Creative Nonfiction," *Writer's Chronicle* 41 (2008): 18.

3. W. B. Yeats, *Memoirs*, transcr. and ed. Denis Donoghue (New York: Macmillan, 1973), 111–112.

4. William Butler Yeats, *The Trembling of the Veil*, in *The Autobiography of William Butler Yeats: Consisting of Reveries over Childhood and Youth, The Trembling of the Veil, and Dramatis Personae* (New York: Macmillan, 1954), 243–244.

5. On the role played by original emotions in memory, see Jonathan W. Schooler and Eric Eich, "Memory for Emotional Events," in *The Oxford Handbook of Memory*, ed. Endel Tulving and Fergus I. M. Craik (New York: Oxford University Press, 2000), 379–392. The influence of one's current mood on memories of the past is briefly treated by Ulric Neisser and Lisa Libby, "Remembering Life Experiences," in *The Oxford Handbook of Memory*, 322, citing D. M. Clark and J. D. Teasdale, who note that "patients with diurnal mood variation tend to recall sadder life events when they are more depressed, happier events when they are less depressed."

6. W. B. Yeats, *Memoirs*, 112.

7. W. B. Yeats, *The Trembling of the Veil*, 244.

8. Denis Donoghue, "Introduction," in W. B. Yeats, *Memoirs*, 13.

9. Vladimir Nabokov, *Conclusive Evidence* (1951; reprint, New York: Grosset and Dunlop, n.d.), vii.

10. *The Nabokov-Wilson Letters, 1940–1971*, ed. Simon Karlinsky (New York: Harper & Row, 1980), 188.

11. See Asher Koriat, "Control Processes in Remembering," in *The Oxford Handbook of Memory*, 333–346, esp. 334, 339–340.

12. Vladimir Nabokov, *Speak, Memory: An Autobiography Revisited* (New York: McGraw-Hill, 1967), 12.

13. For a discussion of how language affects memory, see Katherine Nelson and Robyn Fivush, "Socialization of Memory," in *The Oxford Handbook of Memory*, 288–291.

14. V. Nabokov, *Speak, Memory: An Autobiography Revisited*, 12.

15. V. Nabokov, *Speak, Memory: An Autobiography Revisited*, 12.

16. For a more detailed account of Nabokov's views on memory and will, see John Burt Foster, Jr., *Nabokov's Art of Memory and European Modernism* (Princeton, NJ: Princeton University Press, 1993), 119–120, 205. Tellingly, Nabokov rejected a proposal that the dust jacket of *Conclusive Evidence* include some words from the madeleine passage in *Swann's Way* (p. 206). See Marcel Proust, *Swann's Way*, trans. C.

K. Scott Moncrieff and Terence Kilmartin; rev. D. J. Enright (New York: Modern Library, 1998), 58, where "pan lumineux" is translated as "luminous panel."

17. V. Nabokov, *Conclusive Evidence*, 42; V. Nabokov, *Speak, Memory*, 75.

18. See U. Neisser and L. Libby, "Remembering Life Experiences," 324.

19. See Scott C. Brown and F. Craik, "Encoding and Retrieval of Information," in *The Oxford Handbook of Memory*, 98.

20. Vladimir Nabokov, *Drugie Berega* (1954; reprint, Ann Arbor, MI: Ardis, 1978), 64.

21. V. Nabokov, *Speak, Memory: An Autobiography Revisited*, 73.

22. Vladimir Nabokov, *The Gift*, trans. Michael Scammell in collaboration with the author (New York: Putnam's, 1963), 101.

23. V. Nabokov, *Speak, Memory: An Autobiography Revisited*, 170–171.

24. See K. Nelson and R. Fivush, "Socialization of Memory," 283–295.

25. W. B. Yeats to John Quinn, August 1 [1916], unpublished letter cited in R. F. Foster, *W. B. Yeats: A Life*, vol. 2, *The Arch-Poet, 1915–1939* (New York: Oxford University Press, 2003), 66.

26. V. Nabokov, *Conclusive Evidence*, 31.

27. V. Nabokov, *Speak, Memory: An Autobiography Revisited*, 51.

28. Mary McCarthy, *Memories of a Catholic Girlhood* (New York: Harcourt, Brace, 1957) 3.

29. V. Nabokov, *Speak, Memory: An Autobiography Revisited*, 125, 139.

30. M. McCarthy, *Memories of a Catholic Girlhood*, 63.

31. M. McCarthy, *Memories of a Catholic Girlhood*, 80.

32. M. McCarthy, *Memories of a Catholic Girlhood*, 82.

33. See Henry L. Roediger and Kathleen B. McDermott, "Distortions of Memory," in *The Oxford Handbook of Memory*, 153. Note their remark that this line of research was popular at midcentury, the very time when McCarthy wrote "A Tin Butterfly."

34. M. McCarthy, *Memories of a Catholic Girlhood*, 83.

35. Memory researchers share this skepticism about the accuracy of recalled painful memories, particularly with regard to "recovered memories" involving severe abuse in childhood. See J. Schooler and E. Eich, "Memory for Emotional Events," 386–388.

36. M. McCarthy, *Memories of a Catholic Girlhood,* 83.

37. McCarthy, *Memories of a Catholic Girlhood,* 79.

38. In 1979, McCarthy went so far as to accuse playwright Lillian Hellman of lying in her memoirs, referring chiefly to Hellman's account of the House Un-American Activities Committee hearings in *Scoundrel Time* and the "Julia" section in *Pentimento.*

39. See Colleen M. Kelley and Larry L. Jacoby, "Recollection and Familiarity: Process-Dissociation," in *The Oxford Handbook of Memory,* 215, and A. Koriat, "Control Processes in Remembering," 334.

15   Memory in Theater: The Scene Is Memory

Attilio Favorini

Correspondences between scientific conceptions of memory and the constructions of dramatists have gone almost completely unnoticed. In pursuit of memory, dramatists and scientists historically have led, followed, or marched in step, advancing or withdrawing memory as an attribute of human nature. Memory is a variable, not a constant, in dramatic character, but by the early twentieth century, it had become a system property of character construction, even as it came to be considered a system property of the psyche or, later, of the neuroanatomical connections responsible for the brain's ability to recognize and categorize perceived objects. This chapter pairs Henrik Ibsen, Tennessee Williams, and Samuel Beckett with Sigmund Freud, Jerome Bruner, and Gerald Edelman—three playwrights with three kindred, twentieth-century *memographers* (my own coinage for writers and thinkers about memory, irrespective of discipline). The study of such correspondences can contribute substantively to the histories of both drama and memory.

While Freud was speculating that suppressed memories cause the repetition of neurotic behavior and that neurotics construct false memories to screen a traumatic event, Henrik Ibsen in *When We Dead Awaken* (1899) and his contemporary August Strindberg were already dramatizing the action of such behaviors. By the time cognitive psychologist Jerome Bruner called attention to the interplay of memory and narrative in draw-the-curtain fashion in 1987, playwrights had been exploring the subject for fifty years. Tennessee Williams's *The Glass Menagerie* (1944), a self-styled "memory play," is a great resource for understanding how the self-telling of life narratives can organize memory (and vice versa). For a final example, between the time Samuel Beckett won the Nobel Prize for literature in 1969 and Roger Sperry won the Nobel Prize for Medicine in 1981—the decade during which the formal discipline of cognitive neuroscience was emerging—Beckett explored the embodiment of memory in a way that can be usefully compared with the theories of the neuroscientist Gerald Edelman, whose engagement with memory Beckett and his contemporary Harold Pinter anticipate.

Though twentieth-century memographers are the focus here, Shakespeare offers an early precedent of a dramatist both responsive to and formative of contemporary constructions of memory. Influenced by Giordano Bruno, the poet and deviser of recondite mnemonic systems whose name is anglicized in the character Berowne in *Love's Labor's Lost,* Shakespeare exhibited an almost clinical preoccupation with memory. His varied interests ran from childhood amnesia, as in Prospero's urgent interrogation of Miranda over what she can recall from the "dark backward and abysm of time" (*Tempest* 1.2.38–52) to a curiosity about what we know as "Alzheimer's disease" and its erosion of memory, as in Jacques's observation on "second childishness and mere oblivion" (*As You Like It* 2.7.165). But in two plays not commonly linked, the design of remembrance and its corollary, forgetting, comes dramatically to the fore. *Hamlet* and *Pericles* do not just recall each other but are also antiphonal: Hamlet is an obsessive rememberer of familial devastation; Pericles, a deliberate forgetter of similar distress. *Hamlet*'s triple father-son stories make it a model of masculine, aggressive behavior, even as *Pericles*'s triple father-daughter stories model feminine, compliant behavior. Indeed, Renaissance physiology suggested that the lethargy that overtakes Pericles is sourced in an excess of the moist and cold, characteristic of a woman's body. The Ghost's command to "Remember me" (1.5.91) relentlessly drives Hamlet's tragedy; Pericles turns away from the incest crime hidden in the riddle of Antiochus, confesses, "What I have been I have forgot to know" (2.1.71), and sends his wife's body overboard to the "unfriendly elements [that] forgot thee utterly" (3.1.58–59)—for which he is rewarded with the restoration of his lost wife and child. Hamlet's remembering is metaphorically connected with tablets, books, and volumes—a cluster associated with Aristotle, humanism, and Erasmus. By contrast, the "dumb shews" (pantomimes), tournament imagery, and "Greek" setting of *Pericles* suggest Neoplatonism, medieval mnemotechnics, and Bruno's memory-based occult philosophy, as exampled in his *Seal of Seals* (published when he was in England in 1583), wherein sharp, detailed, and complex images enriched with affect are offered for "the acquiring, arranging and recollecting of all sciences and arts."[1]

As memory-suffused works, *Hamlet* and *Pericles* are like the twin Greek goddesses Mnemosyne and Lesmosyne—one driven by the injunction to remember and the other by the injunction to forget. Better than any memographer between the ancient Greeks and Freud, Shakespeare understood that the members of this binary infuse and are indispensable to each other. *Hamlet* remembers "by the book," *Pericles* by the talismans, emblems and seals of mnemotechnics; the one is "logico-linguistic" and the other "pictorial-imagistic," both forms reflected in Renaissance models of memory.[2] *Hamlet* represents the Erasmian world of the university, ratiocination, mentation, the brain, and the printed book. It stands in opposition to *Pericles*'s occult world of orality, spells, revelation, resurrection, and rhapsody—even as humanism stood against Bruno and the Neoplatonists. Shakespeare manages to hold all this in glorious equipoise, perhaps with a grasp of the therapeutic interaction of remembering and forgetting.

Just as playwrights have drawn on philosophers or psychologists, theatrical metaphors and vocabulary have served other memographers in modeling memory since the Renaissance. In the fifteenth and sixteenth centuries, Giullio Camillo, Giordano Bruno, and Robert Fludd all constructed virtual (in Camillo's case, actual) "memory-theaters" to organize complex categories of knowledge.[3] Concepts of "scene," "script," and "theater" continue to serve as various a group of memographers as Sigmund Freud and Oliver Sacks, cognitive psychologists Martin Conway, Lawrence Barsalou, and Katherine Nelson, and neurobiologists Gerald Edelman and Bernard Baars.

Freud's observation in 1907 that "in my own case the earliest childhood memories are ... regular scenes worked out in plastic form, comparable only to representations on the stage,"[4] suggests that it is the vivid, three-dimensional ("plastic") action of the stage that makes it suitable as a model for memory. More than eighty years later, the fluctuations of a fragile personal selfhood among Oliver Sacks's postencephalitic patients and the vivid, uniquely personal qualities of the memories triggered by L-dopa caused Sacks to speculate on the relationship of consciousness to identity and of memory to both, employing the vocabulary of Pirandellian theatrics. "The person shows forth," he wrote, "in a continual disclosure or epiphany of himself; he is always enacting himself in the theater of his self. Entire memory-theaters are set in motion; long-past scenes are recalled, reenacted, with an immediacy which effaces the passage of time. ... The quality of these recaptured moments shows us the quality of experience itself, and reminds us ... that our memories, our selves, our very existences consist of *a collection of moments*."[5] Less rhapsodically, cognitive psychologists have adduced the notion of a "script" to explain how autobiographical memories are structured and organized into groups. Barsalou posits that event recall is integrated with scripts of generic knowledge that direct individual memories of extended events or activities into "event-memory organizational packets" (E-MOPS).[6] Exploring how individual socialization practices impact autobiographical memory, Katherine Nelson and Robyn Fivush similarly use "scripts" to identify, for example, sequences that children learn for going-to-bed rituals.[7] Stephen Anderson and Martin Conway elaborate the theory of scripts and E-MOPS with "mega-MOPS" (templates by which E-MOPS are created) and a TOP (thematic organizing packet).[8] To some readers, this structuring may begin to resemble literary genre theory, with E-MOPS as story types, mega-MOPS as genres and a TOP akin to a totalizing concept such as Northrop Frye proposed, that genres themselves all partake of a universal quest myth.[9] How the scripting of recollection *narrative* interacts with or diverges from the organization of memory is not considered by these researchers.

When Gerald Edelman writes, "The world can be correlated and bound into a *scene* ... a spatiotemporally ordered set of categorizations of familiar and unfamiliar events,"[10] he returns to a theatrical metaphor with greater promise of reflecting memory's organization. Edelman's concept of a scene entails a *linkage* between the capacities to make perceptual and conceptual categorizations. The "new component of neuroanatomy" enabling this linkage can interject "*a conceptual categorization of concurrent perceptions ... before* these perceptual signals contribute lastingly to that memory."[11] Edelman contends that, though we experience consciousness as a picture or image, "there is no actual image or sketch in the brain. The 'image' is a *correlation* between different kinds of categorizations."[12] Memory scenes do not picture the past, they order, bind, and correlate. Likewise, a dramatic scene organizes stage action-in-time, and it implies and correlates between what comes before it and what comes after in a way that pictures do not, causing us to reevaluate and reconstruct what we "remember" of previous scenes. *Scene* has the further advantage over *image* as a descriptor of memory in that it more readily accommodates intensity and energy, as well as olfactory, tactile, and gustatory events, among its sensuous discriminations.

Less trenchant and more plainly metaphorical, Baars has based his global workspace theory for cerebral processing on "a 'theater model' in which consciousness requires a central workspace, much like the stage of a theater."[13] The theater metaphor is useful to Baars because what happens on stage requires a stage manager, an audience, and so on, which captures the idea of a focal area as well as many other dependent knowledge sources elsewhere in the brain. He goes on to say that *"working memory is like a theater stage"* and that conscious experience is "the spotlight of attention shining on the stage of working memory."[14] Baars manipulates the theater metaphor adeptly enough to account for the interaction of consciousness with experiential context (the stage director is a "context operator") and to (narrowly) avoid the pitfall of identifying consciousness as a homunculus-like controller.

Clearly, theatrical vocabulary continues to have a prominent place in the array of metaphors psychologists and cognitive scientists deploy as explanatory models for memory. To adapt the terminology of Aristotle, who wrote authoritatively on both memory and theater, for many memographers, memory is to the mind as the plot is to tragedy: its "soul" and master organizer. Yet, even though remembering has been heuristically recognized as an exercise of scenic imagination, dramatic representations of memory have not been reckoned as part of its intellectual formation. The following examples, drawn from the twentieth century, go toward filling that gap.

Ibsen and Freud

In the late 1890s, when Freud embarked on his self-analysis, paying particular attention to the significance of fragmentary memories,[15] Ibsen was at work on his last play. In the first act of *When We Dead Awaken*, we meet the world-famous sculptor Rubek and his far younger wife, Maja, at a seaside resort where they encounter Irene, Rubek's former model. In the following two acts, as Maja is lured off to the mountains by the bear hunter Ulfheim, Rubek and Irene reestablish a relationship as fraught with misunderstanding and discrepancy as it had previously been. In the end, Rubek and Irene are killed in an avalanche, virtual suicides. A key incident in the play occurs when the two are grouped momentarily like the sculptor with his masterpiece *The Resurrection Day,* and it has been suggested that the sculpture has fixed or frozen them in a traumatic memory that, as in cases reported by Freud's contemporary, Pierre Janet, triggered obsessive behavior.[16]

Throughout, Ibsen demonstrates an almost clinical interest in how differently Irene and Rubek have dealt with the memory of their relationship. Irene's stiff and measured gait evokes a hysterical symptom noted by Josef Breuer and Freud.[17] Other symptoms—social dysfunction, paranoia causing her to carry a knife with which she secretly threatens Rubek, and what may or may not be delusions of killing her husbands and children— suggest dementia praecox, a diagnosis that eventually replaced the catchall category of hysteria.

Irene is truly locked into repetitive behavior. Ever since parting from Rubek, she has wandered in search of him, wreaking havoc on surrogates of both the artist and his art—the sculpture she insistently calls "our child."[18] She has posed as a naked statue in peep shows in a sordid repetition of her modeling for Rubek. The dagger she now carries with her is another repetition, a surrogate for the sharp needle she concealed in her hair, to fend off Rubek's touches, which she both dreaded and desired, but which never came. This troubling arousal is surely meant to be one source of the subsequent hysteria. Another is an incident unremarkable to Rubek that Irene claims has changed her life. As their artist-model relationship came to a close, Rubek summed it up to Irene as a "delightful episode,"[19] a characterization irredeemably demeaning in her eyes. This double diminution—sexual and social—constitutes the trauma she has spent her life trying to exorcize.

By contrast, Rubek has found a way of working through their relationship, and Irene's reappearance emphasizes how different their lives have been. After they had parted, Rubek had in fact reconfigured the sculpture, making it a larger grouping, with Irene, formerly the sole figure, now occupying the middle ground. Thus Rubek had acted to accommodate the memory of Irene in a larger, changing context, whereas when Irene had fled, her attempts to exorcize the traumatic relationship had only caused her to cling to it, repeating the past. The change in the sculpture signifies, even literalizes, that Irene and Rubek have different memories of their relationship. Ibsen's point is not only that their "reminiscences" are divergent, but also that Rubek's active refashioning of their relationship is productive and in some sense therapeutic, whereas her passive clinging to the memory is pathological: it is while Rubek recounts the remaking of the sculpture that Irene comes closest to stabbing him. Although the Rubek we meet in the play is far from happy, he has continued to create and has moved on in his life, incorporating Irene as an "episode," and sublimating his bitterness in the animal likenesses concealed in the portrait busts he sculpts on commission.

Not surprisingly, my descriptive vocabulary draws on two of Freud's classical essays, "The Aetiology of Hysteria" (1896), published while Ibsen was at work on *When We Dead Awaken*, and "Remembering, Repeating and Working Through," first published in 1914.[20] Freud declares in the earlier essay that the symptoms of hysteria "are determined by certain experiences of the patient's which operate traumatically and are reproduced in his psychic life as memory symbols of these experiences."[21] "Memory symbols" are not true memories but confabulated constructs that may obscure the originating traumatic scene. In the later essay, Freud makes clear that therapeutic remembering, which disentangles the remembered situation from the present one, disposes of patients' compulsion to repeat and frees them for the next stage in their lives. In *When We Dead Awaken*, Rubek's revision of the sculpture is literally a reconstruction of the memory of Irene, psychologically resituating her and converting remembrance, therapeutically speaking, into an auxiliary of forgetting. Irene can make no such adjustment and demonstrates her repetitive behavior in the ways already noticed, but also by confusing in her mind the scene of her traumatic parting with Rubek at Lake Taunitz years ago with the conversation they had just the day before. The inability to distinguish past from present is for Freud the surest sign of pathology, summed up in Freud's oft-quoted pronouncement "Hysterics suffer mainly from reminiscences."[22] Irene's confused recollection comes just minutes before she and Rubek are buried in the avalanche and makes it very difficult to interpret their reunion psychologically as anything but the seduction of Rubek into the world of Irene's dementia.

Irene's behavior differs from the unconscious *reenacting* of a forgotten traumatic incident that Janet describes, but conforms to what Freud refers to as "repetitions," which are acted out as a result of repression: the patient reproduces "what he has forgotten and repressed ... not as a memory but as an action; he *repeats* it, without, of course, knowing that he is repeating it."[23] What he repeats are symbols of memories that display his "inhibitions and unserviceable attitudes and his pathological character traits."[24] The symbols are linked into "memory chains" that lead "*infallibly ... to the realm of sexual experience*" in childhood.[25] Though neither Janet's nor Freud's case studies precisely describe Irene—who has not repressed the memory of her troubling attraction to Rubek—the sexual source of her hysteria certainly evokes Freud. She may have been legally a child when subject to the sexual feelings she could not cope with, for both her vulnerability and youth are emphasized in the text. We are told she left her family and home to go with Rubek, a decision she characterizes as her "childhood's resurrection."[26]

The Memory Play and Narrative Memory

Within the discipline of psychology, Frederic Bartlett's 1932 *Remembering* inaugurated a "brief period of interest in 'ordinary' remembering and forgetting"[27] before memory was reabsorbed into the clinical study of psychopathology, on the one hand, and the laboratory study of educational application, on the other. Bartlett's emphasis on the constructive and social dimensions of remembering naturally pointed to a consideration of memory in the larger context of self-formation. It would be almost fifty years, however, before a series of publications over the course of a decade redirected the attention of psychologists to memory's crucial role in the ongoing self-making of a lived life. In an influential 1977 article, "Flashbulb Memories," Roger Brown and James Kulik examined how surprising, consequential, or emotionally arousing events registered with mnemic intensity, which in turn affected the degree of elaboration in the narration of the memory.[28] Ulrich Neisser's *Memory Observed* (1982) brought together important essays on remembering in natural contexts, while Endel Tulving's *Elements of Episodic Memory* (1983) considered memory of personal events in the context of the development of the self. Finally, Jerome Bruner in "Life as Narrative" (1987) suggested a complex feedback mechanism for the way in which the telling of memories impacted self-formation: "The culturally shaped cognitive and linguistic processes that guide the self-telling of life narratives achieve the power to structure perceptual experience, to organize memory, to segment and purpose-build the very 'events' of a life."[29]

During roughly the same fifty years, from the mid-1930s to the mid-1980s, the scene of autobiographical memory was as crowded in the theater as it was empty in psychology. The interplay of memory and narrative had become a staple, even a cliché of world stages, and the remembering narrator, long a feature of the novel and already embraced by film, took to the stage with full force. Though *The Glass Menagerie* (1944) in declaring itself a "memory play" appears to have launched a genre, it is more likely that, in employing the term, Tennessee Williams was making reference to a tradition in which he thought his audience would readily place his current work: Luigi Pirandello, Eugene O'Neill, and Thornton Wilder all had written memory plays before him.

"Mr. Williams calls his drama a 'memory play,'" reported the *New York Times* on the premiere. "It has a commentator [Tom] who also acts a role. Standing in the present, the commentator glances back, and as he sets the scene the action unfolds."[30] The interplay of remembering narrator and remembered content in *The Glass Menagerie* is deliberately ambiguous, as Williams's stage directions insist memory is *"nonrealistic ... exaggerated ... dim and poetic,"*[31] requiring constant interpretation. Likewise, Williams's setting "An alley in St. Louis. Now and the Past" alerts us to the importance of memory's *negotiation* between past and present. The scrim and projections called for by the playwright attempt to capture the eidetic features of memory. Finally, all the remembering in the play builds to a closing and paradoxical exhortation to forget. It is fair to say that the "shift from an emphasis on atomistic memory traces to multimodal narratives wholes"[32] that took psychology fifty years to effect, happened in the American theater on *The Glass Menagerie*'s opening night.

Tom's struggle for individuation, his sister Laura's sensitivity, and even their mother Amanda's powers of endurance are cause for celebration in the play, despite the failed project of securing for Laura a marriageable Gentleman Caller. Through the sharing device of Tom's narration, the play ultimately strikes us as a small gift from the son to his mother, a commemorative token of his affections. Just as Laura forgives the well-meaning gaucherie of Jim the Gentleman Caller by giving him the glass unicorn he has damaged, Tom lavishes upon his family the creative spirit they unwittingly fostered. Tom has become a "Shakespeare," the play tells us with gentle irony, not by fleeing to the movies but by dwelling again among the familiar images projected on his soul.

The duality of a remembering and remembered Tom may well reflect the psychological circumstances of the playwright: "Tennessee Williams" became the nom de plume for Thomas Lanier Williams III some seven years before he wrote *The Glass Menagerie*. But Williams's assumption of a fabricating persona can guide us beyond psychobiography toward understanding the *construction* of memory as a fictive, though not necessarily falsifying act. Stories, Williams knows, may disguise themselves as memories, and memories—which are quasi or potentially narrative—may be altered in the crucible of narrative form.

Although the playwright's construction of memory is thus more knowing than Tom's, Tom is the most sophisticated rememberer in the play. When Tom remembers Amanda's reminiscing over the seventeen gentlemen callers she received one afternoon on Blue Mountain, he does so in a way that establishes "the tyranny of Amanda's memories over her own life and the lives of her children."[33] Likewise, Tom shows that his sister's memories "lock Laura as securely into the world of the past as her mother's memories of gentlemen callers."[34] In Freudian terms, Tom represents himself as remembering and working through, so as not to repeat, whereas Amanda and Laura are caught in the throes of repetition marked by Jim's catastrophic visit. But Williams does not let us ignore the fact that Tom's memory is idiosyncratic and autobiographical, not omniscient. The projected images and captions, though deployed inconsistently, frequently undercut the studied, photographic memory implied in the remembered episodes. For example, the father's grinning photograph appearing when Tom speaks of escaping from his domestic coffin may suggest an association that Tom's conscious mind does not make. Likewise, the legend "This is my sister: Celebrate her with strings!"[35] introduces a mocking tone belied by the ensuing scene with Laura and Jim, as if Tom was still working through his memories of Laura. Because the self-presence of the rememberer is the most prominent feature of the play's memory frame, we recognize that Tom's closing exhortation, "Blow out your candles, Laura,"[36] is in the nature of a note to self, complex in its motivations: of gratitude, exorcism, premonition, and therapeutic transcendence. The staging of the memory is thus cathartic, or what Janice Haaken calls "transformative," referring "to the recollection of an event that serves as a psychological marker from an earlier to a later form of self-knowledge."[37]

Tom constructs himself as the one who remembers in order to organize his past, make sense of it, and to forget; he "'writes' the play ... because he has not effected that escape from the past which had been his primary motive for leaving."[38] R. B. Parker reads Tom's working through his relationship with Laura as an "obsessive reliving" of Williams's documented transgressive desire for his sister Rose.[39] And David Savran sees Williams's "valorization of eroticism generally" and "endorsement of transgressive liaisons" as the screens "that would allow him to represent his homosexuality in other guises."[40] A persistent strain in criticism of Williams thus pursues the layers of autobiographical memory embedded in his plays, frequently aided by the playwright's exceedingly candid *Memoirs*.[41] "The culturally shaped cognitive and linguistic processes that guide the self-telling" of Tennessee/Tom's life narrative appear to equal in complexity anything described by Jerome Bruner fifty years later.

Memory Made Flesh

How memory both transforms and is transformed by the embodied self and how consciousness materializes are questions taken up by the playwright Samuel Beckett and the Nobel Prize–winning biochemist, Gerald M. Edelman, who succinctly frames the body-based context for consciousness and memory studies by posing the question: "How can the firing of neurons give rise to subjective sensations, thoughts and emotions?"[42] Edelman proposes a theory of cognitive function that is both uncompromisingly physical and consistent with the principles of evolution and individual morphological development. It accounts for the intentionality of consciousness, its "dependency on the activities of multiple parallel brain regions"[43] as in memory, and its place in the transition from a primary to a higher-order state in individuals with a concept of self. Edelman names the evolutionary mechanism "neuronal group selection" and describes his theory as "above all ... a theory of perceptual categorization."[44] It includes an account of how processes of perceptual categorization, including recognition and memory, interact to "mediate the continually changing relations between experience and novelty that lead to learning."[45] And it proposes a detailed model of how neuronal groups are formed and constantly reformed as maps via the reentry of new data that connect neuronal groups. A map of neuronal groups, multiply interconnected, is akin to a species because the firing of neurons in response to environmental stimulus leads to the wiring of those same neurons into groups: "Neurons that fire together wire together."[46]

In this almost infinitely complex system of connectivity, memory is a system property that "depends upon specific neuro-anatomical connections" and that is "exhibited as an enhanced ability to recognize and categorize objects in classes seen before."[47] Like Baars, Edelman virtually identifies working memory with primary consciousness, which depends upon the operation of recategorizing as well as "the capability of temporal ordering and succession. ... Indeed, metaphorically, one might say that the previous memories and current activities of the brain interact to yield primary consciousness as a form of 'remembered present.'"[48] In Edelman's understanding, "scenes" or "new perceptual categorizations are reentrantly connected to memory systems before they themselves become part of an altered memory system. ... The ability to construct a conscious scene in the fraction of a second is the ability to create a remembered present."[49]

For Edelman, the brain operates only procedurally, making consciousness like a musical or theatrical performance. Thus successful performance depends on rehearsal, the reconstruction of relationships previously established but being remade—*in-line, in-place*—with reentered data. We don't remember things; we remember relations. Further, the brain has evolved a sort of redundancy—a capacity Edelman calls "degeneracy"—whereby brain features are selected for the ability to get to the same place by different routes. In terms of memory, Edelman's concept of degeneracy compels the rejection of the ancient metaphor of representational inscription (in wax or stone), in favor of an environmental, nonrepresentational one: "A nonrepresentational memory would be like changes in a glacier influenced by changes in the weather. ... The melting and refreezing of the glacier represent changes in the synaptic response, the ensuing different rivulets descending the mountain represent the neural pathways, and the pond into which they feed represents the output. ... Memory is a system property reflecting the effects of context and the associations of various degenerate circuits capable of yielding a similar output."[50] The differences in what and how individuals remember, then, are based both on biology and on experience (hence culture).

In line with his idea that primary consciousness and working memory are virtually the same—a remembered present—Edelman likewise conceives higher-order consciousness as an evolutionarily new kind of memory: "While the remembered present is, in fact, a reflection of true physical time, higher-order consciousness makes it possible to relate a socially constructed self to past recollections and future imaginations."[51] That is, higher-order consciousness evolved out of primary consciousness as a more sophisticated way to deal with the *not-there*, with absence.

Decades before Edelman, Beckett had embarked on his own cerebral, body-based investigation of memory's role in self-creation. Beckett shows a keen interest in the corporeality of memory and remains topographically engaged with memory as a feature of the mindscape throughout the long casting off of literary resources that characterizes his development from the 1940s to the 1980s. Indeed, Beckett's postures of memory are remarkably fixed,[52] as when Lucky's compulsive, elliptical oration from *Waiting for Godot* (1952) returns in Mouth's monologue of *That Time* (1972), or when Murphy's rocking chair from the eponymous 1938 novel serves *Rockaby* in 1981. Earlier still, in his critical essay *Proust* (1931), Beckett appears to have focused on consciousness as his field of inquiry, like a scientist deciding on a specialization.

Beckett's purpose in the essay is to anatomize and celebrate Proust's use of involuntary memory as a device to recover the "only … real impression"[53] of the past. Surrounding this analysis, however, is what amounts to a theory of consciousness that, remarkably like Edelman's, features different kinds of memory, is body-based, takes into account the value systems satisfying appetitive needs, and even encompasses a rudimentary notion of neuronal remapping, though Beckett never succeeds in escaping a persistent Cartesianism. Beckett theorizes habit as "the generic term for the countless treaties concluded between the countless subjects that constitute the individual and their countless correlative objects."[54] That is, habit is unconscious body-based memory, the continual recategorizations that constitute what Edelman calls the "remembered present." Though Beckett may romanticize involuntary memory as the "pure act of cognition"[55] that occurs in the unguarded mind, he posits it in a way that is compatible with embodied consciousness and evolutionary theory.

Among Beckett's earlier works, *Act without Words I* (1957) demonstrates how memory is connected with value systems governing adaptive survival.[56] The play, in fact, would appear to be a dramatization of a phrase in *Proust*: "periods of transition that separate consecutive adaptations"[57] of habit. When the Player is hurled from the wings out onto the desert, he is offered various tools for survival. A palm tree bestowing shade is dropped in and then flown out; a carafe of water dangled just above his outstretched hand becomes almost, but not quite, accessible from cubes dropped in from above; and so on. Parable this may be, but it is also a lesson in how the brain works: "remembering" the environment based on undertaken action is punctuated by the silent reflections of the Player between each episode; together, they show us primary and higher-order consciousness in successive glimpses. After the Player, Beckett's characters become less able-bodied, their external environment becomes less rich, and they are forced ever more inward and ever more reliant on their subjectivity to provide self-maintenance—to chaotic effect. Higher-order consciousness, unmoored from the sensorimotor feedback provided by external contact, feeds off itself. The effort to bring the self to bear in the world, to alter "the causal relations of objects in a definitive way according to the structure of their memories,"[58] or simply to assert the self/nonself distinction appears at different times ludicrously inadequate (*Krapp's Last Tape*—1957), poignantly heroic (*Happy Days*—1962), and, finally, desperate and pathological (*Not I*—1972; *That Time*—1975).

Indeed, Beckett's intensely memorious *Krapp's Last Tape* carefully connects Krapp's impairments to primary consciousness—he is "very nearsighted" and "hard of hearing,"[59] resorts to numbing alcohol, and lives in a "den" surrounded by darkness—with the impairments to higher-order consciousness that cause him to rely on annual tape recordings to comprehend his life. Krapp's "retrospect"[60] is so deprived of the sense of self-continuity that he cannot grasp the significance of notes in his ledger, has lost vocabulary he once knew, and deliberately skips past a transforming vision he once recorded. The recording/remembering that Krapp undertakes in the present of the play is explicitly aborted when Krapp stops the recorder, rips out the tape, and discards it in favor of the old tape he has been listening to. His way of connecting to the past is to make a categorical break with the present, in effect relinquishing the self-consistency of higher-order consciousness for a state that barely achieves primary consciousness. Krapp is neither fully present nor truly remembering himself, except in the parody of storage-and-retrieval memory the play's punning title alludes to as a sort of playing with the mind's wastes: the tapes are all the Krapp that is left of him. Our impression of a Krapp selfsame over time derives from the fixations his body is subject to: constipation, a fondness for bananas, drinking, and sex. Though Krapp's self-rehearsal may predicate higher-order consciousness, his habits undermine that predication: we see his perspective predicament reduced to the elementary motions of primary consciousness.

The radical division between Krapp then and Krapp now, which neither memory nor its mechanical surrogate can bridge, is exacerbated in *Not I*. Here Beckett's vivisection of memory divides vocal (first person), auditory (second person), and cognitive (third person) functions and presents them in the dramatic equivalent of an isolation tank. A spotlit Mouth spills out a torrent of words, in which autobiographical episodes seamlessly merge with the present situation of the narrator; a motionless, hooded Auditor gestures four times during Mouth's monologue. Thus dispossessed and isolated, the process of self-sustenance in *Not I* is a stream of consciousness with the flow continually recalibrated not by external stimuli but by the brain's own neuronal firings and misfirings ("half the vowels wrong," Mouth testifies).[61] Here is consciousness, voiced in Mouth's constant self-corrections, turning on its own schemata: "Words were coming ... her lips moving!" declares Mouth,[62] never admitting that she is describing her own experience. Thus microscopically fixed and exposed, memory is seen to loop back on itself, revealing nothing so much as its own neuronal networks: "Can't stop the stream ... and the whole brain begging."[63] Precisely this revelation belies Mouth's implied insistence that the third-person subject of her story is "not I." Her *"vehement refusal to relinquish third person,"*[64] as Beckett himself puts it in a stage direction, is like Krapp's return to his tapes: a failure of memory to construct selfsameness.

It is possible, though certainly difficult, to tease out a fragmentary narrative from the stream of words, but the details pale before Beckett's representation of the act of impaired cognition, wherein primary and higher-order consciousness interfere with one another incoherently, like a radio dial set between two frequencies. We are seeing and hearing the words become flesh, Beckett's answer to the question phrased by Edelman as: "How can the firing of neurons give rise to subjective sensations, thoughts and emotions?" What Beckett in his youthful enthusiasm for Proust celebrated as a "miracle" is now a catastrophe, whereby a past "sensation itself annihilating every spatial and temporal restriction, comes in a rush to engulf the subject."[65]

The neuronal mode of *Not I* recurs in *That Time* ("brain" appears nine times in the short text), which seems, however, to reintroduce a Cartesian dualism with an embodied Listener surrounded by disembodied Voices that are "moments of one and the same voice,"[66] Beckett notes, the Listener's own. Beckett specifies that the three voices "relay one another without solution of continuity. ... Yet the switch from one to another must be clearly faintly perceptible."[67] This description might aptly be termed *synaptic*, with the "switch" referring to changes in the scene-making of consciousness: the three relayed voices, each pursuing its own narrative, might be taken as playing along their respective neural networks. Each narrative worries away at the creation of a scene, one associated with an old ruin and a childhood memory, one a glimpse of love lost on a stone bench at the edge of a wood, and one a scene of old age in a portrait gallery. Indeed, the word *scene* or *scenes* tolls through the text.

Each of the three scenes created by Voices A, B, and C lays claim to be a "turning point," "that time" marking the "never the same but the same" when a self might possibly be able to "say I to yourself."[68] Yet none of the scenes in *That Time* quite coalesces. In their fluidity, they put one in mind of Edelman's image of the rivulets of memory running down a glacial mountain: "The melting and refreezing of the glacier represent changes in the synaptic response [and] the ensuing different rivulets descending the mountain represent the neural pathways." Drolly and sardonically, Beckett is suggesting that we can hold onto different self-defining moments at the same time, that different pathways can willy-nilly lead to a sense of self—if not a coherent one.

Edelman links the capacity to construct a scene with the ability to create a remembered present, a facility that both constitutes primary consciousness and enables higher-order consciousness to build upon it. Above all, for Edelman, the brain is constructive, a glorious adaptation that evolved memory to deal with absence, to make something out of nothing, to build a coherent picture of the *once was* and the *could be*. Beckett's view almost seems to be the inverse, a devolutionary view in which higher-order consciousness is ever under threat of degradation to primary consciousness, radically disconnected from environment. Thus Beckett's characters appear fragmented like individuals afflicted with multiple personalities or like pathological patients suffering from the disconnection syndromes resulting from cutting off one part of the brain from another.[69] Beckett contemplates all this with a balance of clinical curiosity, compassion, intellectual enthusiasm, and human interest. His aching engagement with absence, the hallmark of his work, drives his preoccupation with the organ evolved to cope with it. Like Edelman, Beckett has put brain, memory, and consciousness under a microscope.

Ibsen, Williams, and Beckett diverge in their idiosyncratic ways from the strictures of dramatic realism to represent the idea of a coherent self perduring through the successive selves (or, in Beckett's case, "selflets") of a lived life. Paradoxically, one must imagine oneself removed from the present in order to posit a perduring self—making the memory play an ideal vehicle for such an exercise. Although the *I* in the now is responsible for positing the primordial *I*, that *I* in the past is a mental construct that then autonomously impinges on and affects the conceiving *I* in the present. Freud, Bruner, Edelman, and the other scientists considered here, like the playwrights, seek to discover the underlying psychological, cognitive, or neuronal schemata that make this splendid and frustrating exercise possible. It seems timely to introduce one group of memographers to the other.

Notes

1. Giordano Bruno, as quoted in J. Lewis McIntyre, *Giordano Bruno: Mystic Martyr* (Kila, MT: Kessinger, 1992), 37.

2. John Sullivan, *Philosophy and Memory Traces: Descartes to Connectionism* (Cambridge: Cambridge University Press, 1998), 121.

3. On Camillo, see Frances Yates, *The Art of Memory* (London: Routledge, 1966), 145; on Bruno, see Frances Yates, *Giordano Bruno and the Hermetic Tradition* (Chicago: University of Chicago Press, 1964); on Fludd, see Frances Yates, *Theater of the World* (Chicago: University of Chicago Press, 1969).

4. Sigmund Freud, "Childhood Memories and Screen Memories," in *Standard Edition of the Complete Psychological Works of Sigmund Freud,* ed. and trans. James Strachey (London: Hogarth Press, 1957), 6:47.

5. Oliver Sacks, *Awakenings* (New York: HarperCollins, 1990), 259–261

6. Lawrence Barsalou, "The Content and Organization of Autobiographical Memories," in *Remembering Reconsidered: Ecological and Traditional Approaches to the Study of Memory*, ed. Ulrich Neisser and Eugene Winograd (Cambridge: Cambridge University Press, 1988), 193–243.

7. Katherine Nelson and Robyn Fivush, "Socialization of Memory," in *The Oxford Handbook of Memory,* ed. Endel Tulving and Fergus I. M. Craik (Oxford: Oxford University Press, 2000), 283–295.

8. Stephen J. Anderson and Martin A. Conway, "Representations of Autobiographical Memory," in *Cognitive Models of Memory,* ed. Martin A. Conway (Cambridge, MA: MIT Press, 1997), 217–246.

9. See Northrop Frye, *Anatomy of Criticism* (Princeton, NJ: Princeton University Press, 1957).

10. Gerald Edelman, *Bright Air, Brilliant Fire: On the Matter of the Mind* (New York: Basic Books, 1992), 118.

11. G. Edelman, *Bright Air, Brilliant Fire: On the Matter of the Mind*, 119.

12. G. Edelman, *Bright Air, Brilliant Fire: On the Matter of the Mind*, 119.

13. Bernard J. Baars, *The Theater of Consciousness* (Oxford: Oxford University Press, 1997), viii.

14. B. J. Baars, *The Theater of Consciousness*, 41–42.

15. See Peter Gay, *Freud: A Life for Our Time* (New York: Norton, 1988), 97–100.

16. Oliver Gerland, "The Paradox of Memory: Ibsen's *When We Dead Awaken* and *Fin-de-Siècle* Psychotherapy," *Modern Drama* 38 (1995): 450–461.

17. Josef Breuer and Sigmund Freud, "The Aetiology of Hysteria," in *Collected Papers,* ed. Ernest Jones, International Psycho-analytical Library, no. 7 (New York: Basic Books, 1959), 1:137–138.

18. Henrik Ibsen, *When We Dead Awaken* in *The Oxford Ibsen*, trans. and ed. James Walter McFarlane (London: Oxford University Press, 1977), 8:254, 276–278. Subsequent quotations are from this edition.

19. H. Ibsen, *When We Dead Awaken*, 280.

20. Sigmund Freud, "Remembering, Repeating and Working Through," in *Standard Edition of the Complete Psychological Works of Sigmund Freud*, 12:147–156.

21. J. Breuer and S. Freud, "The Aetiology of Hysteria," 185.

22. J. Breuer and S. Freud, "The Aetiology of Hysteria," 7.

23. S. Freud, "Remembering, Repeating and Working Through," 150.

24. S. Freud, "Remembering, Repeating and Working Through," 151.

25. J. Breuer and S. Freud, "The Aetiology of Hysteria," 191, 193.

26. H. Ibsen, *When We Dead Awaken*, 258–259, 261–262.

27. Graham Richards, *Putting Psychology in its Place*, 2nd ed. (New York: Routledge, 2002), 132.

28. Roger Brown and James Kulik, "Flashbulb Memories," *Cognition* 5 (1977): 73–99.

29. Jerome Bruner, "Life as Narrative," *Social Research* 54 (1987): 15.

30. Lewis Nichols, "Glass Menagerie," *New York Times,* April 8, 1945, 39.

31. Tennessee Williams, *The Glass Menagerie,* in *Theater of Tennessee Williams* (New York: New Directions, 1971), 143. This edition contains the more extensive stage directions, production notes and description of characters missing from the Dramatists Play Service Acting Edition. It also contains the directions for the projections cut from the original production. Subsequent quotations are from this edition.

32. Robert W. Schrauf and David C. Rubin, "On the Bilingual's Two Sets of Memories," in *Autobiographical Memory and the Construction of a Narrative Self: Developmental and Cultural Perspectives,* ed. Robyn Fivush and Catherine A. Haden (Mahwah, NJ: Elbaum, 2003), 122.

33. Patricia Schroeder, *The Presence of the Past in Modern American Drama* (Rutherford, NJ: Fairleigh Dickinson University Press, 1989), 108.

34. P. Schroeder, *The Presence of the Past in Modern American Drama,* 109.

35. T. Williams, *The Glass Menagerie,* 193.

36. T. Williams, *The Glass Menagerie,* 237.

37. Janice Haaken, *Pillar of Salt: Gender, Memory and the Perils of Looking Back* (New Brunswick, NJ: Rutgers University Press, 1998), 14.

38. C. W. E. Bigsby, "Entering *The Glass Menagerie,*" in *The Cambridge Companion to Tennessee Williams,* ed. Matthew C. Roudané (Cambridge: Cambridge University Press), 37.

39. R. B. Parker, *The Circle Closed: A Psychological Pleading of "The Glass Menagerie" and "The Two-Character Play,"* ed. and with an introduction by Harold Bloom (Philadelphia: Chelsea House, 1988), 133.

40. David Savran, *Communists, Cowboys and Queers: The Politics of Masculinity in the Work of Arthur Miller and Tennessee Williams* (Minneapolis: University of Minnesota Press, 1992), 83.

41. In Tennessee Williams, *Memoirs,* introduction by John Waters (New York: New Directions, 2006), 119, for example, Williams acknowledges "unusually close relations" with his sister, while denying "carnal knowledge."

42. Gerald Edelman, *Wider Than the Sky: The Phenomenal Gift of Consciousness* (New Haven, CT: Yale University Press, 2004), xiii.

43. Gerald Edelman, *The Remembered Present* (New York: Basic Books, 1989), 18.

44. G. Edelman, *The Remembered Present,* 41.

45. G. Edelman, *The Remembered Present,* 43.

46. G. Edelman, *Wider Than the Sky: The Phenomenal Gift of Consciousness,* 29.

47. G. Edelman, *Wider Than the Sky: The Phenomenal Gift of Consciousness*, 22; G. Edelman, *The Remembered Present*, 60–61.

48. G. Edelman, *Wider Than the Sky: The Phenomenal Gift of Consciousness*, 105.

49. G. Edelman, *Wider Than the Sky: The Phenomenal Gift of Consciousness*, 55, 57.

50. G. Edelman, *Wider Than the Sky: The Phenomenal Gift of Consciousness*, 52–53.

51. G. Edelman, *Wider Than the Sky: The Phenomenal Gift of Consciousness*, 103.

52. I owe the phrase "postures of memory" to Jeanette R. Malkin, *Memory-Theater and Postmodern Drama* (Ann Arbor: University of Michigan Press, 1999).

53. Samuel Beckett, *Proust* (New York: Grove Press, n.d.), 4. For a consideration of Proust's formations of memory, see Suzanne Nalbantian, *Memory in Literature: From Rousseau to Neuroscience* (New York: Palgrave Macmillan, 2003), chap. 4.

54. S. Beckett, *Proust*, 17. Many of Beckett's ideas on memory derive from the philosopher Henri Bergson.

55. S. Beckett, *Proust*, 55.

56. Samuel Beckett, *Endgame* (New York: Grove Press, 1958) includes the play *Act without Words I*.

57. S. Beckett, *Endgame*, 8.

58. G. Edelman, *Bright Air, Brilliant Fire: On the Matter of the Mind*, 169.

59. S. Beckett, *Krapp's Last Tape* (New York: Grove Press, 1960), 9.

60. S. Beckett, *Krapp's Last Tape*, 16.

61. Samuel Beckett, *Not I*, in *Collected Shorter Plays* (London: Faber and Faber, 1984), 219, 222.

62. S. Beckett, *Not I*, 219.

63. S. Beckett, *Not I*, 220.

64. S. Beckett, *Not I*, 215.

65. S. Beckett, *Proust*, 54.

66. Samuel Beckett, *That Time*, in *Collected Shorter Plays*, 227.

67. S. Beckett, *That Time*, 227.

68. S. Beckett, *That Time*, 30.

69. On disconnection syndromes including blindsight, the one most relevant to Beckett, who suffered from glaucoma, see G. Edelman, *Wider Than the Sky: The Phenomenal Gift of Consciousness*, 143.

V Manifestations in the Arts

16   Memory in Art: History and the Neuroscience of Response

David Freedberg

At the center of this chapter stands a historical work of art, one of the great masterpieces of fifteenth-century Flemish painting, Rogier van der Weyden's *Descent from the Cross*. It raises issues that relate to many other historical and contemporary artworks. Like almost all visual images, it poses a large number of difficult questions about the nature and varieties of memory.[1] My current work on the neural bases of empathy and the relationship between emotional and felt motor responses to works of visual art suggests some new ways of thinking about memory, and about the relationship between declarative and procedural memory in particular.

The broader context for this study is provided by recent developments in the neuroscience of the bodily consequences of sight of movement and emotion,[2] and the specific context, by a work of art that effectively illustrates how the question of memory cannot be considered outside the modulating or even preemptive effects of direct (unmediated) and indirect (mediated) responses to such a work. By "direct and indirect" or "unmediated and mediated," I refer to the dialectic between responses which seem to be automatic and predicated on immediate or felt bodily responses, on the one hand , and those which are mediated by concept, reflection, and recollection, on the other.[3] Forms of direct and unmediated response (provisional labels for a variety of immediate and unconscious responses) offer a way of thinking about the continued hold of a centuries-old work of art on contemporary viewers, even in the absence of any particular knowledge or conscious recollection of its subject.[4]

Implicit in this discussion are forms of perception that are either (1) uninflected or uninformed by concept and cognition or (2) cognitive and laden with experience and learning.[5] In the more conventional view, perception is entirely predicated on memory and, more specifically, on stored schematic knowledge. But memory, as we now know, may be explicit or implicit. Explicit memory includes recollection of events and facts, of the textual sources for particular images, and of whatever may be acquired from the oral tradition (*tradition* being an especially salient term when it comes to explicit memory). The kinds of implicit memory most relevant here include the performance of actions (involving motor cortex and cerebellum) and the feeling of emotions (particularly involving the amygdala) without conscious awareness of drawing on experience or memory.

The central problem concerns the integration of experience and forms of explicit knowledge, on the one hand, with responses to sight of the body in movement, even in small movements (such as those of the corrugator and zygomatic muscles or those of the eyelids during blinks), on the other. When we recall a scene from the Bible, for example, and recognize what the scene represents, whether in whole or part, on the basis of accretions of experience and emotions that arise from our personal historical associations with such a scene, or we may react viscerally and corporeally in ways that seem to precede memory. It is these latter ways which need to be taken into account in dealing with artists' strategies, by no means always explicit or conscious, for arousing attention. In such cases, the neural substrate of the connections between vision and touch, or vision and movement, precede all conscious assessment of the iconography of a scene.[6]

Indeed, it's moot whether forms of declarative memory—even the little-discussed implicit forms of such memory—play much of a role in this transaction. Sometimes bodily reactions may actually refute experience and the varieties of declarative memory. But because implicit, nondeclarative memory is predicated on forms of recall that are embedded in the motor skills that underlie procedural memory, the two forms cannot be conflated as conscious. As became well known after studies of patient HM and the consequences of his mediotemporal lesions,[7] amnesia does not preclude muscular learning—indeed, it generally spares forms of learned and habitual movement. Despite damage to the hippocampus (critical for short-term memory and its conversion to long-term memory),[8] the role of the cerebellum (critical for movement conditioning) remains intact.

Underlying this discussion of memory is a commitment to the view that vision originally evolved in the service of movement rather than of perception.[9] Future research on art and memory will need to take into account the relations between the mediotemporal and hippocampal substrates of memory, on the one hand, and the role of the parietal cortex in transforming visual signals into motor activity, on the other.[10] Similarly, the connections between limbic areas relating to emotion (the amygdala in particular)[11] and motor and premotor cortices have generally received more attention than the connections between memory (procedural memory in particular) and the reactions that ensue in movement or felt imitation of seen movement. Such reactions always entail and imply emotional responses.

Experimental familiarity with motor responses to the sight of movement and emotion in works of art brings into question many currently held vague notions about "cultural memory." What follows is a reconception of the problem of memory in the context of past and present emotional responses to a particular work of art, and the felt—and occasionally explicit—motor responses such a work may evoke.

Now that Semir Zeki, who did fundamental work on the areas of the visual cortex in the 1980s and who coined the term *neuroaesthetics* about a decade ago, claims to have found the brain areas dedicated to beauty and love, and Vilayanur S. Ramachandran claims to have identified the neural bases of the principles of art, it remains important not to lose a sense of the historical dimensions of these issues.[12] The functions of both long- and short-term memory must be factored into any consideration of the problems not just of behavioral and emotional responses, but also of the ways in which these might be integrated into whatever it is that people call "the aesthetic." We might also hope to go beyond Jean-Pierre Changeux's stimulating but broad-brush accounts of neuronal networks to account for the individuality that lies at the core of much of what we call "art."[13]

The traditional divide between the sciences and the humanities has long been seen in terms of the tension between naturalist and materialist views, on the one hand, and sensitivity to contextual and social constraints, on the other. But this conventional dichotomy collapses in the face of the evidence for the neural bases of empathetic engagement with works of art. We are in a better position to understand how prefrontal modulation of lower-level cerebral responses offers more flexible and inventive ways of thinking about the relationship between automaticity and experience. Recent research on memory confounds the separation of history and experience from the corporeal and psychological entailments of beholding a visual image, and a work of art in particular. The

subject of embodied responses—much discussed in recent years by humanist scholars—now stands at the intersection of several fields within the
cognitive neurosciences.

In *The Power of Images* (1989), I set out to chart both the historical and
cross-cultural dimensions of a wide range of psychological and behavioral
reactions to images generally, not just to those designated as art.[14] I
became aware of how much art history had neglected the emotions—or
rather, of how systematically it had disregarded them, as though they
would run amok if acknowledged. Indeed, in *The Principles of Art* (1938),
R. G. Collingwood had specifically excluded the emotions as a constitu-
tive factor of art,[15] a position derived of course from Kant's *Third Critique*,
with its firm exclusion of desire and other elements of interest and value
from the definition of art and beauty. In addition, it seemed to me that
empathy had also fallen by the wayside in art history. In the late nineteenth century, writers such as Robert Vischer and Heinrich Wölfflin
dedicated a great deal of attention to their theories of how viewers of
images become physically involved with what they see, or rather of how
visual stimuli from works of art and architecture engender a sense of
embodied involvement in their viewers.[16] A few years later, Theodor Lipps's
briefly influential work took up the still older theme of the understanding
of the emotions through bodily movement.[17] For a long time, these positions were regarded with skepticism, though they were implicit in much
critical writing and were influentially developed by the phenomenological
writers on art. Most notable among these was Maurice Merleau-Ponty,
for whom the body was always implicit in perception, and in the aesthetic
qualities that derive from the corporeal sense made of even abstract
imagery, achieved through the body and the body's perception of movement.[18] It is not hard to understand why Merleau-Ponty's writings have
been so important for students of cubism, for example, as well as for
those interested in making sense of the act of marking two-dimensional
surfaces.

In *Descartes' Error* (1994), Antonio Damasio set out his descriptions of
the neural substrate of the bodily basis of emotion.[19] As William James had
before him,[20] Damasio argued for the ways in which physical responses—
and movement in particular—do not just accompany but actually generate
emotional awareness. Here and in his later books, *The Feeling of What*

Happens (1999) and *Looking for Spinoza* (2003), he developed his neurally grounded theory of the integration of cognition and bodily feeling. Critical to it was his concept of the *as-if body loop*, Damasio's term for the cortical circuits underlying our internally simulated somatic reactions to what we see.[21] Damasio argued that, in observing the physical and emotional behavior of others, our brains—and in particular the somatosensory cortices of their right hemisphere—reorganize themselves in such a way as to assume the same state they *would have* been *if* we were engaged in the same actions—or underwent the same emotions—ourselves. The appeal of such a theory for the understanding of viewers' sense of physical engagement either with the actors in a painted scene, or as subjects of the vicissitudes depicted in a scene (say a stormy seascape) did not escape Damasio, and he briefly suggested the relevance of such as-if responses to a theory of empathy. More specifically, Damasio outlined how the prefrontal cortex (especially the ventromedial prefrontal cortex) and the amygdala (or other relevant limbic region, such as the anterior insula in cases of disgust) signal directly to the somatosensory cortices to organize themselves in the explicit activity pattern they would have assumed had the body actually been placed in the same state. Thus when we see a dramatic action or a dramatic scene in which a body is involved, or even a scene implying bodily movement, the very parts of our motor and somatosensory cortices are activated that would be if we were involved in the scene *ourselves*, even if we do *not actually move.*[22]

But it was the discovery of "mirror neurons" by Giacomo Rizzolatti and colleagues in their Parma laboratory that revolutionized the understanding of embodied responses to the observation of the actions of others, whether in life or in art.[23] Whereas Damasio had left the cortical circuits between vision, motion, and emotion unclear, the initial findings by Rizzolatti and his colleagues Luciano Fadiga, Leonardo Fogassi, and Vittorio Gallese about a class of visuomotor neurons located chiefly in the premotor cortex of the brain—mirror neurons seemed to be fundamental for the understanding of our responses to art.[24]

Although mirror neurons cannot live up to many of the claims currently made on their behalf, they do offer a clearer hold on felt engagement with images than Damasio's body-loop systems. Beyond the viewer's corporeal and emotional involvement with what is seen, there is more specifically the question of the felt imitation of bodily movement and gesture. It is precisely in this domain that the relationship between memory and movement as factors in aesthetic response becomes critically apparent.

After their initial experiments with monkeys, the researchers of Rizzolatti's Parma laboratory proceeded to study mirror circuits in the human brain, which they found in the functional equivalent of monkey F5, that is, in the parietal lobule and frontal operculum of the premotor cortex, and specifically, more or less, in Brodmann's 44, which overlaps with Broca's area, the language region of the brain.[25] At this point, Vittorio Gallese took the implications of the discovery still further. First of all, he realized the implications of mirror responses for the understanding not just of the actions of others, but also of the intentions behind them.[26] He then developed his influential theory of what he called "embodied simulation" to encompass the whole class of imitative sensations felt in the body, whose neural substrate he believed it was now possible to identify.[27] Finally, Gallese, Christian Keysers, and others began to look at the mirror circuits underlying responses to the viewing of touch.[28]

All this took the empathetic implications of mirror theory directly into areas relevant to art. Damasio's hypothesis had already provided a framework for thinking about the viewer's physical involvement with the bodily reactions of the actors in a picture—whether imitating their gestures, having a sense of bodily weight in beholding certain postures, or seeing the objects that bear down, or threaten to bear down, on the protagonists of the scene. Gallese and Keysers, in describing the activation of the secondary somatosensory cortex when their subjects both viewed and experienced touch, raised questions about the kinds of empathetic pain that seem instantly to follow upon the sight of needles piercing the flesh or of even more cutting insults to the body.[29] This seemed to open new perspectives on the kind of sudden start that sometimes occurs when looking at pictures of martyrdom, or at the wounds of Christ in paintings of the Passion. The same sharp sense of empathetic understanding of physical pain may well occur, for example, in response to several of the etchings in Goya's *Desastres de la Guerra*—to say nothing of the photographic images from Abu Ghraib and the war zones of our times and those of others.[30]

But let us turn to a work of art that may serve to focus our attention on some of the key issues at stake: the relationship between bodily movement and the expression of emotion; the ways in which visual perception can turn into a viewer's sense of the weight, feel, and movements of represented bodies; and how emotion can be derived from its expression through movement. The central question is how adopting a perspective predicated on sight, movement, and emotion—rather than one predicated on memory of the story alone—allows for the integration of phenomenological responses with the *historical* claims for physical engagement with the artwork itself.

Rogier van der Weyden's *Descent from the Cross* was painted in the second half of the 1430s for the chapel of the Crossbowmen in the Church of Our Lady outside the Walls in Louvain, Belgium (figure 16.1).[31] On the face of it, the iconography is straightforward enough. Christ's body slumps down from the Cross. Nicodemus holds Him beneath His arms; Joseph of Arimathea lightly holds up His feet; and, from a ladder behind the Cross, a swarthy boy gently holds up His left arm. The Virgin Mary, supported

Figure 16.1
Rogier van der Weyden's *Descent from the Cross*. Deposition, ca 1436. Museo del Prado, Madrid, Spain.
Reproduced with permission from Erich Lessing, Art Resource, New York.

by John the Evangelist and Mary Cleophas, collapses in grief before Him; Mary Salome presses a handkerchief to her tears. On the right, the aged Joseph looks on, while Mary Magdalene, identified by the pot of unguent with which she washed Christ's feet, tightly clasps her hands together in an effort to contain her grief.

There can be no doubt about the artist's skill exhibited in the painting. The folds of every piece of cloth—but especially the whites—are painted with crisp precision; the variety of colors, some saturated, others delicate and subtle (like the lilacs and greens of the Magdalene's garments), testify to the technical prowess of a painter who paints almost every head of hair, every beard in a different way. But it is, above all, his command of the representation of the human body and his ability to convey emotion through bodily and facial expression that signal both Rogier's pictorial skill and the brilliance of his vision. Of course, such a painting was not just meant to impress with its art, but to arouse emotion as well. Made to go above an altar in chapel in a much-used church, it deliberately set out to engage the attention of *all* viewers in such a way that they would feel intimately involved in the scene, in the very suffering of Christ.

Drawing on a rich body of fifteenth-century sources, the art historian Otto von Simson showed how the then prevailing notion of compassion—literally "co-suffering"—was central to the interpretation of the *Descent from the Cross*. At the time it was painted, writers from Dionysius the Carthusian to Bernardino of Siena emphasized over and over again the physical and emotional involvement of the Virgin with the suffering of her Son.[32] Just a few years before the *Descent* was commissioned, a festival of the Compassion of the Virgin was established in Cologne, some 100 miles to the east. It institutionalized centuries of prayer and meditation on the subject of physical and mental compassion for the suffering of Christ.[33] In this tradition, Christ's torments became those of His mother, and writers constantly insisted, in the most graphic ways possible, on the Virgin's corporeal response, precisely in order to elicit the devotees' own affective responses.[34]

The painting shows how emotion can only be fully expressed through the body itself. Previously, painters had shown the Virgin standing or kneeling beside the cross, but in the *Descent*, she collapses in exactly the way Christ descends from the Cross. Rogier gave literal and physical expression to centuries of sentiment about her *compassio*, her sympathetic grieving for her Son by showing how she feels the wounds to His body in her own. Today the *Descent* hangs in the Early Flemish galleries of the Prado. In every respect, it is far from its original context—yet it continues to exert a powerful hold on its viewers. It is surely the sense of bodily presence (of Christ in particular), along with the gestural and physiognomic indices of emotion those bodies so powerfully convey, that continues to draw the attention of viewers of this work. When we see Christ's body slumping down from the Cross, we sense a slumping in our own bodies, and we notice how precisely the Virgin reenacts that same movement, as if to express her grief at the sight of her Son. Furthermore, when we see the gamut of emotions that are so poignantly registered both by the tears on the faces of protagonists of this drama and by the movements of their hands and limbs, we have an immediate sense of the muscular forces that drive these expressions of emotion.

It is often claimed that Rogier exceeded even Jan van Eyck, the great founder of the Early Netherlandish School of painting, in the representation of the emotions.[35] In particular, Rogier had the ability to paint actions and gestures in such a way as to make viewers feel as if they were engaging, or about to engage in, the very same actions and gestures themselves. Hence, for today's viewers, it may not just be the technical skill with which Rogier draws and handles the medium of paint that makes them feel so powerfully engaged in the scene. Instead it is also his ability to convey the outward signs of emotion on the faces of the participants in this drama, in such a way as to make viewers feel as if they are participating in the same emotions and movements themselves. They have no difficulty in recognizing the emotions quite precisely. They do not need to remember even fragmentary details of the story.

How might the new work on mirror neurons, on the corporeal bases of emotional response, and on the felt imitation of the actions of others contribute to a better understanding of the effects of Rogier's picture, especially in terms of viewers' understanding of the emotions of others (and specifically of those represented)? Its hold on its viewers, even in the fifteenth century, would most likely not have depended on knowledge of its subject matter, or even on personal experiences related to the emotional connotations of the scene or of the story represented. Rather, it would have depended, just as it does today, on a set of cortical responses that have

little to do with context, whether historical or connotative, but everything
to do with the connection between sight of the bodies and movements of
others and the viewers' sense of their own bodies and movements. Such
responses may well enhance emotional engagement in a way that in turn
enhances memory.[36] In this regard, following Shaun Gallagher, the body
shapes whatever it is that we call "mind."[37]

How the emotions can either disrupt or reinforce memory has been
much discussed both as a neuroscientific and as a psychological issue, the
latter in terms of repressed or exaggerated (retrospectively heightened)
recollection of trauma.[38] Painters intuitively knew that, by arousing the
emotions through the body, they could reinforce the forms of declarative
memory on which knowledge, say, of a biblical story depended. What is
significant in all such cases is the role of felt corporeal response in the
generation and sustenance of appropriate emotion. It was here that Rogier
excelled. By means of his skills in evoking empathetic response, his work
performed the first of Thomas Aquinas's three functions of art, present in
every aspect of medieval art and theory, namely, to reinforce memory.[39]
The efficacy of the visual arts (especially but not exclusively the static visual
arts) stems not just from the priming possibilities they offer (and the consequent facilitation of implicit memory), but also, mutatis mutandis, from
their ability to elicit the motoric bases of emotional response.

Whatever the formal and decorative attractions of Rogier's work, and
whatever the power its narrative draws from the biblical texts, the range
of emotion it evokes through bodily movement and posture remains its
most compelling feature. Such evocation is not predicated on knowledge
or recollection of the subject of the painting. It would have been activated, then as now, by clear and unconfused awareness of the emotional
expression of the actors in the scene (assuming, of course, that the
picture was well painted). This awareness depends on the activation
(through selective firing of neurons) of the same areas of the motor
cortex as those which *would have been* activated if the painted actors
had been living beings themselves. Understood from this perspective,
action understanding, embodied simulation, and immediate emotional
awareness are more important than declarative memory, the memory of
the details of the story.

Here two questions emerge: How is implicit procedural memory activated by vision? And how might emotional response be reinforced—rather

than activated—by the *combination* of long-term memory and what is now called "emotional memory"?[40] In both cases, deep cortical structures play a critical role: the amygdala in the case of emotional learning, and the cerebellum in the case of motor learning. At stake are not only the roles of the mediotemporal cortex and the hippocampus in memory storage, but the ways in which signals from them, just as those from the amygdala, are processed in the prefrontal cortex. Nevertheless, when it comes to the *continuing* effects of a work of art such as *Descent from the Cross*, what is significant is less the cognitive, prefrontally modulated aspects of memory than the direct amygdalar processing of visual signals (via the superior colliculus) and the multiple ways in which visuomotor signals are processed in the parietal cortex, in the cerebellum, and in the motor cortices—all prior to prefrontal modulation.

A crucial part of Rogier's skill lay in his ability to make his viewers instantly recognize the sadness of those whom he portrays by the evocation of corresponding feelings through the excitation of those parts of the brain responsible for the activation of corresponding movements of the body. In this way, the phenomenology of compassion meets—and reinforces—its iconography. It may be that the effectiveness of the image depends on how knowledge of the suffering of Christ and the recollection of similar (but never, in such scenes, equivalent) forms of travail reinforce preconceptual, precognitive forms of response in which no memory other than perhaps procedural plays a role. Here lies one of the most critical questions raised by the new cognitive neurosciences for the assessment of artistic skill: Does the success of an artwork such as *Descent from the Cross* depend on the artist's ability to evoke our direct emotional responses, irrespective of our historical knowledge? We might say that such an ability is a measure, not of the aesthetic, but rather of all effective images, artistic or not. But to consider the aesthetic independently of how cognition modulates the motoric dimensions of vision is to leave out a critical part of the story. The degree of an artist's skill in conveying conscious or unconscious bodily knowledge is not just a marker of efficacy but an aesthetic one as well.

In 1949, Donald Hebb suggested that emotion results when novel circumstances prevent completion of cued behavior. "Affects," wrote Peter Lang and Margaret Bradley, "are more often *dispositions* to action, than they are the acts themselves."[41] Lesser artists may simply be less good at evoking the motor responses that underlie appropriate emotion. Although a fair experiment might show how artists differ in their ability to use the same actions to arouse their correlative effects—or how the degree of arousal caused by the same actions differs in the hands of different artists—such effects are not confined to verisimilitudinous representations alone. Naturalism is not in itself a criterion of aesthetic quality or effectiveness. Indeed, it may even be an obstacle to it. After all, the suggestiveness of representation does not have to do with the realism of a work of art.

Moreover, there is another, rather different—yet not unrelated—argument against the role of verisimilitude and naturalism in the efficacy of images. It is certainly the case that the phenomenological claims about felt involvement in pictures have never been applied to verisimilitudinous representation alone. Merleau-Ponty devoted many pages to bodily responses to the implied forms of Cézanne's cubism. A strong case can now also be made for embodied responses to works by artists like Jackson Pollock and Lucio Fontana. What is at stake are the implied actions that lie behind—or, rather, that were necessary to execute—the traces of artists' actions on the canvas. A sense of felt bodily response arises not from any seen actions, but from implied ones, where the trace on the canvas or sculpture evokes a response that is predicated on the very actions that produced it. Many viewers have a sense of corporeal engagement with the implied movement of the brushstrokes on many of Pollock's canvases, as well as a felt reaction to Fontana's slashed and punctured canvases.

As for the defining question of gesture, in looking at Rogier's painting, and any number of other visual works, both religious or secular, two issues about the felt imitation of observed movement arise. The first concerns the emulative sense we have of the postures of others, of whole body movement and the consequent emotional feelings that such emulation may arouse or reinforce in ourselves. The second relates to the recognition of particular gestures as invested with particular emotions. The continued understanding of the meaning of such gestures, without any necessary knowledge of story or original function, poses a critical question about the relationship between human motoric capacity and culture.

Many of the non-goal-directed movements like the gestures in Rogier's painting seem to occur almost formulaically across the whole history of art. The question that arises is whether the emotions conveyed by such gestures are culturally conditioned, or whether—and this might explain why the gestures recur so frequently—their particular emotional and connotative freight is prior to and beyond cultural specificity. Examples come to mind: hands thrown up in distress (or sometimes in triumph), palms pressed together in supplication or prayer, the back of the hand wiped across the saddened or tear-filled eye—such as by the angels above Giotto's Padua *Lamentation*, in Claus Sluter's *Well of Moses*, and, to some degree, in Rogier's Louvain altarpiece. This last gesture seems entirely natural and spontaneous. We see it and immediately feel the grief that lies behind it. Thus what many scholars call "cultural memory" may have less to do with the conscious emotional understanding of such gestures than the embodied responses of mirror circuits to an action that is not goal-directed in the way that reaching for food or using an instrument may be.

One of the key concepts outlined by Aby Warburg was that of *Pathosformeln*, the ways in which the outward movements of the whole body were used in works of art to convey inner emotion—as suggested, for example, by Leon Battista Alberti and exemplified by Sandro Botticelli.[42] Warburg gave examples, on the basis of his reading of some remarkable passages about bodily movement in Alberti, of the ways in which the swaying bodies, vigorously flowing drapery, and hair flying in the breeze, conveyed inner states of psychic excitation.[43] Such formulaic movements can be traced back to ancient statues and reliefs, such as those showing the Maenads, the drunken followers of Bacchus. But the notion of *Pathosformeln* was then extended to the variety of apparently repeated gestures that seem to occur throughout the history of art.

Here we can see a role for Gallese's notion of embodied simulation, a form of simulation he regards as preconceptual.[44] Take, for example, Caravaggio's *Entombment of Christ*, in which (as is almost always the case with Caravaggio) emotional effect is significantly predicated on embodied responses. These are evoked by a variety of pictorial strategies, including the way in which the elbow of Joseph of Arimathea juts out into the spectator's space, for example (if you stand before this, you recognize it immediately), and thus commands attention. But what is perhaps most striking are the arms of the Virgin thrown up in a gesture of despair and grief. Does the impact of this gesture lie in its occurring so frequently in the history of art, or in its peculiarly effective way of arousing a sense of inward imitation? The gesture is easily recognizable not only from images of the *Entombment* and *Lamentation*, but also from images such as Goya's famous *Third May, 1808*.[45] It's the inverse of this gesture in, for example, the frontispiece to Goya's *Desastres* or Tyler Hicks's 1997 photograph of a mourning mother in Bosnia and raises similar questions about the relationship between the cultural freight of a gesture and the ways in which it is understood through the body.

For some time now, Fortunato Battaglia and I have been examining the corticomotor networks involved in responses to the sight of particular gestures. That the inward simulation of gestures was not covered by the mirror research led us to design a series of experiments investigating responses to the sight of represented movements. We used single- and paired-pulse transcranial magnetic stimulation (TMS) and more recently electroencephalograms (EEGs) to explore easily locatable cortical responses to the sight of a simple action, like the raising of the wrist.[46] It was then possible to examine subjects' cortical responses to the raising, for example, of Adam's hand in his confrontation with the Angel in Michelangelo's *Expulsion from Eden* in the Sistine Chapel.[47]

We showed subjects the painting itself, a photograph of the identical action, and then a movie of it, and found that sight of the painting and of the movie alone was sufficient to stimulate the same action. In other words, sight of the action in the painting or the movie enhanced the movement-evoked potential (MEP) of the muscle concerned. The effect was considerably weaker in the case of the photograph than in that of either the movie or Michelangelo's painting. We repeated the experiment with artworks that represent a high pitch of emotion—Bellini's *Dead Christ with Angels* in Santi Giovanni e Paolo in Venice, for example—but that show, not a tensed wrist, but a relaxed one. The fact that the movement-evoked potential (MEP) was lower in this case than in that of the Michelangelo painting was sufficient to demonstrate that the responses we found to Adam's gesture could be attributed to sight of the activated wrist alone, and not simply to emotional arousal.

Such experiments as well as a wide variety of phenomenological reports suggest that embodied simulation occurs abundantly in both goal-directed and non-goal-directed movements, such as those found in gestures in real life and as represented in art. What is critical here is not so much the emotional valence of gestures, but the very fact that sight of a gesture activates the same muscles in the viewer as in those of the figures represented, and that the same may be taken for the artist's marks on pictures and sculptures (because of the gestures they imply). Long-term memory is essential for the emotional valence of all gestures; but it is the inevitability of the activation that is crucial. Without this, the valence of the gesture would be limited. The kinds of felt imitation of movement described here suggest how traditional art historical views of imitation as representational mimesis might be expanded and reformu-lated.[48] For Ernst Gombrich, the ability to imitate pictorially depended on the retention of basic artistic schemata handed down by the tradition. These schemata formed the inevitable and indispensable basis for imita-tion conceived of as representational mimesis. But the kinds of imitation arising from sight of a work that implies movement were not anticipated by Gombrich—or by any earlier theorist. It is here that we must seek not only the roots of creativity but also ways of integrating into aesthetic experience a response that is liberated from the shackles of historical memory and personal experience. Despite the pressures of nostalgia, devotion, erudition, and a host of other factors that enter into any appre-ciation of a work of art, it is in this form of felt imitation and engagement of the cortical correlates of movement that some of the most redemptive qualities of art may lie.

This reformulation of the role of memory in aesthetics raises a series of potentially fruitful possibilities and opens up new areas of research. Most of the aesthetic questions remain. If we were to ask to what degree impair-ment of the classical cortical structures of memory—hippocampal, medio-temporal, even prefrontal—would impair emotional recognition (which I still consider, *pace* Collingwood, to be critical to the aesthetic assessment of a work of art), we would have to admit that the consequences would be significant. No one could reasonably exclude experience from aesthetics. But it becomes clear that the fruits of declarative memory might to some degree be dispensable when it comes to aesthetic experience and that it is in the domain of muscular possibility that we may discover what it is that makes certain images transcend the constraints of context and time. The question of procedural memory is fundamental here since implicit memory of bodily possibilities clearly plays a role in felt responses to what is seen in representation. Recently, Beatriz Calvo-Merino and colleagues described the distinctions between expert and nonexpert responses to dance, and to videos of dance, and made it clear that the effects of viewing on motoric circuits are enhanced by prior skill and training.[49] But they only briefly alluded to the ameliorative role that viewing might play on the enhancement of skills. This possibility is suggested by a multitude of other findings, beginning with those from Ramachandran's research on plasticity in the case of phantom limbs, where stimulation of somatosensory regions adjacent to those once associated with working limbs allows for the sensation of movement as if the lost limb itself were operant and functional.[50]

When phenomenology trumps iconography, so action recognition trumps memory—certainly declarative memory, possibly even implicit memory. Memory may often shape embodied responses, but the body shapes memory as well. In these processes, vision plays a central role. It is not just that vision can restore or refresh declarative long-term memory, whether in the case of a picture of Christ's Passion, for example, or a photo of a lost loved one. Even the ancients knew that sight could activate the other senses, but we now have a much clearer idea of how this happens. Thanks to the polymodal consequences of sight, viewing a work of art also restores some of what is truly lost—the vitality of body and hand—and endows movement with the possibilities of emotion. The analysis of how this happens helps to make sense of the relationship between art, memory, and the forces that move the body.

Notes

1. Of course, research on the nature and varieties of memory is vast. For up-to-date accounts of the neuroscience of memory, see *The Cognitive Neurosciences*, 3rd ed., ed. Michael S. Gazzaniga (Cambridge, MA: MIT Press, 2004), chaps. 47–53—a volume that includes a fine brief introduction by Daniel Schacter, whose crucial work on priming and memory is implicit throughout this chapter. See also Larry R. Squire and Eric R. Kandel, *Memory: From Mind to Molecules* (New York: Roberts, 2008).

2. For a survey of the neuroscience of such consequences, see David Freedberg, "Empathy, Motion and Emotion," in *Wie sich Gefühle Ausdruck verschaffen: Emotionen in Nahsicht*, ed. Klaus Herding and Antje Krause Wahl (Berlin: Driesen, 2007), 17–51. For a deeply knowledgeable introduction to some of the philosophical issues at stake on the basis of recent neuroscientific research, see Shaun Gallagher, *How the Body Shapes the Mind* (Oxford: Clarendon Press, 2005).

3. To some extent, the dialectic between these two kinds of responses is reflected in Walter Benjamin's famous remarks on the distinction between *Erfahrung* and *Erlebnis*. See Walter Benjamin, "On Some Motifs in Baudelaire," in *Selected Writings*, vol. 4, *1938–1940*, ed. Howard Eiland and Michael W. Jennings, trans. Edmund

Jephcott et al. (Cambridge, MA: Harvard University Press, 2003), 314 and 329–331, and the discussions in Jonathan Crary, *Suspensions of Perception: Attention, Spectacle, and Modern Culture* (Cambridge, MA: MIT Press, 2001). For a history of the concept of cultural memory, see also Miriam B. Hansen, "Room-for-Play: Benjamin's Gamble with Cinema," *October* 109 (2004): 3–45.

4. Of course, this in turn raises the question of fragmentary recollection, clearly relevant in the case of widely known biblical stories whose *details* have dropped from common memory.

5. For an excellent general introduction to the biology of learning, see Eric R. Kandel, *In Search of Memory: The Emergence of a New Science of Mind* (New York: Norton, 2006), chaps. 10–14.

6. By *iconography*, I mean all the varieties of iconographic understanding. For a basic summary of the possibilities, see Erwin Panofsky's famous introductory essay "Iconography and Iconology," in *Studies in Iconology: Humanistic Themes in the Art of the Renaissance* (Oxford: Oxford University Press, 1939), reprinted as the first chapter in Erwin Panofsky, *Meaning in the Visual Arts* (New York: Doubleday, 1955).

7. The classic study of patient HM is William B. Scoville and Brenda Milner, "Loss of Recent Memory after Bilateral Hippocampal Lesions," *Journal of Neurology, Neurosurgery and Psychiatry* 20 (1957): 1–21.

8. For good overviews of the biological bases of the conversion of short- to long-term memory, see Linda L. Chao and Alex Martin, "Representation of Manipulable Manmade Objects in the Dorsal Stream," *NeuroImage* 12 (2000): 478–484; Larry R. Squire and Eric R. Kandel, *Memory: From Mind to Molecules*, 2nd ed. (New York: Roberts, 2008).

9. See A. David Milner and Melvyn A. Goodale, *The Visual Brain in Action* (Oxford: Oxford University Press, 1995); Melvyn A. Goodale, "Perceiving the World and Grasping It: Dissociations between Conscious and Unconscious Processing," in *The Cognitive Neurosciences*, 1159–1172.

10. Already at the end of the nineteenth century, William James insisted on the interconnectedness of bodily movement and emotion, a theme taken up in a variety of illuminating and convincing ways by Antonio Damasio at the end of the twentieth. See William James, *The Principles of Psychology* (New York: Holt, 1890), 2: 738–766.

11. This, of course, is now an immensely rich and well-studied field. For groundbreaking, accessible accounts, see Joseph E. LeDoux, "Emotion and the Amygdala," in *The Amygdala: Neurobiological Aspects of Emotion, Memory and Mental Dysfunction*, ed. John P. Aggleton (New York: Wiley-Liss, 1992), 339–351; Joseph E. Le Doux, *The Emotional Brain. The Mysterious Underpinnings of Emotional Life* (New York: Simon & Schuster, 1996).

12. See Semir Zeki, *Inner Vision. An Exploration of Art and the Brain* (Oxford: Oxford University Press, 1999); Semir Zeki, "Neural Concept Formation and Art: Dante, Michelangelo, Wagner," *Journal of Consciousness* Studies 9 (2000): 53–76; Vilayanur S. Ramachandran, "The Science of Art: A Neurological Theory of Aesthetic Experience," *Journal of Consciousness Studies* 6 (1999): 6–7; Vilayanur S. Ramachandran, *A Brief Tour of Human Consciousness* (New York: Pi Press, 2004).

13. Changeux was one of the real pioneers in discussing the relationship between art and neuroscience. See Jean-Pierre Changeux, "Art and Neuroscience," *Leonardo* 27 (Fall 1994): 189–201; Jean-Pierre Changeux, *Raison et plaisir* (Paris: Odile Jacob, 1994); Jean-Pierre Changeux, *Du vrai, du beau, du bien* (Paris: Odile Jacob, 2008).

14. See David Freedberg, *The Power of Images: Studies in the History and Theory of Response* (Chicago: University of Chicago Press, 1989). Although *The Power of Images* was indeed about emotional and corporeal responses to works of art, its chief concern was the *symptoms* of such responses. It was not specifically about the relations between how things looked and how people responded to them, especially in light of so much new research about the activity of polymodal neurons, in particular, visuomotor and visuotactile neurons. See the brief outline in David Freedberg and Vittorio Gallese, "Motion, Emotion and Empathy in Aesthetic Experience," *Trends in Cognitive Science* 11 (2007): 197–203.

15. But the views of art historians on the role of emotion in art are rapidly changing. Among the many efforts at reintegration, see Klaus Herding and Bernhard Stumpfhaus, *Pathos, Affekt, Gefühl: Die Emotionen in den Künsten* (Berlin: De Gruyter, 2004); D. Freedberg, "Empathy, Motion and Emotion."

16. The work of Robert Vischer and Heinrich Wölfflin on the subject of empathy is now easily accessible in *Empathy, Form, and Space: Problems in German Aesthetics, 1873–1893*, ed. Harry F. Mallgrave and Eleftherios Ikonomou (Santa Monica, CA: Getty Center, 1994), 89–117, and 149–167. But see also the discussion in D. Freedberg, "Empathy, Motion and Emotion"; Juliet Koss, "On the Limits of Empathy," *Art Bulletin* 88 (2006): 139–157.

17. Theodor Lipps, "Einfühlung, innere Nachahmung, und Organempfindungen," *Archiv für die gesamte Psychologie* 1 (1903–1906): 185–204.

18. See Maurice Merleau-Ponty, *Phénoménologie de la perception* (Paris: Gallimard, 1945).

19. Antonio R. Damasio, *Descartes' Error: Emotion, Reason, and the Human Brain* (New York: Grosset/Putnam, 1994).

20. William James, *The Principles of Psychology* (New York: Holt, 1890).

21. Antonio R. Damasio, *The Feeling of What Happens: Body and Emotion in the Making of Consciousness* (Orlando, FL: Harcourt, 1999): 280–283; Antonio Damasio, *Looking for Spinoza: Joy, Sorrow and the Feeling Brain* (Orlando, FL: Harcourt, 2003), 115–118.

"As-if" responses seem to be fundamental to any aesthetic inquiry; for some stimulating comments on this possibility, see Nicholas Humphrey, *Seeing Red: A Study in Consciousness* (Cambridge, MA: Harvard University Press, 2006).

22. A. Damasio, *The Feeling of What Happens: Body and Emotion in the Making of Consciousness*; Vittorio Gallese, "The 'Shared Manifold' Hypothesis: From Mirror Neurons to Empathy," *Journal of Consciousness Studies* 8 (2001): 33–50. My own sense is that the concept of empathy were better confined to physical empathy—precisely because this may be predicated on procedural memory rather than just on episodic and semantic memory.

23. On the Parma group's initial discoveries, see Giacomo Rizzolatti et al., "Premotor Cortex and the Recognition of Motor Actions," *Cognitive Brain Research* 3 (1996): 131–141; Vittorio Gallese et al., "Action Recognition in the Premotor Cortex," *Brain* 119 (1996): 593–609. On the implications of these discoveries for art, see D. Freedberg and V. Gallese, "Motion, Emotion and Empathy in Aesthetic Experience." One of the very first neuroscientists to appreciate the importance of the discovery of mirror neurons for art was Jean-Pierre Changeux. See note 13.

24. G. Rizzolatti et al., "Premotor Cortex and the Recognition of Motor Actions"; V. Gallese et al., "Action Recognition in the Premotor Cortex." See also *Mirror Neurons and the Evolution of Brain and Language*, ed. Maxim I. Stamenov and Vittorio Gallese (Amsterdam: John Benjamins, 2002).

25. See Giacomo Rizzolatti, "Neurophysiological Mechanisms Underlying the Understanding of Action," *Nature Neuroscience Reviews* 2 (2001): 661–670; see also Giacomo Rizzolatti and Laila Craighero, "The Mirror Neuron System," *Annual Review of Neuroscience* 27 (2004): 169–192.

26. See Vittorio Gallese et al., "The Mirror Matching System: A Shared Manifold for Intersubjectivity," *Behavioral and Brain Sciences* 25 (2002): 35–36; Vittorio Gallese, Christian Keysers, and Giacomo Rizzolatti, "A Unifying View of the Basis of Social Cognition," *Trends in Cognitive Science* 8 (2004): 396–403.

27. Vittorio Gallese, "Embodied Simulation: From Neurons to Phenomenal Experience," *Phenomenology Cognitive Science* 4 (2005): 23–48.

28. Christian Keysers et al., "A Touching Sight: SII/PV Activation during the Observation and Experience of Touch," *Neuron* 42 (2004): 336–346. See also Sarah J. Blakemore et al., "Somatosensory Activations during the Observation of Touch and a Case of Vision-Touch Synaesthesia," *Brain* 128 (2005): 1571–1583.

29. C. Keysers et al., "A Touching Sight: SII/PV Activation during the Observation and Experience of Touch": 342–343.

30. In addition to the discussions by Antonio Damasio (see note 22), a vast literature on empathy has developed in recent years. For a useful discussion when viewing art, see Jean Decety and Philip L. Jackson, "The Functional Architecture of Human

Empathy," *Behavioral Cognitive Neuroscience Review* 3 (2004): 71–100; Philip L. Jackson, Andrew N. Meltzoff, and Jean Decety, "How Do We Perceive the Pain of Others? A Window into the Neural Processes Involved in Empathy," *NeuroImage* 24 (2005): 771–779. A vigorous debate has arisen in the last few years, led by researchers such as Tanya Singer and Chris Frith, about whether the neural substrate of viewers' physical responses to images evoking empathetic pain are located in the specific somatosensory areas correlative to the ones seen, or whether their responses are more generalized affective reactions. See Tania Singer et al., "Empathy for Pain Involves the Affective but Not Sensory Components of Pain," *Science* 303 (2004): 1157–1162. For earlier discussions of experiencing the pain of others, see Elaine Scarry, *The Body in Pain: The Making and Unmaking of the World* (New York: Oxford University Press, 1985); Susan Sontag, *Regarding the Pain of Others* (New York: Farrar, Straus and Giroux, 2003). But these works do not deal in any way with the specific effects of images, or the possibility of distinguishing the aesthetic markers of different kinds of images of emotion and pain. Nor do they consider the reinforcing effects of the memory of other images or iconographies, or the relationship between automatic, immediate, and spontaneous responses unmodulated by prefrontal assessment, on the one hand, and the recollection of similar images, on the other.

31. For a good modern monograph on Rogier, see Dirk de Vos, *Rogier van der Weyden: The Complete Works* (New York: Abrams, 1999).

32. See Otto G. von Simson, "Compassion and Co-redemption in Rogier van der Weyden's *Descent from the Cross*," *Art Bulletin* 35 (1953): 9–16.

33. For a summary of the various festivals and liturgical developments related to the compassion and sufferings of the Virgin, see Carol M. Schuler, "The Seven Sorrows of the Virgin: Popular Culture and Cultic Imagery in Pre-Reformation Europe," *Simiolus* 21 (1992): 5–28.

34. See also Sixten Ringbom, "Devotional Images and Imaginative Devotions," *Gazette des Beaux Arts* 73 (1969): 159–70; Sixten Ringbom, *Icon to Narrative: The Rise of the Dramatic Close-Up in Fifteenth Century Devotional Painting* (Doornspijk, Netherlands: Davaco, 1985).

35. There are other paintings in which Rogier's expressive skill is strongly manifest, such as the Miraflores altarpiece, where he shows the sad surprise of the Virgin upon encountering Christ after His resurrection or the great *Crucifixion* in Vienna, where he signs John, the swooning Virgin, and the sobbing Magdalene with the outward marks of grief.

36. For a recent summary and discussion of research on bodily responses and emotion, see Kevin S. La Bar and Roberto Cabeza, "Cognitive Neuroscience of Emotional Memory," *Nature Reviews Neuroscience* 7 (2006): 54–64; and, more generally, *Memory and Emotion: Interdisciplinary Perspectives*, ed. Bob Uttl, Nobua Ohta, and Amy Siegenthaler (Oxford: Blackwell, 2006).

37. See Shaun Gallagher, *How the Body Shapes the Mind* (Oxford: Clarendon Press, 2005).

38. For a review of the memory-enhancing effects of emotional arousal, see Kevin S. La Bar and Roberto Cabeza, "Cognitive Neuroscience of Emotional Memory," *Nature Reviews Neuroscience* 7 (2006): 54–64.

39. For versions of this position, see, for example, Jean Wirth, *L'image médiévale, naissance et développements, VIe–XVe siècle* (Paris: Méridiens Klincksieck, 1989); Jean Wirth, *L'image à l'époque romane* (Paris: Cerf, 1999).

40. See K. S. La Bar and R. Cabeza, "Cognitive Neuroscience of Emotional Memory"; see also Florin Dolcos, Kevin S. LaBar, and Roberto Cabeza, "The Memory Enhancing Effect of Emotion: Functional Neuroimaging Evidence," in *Memory and Emotion: Interdisciplinary Perspectives*, 107–134.

41. Peter J. Lang et al., "Motivated Attention: Affect, Activation and Action" in: Peter J. Lang, Robert F. Sions, and Marie Balaban, *Attention and Orienting: Sensory and Motivational Processes*, (Hillsdale, N.J.: Lawrence Erlbaum Associates, 1997). See also in this connection Margaret M. Bradley et al., "Remembering Pictures: Pleasure and Arousal in Memory," *Journal of Experimental Psychology: Learning, Memory and Cognition* 18 (1992): 379–390.

42. Aby Warburg, "Sandro Botticellis 'Geburt der Venus' und 'Frühling,'" in *The Renewal of Pagan Antiquity: Contributions to the Cultural History of the European Renaissance*, trans. David Brett (Los Angeles: Getty Research Institute for the History of Art and the Humanities, 1999), 95–156; on *Pathosformeln*, see Aby Warburg, "Francesco Sassetti's Last Injunctions to His Sons of 1907," in *The Renewal of Pagan Antiquity: Contributions to the Cultural History of the European Renaissance* (Los Angeles: Getty Research Institute for the History of Art and the Humanities, 1999), where *Pathosformeln* is simply translated as "emotive formulas."

43. For the passages from Alberti's *Della Pittura* of 1435, see A. Warburg, "Sandro Botticellis 'Geburt der Venus' und 'Frühling,'" 95–196.

44. V. Gallese, "Embodied Simulation: From Neurons to Phenomenal Experience."

45. To what degree can we draw a necessary connection between the gesture and the emotion, irrespective of its social and historical context? Standard gestures for standard emotions, in the manner implied by both Charles Darwin and Paul Ekman, may offer a significantly useful tool for the interpretation of works of art, especially in the absence of further knowledge about them, and in images where the only memories evoked are procedural and implicit.

46. As described in Fortunato Battaglia and David Freedberg, "Art, Imagination and Reality: The Cortical Motor Networks" (forthcoming); the EEG results are presented in Daria Arienzo et al., "Functional Networks Underlying Motor Facilitation during Movement Observation" (forthcoming). See also Fausto Baldissera et al.,

"Modulation of Spinal Excitability during Observation of Hand Actions in Humans," *European Journal of Neuroscience* 13 (2001): 190–194.

47. My hope was to examine a more complex movement, such as the raising of arms in despair or joy, or even still more complex sets of movements, such as those of figures engaged in dance, but testing for felt imitative responses by means of transcranial magnetic stimulation (TMS) would almost certainly be too difficult—there were simply too many different somatotopic areas to locate.

48. See Martin Kemp, "From 'Mimesis' to 'Fantasia': The Quattrocento Vocabulary of Creation, Inspiration and genius in the Visual Arts," *Viator* 8 (1977): 347–398; D. Freedberg, "Imitation and Its Discontents," in *Künstlerischer Austausch / Artistic Exchange: Akten des XVIII Internationalen Kongresses für Kunstgeschichte, Berlin, 1992*, ed. Thomas W. Gaehtgens (Berlin: Akademie Verlag, 1993), 483–491. For a survey of current views on the felt imitation of observed movement, see the excellent volume *Perspectives on Imitation: From Neuroscience to Social Science*, ed. Susan Hurley and Nick Chater (Cambridge, MA: MIT Press, 2005).

49. Beatriz Calvo-Merino et al., "Action Observation and Acquired Motor Skills: An fMRI Study with Expert Dancers," *Cerebral Cortex* 15 (2004): 1243–1249; see also Beatriz Calvo-Merino et al., "Configural and Local Processing of Human Body in Visual and Motor Areas," *2006 Neuroscience Meeting Planner* (Society for Neuroscience Online, 2006, program number 438.5/H2) at http://www.sfn.org/am2006/, who note, "The greater familiarity of experts with their own movement style may lead to stronger activation of brain mechanisms of episodic memory, even when watching another person."

50. See Vilayanur S. Ramachandran and William Hirstein, "The Perception of Phantom Limbs," *Brain* 121 (1998): 1603–1630; Vilayanur S. Ramachandran and Diane Rogers-Ramachandran, "Phantom Limbs and Neural Plasticity," *Archives of Neurology* 57 (2000): 317–320.

17 Memory in Musical Form: From Bach to Ives

David Michael Hertz

Music, the art that unfolds in time, works by triggering the memory. Without memory, musical cognition is not possible. Cognition in music depends on the psychological process of preparing for what is to come by remembering what has already happened. Ernst Hans Gombrich has described this process as "forward matching," whereby each new musical event is compared and contrasted to past ones. The ability to recognize repetition and variation is the key to cognition in music. It is an ability that requires the matching of new musical events with past ones.

The shapes of musical form, and the types of mnemonic cues within them, vary as musical styles evolve. Johann Sebastian Bach, Ludwig van Beethoven, Wolfgang Amadeus Mozart, and Joseph Haydn carefully crafted repetition into their preludes, fugues, sonatas, and other musical forms to balance the complex mental processes necessary for fully functioning memory, including both short- and long-term memory. Although Beethoven wrote long-term memory into musical structure in new ways, bringing the act of remembering clearly into his compositions, his architectonic sense of form based in tonality still dominated all musical activity. The older structural hierarchies of the Baroque and Classical periods began to unravel with Robert Schumann, who experimented with new harmonic freedoms, instrumental color, and texture in his most radical cyclic pieces. Following him, the Romantics invented more idiosyncratic formal schemes to integrate short-term memory and other faculties of memory, although they retained the phrase structure and tonal language even as they undermined it. With Claude Debussy, the integration of rhythm, pitch, and timbre could no longer be counted on as a coordinated plan to prompt memory, especially in terms of organizing musical architecture with a teleological structure. Arnold Schoenberg and Igor Stravinsky introduced even more radical innovations. Finally, with Charles Ives, music became the site of memory itself, as older forms of music, now appearing as "memory-fragments," were recalled within a Modernist structure.

Although research has shown that the visual arts depend on temporal scanning,[1] all forms of visual art—whether in two dimensions (paintings or drawings) or in three (sculpture or architecture)—have the complete pattern presented in place, allowing the eye to refer to various points of comparison. In sharp contrast, music, like poetry, depends on memory, since scanning backward and forward in time is not possible. But poetry establishes meaning within the larger culture of language, with all of its symbolic processes, while music, unique among the arts, relies chiefly on self-reference to its own structures to establish meaning.

Sequence, Motive, Melody, and Other Types of Forward Matching

Celebrated for his work on the intersection of art and the psychology of perception, art historian E. H. Gombrich also possessed a deep knowledge of European musical culture. He was trained as a cellist and grew up in a musical family. Gombrich brought his interests in music and art together in a late book, *The Sense of Order*, in which he explains how musical cognition requires an aural forward matching that both resembles and differs from the eye's temporal scanning in visual cognition. For Gombrich, *forward matching* is the internal neural patterning that balances with "the regularities of the external movement," which he likens to adjusting our posture while in a saddle to the movements of a galloping horse.[2] We prepare for what is to come by judging what has already happened. Music continually plays on this continual adjustment of the mind as it gets ready for future sound events, at some times giving us the expected, and at many others, the unexpected. Will symmetry and resolution be granted, or will they be denied for further adventure? The composer knows how to make these questions continually exciting. Sometimes listeners may be successful at predicting what will happen, and sometimes not. Without the interplay of memory, this would not be possible.

The simplest and probably the oldest device in music for extending musical form into time is the echo, usually described by musicians as "literal imitation" of earlier sound at the same pitch level. Such imitation is also the simplest form of forward matching in music. The canon, which is basically an overlapping echo, may have evolved from the natural phenomenon of the echo. Canons range in complexity from "Row, Row, Row Your Boat" to the sublime canon on the unison in J. S. Bach's *Goldberg Variations* (1741). Next in complexity is the sequence, in which the same musical idea is repeated at *different* pitch level, with no canonic overlap. A good example of sequence without canonic overlapping is Mozart's aria for the Queen of the Night in *The Magic Flute* (*Die Zauberflöte*; 1791), where the vowel sounds of the great solo are repeated at different pitch levels. The motive, the smallest unit of musical structure, is related to the sequence. The most famous example of a motive is probably the first four notes of the Beethoven's Fifth Symphony, which quickly appear at many different pitch levels in the opening bars of the symphony, giving listeners an immediate sense of the symphony's coherence and propulsive power.

Sometimes these elements combine in novel ways. For example, Bach also includes eight more canons in his *Goldberg Variations*, which repeat a musical idea at every interval from the second to the ninth, essentially combining elements of the canon and sequence in some of the most intricate musical structures every devised. Repetition by echo (imitation at pitch), canon, motive, and sequence, designed to stimulate the short-term memory, enables listeners to grasp and remember a short musical idea. Without these types of encoded repetition, the masterworks of Bach, Mozart, Haydn, and Beethoven would not have been possible, and neither would many of the large-scale musical compositions of the Romantic period, which immediately followed the Classical. In these later compositions, memory is prompted by what might be called "sound architecture." A clear musical form is presented in time, then re-presented in different ways, but the clear shape is always discernible. The initial presentation of the motivic form is the code of the piece, generating the shapes to come. Musical shapes form into symmetrical units, most commonly in phrases of two, four, eight, sixteen, and thirty-two bars. The even numbers in the structures of the phrases are further proof that the composers who wrote them knew they were intended to be easy to remember. Short-term memory (about 15–20 seconds) is carefully prompted to project into larger time frames, aiding the collaborative functioning of the different parts of the brain, which recent research has shown to be required for the memory process (see chapter 18 in this volume).[3]

A melody occurs when a composer forms a single musical line that dominates all other musical activity, including rhythm and harmony. By its very nature, a melody is a series of notes that is particularly likely to be remembered, sometimes even forming what has been described by Oliver Sacks as a "brainworm," a musical segment that sounds incessantly in the mind, day and night.[4] Although experienced by many musicians, when such brainworms disrupt sleep or other activities, they can become pathological, as Sacks illustrates.

Every composer who wants to write music that is impossible to forget knows that echo and sequence, proportion and symmetry, and attention to the tendency of musical pitches to organize around a central pitch, or tonality, are crucial to most melodies. Most melodies are short, from eight to thirty-two bars, but some are longer, spinning out into musical time for an extended period, as many as fifty-six bars or more. A good example of one with carefully crafted repetition is the sixteen-bar melody Beethoven composed for his "Ode to Joy." With its stepwise motion (no difficult leaps), simple AABA format, and frequent reiteration of its tonal pitch (D), it is easy both to sing and to remember. It sounds uncannily familiar even on first hearing. But this is just what Beethoven, who worked extremely hard to craft such melodies, intended—and just what he needed to build on for the colossal last movement of his Ninth Symphony (1824), with its complex choral interludes.

The first prelude in Bach's *Well-Tempered Clavier*, Book One (1722) has the simplest form of Gombrich's "forward matching." Eight notes are stretched out in time to outline a chord, and then played exactly again. Then comes a new chord and then it, too, is played again (figure 17.1).

The first eight notes of the prelude prepare the ear for the second iteration of eight notes. The second affirms the importance of the first. Each chord, always repeated immediately, has a clear function and description within the framework of C major, the tonality that is clearly articulated at the beginning and the end of the piece. Each new chord is sounded exactly

Figure 17.1
Bach Prelude no. 1, measures 1–3, from the *Well-Tempered Clavier*, Book One. Reproduced from *Das Wohltemperirte Clavier*, p. 3 in Volume 14 of *Johannn Sebastian Bachs Werke*, published by the Bach-Gesellschaft, Leipzig, 1866.

twice, always taking up eight notes and always referring to the overall organizing key of C. Aural satisfaction is achieved with each repetition of the expected rhythmic unit, matched against the first. This elemental type of forward matching, a highly structured, written-out form of an echo, is easy to discern.

An unfolding section of musical time, even one as clear as the Bach prelude excerpt, is not like a spatial form in architecture, where there is a demarcated area that can be visually scanned and compared to another symmetrically balanced area. In a spatial form, the evidence is always there, available for comparison and contrast in the present, whereas, in a temporal form, the evidence is heard and then gone. In a musical performance, various types of memory are called into play. Our emotional response to repetition should not be underestimated; it is a powerful element of musical cognition. When Bach writes something twice, the second iteration has a role quite different from the first.[5] Spatial relations are everywhere in musical style, but they can only be understood and expressed with metaphor. This is because musical space is contingent on the mutable experience of passing time. For this reason, it is probably most accurate to think of musical forms as temporal shapes.

That the repetition comes at a later point in time, even if immediately after, makes it different. If the motive of the prelude is played without the repetition, the prelude loses all of its hypnotic power. Why does it sound so bad without the repetition? The answer has much to do with how we remember sound. Bach begins his first prelude in his masterwork collection of twenty-four preludes and fugues by stimulating short-term memory.

In the intricate fugue that follows the prelude in C major, Bach's elusive theme, remarkably open ended and harmonically ambiguous, in contrast with the fixed chordal shapes of the prelude, is interwoven twenty-four times into the piece in an intricate contrapuntal texture (a subtle compositional statement of his intention to explore all twenty-four keys of the clavier). There are *stretti* (literally, "narrowings") in which many entries are heaped together to build up to a climax, one of the features of the great Baroque fugue in general. The entries of the theme, first heard spread out spaciously in time and sounded separately in each voice (with no overlap), soon come more frequently, eventually seeming to be everywhere. Memory of the initial sounding of the theme enables us to understand the increasing drama as we hear the many entries of the theme crowded together.

Occurring at different pitch levels and beginning at different instances, they create a staggered pattern. No average musician could have predicted the intricate *stretti* of Bach's fugue, and only Bach could have written them. But he has prepared his listeners and students (the preludes and fugues were originally written for study, not public performance) with the careful presentation of his fugue theme in different voices.

As the simple echoes in Bach's prelude illustrate, the great composers can captivate listeners with startling simplicity. But they can also challenge our ability to remember with a complexity that we can understand only with study, even though the psychological process of remembering musical sounds is in play whether we understand that complexity or not. One example of this in the family of musical forms is the *cancrizans*, where a pattern is played in reverse. Thus in this form a pattern of notes first played in the order ABCD, for example, is then played in the order DCBA. Such musical reversal, though it resembles the balanced stasis of symmetrical patterns in the visual arts, also differs in one crucial respect—DCBA is played at a later point in time than ABCD.

Very few listeners can discern the complex *cancrizans* in the fugue of Beethoven's Piano Sonata no. 29 in B-flat major (*Hammerklavier*, op. 106; 1817–18), for example. Here the intricate fugal theme is played backward and at different pitch levels. Only the rare musician with unusual aural abilities can absorb this on the first hearing or clearly relate the backward version of the theme to a clear recalling of the initial theme, last played in its full form about two minutes before. Still, even those who have neither musical education nor special aural abilities can probably sense the music's coherence and unity from the architectonic shape of the reversed version of the theme, which is rhythmically similar to its original form.

Beethoven's Sense of Time and Memory

The great master of time in musical form, Beethoven makes memory itself a subject for expression in his works, opening up new paths later taken by the Romantics and the moderns. As Charles Rosen explains in his published Norton lectures: "Beethoven is the first composer to represent the complex process of memory—not merely the sense of loss and regret that accompanies visions of the past, but the physical experience of calling up the past within the present."[6] Or, in neuroscientific terms, he is the first composer to express the activation of long-term memory (hours to days to years) in musical form, using intermediate-term memory (minutes to hours) to create the effect of calling up events from the remote past.[7]

Beethoven took the simple Classical structures he inherited from Haydn and Mozart and stripped them down to the bare minimum, allowing the propulsive force of simple ideas to project forward into time. More than any other composer before or after him, Beethoven made the forward push of time his main compositional concern—which is to say, he made music teleological. In the music he wrote from 1800 to 1810, he expressed the quickened pace of "felt time," as George Steiner once put it, a musical innovation possibly stimulated by the upheavals of the Napoleonic wars.[8] But, in developing his new method, Beethoven eventually found it necessary to change the interaction of short- and long-term memory in musical form.

It was, in fact, Joseph Haydn, Beethoven's master teacher, who first introduced the recalling of a theme in different movements of a Classical musical composition.[9] Beethoven developed it into something more, and it became a norm in his late works. We first find the introduction recalled in both the development and recapitulation of the first movement of his *Sonata Pathétique* (op. 13; 1797–98). This is an early version of Beethoven's expression of recalling a past even in the present. It then appears in later, more important works: his Fifth Symphony (1807–8), his *An die ferne Geliebte* (op. 90; 1818), with which he invented the song cycle and perhaps also his miraculous "late style" (*spät Stil*), and, notably, in his Ninth Symphony (1824), where Beethoven forces his listeners to remember each of the first three movements before he presents his "Ode to Joy" and the final movement. The expansion of forms he devised toward the end of his life created new ways to express memory in music and new ways to use it. Piano Sonatas no. 28 (op. 101; 1816) and no. 31 (op. 110; 1821) are important examples of these innovations in musical form and memory. In opus 101, the lyrical first movement is recalled just before the boisterous last movement, first literally, then as remembered fragments that are something like stream of consciousness in musical sound. In opus 110, the great fugue comes back upside down and augmented (spread out in expanded time values), recurring in new ways that are more accessible to forward matching than the *cancrizans* of the *Hammerklavier*.

The Austrian musicologist Viktor Zuckerkandl believed that we enter a kind of "expanded now" when we sing a melody: "The hearing of a melody is a hearing *with* the melody. ... It is even a condition of hearing melody that the tone present at the moment should fill consciousness *entirely*."[10] But that is not the complete story of musical memory. Oliver Sacks has made this distinction obvious in his account of a number of musicians who have sustained serious brain damage, including partial amusia (the inability to recognize or reproduce musical tones), but who can nonetheless continue to function as musicians in at least some limited sense.[11]

Sacks's description of the impaired skills of these musicians is reminiscent of William James's "specious present." It was James who wrote that "the practically cognized present is no knife-edge, but a saddle-back,"[12] which is closely related to Zuckerkandl's notion of the presentness of melody, contingent on the mental ability to match sounds in the present with those extending a few seconds back in time and also to forward match sounds in the present with those a few seconds ahead in time. The impaired musicians seem to have retained strong short-term memory skills, musically stuck in the specious present. But memory in music is not just about the contiguous association of notes, necessary for playing a melody, a single line, or a short piece. Research now shows that it requires an interrelation of skills and the activity of several areas of the brain. To absorb new and unexpected sounds as well as contiguous and similar musical events, we must also be able to employ our *episodic memory*, which Oliver Sacks defines as "a conscious memory of events." Long stretches of remembered time have to be accounted for. The final movement of the Fifth Symphony with its endless series of crashing C chords makes no sense without the remembered context of the astonishing first movement, with its famous reiterated four notes (figure 17.2).

The sound experience of this last movement, in the phenomenology of realized performance, includes all the movements in between, including a long and slow theme and variations followed by a rich and varied scherzo. In one of the most innovative moments in the history of music, following a long, suspended pedal transition from the scherzo to the ebullient finale, Beethoven creates "the physical experience of calling up the past within the present"[13] when the scherzo is recalled in the final allegro. Only after it is remembered in musical time, only after the piece quotes from itself, does the rush to the finish of the last movement finally begin.

In the last 30 seconds of this gigantic symphony, there are fifty bars of just two chords, dominant and tonic, with a few measures of silence

Figure 17.2
Beethoven's Fifth Symphony, first movement, measures 1–20, in Liszt's piano reduction.
Reproduced from *Symphonies de Beethoven, Partition de Piano, par Franz Liszt*, p. 169.
Leipzig: Breitkopf and Härtel, 1865.

distributed here and there. The last twenty-nine bars are only repeated C chords, tonic chords (just one repeated sonority) together with four bars of silence (our ringing ears still hear the C chords then). To some, this aspect of Beethoven is obsessive, but it could also be argued that the driving power of the famous first movement, in which the best-known four notes in history are propelled through almost every bar, needs to be balanced and resolved and summed up. The overall time it takes to perform the symphony is about 33 minutes. The time span between the last "duh-duh-duh-*dah*" of the first movement and the final, heavily repetitious closing sections (Allegro and Presto) of the symphony is about 28 minutes. Our memory of the musical events demands balance. There can be no other justification for the excessive repetition.

Equipped with the knowledge of a few innovative moments in the music of Joseph Haydn, Beethoven started a revolution in European musical form by going beyond the strictures of movements into cyclic memory in a sustained exploration, one that intensified as he evolved into his late period. When Beethoven began his career, musical forms in the sonata were presented, developed, resolved, and then dispensed with as the composition went from one movement to the next. When he finished, things were completely different. Cognition of musical form now required new interactions of short- and long-term memory. Despite his innovations, however, Beethoven inscribes memory in a highly structured manner, using his forms to heighten the gravitational pull of tonality. Tonal focus was the most important mnemonic device in his music. His clear reference to keys and symmetrical phrases make his music easy to remember. He always justifies every note in his musical architecture in relation to a clearly established central tonality—and to the triad of tonic, mediant, and dominant pitches built on it—that functions as a center of gravity for all his composed sounds.

Short-Term Memory and the Romantic Attack on Musical Form

Robert Schumann launched an attack on the architectonic structure of the Classical style, which had been brought to its zenith by Beethoven. Although he also drew on certain innovations he found in late Beethoven, extending them and expanding their implications. Schumann was a composer interested in literary structure, which perhaps contributed to his strange cyclic forms. We remember Schumann today, not for his sonatas, which are mediocre when compared to Beethoven's, but for his collections of character pieces, revolutionary masterpieces that represent a concentrated attack on Beethoven's musical forms. The assault was carried out in the 1830s, when Schumann produced his *Papillons* (op. 2; 1831), *Davidsbundlertänze* (op. 6; 1837), *Carnaval* (op. 9; 1834–35), *Fantasiestücke* (op. 12; 1837), *Kinderszenen* (op. 15; 1838), and *Kreisleriana* (op. 16; 1838), along with other, less famous works. It culminated with the great *Fantasie* (op. 17; composed in 1836–38, but not published until 1839), a piece written as a memorial to Beethoven that even quotes some of his music, a melody from the song cycle *An die ferne Geliebte*. This is one of several important cases of musical memory connecting two pieces of music, where one great composer specifically quotes the music of another, repositioning the earlier music in a distinctly different, freshly created musical texture.

Davidsbundlertänze (1837) offers intriguing examples of how Schumann encodes memory in a musical composition in a very different way from Beethoven or Mozart. Here we no longer have an organized sonata, a well-crafted form designed to direct memory in carefully channeled ways. Instead, we have eighteen interconnected character pieces that require some 35 minutes to perform. Here form almost breaks down, but not quite. Rather than appearing in separate boxes of time called "movements," musical forms now accumulate organically, with reference to the past as needed. After the first piece is performed, its musical ideas are set aside, never to be replayed in the later sections of the composition. But the second piece, the important one for this musical form, is then exactly quoted in the seventeenth or penultimate piece, where it builds into a tremendous climax in B minor. For its part, the last piece, which seems to be about something completely different, is in a completely different key—the wrong key according to the memory codes of Classical form—C major, which sends the ear in a completely new direction. Beethoven, who had died in 1827, less than a decade before Schumann produced this strange work, surely would have been horrified.

Schumann's experiments with memory and form in music gave artistic expression to his bipolar musical personality, for which Schumann invented two imaginary literary characters, Florestan (the fiery madman-adventurer) and Eusebius (the dreamy poet). Thus Schumann signed each piece of the *Davidsbundlertänze* with the initial of one or the other side of his personality, using an "F" for Florestan or an "E" for Eusebius. Sometimes the two collaborated and Schumann signed a piece with both initials (four in the set of eighteen are signed "F and E").

Rebellious as he was, Schumann followed Beethoven as a slavish disciple in one important detail. If anything, using motives to stimulate short-term memory was more important in Schumann than it was in Beethoven, as is clear in Schumann's great *Fantasie*, which even quotes from Beethoven's song cycle. But Schumann knowingly undermined the clear architectonic structures of the earlier Classical forms by creating his revolutionary new cycles of character pieces. That is probably why he at first planned to call the *Fantasie* by another title—*Ruines* (*Ruins*). It was Schumann who instigated the rebellion against teleology in music, championing the sensuous present as the norm for musical form. In various ways, Frédéric Chopin, Franz Liszt, Richard Wagner, and Johannes Brahms followed his example.

Memory Fragments and the Modernist Rebellion

Schumann had started something that could not be stopped. For the French group of composers led by Claude Debussy and Maurice Ravel, who concentrated on the sensuous pleasures of sound, the forward thrust of time was not important. This change in musical purpose can be most specifically attributed to Debussy's innovations of the late nineteenth century. Upon hearing a Beethoven symphony, Debussy once said, "Ah, the development section is beginning; I can go out for a cigarette."[14] In addition to being one of the great composers Debussy was also a brilliant critic who knew exactly how to pinpoint the weakness of the great Beethoven. He repeatedly poked fun at Beethoven's architectonic forms and was especially critical of the late sonatas. Why so much repetition? Why must a theme always be developed with a long series of exact or close to exact repetitions or sequences? Debussy continued Schumann's attack on the balanced interplay of short- and long-term memory in the forms of Beethoven. His breakthrough masterpiece, the *Prélude à l'après-midi d'un faune* (1892), which unquestionably established his emergence as a great composer, is based on a continuously evolving theme first played in the flute. It is a notoriously difficult work to analyze, let alone to comprehend on a first hearing. There are no easy forward matching aids for the first-time listener in this Debussy piece. It takes work to unravel the form. Inspired by Stéphane Mallarmé's poem "L'Après-midi d'un faune," a poem about the birth of music out of the spirit of desire, Debussy's piece is a prelude to the poem, not an exact setting of the text. It was composed a short time after Debussy heard Javanese gamelan music at the 1889 World Exposition in Paris. Some of its distinctive features are its new sense of slow-motion time, perhaps inspired by gamelan theater performance, and the odd juxtaposition of solo and ensemble sounds, so unlike Western orchestration, transparent and rich at the same time. Instead of traditional development, the faun theme undergoes kaleidoscopic transformations. It never goes away, appearing sometimes in the unstable C-sharp to G tritone, sometimes in more harmonious fourths. E major appears at the end as a final sigh of resignation. The tonality of the theme and its balanced symmetrical repetition no longer reinforce the prompting of memory within the score, as it had in Beethoven. Listeners had to navigate Debussy's newly asymmetrical patterns and find a way to make sense of them. This is why the piece horrified some of the first distinguished critics who heard it.

Debussy opened the path to the new music and to new intersections of music and memory. Arnold Schoenberg and Igor Stravinsky, two of the greatest musical Modernists, both decided to deny (but in different ways) the usual paths of memory prompting in musical forms by avoiding tonal tension and resolution and even the centuries-old tradition of sequence making. It was the sequence that made forward matching easy on the listening mind; that ease would end with Modernism. Famous examples of the assault on the sequence are Schoenberg's *Pierrot Lunaire* and Stravinsky's *Petrouchka*. Isolated pitches and patterns of timbre in *Pierrot Lunaire* (1912), written in Schoenberg's Expressionist period, are promoted to new importance, breaking away from the clearly structured sequencing of older music. Schoenberg even challenges the importance of pitch, creating strange moans and cries with his new "speak-voice" (*Sprechstimme*). *Pierrot Lunaire* is written for voice and chamber orchestra, and its singer must slip and slide up and down the scale every time Schoenberg writes an *x* in the score. Schoenberg completes the divorce between rhythmic repetition and tonal repetition; timbre becomes as important as pitch and even the human voice is newly valued, as much for tone color as for its ability to hit a specific note on a scale or in a key. This is what makes it hard for listeners' short-term memory to be stimulated. Hard, that is, but not impossible, for Schoenberg, too, finds a way to repeat musical events and textures for emphasis and meaning.

Stravinsky also launched an attack on traditional repetition in music in his early masterpieces for the ballet, fragmenting musical rhythm into frequently changing patterns. All of this made musical forms harder to remember. Stravinsky is in this one respect even more radical than Schoenberg because he undermines the unity of the motive. Stravinsky's famous Russian Dance from *Petrouchka* (1911) is an example of a Modernist attack on the traditional sequence of music in the Classical style. The opening motive is always changing and yet part of it is always the same. The little changes make it difficult for the musician to memorize. Also, Stravinsky writes much of the score in two simultaneous keys, C and F-sharp, a famous early example of twentieth-century bitonality. This bitonality makes pitch less important than it was in Beethoven, pulling rhythm and pitch away from its traditionally collaborative function in orienting the listeners' memory. Now two keys compete with each other, making pitch less important for mnemonic cues, which, again, made it harder for the mind to know what to remember. The ear is sent, after all, in two directions at once. Chords seem scattered and stagnant, no longer linked by the gravitational pull of a harmonic structure in a clear tonality.

Perhaps an even more radical assault on the traditional appeal to the powers of memory in musical form was launched by the American composer Charles Ives. In his compositions, Ives supplants the clearly structured sequences of an architecture unfolding in time with a new sense of musical organization. He inserts older music, music written by others, often in the form of fragmented sequences into his new musical scores. He pulls apart the older music, cutting it up into fragments so he can examine it as part of his composing process. Eventually, he puts it back together again, but in an entirely new way. Ives evokes a remembering mind calling up the past in the musical present. We hear him thinking about remembered sound. We hear him engaging in the activity of memory itself. Expressing the process of musical cognition becomes a central concern of Ives's compositional design.

The effect may at first seem like a collage of sound, but it is more complex than that. Ives creates a Modernist context in his new musical work for reconsidering and reevaluating the music of the past. Ives's freshly composed music seems to be ruminating on remembered older music. This older music is drawn from his cultural heritage, a mixture of American popular music and European masterworks from the nineteenth century. Ives's Piano Sonata no. 2, *Concord, Mass., 1840–1860*, commonly known as the *Concord Sonata* (and composed chiefly between 1911 and 1920), features the most obvious example of what musicologist James Hepokoski has called a "connotationally loaded memory-fragment"—the first four notes of Beethoven's Fifth Symphony.[15] The sonata is a kind of musical Mount Rushmore, made up of movements dedicated to Ives's favorite American transcendentalist writers: "Emerson, "Hawthorne," "The Alcotts" and "Thoreau," "Emerson," the daunting first movement, alone takes some 17 minutes to perform, and the entire sonata almost an hour. Beethoven's music is quoted throughout "Emerson" (and in the other three movements), but much more conspicuously than in the music of Schumann. From the first moments of "Emerson," the famous four notes of Beethoven's Fifth Symphony resound in a thicket of middle-range voices, rumble in the bass, or erupt in the upper reaches of the piano. Finally, in the closing moments, the Fifth Symphony "memory-fragment" occurs in a haunting coda of mysterious echoes (figure 17.3), forming a powerful conclusion to the piece. But the harmonic relationships of Beethoven's four notes have been pulled apart in startling new ways. There is no organizing C minor. Now the sounds of Beethoven are recast to indicate new musical dimensions that Beethoven could never have imagined, quartertone relationships and pitches beyond the limitations of the piano.

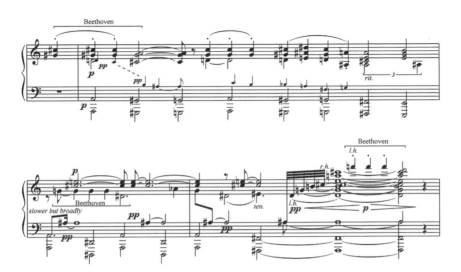

Figure 17.3
Ives's "Emerson" coda showing quotations from Beethoven's Fifth Symphony.
Reproduced from Piano Sonata no. 2 (Concord Sonata) by Charles Ives. Copyright
© 1976 (Renewed) by Associated Music Publishers, Inc. (BMI). International Copyright Secured. All Rights Reserved. Used by Permission.

Later, in the far more accessible third movement ("The Alcotts"), we
hear Beethoven's Fifth again. Here Ives has merged it with a tune from a
Protestant hymnal, the *Missionary Chant* of H. Charles Zeuner, a short
choral work with a highly similar rhythmic structure, but obviously written
to be performed at a much slower tempo and in a humble New England
church setting. At the climax of "The Alcotts" movement, he merges the
two with another melodic fragment, one of his own creation and commonly identified by musicologists as "the human faith melody,"[16] This
theme, too, has been echoing and murmuring in the *Concord* since the first
moments of "Emerson," and it now emerges in its full, clarified statement,
in combination with other musical materials, such as a probable reference
to Beethoven's *Hammerklavier*. Over time, Ives's themes accumulate
meaning and are clarified in a procedure most aptly described by J. Peter
Burkholder as "cumulative form." We might think of "cumulative form"
in terms of how it relates to a musical conceptualization of a memory
process. The meanings of Ives's fragments are slowly revealed as he recalls
them in his composition. Finally, his themes emerge as a newly formed,
complete whole. The musical past is now part of a new musical present,
and the past is recalled within it.

For Beethoven, this would have been composing backward, but not for Ives. Inspired by Beethoven's earlier innovations, Ives discovered a new way to combine short- and long-term memory and to make memory the center of his compositional procedure. Musical form became a gradual accumulation of significance as a particularly important fragment emerges out of a musical background into a foreground over a great expanse of musical time. Fixed architectural form unfolding in time (Beethoven's method) was no longer as important as other musical matters. Some of the iterations of the fragment are obvious, easy to hear. Others are not. Bits and pieces of memory-fragment, perhaps the residue of a short-term memory experience, are at first scattered and diffuse. Because the fully formed melodic material is only heard in the closing bars, as if finally gaining access to a long-lost recollection of great lyric significance, long-term memory emerges triumphant at the end of Ives's larger works. Thus the fullest expression of Ives's thematic material in the *Concord Sonata* comes in the final moments of "The Alcotts" and "Thoreau," the last two movements of the massive work. Although the full significance is eventually achieved, the actual exposure to what must be remembered—and its full, meaningful expression—is held back, denied as long as possible. But it works perfectly well.

The great composers have shown a variety of ways in which memory is essential to musical forms. Over time, these forms change, but the powerful role of memory in musical understanding remains central. Long before scientists could dream of showing the complex cognitive processes essential for memory in music and how the various parts of the brain collaborate to make musical cognition possible, the great composers wrote musical scores intricately designed to set off and engage memory, whether short-, intermediate-, or long-term, in their listeners.

Notes

1. E. H. Gombrich, "Moment and Movement in Art," *Journal of the Warburg and Courtauld Institute* 27 (1964): 293–306.

2. E. H. Gombrich, *Sense of Order: A Study in the Psychology of Decorative Art* (1979; reprint, Ithaca, NY: Cornell University Press, 1984), 10, 289.

3. Gottfried Schlaug has conducted impressive research that indicates how the brains of musicians develop differently from those of nonmusicians. See Gottfried Schlaug, "The Brain of Musicians," in *The Cognitive Neuroscience of Music*, ed. Isabelle

Peretz and Robert Zatorre (New York: Oxford University Press, 2003), 366–381. The collection in general is seminal in the field. See also Christian Gaser and Gottried Schlaug, "Gray Matter Differences between Musicians and Nonmusicians" in *The Neurosciences and Music*, ed. Giuliano Avanzini et al. (New York: New York Academy of Sciences, 2003), 514–517. A useful survey of the topic of music and brain function is Bob Snyder, *Music and Meaning: An Introduction* (Cambridge, MA: MIT Press, 2000).

4. The "brainworm," first described in German as an *Ohrwurm* (earworm), can become like a tic. See Oliver W. Sacks, *Musicophilia: Tales of Music and the Brain* (New York: Knopf: 2007), 41–48.

5. Charles Rosen, *The Classical Style: Haydn, Mozart, Beethoven*, 2nd ed. (New York: Norton, 1997), 75, is quite clear on why musical repetition can never be equated exactly with repetition in the sense of the plastic arts: "Temporal proportions are not like spatial ones: we cannot refer back and forth at a performance, and we must rely on memory, emotional and sensuous as well as intellectual, for comparison."

6. Charles Rosen, *The Romantic Generation* (Cambridge, MA: Harvard University Press, 1998), 166.

7. Raymond Kesner provides these time lengths for long- and intermediate-term memory, which he admits are approximate, in "Neurobiological Views of Memory," in *Neurobiology of Learning and Memory*, 2nd ed., ed. Raymond Kesner and Joe Martinez, Jr. (New York: Elsevier, 2007), 284. See also David Huron, *Sweet Anticipation: Music and the Psychology of Expectation* (Cambridge, MA: MIT Press, 2008), 238. Huron comments on the interaction of long-, intermediate-, and short-term memory.

8. George Steiner, *In Bluebeard's Castle* (New Haven, CT: Yale University Press, 1971), 11–12.

9. In Haydn's Symphonies 45 and 46, the finale quotes the earlier minuet. See Lewis Lockwood, *Beethoven: The Music and the Life* (New York: Norton, 2003), 220.

10. Viktor S. Zuckerkandl, *Sound and Symbol: Music and the External World.* (Princeton, NJ: Princeton University Press, 1956), 1:231. Sacks quotes this passage, too, but the scholarly reader would do well to read Zuckerkandl's entire section on melody as temporal gestalt, 229–235.

11. O. Sacks, *Musicophilia*, 112–119, 187–213.

12. William James, *The Principles of Psychology* (New York: Holt, 1890), 1:609.

13. C. Rosen, *The Romantic Generation*, 166.

14. Claude Debussy, as quoted in Charles Rosen, *Critical Entertainments: Music Old and New* (Cambridge, MA: Harvard University Press, 2000), 118. Debussy's numerous, often hilarious remarks on Beethoven and Wagner, written under the penname of "Monsieur Croche," reflect his determination to find his French identity in a field dominated by great German composers.

15. Hepokoski defines the "connotationally-loaded" musical-*fragment* as "the allusion to or paraphrase of a pre-existing musical piece with strong public or private associations (or, more normally, both)." See James Hepokoski, "Temps Perdu," *Musical Times* 135 (December 1994): 746.

16. For a more elaborate treatment of the various structural materials in the *Concord Sonata* and how they work together, see David Michael Hertz, "Ives's *Concord Sonata* and the Texture of Music, in *Ives and His World*, ed. J. Peter Burkholder (Princeton, NJ: Princeton University Press, 1996), 75–117. See also David Michael Hertz, *Angels of Reality: Emersonian Unfoldings in Ives, Stevens and Wright* (Carbondale: Southern Illinois University Press, 1993), 93–137. One of the best discussions of the *Concord Sonata* is in J. Peter Burkholder's *All Made of Tunes: Charles Ives and the Uses of Musical Borrowing* (New Haven, CT: Yale University Press, 1995), 350–357. This study as a whole is the fullest account of Ives's use of earlier music in his compositional technique and his method of composing in general.

18 Neurocognitive Approaches to Memory in Music: Music Is Memory

Barbara Tillmann, Isabelle Peretz, and Séverine Samson

Musical memory has remarkable features and a wide-ranging scope. For example, it has the capacity to recognize melodies even after long time spans and within a couple of notes. Music is a complex, highly structured, acoustic material that unfolds over time. Memory for musical material includes the capacity to remember a wide range of features, from the pitch of tones and musical timbres to their rhythmic and metric patterns, from associated lyrics and evoked emotions to the combination of these and other features in larger, integrated structures and representations. Psychologists and neuroscientists investigate how such features are encoded, stored, and combined in a memory representation and then reactivated at recognition and recall. The study of musical memory can make a unique contribution to further understanding short-term memory, long-term memory, and emotional memory. Notably, musical long-term memory provides considerable connections to listeners' autobiographical past. This chapter, drawing from multiple findings, presents the specific feature of musical memory and its neural correlates and compares them to memory in language and other domains.

As with memory models involving auditory features in nonmusical contexts, we can differentiate memory storage as a function of time. Sensory memory acts on extremely short timescales—up to hundreds of milliseconds; short-term and working memory maintain musical information for up to about 15–20 seconds; and long-term memory, which contains listeners' knowledge about the musical system of their culture and about specific musical pieces experienced as familiar, for many years. Auditory perception is directly linked to memory: to perceive a melody, for example, individual notes are encoded and held in an auditory sensory memory buffer, allowing listeners to combine the incoming information over time.

In our neurocognitive study of musical material, first we present research investigating musical information in short-term and working memory. As observed for short-term memory of verbal and visual materials, short-term memory of musical material suffers from interference due to additional information and from forgetting over time. However, the investigation of short-term memory for musical material during the continuous listening of an ongoing musical piece has shown that memory traces of music can improve and become more precise over time. Research has also shown that even nonmusician listeners have knowledge about the musical system of their culture. Their knowledge of pitch relations and regularities is acquired through mere exposure to the music of their culture and is stored in long-term memory. Such knowledge allows listeners to develop culturally generic and automatic expectations, which influence their perception of musical sequences, whether familiar or new to them, and which play an important role in musical expressiveness. Second, we consider listeners' long-term knowledge about specific familiar melodies, also referred to as the "musical lexicon." Such long-term knowledge of specific musical pieces gives rise to a feeling of familiarity or a sense of "knowing" that occurs upon hearing even a short excerpt of a tune, particularly its beginning. This knowledge allows most listeners to anticipate—creates *veridical expectations* for—the next tones of that melody. Third, we review research on musical memory and emotions and consider its clinical implications for the rehabilitation of patients with cognitive impairment, particularly those suffering from Alzheimer's disease.

Short-Term Memory and Working Memory of Musical Material

Research on short-term memory has shown that the cognitive capacity to retain information over time depends on the structure of the material, the presence of interfering material, and the possibility of rehearsal. Short-term memory traces decline over time and additional material occurring during the retention delay may interfere with memory performance. Most of this research has investigated short-term and working memory for verbal and visual materials and has proposed memory models designed for such materials, as, for example, the influential working memory model proposed by Alan D. Baddeley.[1] Studying the capacity to remember tones, tone sequences, and tonal melodies not only extends the investigation of short-term and working memory to musical material, but also serves to test previously proposed models for modality and domain specificity.

The performance of listeners asked to compare the pitch of a standard and a comparison tone is perfect when the two tones are separated by short silent delays, of 5 seconds, for example. Performance decreases to chance level when the intervening delay is filled with other tones of similar pitch, even when participants are told to ignore these tones. The amount of interference depends on the similarity in pitch or timbre, for example, between the tones to be remembered and the intervening material. Intervening verbal material such as spoken numbers does not create the interference that pitch information creates.[2] These findings suggest that verbal and tonal information might be, at least partly stored separately, and thus be functionally or perhaps even anatomically dissociated.

Memory capacity depends on the structure of the material to be remembered: learning and memory are facilitated when tone sequences are based on hierarchical structures or follow rules and regularities of the musical system, such as scale structures.[3] This finding is similar to those obtained for visual or verbal materials. For musical material, it has been further shown that listeners' tonal knowledge (stored in long-term memory) influences memory performance. For example, memory for single tones is affected by a musical context: memory performance is better when the pitches of the context define a tonality than when they describe an atonal sequence. Furthermore, when the pitches of the context define a tonality, memory performance is better for stable than for unstable tones. When comparing tone (or chord) sequences by pair with the instruction to detect whether one tone or chord in a pair of sequences is changed, subjects perform better overall for tonal than for atonal sequences.

Research by W. Jay Dowling investigating short-term memory for melodies is probing the respective roles of pitch, interval (distance between pitches), melodic contour (pattern of ups and downs), and tonality (tonal scales).[4] Melodic contour, independently of exact interval sizes, is an important feature for immediate recognition of tonal melodies and also of atonal melodies, which are lacking a tonal schema. In tonal melodies, pitch information is stored in a representation combining melodic contour and tonal scale information of the tones. Melodic contour and tonality are thus not encoded independently: listeners' ability to recognize melodies is influenced by their knowledge of tonality and of the distances between tonalities. This influence leads to increased confusion errors in recognition paradigms, notably when the melody to be remembered and the test melody presented are based on closely related tonalities in contrast to tonalities that are distant and unrelated.

Delayed recognition tests for tonal melodies have revealed changes in the effectiveness of retrieval cues over time. At immediate testing and after short retention delays, global contour information is the important retrieval cue. Over time, for example, after delays of 30 seconds, exact interval sizes become more important: listeners recognize a melody more exactly—and reject more correctly a test melody that differs in interval sizes from the melody to be remembered—after a longer retention delay. Most important, this memory improvement is observed even when listeners are presented other musical information, such as a continuously played musical piece, during that delay. Consequently, the memory improvement observed for musical material contradicts well-established observations for memory of verbal material, where recognition of items in short-term memory declines with delay and even more so when subjects are presented additional, similar interfering material during the delay.

Although the neural correlates of memory improvement for musical material over time, particularly for the exact interval sizes of a melody, have not yet been investigated, some research has been done on the neural correlates of interval and contour processing (also referred to as "local" and "global auditory processing"). Data from right- and left-brain-lesioned patients suggest that local and global auditory processing is lateralized to left and right hemispheres, respectively, whereas data from functional magnetic resonance imaging (fMRI) of healthy participants suggest the opposite lateralization pattern.[5] Differences in lateralization patterns for local and global processing have also been reported in the visual modality and have been attributed to influences of experimental materials and tasks.[6]

On the other hand, neural correlates of memory for tones have been investigated with same-different paradigms. Participants were asked to judge whether two tones were the same or different in various conditions, for example, with immediate testing or short empty delays (low memory load) or with delays filled with other interfering tones (high memory load). Functional brain imaging studies conducted by Robert J. Zatorre and colleagues have revealed that pitch comparisons with low-memory load involve the right frontal cortices, whereas comparisons with high-memory load involve the interaction of right temporal and frontal cortices, along with parietal cortex activation.[7] Temporal-frontoparietal activations have also been reported for music perception with high attentional load, as when listeners focused on one melodic line in a polyphonic musical passage. Music perception can thus involve the more general circuitry of working memory, such as the frontoparietal networks that have been reported in working memory tasks for various types of materials (verbal, spatial, and visual objects).[8]

In fMRI studies, performance on tonal working memory tasks decreased in patients with right temporal or frontal lesions, but not in the left hemisphere.[9] The importance of interactions between right temporal and frontal cortices for the processing of pitch patterns, including online maintenance and encoding of tonal patterns has been further suggested by recent anatomical studies investigating brain anomalies in congenital amusia, a life-long disorder for music perception, memory, and production. The brains of individuals with congenital amusia show anomalies in white matter concentration, cortical thickness, and fiber tracks in the right hemisphere, notably in the right inferior frontal and temporal auditory cortices.[10]

The implication of right hemispheric networks for the memory of melodic material extends to longer retention delays, which go beyond short-term memory and tap into newly acquired knowledge stored in long-term memory. Séverine Samson and Robert Zatorre used a delayed recognition test taken 24 hours after the memorization phase.[11] Patients with a right or left anterior temporal lobectomy (focal cerebral excision for the relief of intractable epilepsy) and a group of healthy control participants performed the delayed recognition task for unfamiliar melodies and nonsense words. Although all patients performed worse than control participants, patients with left resection performed better in recognizing melodies than they did in recognizing words, and the reverse pattern was observed for patients with right resection.

These data patterns show the importance of both right and left temporal lobes for memory, with the right hemisphere seeming to be more strongly involved in memory for melodies and the left hemisphere more strongly involved in memory for words. Other data from patients with acquired lesions further suggest at least partial separation of musical and verbal long-term memory: some patients cannot recognize familiar melodies, although they can recognize the associated lyrics. In contrast, brain-imaging data from healthy participants have shown overlapping activation patterns for music and language perception and memory, although the observed bilateral networks often include asymmetric hemispheric activations: notably, with a left-weighted activation pattern for language and a right-weighted activation pattern for language. It has been suggested that this might be partly related to the temporal and spectral acoustic characteristics of the materials, shaping higher-order process specialization.[12]

Perception and memory of musical material involve listeners' schematic knowledge about the musical system of their culture, which is stored in long-term memory. This knowledge is acquired by mere exposure to music in everyday life (at least for nonmusician listeners) due to the cognitive capacity of implicit learning. It remains on an implicit level (nonmusicians cannot verbalize this knowledge) and involves the regularities and structures specific to the musical system, such as the musical function of tones and chords as well as their tonality structures. When listening to a musical sequence, listeners develop expectations for musically appropriate events coming up later on in the melody. An acoustic event such as a tone can be appropriate in one context but not in another, where the same tone is perceived less accurately and more slowly, and where its processing involves increased brain activation in the inferior frontal cortex.[13] Interestingly, these observations mirror behavioral and neural data patterns reported for listeners' processing words that differ in contextual expectedness or appropriateness on the basis of the listeners' knowledge about verbal structures, such as syntax or semantics. Aniruddh D. Patel proposes that, even though knowledge representations of music and language differ, music and language processing share neural resources necessary for the integration of the perceived structures—a hypothesis that allows researchers to integrate patient and brain imaging data on music and language processing.[14]

Long-Term Memory of Music: They're Playing Our Song

From infancy to old age, we are able to recognize a familiar tune; we associate many moments of our lives with particular songs or other music. Yet this commonly experienced association of music with episodic, autobiographical memory is far from simple. Successful recognition of a familiar tune depends on a selection procedure that takes place in a memory system—the musical lexicon—that contains representations of specific musical phrases to which each of us has been exposed during our lifetime. The musical lexicon is best understood as a perceptual representational system for isolated tunes, much in the same way as the mental word lexicon represents isolated words. These long-term memory representations embody some of the invariant properties of the familiar tunes to allow recognition despite transposition to a different register, change in instrumentation, and change in tempo. The stored representations can nonetheless preserve some surface features, such as absolute pitch, precise tempo, and timbre. Thus, both surface and structural features may be contained in the stored representation of familiar tunes.[15]

We can examine access to these memory representations with the gating paradigm used in psycholinguistic research to study the verbal lexicon. In this paradigm, a stimulus of increasing length is presented to subjects, who are asked to indicate whether they recognize the stimulus or to judge its familiarity. For the musical material, the increasing length of the stimulus can be created note by note or by sections of short duration (slices of 500 milliseconds, for example). Access to the musical lexicon is relatively quick, often requiring just the first few notes, Depending on the material (e.g., keeping original timbre and orchestrations vs. piano tones only), the estimated amount of required information ranges from hundreds of milliseconds to several notes.[16]

Retrieval of information from memory representations is conceived as automatic and incremental through three stages: access, selection, and integration. In the access stage, the beginning of the music activates a series of potential tune candidates, determined solely on the basis of perceptual information deriving from the analysis of the musical input. In the selection (or discrimination) stage, the cohort of tune candidates is progressively reduced in number with the increase in available musical information about the specific tune. Singing from memory or inner singing can be initiated at this stage. The level of activation of the candidates is raised or lowered depending on their compatibility with the musical input, until the best-fitting match is selected and hence recognition is achieved. This cohort model, originally developed for word recognition by William D. Marslen-Wilson, has been shown to account for tune recognition as well.[17]

In the final or integration stage, the position and function of the selected tune or musical phrase are integrated into a larger musical context, that is, into a higher-level representation of the musical piece. This stage may involve musical tonal regularities, as seen above, and extramusical associations. Here we focus on the neural correlates of the first two stages of the access and selection phase in the musical lexicon.

The neural correlates of the musical lexicon point to the superior temporal sulcus as a key brain structure.[18] Long ago, Wilder Penfield and Phanor Perot reported that electrical stimulation of the exposed surface of the auditory cortex could elicit music-specific memories in the form of a musical hallucination.[19] Stimulation on both sides of the temporal lobes, with slightly greater stimulation on the right side, could result in the patients reporting illusory musical memories. Similarly, bilateral brain damage to the auditory cortex can result in persistent loss of the ability to recognize music despite normal or near normal perception. Such memory loss can be limited to music, as reflected in some cases of amusia for those patients who show deficits in memory processing. For instance, a female amusia patient with bilateral damage to the auditory cortex performed normally in recognizing and memorizing spoken lyrics, whereas she could not recognize or relearn the corresponding melody played without lyrics. The deficit was selective and quite specific: the patient had no difficulties with other nonmusical auditory materials, such as voices and animal cries, and had no memory impairment for visual stimuli.[20]

Deficits in recognizing familiar melodies can occur after damage to either left or right superior temporal brain structures.[21] Thus several recent neuroimaging studies have emphasized the participation of the left superior temporal structure and of the right superior temporal sulcus in such deficits.[22] Left lateralization may be attributed in part to the association of familiar melodies with extramusical and extraexperimental events that may contribute to recognition. For instance, song melodies (played without lyrics) automatically trigger the lyrics with which they are typically paired.[23] The presence of these associated memories may even confer an advantage in the case of lesion. It has been shown that brain damage can impair recognition of instrumental music, but spare recognition of song melodies.[24]

Another way to tap into the musical lexicon is to study *musical imagery,* the neuropsychological term for the subjective experience of imagining music in the absence of actual sound input. Patient studies have suggested the implication of right auditory cortical areas in imagining music since damage of these cortical areas leads to deficits in such imagining.[25] This observation has been supported in research using functional neuroimaging, which consistently indicates that secondary auditory cortices are recruited during a variety of tasks that involve the imagining or rehearsal of melodies.[26] Further evidence comes from electrophysiological measures showing that the scalp topography elicited by imagining the continuation of a melody is similar to the N100 component elicited by a real tone.[27] These demonstrations of auditory cortex activity in the absence of an acoustical stimulus, or at least not driven solely by external input, suggest that access to the memory representations in the musical lexicon is determined by perceptual processes. In addition, it has been found that a familiar tune tends to engage inferior frontal regions and the supplementary motor area, which may relate to subvocalization or inner singing.[28] In sum, listeners' long-term knowledge about specific musical pieces is stored in the musical mental lexicon, where it can be accessed rapidly with few external stimulations, leading to the feeling of familiarity, to recognition, and to the mental imagery of the melody's continuation.

Musical Memory and Emotion: Clinical Implications

Although numerous neuroscientific studies have investigated the connection between memory and emotion, surprisingly few have extensively examined its relation to musical material. Since emotion is ever present and powerful in music, the interaction between emotion and memory processes should be stronger in musical than in nonmusical domains, such as visual scenes. We can first consider how the felt emotion elicited by listening to music can modify memory. A leading question is whether such musical experiences convey specific emotional feelings that verbal or visual experiences are not able to trigger. To illustrate the kind of emotional memory that is witnessed in music, we can also consider the effect of prior exposure on liking or preference ratings.

But let's first consider an especially significant influence of emotion on memory for music, notably in the trigger of autobiographical memories by musical listening. Pieces of music are frequently embedded in specific episodes of our life. Such associations serve to link a personal event and a specific piece of music, the latter being used as a retrieval cue for autobiographical memory. Examining long-term memory for popular songs in both young and older normal subjects and the emotions associated with these pieces of music, Matthew D. Schulkind and colleagues reported a positive correlation between the emotional rating of well-known popular songs and the retrieval of autobiographical memory and title or performer's name.[29] Since music relates to our everyday lives, hearing these pieces of music can be linked to autobiographical episodes with a specific emotional context. The more emotionally moved by a song the subjects reported themselves to be, the more details about their lives and about the song they retrieved. Although these results confirm a direct relation between emotion and long-term memory for music, it remains unclear whether emotion elicited memory or vice versa. Schulkind and colleagues further reported that, in older subjects, emotional ratings for popular songs showed no signs of decline over long retention intervals, which is not the case for declarative memory abilities. Thus the effect of emotion on memory becomes more pronounced as the retention interval increases.

Investigating the experiences elicited by music in a group of more than three hundred students, Petr Janata and colleagues showed that approximately one-third of the songs presented were associated with precise phenomenological descriptions that were autobiographically salient. Interestingly, it was found that the majority of these songs evoked strong and pleasant emotions.[30] These findings are consistent with findings on memory for nonmusical events, such as pictures and words, which can also show high arousal and emotional valence.[31] They also support the longstanding hypothesis that emotional feelings associated with events that have been memorized are used as an affective context for cuing memories. According to Gordon H. Bower, an emotion serves as a memory unit that can be part of the associations stored in a semantic network.[32] By creating a robust emotional memory marker, music can facilitate retrieval of related emotional and personal events. Generally experienced as pleasant or neutral, familiar songs appear to be an appropriate tool for probing autobiographical knowledge.

To further explore the effect of emotion on music recognition, Eckhart Altenmuller and colleagues conducted two successive studies.[33] In both, nonmusician subjects were asked to rate arousal (from very calm to very arousing) and valence (from unpleasant to pleasant or from negative to positive feelings) induced by classical piano pieces and symphonic film music. Recognition of these musical pieces was tested two weeks later. Again, the results showed that well-recognized pieces were associated with higher arousal ratings and received a higher positive valence rating. It seems therefore that emotional arousal and valence both influence long-term memory for music. In patients with temporal lobe dysfunction, for instance, memory performance for musical samples intended to induce specific emotions (happiness, sadness, anxiety, peacefulness) is better than for verbal information.[34] There is consistency here with the hypothesis that emotion facilitates encoding and retrieval of long-term musical memory. Although the neural correlates of musical memory have already been described, no study, to our knowledge, has investigated the correlates of memory for musical emotion. Neurophysiological findings in nonmusical domains suggest that the medial temporal lobe structures may be critical to the modulating role of emotion on declarative memory, and that the amygdala, which is involved in emotional processing of frightening or arousing music, may modulate both the encoding and the storage of hippocampus-dependent memories.[35] Elizabeth A. Phelps suggests that the medial temporal lobe structures may act in concert when emotion meets memory.[36]

Other studies have examined the influence of unconscious memory on emotion. The simple presentation of a stimulus is sufficient to increase preference for this stimulus as compared to one that has never been encountered before. According to Robert B. Zajonc, the "mere exposure effect," which reflects a preference for presented over unpresented stimuli without conscious recognition of previously encountered stimuli, involves a precognitive emotional system that could precede and operate independently of cognition and memory.[37] Exposure induces various behavioral changes and shapes emotional judgments by increasing positive affects toward presented stimuli. In the classical paradigm, exposure to unfamiliar material during the study phase is followed by a preference task in which studied and unstudied stimuli are presented. Typically, subjects prefer previously encountered stimuli over new stimuli even in the absence of stimulus recognition. Such a preference for previously studied items is a very robust finding. Initially described by Max Meyer back in 1903,[38] the increase of positive ratings with familiarity reveals a direct relation between emotional valence and memory. This phenomenon, which has been well documented in the visual domain, has been also observed with musical stimuli.

Isabelle Peretz and colleagues have characterized the "mere exposure effect" as an expression of implicit memory that is dissociated from explicit memory.[39] This dissociation between implicit and explicit mechanisms has been supported by effects obtained in recognition tasks, testing for explicit memory, and in preference tasks testing for implicit memory. It has been shown that familiarity and encoding processing of the stimuli as well as the age of subjects differently affect performances in both tasks. In neuropsychology, a similar dissociation has been reported. Except for a study by Andrea R. Halpern and Margaret G. O'Connor,[40] the scant research on "mere exposure" in music has shown a spared exposure effect on liking judgments in patients with severe explicit recognition disorders (alcoholic Korsakoff's or bitemporal amnesic syndrome, Alzheimer's disease). Results consistent with the existence of different processes for preference and recognition judgments have also been reported in patients with unilateral temporal lobe lesion.[41] Although patients with left temporal lobe lesion and matched control participants presented an exposure effect on liking judgments of music, patients with a similar lesion on the right side failed to exhibit this effect. However, a different result pattern was shown for recognition judgments; here patients with either right or left temporal lobe lesion were impaired. On the basis of these findings, we have suggested that the right temporal lobe plays a critical role in the formation of musical representations that support both priming and memory recognition (implicit and explicit retrieval), whereas the left temporal lobe is mainly involved in the explicit retrieval of music. Research in this area has only just begun, and further studies will be necessary to better understand the relation between memory and the emotional response to music as well as to art in general.

Finally, studies on musical memory and its relation to emotion open up paths for new strategies in cognitive rehabilitation and highlight the importance of examining interactions between cognitive and clinical neuroscience. The strong emotional power of music may well be able to mobilize the underestimated cognitive skills of persons with various neurological, psychiatric, or developmental disorders. Several lines of evidence indicate that Alzheimer patients can succeed in learning new songs; this shows that some memory for music can be retained, despite severe verbal disorders.

More important, several neuropsychological studies have shown that musical memory can be lasting in patients with Alzheimer's disease and that music listening can increase autobiographical recall even in dementia. The enhanced autobiographical recall associated with music listening might be due to the emotional or arousal effects of the music.[42] However, given the lack of methodological rigor in much of this research, as discussed by Annemiek C. Vink and colleagues, this viewpoint has not been fully validated. [43]

The powerful and long-lasting memory-enhancing effect of musical stimuli points to the potential benefits of using musical stimuli in the rehabilitation of brain-damaged patients. Music elicits emotional experiences of positive or negative valence that cannot always be conveyed by language and that might remain accessible in brain-damaged patients. Since the emotional power of music can strengthen autobiographical memory, music seems to provide a privileged pathway to the past for those with severe memory disorders, such as Alzheimer's or amnesic patients. In this respect, the emotional power of music might go beyond enhancing autobiographical memory. It might also improve cognitive function in general. It could also change mood, notably by reducing anxiety, and thus be used for cognitive rehabilitation programs in clinical settings. For example, music listening has been shown to help older adults with cognitive impairment, including Alzheimer's disease, to maintain attention.[44] Furthermore, evidence has recently emerged that, for stroke patients in early poststroke periods, music listening enhances cognitive recovery and prevents negative moods.[45]

In conclusion, there is increasing evidence that memory for music is a comparatively strong form of memory. Research on musical memory has shown that, on short timescales, detailed surface information can resist temporal decay and interference. On longer timescales, musical material stored in the mental lexicon can be accessed rapidly and can resist aging and diseases that lead to memory deficits for verbal material. Overall, these findings support the use of music in cognitive rehabilitation programs that involve training, learning, memory, and attention. To develop clinical applications, researchers are now investigating how and why musical memory, as distinct from other kinds of memory, seems to be less vulnerable to cerebral damage, more efficient, and more lasting.

Acknowledgments

Barbara Tillmann and Séverine Samson were supported by grant NT05-3-45978, "Music and Memory," from the National Research Agency (ANR) of the French Ministry of Higher Education and Research, and Isabelle Peretz, by a Canada Research Chair in Neurocognition of Music.

Notes

1. Alan D. Baddeley, *Human Memory: Theory and Practice* (Hove, UK: Erlbaum, 1990).

2. Diana Deutsch, "Tones and Numbers: Specificity of Interference in Immediate Memory," *Science* 168 (1970): 1604–1605. For a review, see Diana Deutsch, "The Processing of Pitch Combinations," in *The Psychology of Music*, 2nd ed., ed. Diana Deutsch (San Diego: Academic Press, 1999), 349–412. See also Catherine Semal et al., "Speech versus Nonspeech in Pitch Memory," *Journal of the Acoustical Society of America* 100 (1996): 1132–1140.

3. Carol L. Krumhansl, "The Psychological Representation of Pitch," *Cognitive Psychology* 11 (1979): 346–374; Jamshed J. Bharucha and C. L. Krumhansl, "The Representation of Harmonic Structure in Music: Hierarchies of Stability as a Function of Context," *Cognition* 13 (1983): 63–102; Kathryn M. Dewar, Lola L. Cuddy, and Douglas J. K. Mewhort, "Recognition Memory for Single Tones with and without Context," *Journal of Experimental Psychology: Human Learning and Memory* 3 (1977): 60–67.

4. For a review of his work, see W. Jay Dowling, "Music Perception," in *Oxford Handbook of Auditory Science: Auditory Perception*, ed. Chris Plack (Oxford: Oxford University Press, 2010).

5. Isabelle Peretz, "Processing of Local and Global Musical Information by Unilateral Brain-Damaged Patients," *Brain* 113 (1990): 1185–1205; Lauren Stewart et al., "fMRI Evidence for a Cortical Hierarchy of Pitch Pattern Processing," *PLoS ONE* 3 (2008): 1470.

6. Galit Yovel, Jerre Levy, and Iftah Yovel, "Hemispheric Asymmetries for Global and Local Visual Perception: Effects of Stimulus and Task Factors," *Journal of Experimental Psychology: Human Perception & Performance* 27 (2001): 1369–1385.

7. Robert J. Zatorre, Alan C. Evans, and Ernst Meyer, "Neural Mechanisms Underlying Melodic Perception and Memory for Pitch," *Journal of Neuroscience* 14 (1994): 1908–1919.

8. Petr Janata, Barbara Tillmann, and Jamshed J. Bharucha, "Listening to Polyphonic Music Recruits Domain-General Attention and Working Memory Circuits," *Cognitive, Affective & Behavioral Neuroscience* 2 (2002): 121–140.

9. R. J. Zatorre and Séverine Samson, "Role of the Right Temporal Neocortex in Retention of Pitch in Auditory Short-Term Memory," *Brain* 114 (1991): 2403–2417.

10. Krista L. Hyde et al., "Cortical Thickness in Congenital Amusia: When Less Is Better Than More," *Journal of Neuroscience* 27 (2007): 13028–13032.

11. Séverine Samson and Robert J. Zatorre, "Learning and Retention of Melodic and Verbal Information after Unilateral Temporal Lobectomy," *Neuropsychologia* 30 (1992): 815–826.

12. Robert J. Zatorre, Pascal Belin, and Virginia B. Penhune, "Structure and Function of Auditory Cortex: Music and Speech," *Trends in Cognitive Sciences* 6 (2002): 37–46.

13. B. Tillmann et al., "Cognitive Priming in Sung and Instrumental Music: Activation of Inferior Frontal Cortex," *NeuroImage* 31 (2006): 1771–1782; Barbara Tillmann, "Implicit Investigations of Tonal Knowledge in Nonmusician Listeners," *Annals of the New York Academy of Sciences* 1060 (2005): 100–110.

14. Aniruddh D. Patel, "Language, Music, Syntax and the Brain," *Nature Neuroscience* 6 (2003): 674–681.

15. W. J. Dowling and Diane S. Fujitani, "Contour, Interval, and Pitch Recognition in Memory for Melodies," *Journal of Acoustical Society of America* 49 (1971): 524; Gabriel A. Radvansky, Kevin J. Flemming, and Julie A. Simmons, "Timbre Reliance in Nonmusicians' Memory for Melodies," *Music Perception* 13 (1995): 127–140; Daniel J. Levitin and Perry R. Cook, "Memory for Musical Tempo: Additional Evidence that Auditory Memory Is Absolute," *Perception & Psychophysics* 58 (1996): 927–935; Andrea R. Halpern, "Memory for the Absolute Pitch of Familiar Songs," *Memory & Cognition* 17 (1989): 572–581.

16. E. Glenn Schellenberg, Paul Iverson, and Margaret C. McKinnon, "Name That Tune: Identifying Popular Recordings from Brief Excerpts," *Psychological Bulletin Review* 6 (1999): 641–646; Simone Dalla Bella, Isabelle Peretz, and Neil Aronoff, "Time Course of Melody Recognition: A Gating Paradigm Study," *Perception & Psychophysics* 65 (2003): 1019–1028; Matthew Schulkind, Rachel Posner, and David C. Rubin, "Musical Features That Facilitate Melody Identification," *Music Perception* 21 (2003): 217–249.

17. William D. Marslen-Wilson, "Functional Parallelism in Spoken Word-Recognition," *Cognition* 25 (1987): 71–102. This model has been applied to music by M. Schulkind, R. Posner, and D. C. Rubin, "Musical Features That Facilitate Melody Identification," and by S. Dalla Bella, I. Peretz, and N. Aronoff, "Time Course of Melody Recognition: A Gating Paradigm Study."

18. Isabelle Peretz et al., "Musical Lexical Networks: The Cortical Organization of Music Recognition," *Annals of the New York Academy of Sciences* 1169 (2009): 256–265.

19. Wilder Penfield and Phanor Perot, "The Brain's Record of Auditory and Visual Experience," *Brain* 86 (1963): 596–696.

20. Isabelle Peretz, "Can We Lose Memories for Music? The Case of Music Agnosia in a Nonmusician," *Journal of Cognitive Neurosciences* 8 (1996): 481–496.

21. Julie Ayotte et al., "Patterns of Music Agnosia Associated with Middle Cerebral Artery Artefact," *Brain* 123 (2000): 1926–1938.

22. Jane Plailly, Barbara Tillmann, and Jean-Pierre Royet, "The Feeling of Familiarity of Music and Odors: The Same Neural Signature?" *Cerebral Cortex* 17 (2007): 2650–2658; David J. M. Kraemer et al., "Sound of Silence Activates Auditory Cortex," *Nature* 434 (2005): 158; Hervé Platel et al., "Semantic and Episodic Memory of Music Are Subserved by Distinct Neural Networks," *NeuroImage* 20 (2003): 244–256; H. Platel et al., "The Structural Components of Music Perception: A Functional Anatomical Study," *Brain* 120 (1997): 229–243.

23. Isabelle Peretz, Monique Radeau, and Martin Arguin, "Two-Way Interactions Between Music and Language: Evidence from Priming Recognition of Tune and Lyrics in Familiar Songs," *Memory & Cognition* 32 (2004): 142–152.

24. Willi R. Steinke, Lola L. Cuddy, and Lorna S. Jakobson, "Dissociations among Functional Subsystems Governing Melody Recognition after Right-Hemisphere Damage," *Cognitive Neuropsychology* 18 (2001): 411–437.

25. Robert J. Zatorre and Andrea R. Halpern, "Effect of Unilateral Temporal-Lobe Excision on Perception and Imagery of Songs," *Neuropsychologia* 31 (1993): 221–232.

26. Andrea R. Halpern, "Organization in Memory for Familiar Songs," *Journal of Experimental Psychology: Learning, Memory & Cognition* 10 (1984): 496–512; Robert J. Zatorre et al., "Hearing in the Mind's Ear: A PET Investigation of Musical Imagery and Perception," *Journal of Cognitive Neuroscience* 8 (1996): 29–46.

27. Petr Janata, "Brain Electrical Activity Evoked by Mental Formation of Auditory Expectations and Images," *Brain Topography* 13 (2001): 169–193.

28. Andrea R. Halpern and Robert J. Zatorre, "When That Tune Runs through Your Head: A PET Investigation of Auditory Imagery for Familiar Melodies," *Cerebral Cortex* 9 (1999): 697–704; Andrea R. Halpern et al., "Behavioral and Neural Correlates of Perceived and Imagined Musical Timbre," *Neuropsychologia* 42 (2004): 1281–1292.

29. Matthew D. Schulkind, Laura K. Hennis, and David C. R. Rubin, "Music, Emotion, and Autobiographical Memory: They're Playing Your Song," *Memory and Cognition* 27 (1999): 948–955.

30. Petr Janata, Stefan T. Tomic, and Sonja K. Rakowski, "Characterization of Music-Evoked Autobiographical Memories," *Memory* 15 (2007): 845–860.

31. Tony W. Buchanan, "Retrieval of Emotional Memories," *Psychological Bulletin* 133 (2007): 761–779; Kevin S. LaBar and Roberto Cabeza, "Cognitive Neuroscience of Emotional Memory," *Nature Reviews Neuroscience* 7 (2006): 54–64.

32. Gordon H. Bower, "Mood and Memory," *American Psychologist* 36 (1981): 129–148.

33. Susann Eschrich, Thomas F. Munte, and Eckhart Altenmuller, "Unforgettable Film Music: The Role of Emotion in Episodic Long-Term Memory for Music," *BMC Neuroscience* 9 (2008): 48; Susann Eschrich, Thomas F. Munte, and Eckhart Altenmuller, "Remember Bach: An Investigation in Episodic Memory for Music," *Annals of the New York Academy of Sciences* 1060 (2005): 438–442.

34. Séverine Samson, Delphine Dellacherie, and Hervé Platel, "Emotional Power of Music in Patients with Memory Disorders: Clinical Implications of Cognitive Neuroscience," *Annals of the New York Academy of Sciences* 1169 (2009): 245–255.

35. Nathalie Gosselin et al., "Impaired Recognition of Scary Music Following Unilateral Temporal Lobe Excision," *Brain* 128 (2005): 628–640; Nathalie Gosselin et al., "Amygdala Damage Impairs Emotion Recognition from Music," *Neuropsychologia* 45 (2007): 236–244.

36. Elizabeth A. Phelps, "Human Emotion and Memory: Interactions of the Amygdala and Hippocampal Complex," *Current Opinion in Neurobiology* 14 (2004): 198–202.

37. Robert B. Zajonc, "Attitudinal Effects of Mere Exposure," *Journal of Personality and Social Psychology* 9 (1968): 1–27.

38. Max Meyer, "Experimental Studies in the Psychology of Music," *American Journal of Psychology* 14 (1903): 456–478. For a review, see: Robert F. Bornstein, "Exposure and Affect: Overview and Meta-analysis of Research," *Psychological Bulletin* 106 (1989): 265–289.

39. Isabelle Peretz, Danielle Gaudreau, and Anne-Marie Bonnel, "Exposure Effects on Music Preference and Recognition," *Memory & Cognition* 26 (1998): 884–902.

40. Andrea R. Halpern and Margaret G. O'Connor, "Implicit Memory for Music in Alzheimer's Disease," *Neuropsychology* 14 (2000): 391–397.

41. Séverine Samson and Isabelle Peretz, "Effects of Prior Exposure on Music Liking and Recognition in Patients with Temporal Lobe Lesions," *Annals of the New York Academy of Sciences* 1060 (2005): 419–428.

42. Amee Baird and Séverine Samson, "Memory for Music in Alzheimer's Disease: Unforgettable?" *Neuropsychological Review* 19 (2009): 85–101.

43. Annemiek C. Vink et al., "Music Therapy for People with Dementia," *Cochrane Database of Systematic Reviews* CD003477 (2003).

44. Nicholas A. Foster and Elizabeth R. Valentine, "The Effect of Auditory Stimulation on Autobiographical Recall in Dementia Clients," *Experimental Aging Research* 27 (2001): 215–228.

45. Teppo Särkämö et al., "Music Listening Enhances Cognitive Recovery and Mood after Middle Cerebral Artery Stroke," *Brain* 131 (2008): 866–876.

19 Memory, Movies, and the Brain

Fernando Vidal

Films variously display memory and brain theories and situations, particularly through conditions of amnesia. Although many movies concerned with memory have appeared over the years, relatively few deal directly with the brain, and most of these few concern an amnesic protagonist. Memory and especially forgetting have served dramatic and comical purposes from cinema's earliest days, but it was mainly in the 1980s, with the convergent rise of cyberpunk and the cognitive neurosciences, that they began to connect memory explicitly to the brain and to various neurotechnologies. Most of the films examined or mentioned in this chapter have been produced since then: *Blade Runner* (1982), *Brainstorm* (1983), *The Bourne Identity* (1988, 2002), *Total Recall* (1990), *Johnny Mnemonic* (1995), *Strange Days* (1995), *Dark City* (1998), *Memento* (2000), *I Know Who You Are* (2000), *Paycheck* (2003), *The Manchurian Candidate* (2004 remake compared to its 1962 original), *Eternal Sunshine of the Spotless Mind* (2004), *Final Cut* (2004), *Magdalena's Brain* (2006), and *The Bourne Ultimatum* (2007). A central feature of these movies, and one whose implications we shall ponder, is that, although amnesia is often attributed to brain damage, it makes sense only in the light of protagonists' personal histories, experiences, and existential quests. Both before and after making a cerebral diagnosis, films (like short stories, novels, and the sciences of memory themselves) must turn toward the mind.

Movies offer thought-provoking characterizations of the function of memory, however unscientific these are judged to be. The gap that separates films from psychology, psychiatry, and the neurosciences reflects the beliefs and concerns of the cultures where they are produced and consumed. In particular, films often mix discredited theories (e.g., about discrete memory localizations in the brain) with others that have been accepted (e.g., about the effect of emotional arousal on encoding, storage, and retrieval). Both their "mistaken" and their accurate representations tend to go hand in hand with a certain inconclusiveness regarding scientific and philosophical positions. This may be a positive feature if it throws viewers off balance. For example, the memory erasure procedure in *Eternal Sunshine of the Spotless Mind* requires memories to be localized in circumscribed clusters of neurons. At the same time, the protagonist's "resistance" to erasure suggests that memory processes are more dynamic and distributed than the localization theory implies. Beyond science-related beliefs and theories, films incorporate elements of larger cultural views, in particular those about the primordial role of memories in defining the individual self, and of the brain in constituting human personhood.

Filmic Fiction and Scientific Fact

Commentators with backgrounds in psychology or neuropsychology tend to follow the "deficit model" of film analysis, emphasizing the gap that separates filmic fiction from scientific fact. This gap obviously exists. Indeed, as Sallie Baxendale aptly observes, "most amnesic conditions in films bear little relation to reality."[1] In contrast to filmic portrayals, personality and identity are relatively unaffected in amnesic syndromes, most of which develop as a result of a stroke, neurosurgery, or brain infection.

The prevalence of a certain type of amnesia provides another instance of cinematographic "misrepresentation." Anterograde amnesia, an inability to recall events that take place after the onset of the disease, is a far more common and incapacitating condition than retrograde amnesia (the inability to recall events that preceded the onset of the disease). Nevertheless, films have overwhelmingly focused on loss of memories of the past.

A notable exception is *Memento* (2000), in which former insurance claims investigator Leonard "Lenny" Shelby suffers from anterograde amnesia as a consequence of a head injury sustained while defending his wife from a robber. Her murder by that robber is the last thing Lenny remembers, and his life's goal is to take revenge. To compensate for his condition, he tattoos important information on his body, makes notes to himself, and takes Polaroid pictures. The film alternates color sequences that tell the events in reverse chronological order, and black-and-white sequences that move forward in time; events are repeated in scenes that add detail or perspective to the previous version. The result is so labyrinthine that we never know what "actually" happened. Yet, as director Christopher Nolan pointed out, *Memento* is "an extremely linear film" in which scenes are so strongly linked to each other that they could be hardly be moved around.[2]

Indeed, the confusion we experience is supposed to make us feel the fragility of memory. Nolan wanted to put the audience in the hero's head— "and that's why the story is told backwards, because it denies the information that he's denying."[3] The movie conveys the recurrences and the immobility that characterize Lenny's existence as he goes from one short-term memory to the next, with his identity frozen in a last, painful recollection. In the original story, such a predicament is summarized by the unidentified narrator, who tells the protagonist, "Time is three things for most people, but for you, for us, just one. A singularity. One moment. This moment ... Time moves about you but never moves you. It has lost its ability to affect you."[4]

The scientific response to *Memento* has been overwhelmingly positive.[5] High-profile neuroscientist Christopher Koch declared *Memento* "by far the most accurate portrayal of the different memory systems in the popular media," and there seems to be consensus on that opinion.[6] Esther M. Sternberg from the National Institute of Mental Health explained how *Memento*'s plot, dialogue, and technique "expose the different kinds of memory that we take for granted, unless they are suddenly lost."[7] Lenny's semantic, implicit, working, procedural, and emotional memory still function. The movie passingly informs us that his anterograde amnesia is due to hippocampal damage; like other commentators, Sternberg notes that his condition is consistent with the case of the "unforgettable" amnesic HM.[8] In 1953, the 27-year-old patient underwent a bilateral temporal lobe resection, involving removal of most of the hippocampus, in the hope of alleviating uncontrollable epileptic seizures. The operation produced "a grave loss of recent memory" and partial retrograde amnesia, while leaving early memories "apparently vivid and intact."[9] Until his death in 2008, HM remained one of the most intensively studied subjects in the history of the neurosciences; without evidence, some blogs maintain that he inspired *Memento*.

As portrayed in *Memento*, Lenny's condition is consistent not only with HM's but also with other documented cases of amnesia with hippocampal lesion. The film thus stands in stark contrast to almost all others of its kind, which stage retrograde memory loss in the absence of anterograde amnesia, even though such a condition is extremely rare.[10] Commentators have good reason to praise *Memento* and to underscore the psychiatric and clinical inaccuracies of most other filmic amnesia.

Nevertheless, a major reason for *not* concentrating on the potential of cinema to mislead the public is that its science-fictional portrayals are one of the ways the neurosciences become known outside the laboratory. When the organizers of the "European Citizens' Deliberations on Brain Science" claimed that science fiction is "becoming reality" and that future neuroscientific developments "will probably go beyond our wildest expectations"—"as far as changing the very nature of the human being"— they were voicing beliefs often expressed by neuroscientists themselves.[11] Such hyperbolic rhetoric helps shape the cultural meaning of science.[12] "Outside the laboratory," moreover, includes a universe of "neurocultures" whose common denominator is the conviction that the human being is essentially a "cerebral subject," and that personhood may be ultimately assimilated to "brainhood."[13]

Emphasizing the distinction between fact and fiction in cinema or other nonacademic contexts suggests that scientific knowledge is totally isolated from those contexts. But the reviled process of "dumbing down" is part of how that knowledge exists in society. Moreover, in fiction film, entertainment appeal, "filmability," and storytelling take precedence over scientific accuracy. Although filmmakers consult scientists because they want verisimilitude, scientific expertise does not determine a movie's factual and scientific content.[14]

The "Cerebrality" of Self and Memory

Placed in a long-term historical perspective, cinema's penchant for retrograde amnesia reflects lasting beliefs about the relationship of personhood and memory. Yet it differs in fundamental ways from neuroscientific discourses about the self. Neuroscientist Joseph LeDoux, for example, considers that since the self "reflects patterns of interconnectivity between neurons in your brain," it should "practically be a truism to say that the self is synaptic."[15] He acknowledges that the self may be characterized as psychological, social, moral, aesthetic, or spiritual, but his final goal is "a complete synaptic theory of personality."[16] Such a theory would involve implicit and explicit, unconscious and conscious memory, as well as the corresponding brain systems, for memory, asserts LeDoux, "does indeed make us who we are."[17]

Movies also assume an inherent connection between self and memory, which they, too, locate in the brain. At the same time, by their attention to experiential, interpersonal, and social aspects, they suggest that neuro-scientific explanations are, perhaps intrinsically, incapable of solving "hard problems" such as those posed by consciousness and personal identity.[18] Though memorial, filmic selves are so anchored in lived experience that, in most movies, "memory of a 'real' past remains a defining criterion of being a 'real' person."[19] But before dealing with the crucial issue of reality and authenticity, we should ask why filmmakers have been so fond of memory loss.

One reason may be that memory has become so much "a shorthand for identity" that, without it, "we cease to exist as who we are and become only receptors of current data."[20] Such a view derives largely from John Locke, who argued in 1694 that personal identity only requires the continuity of memory and consciousness.[21] Since the brain was known to be somehow the seat of those psychological functions, it became the only organ essential to our selves as *persons*. Brain research would later reinforce the assimilation of personhood to brainhood, which in turn would become an autonomous cinematographic theme. In plots where cerebral information, a brain, or even an entire head is transplanted, the operation invariably transfers the donor's identity to the receiver.[22]

Remakes illustrate the cerebralization of the psyche since the mid-twentieth century. *The Manchurian Candidate*, for instance, deals with soldiers brainwashed to have false memories of their commander's behavior. In the 1962 original version, they were manipulated with hypnosis and behavioristic conditioning. In the 2004 remake, these means were augmented by implanting a microchip in the brain. The miniaturized and computerized procedures give mind an unmistakably cerebral materiality. Thus, although microtechnology and the brain fluids some films use as extracerebral memory storage are a far cry from the invasive surgeries and the naked brains of earlier movies, they suggest the extent to which the "person as memory in the brain" theory of identity has become the predominant position about personhood in contemporary Western and Westernized cultures.

In *Total Recall* (1990), set in the year 2084, construction worker Douglas Quaid has recurrent dreams about Mars, where, as far as he knows, he has never been. At a holiday agency that implants artificial memories of visits to exotic places, Quaid signs up for a vacation as a secret agent to the red planet. It turns out, however, that he actually has been a secret agent on Mars. Another personality surfaces during implantation, and, for most of the movie, it is difficult to tell whether the events we see are "reality" or programmed memories. A video of someone identical to Quaid announces "the big surprise: you are not you, you are me." This "me" is Hauser, an agent for the dictator of Mars; they used Quaid to lead them to a rebel leader, and after the leader is killed, Hauser wants his body back. Quaid, however, manages to escape, and in the end, he contemplates the fertile landscape of a liberated Mars together with a lovely woman who also appeared in his dreams. Throughout the movie, tormented by doubts about the reality of his memories (which, a character reminds him, lie in "that black hole you call brain"), Quaid keeps looking for his "real" self— "If I'm not me, who the hell am I?"—but never finds it. We recognize one moral of the film in the rebel leader's dictum: "A man is defined by his actions, not his memories."

How, then, do movies localize memory in the brain? Films of the 1950s to 1970s often show garishly material encephala. After the 1970s, most cerebral manipulations are slightly physicalized forms of mind transfer. In *Magdalena's Brain* (2006), the protagonist's husband, Arthur, is a paralyzed Stephen Hawking–type genius. Magdalena helps him continue his work in Artificial Intelligence—now with the goal of developing an artificial brain "smart enough to repair [his] mind and get [him] out of this chair." This involves a "memory transfer" in which Arthur's mind contents are downloaded into a bluish liquid. A small amount of the fluid is to be injected into the brain of a muscular, good-looking young man who suffers from a brain tumor; once the material is "integrated," the young man's tumor will be removed, and Magdalena will benefit from having her husband's mind in a sexy body. (None of this happens, and somehow Arthur gets back on his feet.)

We are not told how the fluid encodes information, but the point is that memory must appear as a physical cerebral substance. Simple visuals (a glass container with colored liquid) suffice to demonstrate that manipulating memory amounts to handling matter. Only at the cost of completely disrupting the progress of its action could a fiction movie do justice to, say, the recent hypothesis that posttranslational modifications of synthesized proteins are required for long-term memory storage.[23] Such specialized detail, however, is not necessary to communicate the idea that persons are their memories, and that memories are brain substance.

Dark City (1998) takes a similar approach. A race of Strangers has invaded the earth. Once a day, they engage in "tuning": they stop everything, make everybody lose consciousness, and refashion a Metropolis-like artificial city; they then change people's identities by injecting other individuals' memories into their brains, a process they call "imprinting." The Strangers, who use dead human bodies as "vessels," are a vanishing race of jellyfish-like intelligent creatures that must become like humans in order to survive. But they do not know what defines humanity, and manipulating memories is the means of finding out. The work is carried out by a human doctor, Daniel P. Schreber, namesake of the German judge on whom Sigmund Freud based his 1911 monograph about paranoia.[24] Using a drilling syringe, the doctor first extracts memory fluids through people's foreheads. He mixes them—the painful memory of a great love, a dose of unhappy childhood, youthful rebellion, a death in the family—and injects the preparation into other individuals.

Personal Identity and the Authenticity of Memory

Dark City conveys another filmic leitmotif: the authenticity of memories. The humans whose identity is transformed have no way of knowing that their recollections do not correspond to their own lived experiences. There are, however, two exceptions: Schreber, who knows the entire truth; and John Murdoch, who is partly immune to the Strangers' manipulation and is even able to "tune." Murdoch simply ignores whether his remembered past actually happened, or whether a beloved wife called "Emma" ever existed. Yet, unlike other humans, he is aware of the problem, knowing for example that he is not a serial prostitute killer (the imprint attempted on him), and faintly longing for a place called Shell Beach. Together with Schreber, he embarks in the quest to find that town, only to reach a brilliantly colored billboard behind which there is nothing but deep space.

Schreber eventually helps Murdoch defeat the Strangers, reshape the city, bring back the sun, and restore the natural landscapes. At a recreated

Shell Beach, Murdoch meets Emma; the fact that she has been imprinted as Anna and has no recollection of him does not prevent a happy ending. Except for Schreber and Murdoch, nobody's personal identity in the new world is made up of personal memories; for those already imprinted, like Emma/Anna, life goes on, and nothing qualifies it as inauthentic. Similarly, in *Blade Runner* (1982), Rachel, a genetically manufactured "replicant," is fitted with long-term implanted memories that go back to childhood. That those memories are someone else's does not make them any less significant for her sense of self. On the contrary, the psychological continuity between the alien memories and her own coalesce into one personality.

In film, therefore, amnesia disrupts personal identity more than false memories do. The integrity of the self largely depends on the integrity of memory; memory lost is more problematic than memory received.

In this connection, *Johnny Mnemonic* (1995) illustrates childhood's special significance. As a "mnemonic courier," Johnny had "to dump a chunk of long-term memory: [his] childhood" to make room for the data he would carry in his brain implant. He now wants to recover that memory, and in order to pay for the necessary surgery, he agrees to carry a dangerously large amount of information about the treatment of a pandemic nerve attenuation syndrome. In addition to the gangs who want to seize the information for their profit, there are rebels who wish to make it freely available to all. It turns out, however, that the memory-retrieval surgery cannot take place; Johnny is told that "the only way left is to hack your own brain." When he enters the virtual reality of his implant, however, its contents are broadcast worldwide to the tune of appropriately stirring music, thus proclaiming the rebellion's victory. Thanks to the brain space made available, Johnny relives his joyous childhood memories, and this recovery of identity opens the way for a happy ending. Oblivion amounts to a paradise lost; remembering, to a paradise regained.

Johnny Mnemonic presupposes that memory is a collection of fixed data items that can be stored and recovered. Such a view has been called into question by cognitive neuroscience, with its emphasis on plasticity and its demonstration that long-term memories are embodied, not in singular locations, but in neural connections—as well as in different types of memory processed by different brain systems spread throughout the brain.[25] At the same time, like most movies of its kind, *Johnny Mnemonic* highlights the connection between memory and emotion, which the neurosciences have also been exploring. For several decades now, research has shown that emotion may enhance memory (though emotional memories are not more accurate in their details than nonemotional ones); that emotional arousal increases the likelihood of memory consolidation (though amnesia can also occur for emotionally charged events); that autobiographical memories of events experienced as emotional are more vivid than those of experientially neutral events; and that, in short, emotion plays a crucial role in encoding and retrieval.[26]

Like neuroscience, film has given new forms to the notion that an event or a memory is not traumatizing in itself, but by virtue of the accompanying affect. In *Brainstorm* (1983), for example, a company has developed a machine to record sensory and mental experiences directly from people's brains, and to play them into other people's brains, projected as though filmed through the experiencing subject's eyes (i.e., as "point of view," or POV, scenes, through the lens of the so-called subjective camera). The sensory and mental videotapes record not only good sex and other fun activities, but also fear, early trauma, nightmares, physical pain, anxiety, psychosis, and even someone's death.

Released two decades after *Brainstorm*, *Final Cut* (2004) takes place in a world where implanted microchips, called "Zoe [i.e., life] implants," record every moment of a person's life, again filmed in subjective camera. After that person's death, the Zoe recording can be "cut" as an individual "rememory" to show the best moments in the life of the deceased. The hero of *Final Cut* is the cutter Alan Hakman, whose lifelong misery results from the guilt he feels for the death of a childhood playmate. One day, he recognizes his childhood friend as a grownup in someone's rememory and decides to track him down. After Hakman discovers that his memory of the traumatizing event was false, viewing his own recording leads to a dramatic moment of catharsis.

Can a false memory constitute a subject's "truth"? Whatever the nuances of their answers, movies tend to imply that personal identity requires a repertoire of long-term eidetic or "photographic" episodic memories of real autobiographical events stored in discrete brain locations. This position, more evocative of the memory palaces of the late Renaissance than of modern neuroscience and its chemical pathways, has the distinct advantage of being eminently representable. A conceptualization of the mind that emphasizes experience and interaction with objects, persons, and events is far more translatable into film than one that focuses on the empty space of the synapses. In his pioneering work *The Photoplay: A Psychological Study* (1916), Harvard psychologist Hugo Münsterberg's examined film's capacity to "objectify" the functioning of the human mind. The close-up objectified attention; the flashback, remembering; the combination of flashbacks with "forward glances" (equivalent to expectation and imagination) showed how past and future become mentally "intertwined" with the present.[27] We do not need to agree that film obeys the same laws as the mind to see that, if these laws are to be embodied in film, the mind must be portrayed as though consistent with the constraints and possibilities of filmmaking.[28]

On the other hand, psychological processes can be given many different visual forms. We have already mentioned how *Memento* went beyond flashbacks and flashforwards to capture an experience of time and memory. A more conventional example is offered by *Final Cut*'s displaying the past in black-and-white monochromes. The scenes exhibit contrasting versions of the traumatizing childhood episode: the first one shows Hakman's memory and how he believes things happened; the second, his Zoe implant recording, filmed in subjective camera. The fact that the *subjective* camera is meant to give us the *objective* picture of events raises the question of what exactly makes up a human memory.

The reconstructive, malleable, and manipulable nature of memory has been the object of outstanding research, since Frederick Bartlett's 1932 *Remembering* and since virulent discussions during the "false memories" controversy of the 1990s.[29] With Akira Kurosawa's *Rashomon* (1950), Alain Resnais's *Hiroshima mon amour* (1959), and the oeuvre of Andrey Tarkovsky (1932–86)—who defined the filmmaker's work as "sculpting in time," and time and memory as "the two sides of a medal"[30]—cinema has brilliantly explored memory and how it engages forgetting, the present and the future.

Beyond these classics, and in a sci-fi cyberpunk mode, *Strange Days* (1995) is particularly interesting. Its protagonist deals in illegal recordings of experiences made directly from the cerebral cortex, allowing future viewers to live those experiences as if they were their own. The recordings include the entire experience as mediated by the brain and filmed as POV scenes. Since the experience is transmitted and relived as the same POV scenes, the subjective camera in effect transfers a fixed memory from cortex to cortex without distortion.

Despite the ideological and filmic significance of their brain motifs, these cinematic dramas and others like them are psychological, not neurological. Yes, Zoe implants are in the brain; Johnny recovers his childhood memory only by hacking his brain; the *Strange Days* devices record from one brain and deliver to another; and Schreber engineers memories by manipulating a cerebral fluid. Like the neurosciences, movies proclaim that memories are brain mechanisms and that experiences have neural correlates; and yet, also, like the neurosciences, movies must place psychology center stage if those mechanisms and these correlates are to have any meaning. Thus *Memento*, though hailed as being "close to a perfect exploration of the neurobiology of memory," in fact reduces that neurobiology to Lenny's distressing awareness that he suffers from a brain disorder.[31]

Erasing Memories

Since about 2000, neuroscientists have revived a minority opinion among researchers of the 1960s and 1970s that a temporally graded retrograde amnesia could be obtained in rodents for a memory that was reactivated or retrieved just before the amnestic procedure.[32] Research with laboratory rats subjected to Pavlovian fear conditioning has suggested that, when reactivated, memories become labile and must undergo "reconsolidation," a process involving protein synthesis.[33] If the memory is reactivated and protein production inhibited immediately afterward, however, the memory is lost.[34] Thus, after memory retrieval, activating production of a certain protein in the amygdala enhances memory reconsolidation and strengthens an established fearful memory, whereas inhibiting its production impairs reconsolidation.[35] The fact that disrupting reconsolidation appears to erase "initial encoded plasticity" (e.g., the association between a musical tone and an electric shock) may "lend some validity for therapeutic use of agents that disrupt reconsolidation to reduce the fear-arousing aspects of emotional memory in posttraumatic stress disorder."[36] Neuroscientists have debated whether reconsolidation is universal, how it works, and what its clinical applications might be.[37]

The discussion took a new direction in 2007, after the discovery that inhibiting a certain enzyme in the cortex of the laboratory rat results in the erasure of long-term associative memories. Since no reactivation is needed to render the memory trace susceptible to the inhibitor, the persistence of memory seems to depend on the ongoing activity of the enzyme long after the memory is regarded as consolidated into a long-term stable form.[38] Yadin Dudai, one of the authors of the discovery, remarked that "what the field attempts to do at the end of the day is to erase not necessarily a single complete chunk of memory but ... to blunt or erase the extremely annoying emotional burden of the traumatic experience."[39]

Thus, even if long-term memory can be erased, medical applications aim to "dull" or to "dampen" memories rather than erase them. This is the case even in connection with the most recent findings about extinction training in humans: when a stimulus already associated with a mild but painful electric shock is presented again to the experimental subject in the absence of the shock, and during the "reconsolidation window," the stimulus-pain association ("fear memory") is "edited out," without eliminating the subject's recollection of the stimulus itself.[40]

Yet, in a wonderful instance of how movies become part of the "technoscientific imaginary," research on reconsolidation has been often associated with *Eternal Sunshine of the Spotless Mind* (2004), where two former lovers, Joel and Clementine, have their memories of each other erased. *Forbes.com* reported: "A scientist asks you to recall a memory, gives you a pill and alters your recollection. It sounds like a scene from the 2004 film *Eternal Sunshine.* ... But it's exactly what McGill neuroscientist Karim Nader is doing with folks who suffer from post-traumatic stress disorder."[41] Nader is the first author of the *Nature* article on fear memories that resurrected the notion of reconsolidation.[42] In light of his research, declared the *McGill Daily*, "science fiction proves to be more science than fiction."[43] Or in connection with the success of Joseph LeDoux's team in preventing the transfer of a fearful memory from short- to long-term storage in rats, a neurophilosophy blog asserted that "the ability to erase memories is no longer restricted to Hollywood script-writers." [44]

Given that *Eternal Sunshine* has generally been discussed as a science-fiction romance about memory erasure, what, if any, are its connections to research? Although the movie is supposed to have a "remarkably nuanced" understanding of how the brain forms memories of intense emotional experiences, how traces of those experiences may resurface in amnesia, and how targeted memory erasure could take place in conformity with the reconsolidation theory, it "contains almost no dialogue that sounds like actual neuroscience."[45] Moreover, its supposed convergence with neuroscience coexists with a "focused erasure" of troubling memories that proceeds, unrealistically, by destroying, one per memory, localized clusters of neurons.

Commentators' emphasis on memory erasure is symptomatic of current neurocultural obsessions, but overlooks one of the film's crucial features.[46] Erasure is of course essential to the film—but chiefly because both the narrative and the filmic textures are motivated by its *failure*. At one point during the procedure, Joel, who is unconscious, wants to call it off and preserve certain targeted memories. His desire to do so is conveyed in dreamlike scenes in which he and Clementine run away from settings that dissolve around them. When, for example, they are in a bookstore, the names of the book sections fade, pages turn blank, and the image blurs. When they sit in a car watching a movie, they must rush out before the vehicle vanishes. And when Clementine asks Joel to find a hiding place where there are no memories of her, they land in his childhood home, which eventually also disintegrates. *Eternal Sunshine* differs significantly from other movies in that it focuses on resistance to erasure rather than on what happens after a protagonist's memories have been erased or falsified (though this too is essential to the film).

In contrast to resistance against forgetting, the certainty that natural memories are never totally lost is a major theme of filmic amnesia. In *Johnny Mnemonic*, where the erasure is voluntary, the memory of the protagonist's childhood is entirely retrievable. In other cases of premeditated memory loss, traces remain operational. *Eternal Sunshine* opens with Joel impulsively taking the train to the forgotten place where he first met Clementine. In *Paycheck* (2003), a reverse engineer agrees to have the three years when he cracked the design of a machine to see into the future erased from his memory. But when he attempts to claim the millions owed him, he discovers he has signed away the money, and in exchange receives an envelope with miscellaneous everyday objects. Presumably thanks to his work, he knew those things would help him escape from the killers that would chase him; after memory erasure, the nonconscious traces of such knowledge serve him well.

Jason Bourne of *The Bourne Identity* (2002), a spy whom his bosses want to eliminate, has no idea who he is or why he is being hunted down. Amnesia does not prevent him, however, from putting his linguistic, lethal, and other secret-agent skills into high gear while he crisscrosses Europe evading assassination attempts and searching for his identity. Bourne is the killing-machine avatar of David Webb, who in the 1988 TV version was endowed with the same skills, but had, in addition, undergone plastic surgery, remembered episodes from the days before the onset of amnesia, and hoped to "put the pieces back together, some of them at least." In the third and final Bourne movie (*The Bourne Ultimatum*, 2007), the hero, when not involved in chases and fights, experiences flashbacks that reveal the causes of his condition in the "behavior modification" program that transformed Webb into Bourne. After "three years trying to find out who I am," he remembers—and ceases, from his own viewpoint, to be Jason Bourne. Once again, recovering true memories coincides with regaining true identity. In the meantime, there is often not much about their past that our amnesic heroes can put into words (declarative memory), but their implicit memory, especially procedural, is efficient enough to drive much of the action.

Whereas the pathological condition of *Memento*'s Lenny results from injuries, and Bourne's amnesia from manipulation, the protagonist of *I Know Who You Are* (2000) combines two etiologies. Mario is said to suffer from alcohol-related Korsakoff's syndrome, whose onset is dated to 1980. Yet his psychiatrist, Paloma, discovers that Mario's retrograde amnesia actually began in 1977. Hypothesizing that he became an alcoholic due to a traumatic event he unconsciously "prefers to erase from his memory," Paloma researches his past and gives him methylphenidate (a psycho-stimulant used for attention-deficit hyperactivity disorder). After discovering the truth, she makes Mario remember it. Hired by right-wing Spanish generals to assassinate one of their pro-democracy colleagues, Mario also killed the victim's little daughters, and saw one of them die before his eyes. In the end, Mario recovers his past and forms new memories. Thus the retrieval of repressed memories goes hand in hand with the recovery from anterograde amnesia to give Mario back his personal identity and possibilities for a future life.

For most of the movies that have rehearsed thought experiments about memory, identity, and the brain since the 1980s, humans are, above all, memorial subjects essentially defined by the relationship of their present to their remembered past. Like the ancient legend that, before being reincarnated, souls must drink from Lethe, the river of forgetfulness, most of these films postulate that total oblivion of a person's past turns that person into a different being. A second shared feature is the tendency to assume a storehouse model of memory, which has the virtue of being a recognizable commonplace, avoiding complicated explanations, and thus facilitating figurability. Discrete locations are more straightforward than neuronal networks, and gray matter is more visible and tangible than synaptic gaps.

The indestructibility of memory is a third common theme. Protagonists are driven by the conviction that their erased memories can be eventually retrieved intact. "The most faithful memory" may well be, as Yadin Dudai remarked, "the one which is never used."[47] But how could something that neither materializes nor arouses existential interest provide good cinematic material? In contrast to the whole-brain-transplantation movies of an era before microtechnologies and computers, post-1970s science fiction film fragments and commodifies identity through the transfer or elimination of chosen memories, and tends to treat forgetting mainly in connection with trauma and amnesia. It has not dealt with hypermnesia and its disabling consequences, as depicted in Alexander Luria's case history *The Mind of a Mnemonist* (1968) or fictionalized in Jorge Luis Borges's short story "Funes the Memorious" (1942). Nor has it explored how the inhibition of memory items is essential for the adequate retrieval and adaptive use of others.[48]

A fourth shared feature consists of conflicting characterizations of memorial experiences and of memories themselves. Although movie characters relate their recollections to events that actually happened, and when in doubt look for empirical truth, films also portray memories as fundamentally constructed, whether by their subjects' unconscious or by malevolent masterminds. The same film may insist on two properties that are in conflict with each other: the authenticity of memories as criterion for a genuine self, on the one hand, and on the other the primacy of a *psychic reality* (Freud's term) that eludes the dichotomies of objective and subjective, natural and artificial, true and false. Thus, even alien or fabricated memories are given a "flashbulb" appearance, as well as the eidetic and visual qualities that usually suggest veracity and authenticity; such emphasis, however, misses the filmic potential of autobiographical memory research.[49]

Given the nature of cinema, memory in the movies must be primarily visual; but the films examined here also assume that images are in the mind, and that mind is what the brain does. *Eternal Sunshine*, for example, invests most of its visual riches in displaying what goes on in Joel's mind while "he" runs away from memory erasure. Although what we see as "mind screen" (projection of the contents of a character's mind) is also "brain screen," the movie illustrates the impossibility of finding happiness by destroying small clusters of neural tissue. Films rarely offer a single, unequivocal position or body of information, which could be easily checked against scientific knowledge. This is, perhaps, simply because they are concerned with human beings, while the neurobiology of memory uses animal models where "memory" often designates no more than conditioned fear or taste aversion. Methodological reductionism has proven crucial for understanding the plasticity that subserves memory—but not for exploring the contents and meanings that matter most to human beings.[50]

Movies, for all their visual and narrative manifoldness, still adhere to the classical Lockean theory of personal identity. Only when he can say, "I remember, I remember everything," can the hero of *The Bourne Ultimatum* declare, "I'm no longer Jason Bourne." It is as if the whirlwind performance of his procedural memory were of no moment; only when ostensibly accurate visual-emotional memories of an experienced past reach his consciousness does he revert to his authentic identity as David Webb. Memory's role in cinema is thus anchored in its protagonists' past lives. Memory is usually assumed to be permanently stored in their brains, at the expense of its adaptive, plastic, transformative, present- and future-oriented offscreen functions.[51] At the same time, cinema embodies the multiplicity of perspectives from which memory can be approached, displays the heterogeneity of insights about it, and enacts its conceptual and phenomenological complexity.

Acknowledgments

I'm grateful to Joelle Abi-Rached, Suzanne Nalbantian, and Claudia Passos for their comments.

Notes

1. Sallie Baxendale, "Memories Aren't Made of This: Amnesia in the Movies," *British Medical Journal* 329 (2004): 1480.

2. Christopher Nolan, as quoted in Anthony Kaufman, "Christopher Nolan Remembers 'Memento'" (an interview), *indieWIRE*, March 16, 2001, http://www.indiewire.com/article/interview_mindgames_christopher_nolan_remembers_memento/.

3. C. Nolan, as quoted in A. Kaufman, "Christopher Nolan Remembers 'Memento'." See also http://www.bbc.co.uk/films/2000/10/16/christopher_nolan_i_interview.shtml/; http://www.christophernolan.net/interviews_m_virgin.php/.

4. Jonathan Nolan, "Memento Mori," *Esquire*, March 1, 2001, http://www.esquire.com/fiction/fiction/memento-mori-0301.

5. On scientific inaccuracies in *Memento*, see Daniel Pendick, "Memory Loss at the Movies," *Memory Loss & the Brain* (newsletter of the Memory Disorders Project at Rutgers University, Newark), Spring 2002, http://www.memorylossonline.com/spring2002/memlossatmovies.htm/.

6. Christof Koch, *The Quest for Consciousness: A Neurobiological Approach* (Greenwood Village, CO: Roberts, 2004), 196n16.

7. Esther M. Sternberg, "Piecing Together a Puzzling World" (review of *Memento*), *Science* 292 (2001): 1661–1662.

8. Benedict Carey, "H. M., an Unforgettable Amnesiac, Dies at 82," *New York Times*, December 4, 2008, http://www.nytimes.com/2008/12/05/us/05hm.html/. HM was Henry (Gustav) Molaison (1926–80).

9. William Beecher Scoville and Brenda Milner, "Loss of Recent Memory after Bilateral Hippocampal Lesions," *Journal of Neuropsychiatry and Clinical Neuroscience* 12 (2000): 106. The original article appeared in *Journal of Neurology, Neurosurgery and Psychiatry* 20 (1957): 11–21.

10. See Beatriz Vera Poseck, *Imágenes de la Locura: La psicopatología en el cine* (Madrid: Calamar Ediciones, 2006), 127.

11. See "Meeting of Minds," European Citizens Deliberatins on Brain Science, http://www.meetingmindseurope.com/, French pages.

12. For "cultural meaning" in connection with genomics, see Dorothy Nelkin and Susan M. Lindee, *The DNA Mystique. The Gene as a Cultural Icon* (New York: Freeman, 1996).

13. See Fernando Vidal, "Le sujet cérébral: Une esquisse historique et conceptuelle," *Psychiatrie, Sciences Humaines, Neurosciences* 3 (2005): 37–48. Fernando Vidal, "Brainhood, Anthropological Figure of Modernity," *History of the Human Sciences* 22 (2009): 5–36.

14. See David Kirby, "Scientists on the Set: Science Consultants and Communication of Science in Visual Fiction," *Public Understanding of Science* 12 (2003): 261–278; David Kirby, "Cinematic Science: The Public Communication between Scientific and

Entertainment Cultures," in *Handbook of Public Communication of Science and Technology*, ed. Massimiano Bucchi and Brian Trench (London: Routledge, 2008), 165–181.

15. Joseph LeDoux, *Synaptic Self: How Our Brains Become Who We Are* (New York: Viking, 2002), 2.

16. J. LeDoux, *Synaptic Self: How Our Brains Become Who We Are*, 26, 3.

17. J. LeDoux, *Synaptic Self: How Our Brains Become Who We Are*, 133.

18. A problem of this sort is "hard" when it persists even after the mechanisms involved in the performance of the relevant functions have been specified. See David Chalmers, "Facing Up to the Problem of Consciousness," *Journal of Consciousness Studies* 2 (1995): 200–219.

19. Sky Marsen, "Against Heritage: Invented Identities in Science Fiction Film," *Semiotica* 152 (2004): 144.

20. James Bowman, "Memory and the Movies," *New Atlantis: A Journal of Technology and Society* 5 (Spring 2004): 85, 88.

21. See John Locke, *An Essay Concerning Human Understanding*, 2nd ed. (1694), ed. Peter H. Nidditch (1694; rpt., Oxford: Clarendon Press, 1979). New York: Dover, 1959), vol. 2, chap. 27.

22. See Fernando Vidal, "Ectobrains in the Movies," in *The Fragment: An Incomplete History*, ed. William Tronzo (Los Angeles: Getty Research Institute, 2009), 193–211.

23. See Aryeh Routtenberg, "The Substrate for Long-Lasting Memory: If Not Protein Synthesis, Then What?" *Neurobiology of Learning and Memory* 89 (2008): 225–233; Aryeh Routtenberg and Jerome L. Rekart, "Post-Translational Protein Modification as the Substrate for Long-Lasting Memory," *Trends in Neuroscience* 28 (2005): 12–19.

24. Freud's *Psychoanalytic Remarks on an Autobiographically Described Case of Paranoia* (1911) was based on Judge Schreber's 1903 memoirs. See Sigmund Freud, *The Schreber Case*, trans. Andrew Webber (London: Penguin Books, 2003). David H. Wilson argues that *Dark City* represents Judge Schreber's experience of mental pathology through the metaphor of the city. See David H. Wilson, "The Pathological Machine: *Dark City*'s Translation of Schreber's *Memoirs*," *Journal of the Fantastic in the Arts* 15 (2005): 153–164.

25. See Howard Eichenbaum, *The Cognitive Neuroscience of Memory: An Introduction* (New York: Oxford University Press, 2002).

26. For recent overviews of research into emotion and memory, see Tony W. Buchanan, "Retrieval of Emotional Memories," *Psychological Bulletin* 133 (2007):

761–779; Elizabeth A. Phelps and Tali Sharot, "How (and Why) Emotion Enhances the Subjective Sense of Recollection," *Current Directions in Psychological Science* 17 (2008): 147–152.

27. Hugo Münsterberg, *The Photoplay: A Psychological Study* (1916) in *Hugo Munsterberg on Film: The Photoplay: A Psychological Study and Other Writings*, ed. Allan Langdale (New York: Routledge, 2002), chap. 5. *Flashback* denotes both a narrative technique and a psychological phenomenon; *cutback*, the term used by Münsterberg, emphasizes instead the editing procedure. The more usual term for *forward glance* is *flashforward*.

28. In contrast to Münsterberg's psychology of film, which saw in the various ways of framing, shooting, and editing an embodiment or "objectification" of mental faculties and mechanisms, the emerging field of "neurocinematics" is mainly about film reception and its brain-mediated mechanisms. It uses fMRI to assess the effect of film on viewers' brain activity, and considers film as a multimodal stimulus to analyze brain circuits that process perceptual and affective information in situations said to mimic aspects of real-life learning and memory. See Uri Hasson et al., "Neurocinematics: The Neuroscience of Film," *Projections* 2 (2008): 1–26; Orit Furman et al., "They Saw a Movie: Long-Term Memory for an Extended Audiovisual Narrative," *Learning & Memory* 14 (2007): 457–467. Neurocinematics also aims at developing models of the brain-film match. Yadin Dudai, for example, argues that "the generic attributes of film resonate optimally with the capabilities of WM [working memory], while WM can exploit efficiently information in movie stimuli." See Yadin Dudai, "Enslaving Central Executives: Toward A Brain Theory of Cinema," *Projections* 2 (2008): 28.

29. Frederic C. Bartlett, *Remembering: A Study in Experimental and Social Psychology* (1932; reprint, London: Cambridge University Press, 1967). Among the many books produced in the context of the repressed-recovered memory wars see Elizabeth Loftus and Katherine Ketcham, *The Myth of Repressed Memory: False Memories and Allegations of Sexual Abuse* (New York: St. Martin's, 1994).

30. Andrey Tarkovsky, *Sculpting in Time: Reflections on the Cinema*, trans. Kitty Hunter-Blair (London: Faber and Faber, 1986), 63, 57.

31. E. M. Sternberg, "Piecing Together a Puzzling World." Given that *Memento's* science boils down to Lenny's knowing he has a brain condition, the film's conceptual potential seems more philosophical or psychological than neuroscientific. See for example, Basil Smith, "John Locke, Personal Identity, and *Memento*," in *The Philosophy of Neo-Noir*, ed. Mark T. Concord (Lexington, KY: University Press of Kentucky, 2007), 38.

32. See Susan J. Sara, "Retrieval and Reconsolidation: Toward a Neurobiology of Remembering," *Learning & Memory* 7 (2000): 73–84.

33. See Karim Nader, Glenn E. Schafe, and Joseph E. LeDoux, "Fear Memories Require Protein Synthesis in the Amygdala for Reconsolidation after Retrieval," *Nature* 40 (2000): 722–726.

34. See Jacek Debiec, Joseph E. LeDoux, and Karim Nader, "Cellular and Systems Reconsolidation in the Hippocampus," *Neuron* 36 (2002): 527–538.

35. See Natalie C. Tronson et al., "Bidirectional Behavioral Plasticity of Memory Reconsolidation Depends on Amygdalar Protein Kinase A," *Nature Neuroscience* 9 (2006): 167–169.

36. Valérie Doyère et al., "Synapse-Specific Reconsolidation of Distinct Fear Memories in the Lateral Amygdala," *Nature Neuroscience* 10 (2007): 415.

37. See Yadin Dudai, "The Neurobiology of Consolidations, or How Stable is the Engram?" *Annual Review of Psychology* 55 (2004): 51–86; Yadin Dudai, "Reconsolidation: The Advantage of Being Refocused," *Current Opinion in Neurobiology* 16 (2006): 174–178; Yadin Dudai and Mark Eisenberg, "Rites of Passage of the Engram: Reconsolidation and the Lingering Consolidation Hypothesis," *Neuron* 44 (2004): 93–100.

38. Reut Shema, Todd Charlton Sacktor, and Yadin Dudai, "Rapid Erasure of Long-Term Memory Associations in the Cortex by an Inhibitor of PKMζ," *Science* 317 (2007): 951–953; Reut Shema et al., "Boundary Conditions for the Maintenance of Memory by PKMζ in Neocortex," *Learning & Memory* 16 (2009): 122–128.

39. Joelle M. Abi-Rached, "The Implications of Memory Research and 'Memory Erasers': A Conversation with Yadin Dudai," *BioSocieties* 4 (2009): 85.

40. Daniella Schiller et al., "Preventing the Return of Fear in Humans Using Reconsolidation Update Mechanisms," *Nature* 463 (2010): 49–53; Gregory J. Quirk and Mohammed R. Milad, "Neuroscience: Editing Out Fear," *Nature* 463 (2010): 36–37.

41. Elisabeth Eaves, "Altering Human Memory," *Forbes.com*, May 24, 2007, http://www.forbes.com/2007/05/23/karim-nader-memory-tech-cx_07rev_ee_0524nader.html/.

42. K. Nader, G. E. Schafe, and J. E. LeDoux, "Fear Memories Require Protein Synthesis in the Amygdala for Reconsolidation after Retrieval."

43. Rosie Aiello, "The Spotless Mind: Can We Erase Memories?" *McGill Daily*, April 10, 2006, http://www.mcgilldaily.com/view.php?aid=5146

44. V. Doyère et al., "Synapse-Specific Reconsolidation of Distinct Fear Memories in the Lateral Amygdala"; "Eternal Erasing of the Scary Memory," Neurophilosophy at ScienceBlogs.com, March 13, 2007, http://neurophilosophy.wordpress.com/2007/03/13/eternal-erasing-of-the-scary-memory/. For a more skeptical account of memory erasure, see Rob Stein, "Is Every Memory Worth Keeping? Pills to Reduce Mental Trauma Raise Controversy," *Washington Post*, October 19, 2004, A01, http://www

.washingtonpost.com/wp-dyn/articles/A43210-2004Oct18.html/, where *Eternal Sunshine* is criticized for taking the notion of therapeutic forgetting "to science fiction extremes."

45. Steven Johnson, "The Science of *Eternal Sunshine*. You Can't Erase Your Boyfriend from Your Brain, but the Movie Gets the Rest of It Right," *Slate*, March 22, 2004, http://www.slate.com/id/2097502.

46. See Fernando Vidal, "Eternal Sunshine of the Spotless Mind and the Cultural History of the Self," *Werkstatt Geschichte* 45 (2007): 96–109.

47. Yadin Dudai, as quoted in J. M. Abi-Rached, "The Implications of Memory Research and 'Memory Erasers': A Conversation with Yadin Dudai," 88.

48. See discussion in Robert A. Bjork, "Inhibition: An Essential and Contentious Concept," in *Science of Memory: Concepts*, ed. Henry L. Roediger III, Yadin Dudai, and Susan M. Fitzpatrick (New York: Oxford University Press, 2007), 307–313. For one experimental illustration among others, see Benjamin C. Storm, Elizabeth Ligon Bjork, and Robert A. Bjork, "Accelerated Relearning after Retrieval-Induced Forgetting: The Benefit of Being Forgotten," *Journal of Experimental Psychology: Learning, Memory, and Cognition* 34 (2008): 230–236.

49. See Avi Mendelsohn et al., "Subjective vs. Documented Reality: A Case Study of Long-Term Real-Life Autobiographical Memory," *Learning & Memory* 16 (2009): 142–146. The term *flashbulb memories* was coined to convey the vividness with which highly emotional memories are recalled. See Roger Brown and James Kulik, "Flashbulb Memories," *Cognition* 5 (1977): 73–99.

50. On reductionism and memory research, see Yadin Dudai's perceptive review of Eric R. Kandel, *In Search of Memory* (2006), in *Nature* 442 (2006): 157–159.

51. See Yadin Dudai, "Predicting Not to Predict Too Much: How the Cellular Machinery of Memory Anticipates the Uncertain Future," *Philosophical Transactions of the Royal Society* B 364 (2009): 1255–1262.

About the Authors

Editors

Suzanne Nalbantian is professor of comparative literature at Long Island University. An interdisciplinary scholar, she conceived and organized this book. Her pioneering book *Memory in Literature: From Rousseau to Neuroscience* (2003) forged new pathways linking literary memory studies to neuroscience. She is also the author of *The Symbol of the Soul from Hölderlin to Yeats* (1977), *Seeds of Decadence in the Late Nineteenth-Century Novel* (1983), *Aesthetic Autobiography: From Life to Art in Marcel Proust, James Joyce, Virginia Woolf, and Anaïs Nin* (1994) and the editor of *Anaïs Nin: Literary Perspectives* (1997). She has taught interdisciplinary courses on memory and neuroscience at the Universities of Tübingen and Würzburg in Germany. She has given invited lectures on the interdisciplinary study of memory at Harvard, Yale, Stanford, Columbia, Indiana, Carnegie Mellon, University of the New Sorbonne (Paris III), Collège de France (Paris), as well as at laboratories such as Cold Spring Harbor (New York), Max-Planck (Tübingen), the Pasteur Institute (Paris), and the European Science Foundation (Strasbourg). In 2007, Nalbantian created and directed the Interdisciplinary Memory Symposium in Neuroscience and the Humanities at Cold Spring Harbor Laboratory.

Paul M. Matthews is vice president for imaging and head of the GlaxoSmithKline (GSK) Clinical Imaging Center within GSK's Drug Discovery Division and honorary consultant neurologist at the Hammersmith Hospital and in the Radcliffe Infirmary Hospitals Trust, Oxford. A full professor of clinical neurosciences at Imperial College, London, he is also fellow by special election of St. Edmund Hall, Oxford, honorary university professor at the Institute of Neurology, University College, London, and adjunct professor of neurology at McGill University, Montreal. He has coauthored more than 250 peer-reviewed research reports on problems of imaging for drug discovery and on mechanisms of systems level plasticity for motor control and four books, including *The Bard on the Brain: Understanding the Mind through the Art of Shakespeare and the Science of Brain Imaging* (with Jeff McQuain; 2003). In 2008, Matthews was made an honorary officer in the Order of the British Empire by the Queen for services to neuroscience.

James L. McClelland is professor and chair of the Department of Psychology and the founding director of the Center for Mind, Brain, and Computation at Stanford University, having served as a founding codirector of the Center for the Neural Basis of Cognition, a joint project of Carnegie Mellon University and the University of Pittsburgh. His research focuses on connectionist / parallel distributed processing models for perception theory, cognitive development, and the neurobiology of memory. He has written scores of articles, including the landmark "Constructive Memory and Memory Distortions: A Parallel-Distributive Processing Approach" (1995); he coauthored, with Timothy T. Rogers, *Semantic Cognition: A Parallel Distributed Processing Approach* (2004). McClelland received the Association for Psychological Science William James Fellow Award for lifetime contributions to the basic science of psychology and, in 2009, he was awarded the David E. Rumelhart Prize for significant contributions to the theoretical foundations of human cognition.

Other Contributors

John Bickle is professor and head of the Department of Philosophy and Religion at Mississippi State University. He was previously professor and head of philosophy, professor in the Neuroscience Graduate Program, and director of the Undergraduate Neuroscience Program at the University of Cincinnati. He is the author of *Psychoneural Reduction: The New Wave* (1998), *Philosophy and Neuroscience: A Ruthlessly Reductive Account* (2003); he is coauthor, with Ronald Giere and Robert Mauldin, of *Understanding Scientific Reasoning*, fifth edition (2006), and, with Alcino J. Silva and Anthony Landreth, of *Engineering the Next Revolution in Neuroscience* (2010). Bickle is the author of numerous articles on philosophy and neuroscience, and is the editor of *The Oxford Handbook of Philosophy and Neuroscience* (2009).

Jean-Pierre Changeux is emeritus professor at the Collège de France and at the Pasteur Institute, where he successively directed, from 1967 to 2006, the Molecular Neurobiology and the Receptors and Cognition Laboratories. His main discoveries in the past forty years are centered on the general theme of the molecular and cellular mechanisms of signal recognition, and transduction, also referred to as "receptor mechanisms," primarily in the nervous system. He is the author of the 1983 pathbreaking book *Neuronal Man: The Biology of the Mind* and numerous subsequent books, including *The Physiology of Truth: Neuroscience and Human Knowledge* (2002) and *Acetylcholine Nicotinic Receptors: From Molecular Biology to Cognition* (with Stuart J. Edelstein; 2005). His book on neuroaesthetics, *Raison et plaisir* (1994), and *Du vrai, du beau, du bien* (2008) have established fundamental links between neuroscience and the humanities. Changeux has headed the National Advisory Committee on Bioethics in France and has chaired a high-level commission at the Louvre. He is the winner of numerous prizes, including the Dart / New York University Biotechnology Achievement Award, the National Academy of Sciences Award in the Neurosciences, the Balzan Prize, the Linus Pauling Medal, the Gold Medal of the French National Center for Scientific Research (CNRS), and the Goodman and Gilman Award in Drug Receptor Pharmacology.

Valérie Doyère is senior scientist at the French National Center for Scientific Research (CNRS), working in the Neurobiology of Learning, Memory, and Communication Laboratory (Paris-Sud 11 University). A recognized expert in amygdala plasticity, she has been collaborating closely with Joseph LeDoux at New York University's Center for Neural Science since 1999, starting with a three-year stay in his laboratory as a visiting scholar. Doyère has coauthored numerous articles, including "Long-Term Potentiation in Freely Moving Rats Reveals Asymmetries in Thalmic and Cortical Inputs to the Lateral Amygdala" and "Synapse-Specific Reconsolidation of Distinct Fear Memories in the Lateral Amygdala."

Yadin Dudai is Sela Professor of Neurobiology and chair of the Department of Neurobiology at the Weizmann Institute of Science, Rehovot, Israel, and Albert and Balanche Willner Family Global Distinguished Professor of Neural Science at New York University. As a research fellow in the laboratory of Seymour Benzer at the California Institute of Technology, he was on the team that pioneered modern neurogenetics; he is currently studying brain mechanisms of learning and memory. Dudai is author of some 200 professional publications and several books in the field of memory, including *The Neurobiology of Memory* (1989) and *Memory from A to Z: Keywords, Concepts and Beyond* (2002), as well coeditor, with Henry L. Roediger III and Susan M. Fitzpatrick, of *Science of Memory: Concepts* (2007).

Attilio Favorini is professor of theater arts at the University of Pittsburgh, whose Department of Theater Arts he founded and chaired for many years. He also founded the Three Rivers Shakespeare Festival, serving as its producing director from 1980 to 1992. He edited *Theatre Survey: The American Journal of Theatre History* (1969–79) and *Voicings: Ten Plays from the Documentary Theater* (1995). His play *Steel/City* was voted Best Production of 1992 by the *Pittsburgh City Paper*, and his *In the Garden of Live Flowers* won the David Mark Cohen Playwriting Award in 2002. Favorini is the author of *Memory in Play: From Aeschylus to Sam Shepard* (2008).

John Burt Foster, Jr. is university professor of English and cultural studies at George Mason University. As a comparative literature scholar, he has taught at Stanford, Harvard, and New York University. He is the author of *Nabokov's Art of Memory and European Modernism* (1993) and of numerous articles on world literature and modern literature and thought; he is co-author, with Wayne J. Froman, of *Thresholds of Western Culture: Identity, Postcoloniality, Transnationalism* (2002). Editor of the award-winning journal *The Comparatist* from 1999 to 2004, Foster has recently assumed the editorship of *Recherche Littéraire / Literary Research*, the annual journal of the International Comparative Literature Association.

David Freedberg is the Pierre Matisse Professor of the History of Art at Columbia University and Director of the Italian Academy for Advanced Studies in America. After his initial work on iconoclasm, censorship, and painting during the Reformation and Counter-Reformation, he embarked on the study of psychological responses to art and the role of images in the history of science. His best-known books are *The Power of Images: Studies in the History and Theory of Response* (1989) and *The Eye of the Lynx: Galileo, His Friends, and the History of Natural History* (2003). For the last decade, Freedberg has turned his attention to the neuroscience of embodied responses to visual images, and he is producing a book on the subject.

Walter Glannon is Canada Research Chair in Medical Bioethics and Ethical Theory at the University of Calgary, where he is associate professor of philosophy and associate professor of community health sciences. Glannon has published over seventy articles, authored *Genes and Future People: Philosophical Issues in Human Genetics* (2001), *The Mental Basis of Responsibility* (2002), *Biomedical Ethics* (2005), and *Bioethics and the Brain* (2007), and edited *Contemporary Readings in Biomedical Ethics* (2001) and *Defining Right and Wrong in Brain Science: Essential Readings in Neuroethics* (2007).

David Michael Hertz is a professor of Comparative Literature at Indiana University in Bloomington. He is the author of *The Tuning of the Word: The Musico-Literary Poetics of the Symbolist Movement* (1987), *Angels of Reality: Emersonian Unfoldings in Wright, Stevens, and Ives* (1993), and *Frank Lloyd Wright in Word and Form* (1995). He has written essays on Arnold Schoenberg, Claude Debussy, lectured at the Bard Music Festival, and published an article on Charles Ives in its book series. A composer and pianist, Hertz is the cofounder of the Center for Comparative Arts at Indiana University. He has served as departmental chair of comparative literature at Indiana University, and he has been on the National Council of the National Endowment for the Humanities in Washington, D.C. At Indiana University, Hertz teaches a long-running series on composers in their cultural context, offering courses on Mozart, Beethoven, Charles Ives, Claude Debussy, and other major figures.

William Hirstein is professor and chair of the Philosophy Department at Elmhurst College in Illinois. His graduate and postdoctoral studies were conducted under the supervision of John Searle, Vilayanur S. Ramachandran, and Patricia Churchland. He is the author of *On Searle* (2001), *On the Churchlands* (2004), and *Brain Fiction: Self-Deception and the Riddle of Confabulation* (2005); he is the editor of *Confabulation: Views from Neuroscience, Psychiatry, Psychology, and Philosophy* (2009). His articles include "Self-Deception and Confabulation" and, with Vilayanur S. Ramachandran, "Three Laws of Qualia: What Neurology Tells Us about the Biological Functions of Consciousness" and "The Perception of Phantom Limbs: The D. O. Hebb Lecture." Hirstein's research interests include autism, sociopathy, brain laterality, and the misidentification syndromes.

Joseph E. LeDoux is the Henry and Lucy Moses Professor of Science and professor of neuroscience and psychology at New York University. He is also the director of the multiuniversity Center for the Neuroscience of Fear and Anxiety in New York City, devoted to using animal research to understand pathological fear and anxiety in humans. He is the author of *The*

Emotional Brain: The Mysterious Underpinnings of Emotional Life (1996) and *Synaptic Self: How Our Brains Become Who We Are* (2002); he is coeditor, with Jacek Debiec and Henry Moss, of *The Self: From Soul to Brain* (2003) and, with Priyattam J. Shiromani and Terence M. Keane, of *Post-Traumatic Stress Disorder: Basic Science and Clinical Practice* (2009). LeDoux is also the singer and songwriter in the rock band the Amygdaloids, who play music inspired by brain research.

Isabelle Peretz is professor of psychology at the University of Montreal and a cognitive neuropsychologist. Known for her work on congenital and acquired musical disorders (amusia) and on the biological foundations of music processing, she has published more than 150 scientific papers on topics ranging from perception, memory, and emotions to performance. She is coeditor, with Robert J. Zatorre, of *The Biological Foundations of Music* (2001) and of *The Cognitive Neuroscience of Music* (2003). In 2004, she was the University of Montreal's endowed Casavant Chair in Neurocognition of Music and subsequently a Canada Research Chair in Neurocognition of Music. In 2005, Peretz became a founding codirector of the International Laboratory for Brain, Music, and Sound research (BRAMS), a unique multiuniversity consortium that is jointly affiliated with McGill University and the University of Montreal.

Alan Richardson is professor of English at Boston College. He has published extensively on the literature and culture of the British Romantic era. He is the author of *The Neural Sublime: Cognitive Theories and Romantic Texts* (2010), *British Romanticism and the Science of the Mind* (2001) and coeditor, with Thomas Uebel, of *The Cambridge Companion to Logical Empiricism* (2007). His current research involves Romantic theories and representations of subjectivity, embodied agency, and language in relation to eighteenth- and early nineteenth-century neuroscientific speculation and experimentation. Richardson cofounded and has codirected both the Seminar on Romantic Literature and Culture and the Seminar on Cognitive Theory and the Arts at the Humanities Center of Harvard University.

Edmund T. Rolls is a researcher at the Oxford Center for Computational Neuroscience. His research interests include the operation of real neuronal networks in the brain; functional neuroimaging of vision, taste, olfaction, feeding, and the control of appetite, memory, and emotion; neurological, emotional, and psychiatric disorders; and the brain processes underlying consciousness. He was professor of experimental psychology at the University of Oxford and fellow and tutor in psychology at Corpus Christi College, Oxford, from 1973 to 2008. Rolls is author of *The Brain and Emotion* (1999), *Emotion Explained* (2005), and *Memory, Attention, and Decision-Making: A Unifying Computational Neuroscience Approach, Neural Networks and Brain Function* (2007) and coauthor of *Introduction to Connectionist Modelling of Cognitive Processes* (with Peter McLeod and Kim Plunkett; 1998), *Computational Neuroscience of Vision* (with Gustavo Deco; 2002), and *The Noisy Brain: Stochastic Dynamics as a Principle of Brain Function* (with Gustavo Deco; forthcoming).

Séverine Samson is a professor of psychology at the University of Lille, whose faculty she joined in the 1990s. Recently nominated senior member at the University Institute of France, she specializes in the neuropsychological and perisurgical evaluation of epileptic patients. Samson's research focuses on the role of the temporal lobes in memory, perception, and emotion in musical domains using methods taken from psychophysics, cognitive psychology, and neuroimagery.

Alcino J. Silva is professor in the Departments of Neurobiology, Psychiatry, Psychology, and Brain Research Institute at the University of California, Los Angeles, where he is studying hippocampal/prefrontal memory mechanisms with a focus on synaptic plasticity and learning. He is the author or coauthor of numerous articles, including "Genetic Substrates of Memory" and "Gene Targeting and the Biology of Learning and Memory," in journals such as *Learning and Memory*, *Nature*, *Neuron*, and *Nature Neuroscience*. Silva is also coauthor, with John Bickle and Anthony Landreth, of *Engineering the Next Revolution in Neuroscience* (2010).

Robert Stickgold is associate professor of psychiatry at Beth Israel Deaconess Medical Center and Harvard Medical School. He is coeditor, with Pierre Maquet and Carlyle Smith, of *Sleep and Brain Plasticity* (2004), which contains his articles "Memory, Cognition and Dreams" and "Human Studies of Sleep and Off-Memory Reprocessing." He has published two science fiction novels and over seventy-five scientific articles, including "Sleep-Dependent Memory Consolidation" and "Sleep: The Ebb and Flow of Memory Consolidation." His work has been written up in *Time*, *Newsweek*, the *New York Times*, and the *Boston Globe Magazine*. Stickgold's current research examines the nature and function of sleep and dreams from a cognitive neuroscience perspective, with an emphasis on the role of sleep and dreams in memory consolidation and integration.

Barbara Tillmann is a CNRS researcher at Joint Research Unit 5020 of the National Center for Scientific Research (CNRS-UMR 5020) in Lyon. In 2004, Tillman received the CNRS Bronze Medal for her research. Leader of the Auditory Cognition and Psychoacoustics Team since 2007, she is currently an eminent visiting researcher at the University of Western Sydney, investigating how the brain acquires knowledge about complex sound structures and how this knowledge shapes perception and memory. Tillmann is coauthor of the book *Perception des structures musicales* (with M. Pineau; 2001) and of numerous journal articles, such as "Memory and the Experience of Hearing Music," as well as book chapters, including "Music Perception from a Connectionist Perspective" in *The Biological Foundations of Music* (2001).

Fernando Vidal is senior research scholar at the Max Planck Institute for the History of Science, Berlin. A former Guggenheim Fellow, Vidal has worked on various topics in the history of the human sciences, including early-modern and Enlightenment psychology, psychoanalysis and psychiatry in the early twentieth century, and the progressive education movement in the interwar years. His books include *Piaget before Piaget* (1994), *Piaget neuchâtelois* (1996), and *Les sciences de l'âme, XVIe–XVIIIe siècle* (2006). He has also edited *Las razones del cuerpo* (1999), a collection of Jean Starobinski's writings on the history of the body, and coedited *The Moral Authority of Nature, Believing Nature, Knowing God* (with Lorraine Daston; 2004), a thematic issue of *Science in Context* (with Bernhard Kleeberg; 2007), and *Neurocultures: Glimpses into an Expanding Universe* (with Francisco Ortega; forthcoming). Vidal is currently at work on a cultural history of the "cerebral subject" in collaboration with the Institute for Social Medicine of the State University of Rio de Janeiro, a project discussed in his article "Brainhood: Anthropological Figure of Modernity" (2009).

Index